Mastering QuickBooks 2024
Fifth Edition

Bookkeeping with US QuickBooks Online
for small businesses

Crystalynn Shelton, CPA

BIRMINGHAM—MUMBAI

Mastering QuickBooks 2024

Fifth Edition

Copyright © 2023 Packt Publishing

Senior Publishing Product Manager: Larissa Pinto
Acquisition Editor – Peer Reviews: Jane Dsouza
Project Editor: Namrata Katare
Content Development Editor: Matthew Davies
Copy Editor: Safis Editing
Technical Editor: Aneri Patel
Proofreader: Safis Editing
Indexer: Tejal Daruwale Soni
Presentation Designer: Ajay Patule
Developer Relations Marketing Executive: Sohini Ghosh

First published: December 2019
Second edition: January 2021
Third edition: January 2022
Fourth edition: November 2022
Fifth edition: December 2023

Production reference: 1211223

Published by Packt Publishing Ltd.
Grosvenor House
11 St Paul's Square
Birmingham
B3 1RB, UK.

ISBN 978-1-83546-995-8

www.packt.com

To my mother, Mary A. Moore, and my mother-in law, Florence J. McGrue, who are smiling down on me from heaven; to my husband, Charles, for always being loving and supportive; to my siblings, Cynthia, James, and Jay; and to my niece and nephews, Jonathan, Dante, Taelor, and Braylon, who make me proud to be their aunt!

To my fellow accountants, bookkeepers, and tax professionals who spend countless hours doing their part to help small businesses succeed – I salute you.

Finally, thank you to the Packt Team who worked tirelessly on this edition with me. Particularly Larissa Pinto, Namrata Katare, Matthew Davies, Steven A. Windsor, Valerie Armstrong, and Sohini Ghosh.

– Crystalynn Shelton, CPA

Contributors

About the author

Crystalynn Shelton provides training, consulting, and coaching services to small businesses looking to get a handle on their bookkeeping. She is also an adjunct instructor at UCLA Extension, where she teaches accounting, bookkeeping, and QuickBooks to hundreds of small business owners and accounting students each year.

Crystalynn is the author of four Amazon Bestsellers: *Mastering QuickBooks 2020*, *Mastering QuickBooks 2021*, *Mastering QuickBooks 2022, and Mastering QuickBooks 2023*. She has a degree in accounting from the University of Texas, Arlington, and she is a licensed CPA and an Advanced Certified QuickBooks ProAdvisor. She has managed accounting teams at Fortune 500 companies such as Texaco and Paramount Pictures, ran her own bookkeeping practice for 3 years, and worked for Intuit (QuickBooks) for 3 years as a senior learning specialist.

Visit her website at https://crystalynnshelton.com/ for more information on the services that she offers to small business clients and to sign up for her weekly newsletter where she shares QuickBooks tips and tricks. You can find her on social media using @CrystalynnShelton.

To the small business owners all over the world, you are my inspiration for writing this book. I hope it helps you to understand how important it is to stay on top of your business finances.

About the reviewers

Steven A. Windsor is a Chartered Certified Accountant who currently works as a business advisory manager for Pascoe Partners Accountants in West Perth, Western Australia. He is also the President of the Wanneroo Business Association, one of the premier business associations in Western Australia with over 400 business members. Steven is passionate about working with small-to-medium businesses owners and community groups on planning, strategy, and problem solving to enable them to overcome their challenges in order to grow and meet their dreams and goals.

Steven has been using QuickBooks for over 20 years in both the Desktop and Online versions, and holds the QuickBooks Online Advanced Certification. He enjoys training people in bookkeeping and finds QuickBooks Online to be one of the most intuitive cloud software packages available.

In the past, Steven has reviewed previous editions of *Mastering QuickBooks*. He hopes the readers will find it as useful and informative as he did.

Valerie Armstrong is a master fixer at Bon Vie Bookkeeping LLC, a bookkeeping firm specializing in clean-up project work and mentoring for accounting and bookkeeping professionals. At Bon Vie Bookkeeping, she runs a unique bookkeeping practice focused solely on the sorting of untidy books. Her clients benefit from her strengths in strategic thinking and creating custom solutions for each situation. Valerie also joined Brian Walters & Associates as a valuation analyst in 2021 after working closely with CEO Brian Walters on a complex business appraisal.

Valerie graduated from the University of Texas with a degree in Business Management, and after over twenty years in the field of residential real estate, she turned her focus to business accounting and advisory services. She is a Certified Digital Bookkeeper, as well as a QuickBooks Online Advanced ProAdvisor. She is a lifetime member of the **Digital Bookkeepers Association (DBA)**, and she receives continuing education throughout the year to stay up to date with the latest industry and cloud accounting technology developments.

She lives in Austin, Texas, with her dachshund, Lucy, and is the proud mom of college-going son, Graham.

Join our community on Discord

Join our community's Discord space for discussions with the authors and other readers:

`https://packt.link/quickbooks`

Table of Contents

Chapter 4: Customizing QuickBooks for Your Business   85

Section 3: Generating Reports in QuickBooks Online   289

Chapter 10: Reports Center Overview   291

Chapter 11: Business Overview and Cash Flow Reports   319

Preface

Intuit QuickBooks is an accounting software package that helps small business owners manage all their bookkeeping tasks. Its complete range of accounting capabilities, such as tracking income and expenses, managing payroll, simplifying taxes, and accepting online payments, makes QuickBooks software a must-have for business owners and aspiring bookkeepers.

The goal of this book is to teach small business owners, bookkeepers, and aspiring accountants how to properly use QuickBooks Online. Using a fictitious company, we will demonstrate how to create a QuickBooks Online account; customize key settings for a business; manage customers, vendors, and products and services; enter transactions; generate reports; and close books at the end of the period. QuickBooks records debits and credits for you so that you don't have to know accounting. However, we will show you what's happening behind the scenes in QuickBooks so that you can understand how your actions in QuickBooks impact financial statements. We will also provide you with tips, shortcuts, and best practices to help you save time and become a QuickBooks pro.

The US edition of QBO was used to create this book. If you are using a version that is outside of the United States, results may differ.

Who this book is for

If you're a small business owner, bookkeeper, or accounting student who wants to learn how to make the most of QuickBooks Online, this book is for you. Business analysts, data analysts, managers, professionals working in bookkeeping, and QuickBooks accountants will also find this guide useful. If you are planning to take the **QuickBooks Certified User (QBCU)** exam, this book is an excellent study guide. No experience with QuickBooks Online is required to get started; however, some bookkeeping knowledge would be helpful.

What this book covers

Section 1: Setting Up Your Company File

Chapter 1, Getting Started with QuickBooks Online, starts off with a brief description of QuickBooks Online, then it outlines the key features in all four editions of the software. We also explain how to choose the right edition for your business. There are step-by-step instructions on how to create a QBO account and how to navigate the software. Finally, we provide you with some basic bookkeeping knowledge to help you understand what's going on behind the scenes in QuickBooks.

Chapter 2, Company File Setup, shows you how to customize the QuickBooks Online account created in *Chapter 1* to meet your business needs. First, we explain the documents and key information you will need to have handy for the setup. Next, we walk you through all of the available preferences in QBO and explain the purpose and benefit of utilizing the various options available.

Chapter 3, Migrating to QuickBooks Online, gives you all the information required to migrate to QuickBooks Online from platforms such as Excel, QuickBooks Desktop, or another accounting/bookkeeping software.

Chapter 4, Customizing QuickBooks for Your Business, introduces customization for the chart of accounts and then dives into the different ways of connecting bank accounts and credit cards to your QuickBooks Online account, followed by granting users access to your QuickBooks data. Finally, you will learn how to discover and install apps in QuickBooks Online. Apps are a great way to help you streamline day-to-day business tasks that can otherwise be time-consuming.

Chapter 5, Managing Customer, Vendor, and Products and Services Lists, gives you a detailed insight into how to manage your customers, vendors, products, and services. This includes importing customer, vendor, and product and service data from an Excel spreadsheet and manually entering it into the software.

Section 2: Recording Transactions in QuickBooks Online

Chapter 6, Managing Sales Tax, covers how to set up sales tax for the various tax jurisdictions you are required to collect sales tax for, how to create an invoice with sales tax, and what reports will help you to report and pay the appropriate sales tax amount when it becomes due.

Chapter 7, Recording Sales Transactions in QuickBooks Online, starts by giving detailed information on different forms of sales, followed by information on how the customer can record payments using different methods, and finally teaches you how to initiate refunds for your customers. You will also learn how to customize sales templates with your company branding, such as adding a name and logo.

Chapter 8, Recording Expenses in QuickBooks Online, teaches you how to enter and pay bills for your QuickBooks Online account. Then, we'll start exploring how to manage recurring expenses, followed by writing and printing checks.

Chapter 9, Reconciling Uploaded Bank and Credit Card Transactions, gives you an overview of the Banking Center in QuickBooks Online and an understanding of how the bank rules work, followed by how to edit QuickBooks Online transactions and how to reconcile bank accounts. We wrap this chapter up with a few troubleshooting tips for reconciling bank/credit card accounts.

Section 3: Generating Reports in QuickBooks Online

Chapter 10, Report Center Overview, highlights the key reports that you need in order to keep track of your business finances. It takes you through the Report Center, its purpose, and how to navigate it. You will then go through instructions for generating and customizing the main reports that are available, as well as how to export reports and send them via email. You will learn how regularly you need to check these reports, what to look out for, and what actions or decisions these findings might prompt.

Chapter 11, Business Overview and Cash Flow Reports, discusses the three primary reports that provide a good overview of your business: the profit and loss statement, balance sheet report, and statement of cash flows. You will learn when to check these reports and how to use them to evaluate your business's performance. It also introduces you to the Cash Flow Center, where you can find important tools like the Cash Flow Planner and audit log.

Chapter 12, Customer Sales Reports in QuickBooks Online, focuses on reports that will give you insight into your customers and sales. We will discuss what information you will find on each report, how to customize the reports, and how to generate each report. Once they are generated, we will observe when to check these reports and what decisions they might encourage us to make.

Chapter 13, Vendor and Expenses Reports, dives into reports that help you manage your outgoings and have a clearer view of your profitability. The main reports that are covered are the accounts payable aging report, unpaid bills report, expense by vendor summary report, and bill payments report. You will learn how to generate and customize these reports to help you manage your expenses and cash flow.

Section 4: Managing Employees and Contractors

Chapter 14, Managing Employees and 1099 Contractors in QuickBooks Online, shows you what information and key documents are needed to set up payroll, how to sign up for an Intuit Payroll subscription plan, and how to generate payroll reports.

You will also learn how to file payroll tax forms and payments. You will be introduced to 1099 contractors, how to define them, what forms to use, and how to make payments to them.

Section 5: Closing the Books and Handling Special Transactions

Chapter 15, Closing the Books in QuickBooks Online, covers the steps needed to close your books each month or for the year; including but not limited to reconciling all bank and credit card accounts, making year-end accrual adjustments (if applicable), recording fixed asset purchases made throughout the year, recording depreciation, taking a physical inventory, adjusting retained earnings, and preparing financial statements.

Chapter 16, Handling Special Transactions in QuickBooks Online, covers some of the more complicated or uncommon transactions that you may need to handle in your business. It covers how to set up business loans and lines of credit, including how to make payments on a loan. You will also learn how to keep track of petty cash and record delayed charges.

Chapter 17, QuickBooks Online Advanced, takes a deep dive into the features included in this top-tier QuickBooks Online subscription. We show you how to access the QuickBooks Online Advanced test drive account, use the new fixed asset manager to automatically calculate and record monthly depreciation, add custom fields, manage customized user permissions, what workflow automation is and how to use it, how to import invoices and budgets, and much more.

Appendix

At the end of the book, there is a brief section called *Shortcuts and Test Drive,* which summarizes the keyboard shortcuts you can use in QuickBooks Online to save time, and also provides links to the QBO test drive account as well as a QBO discount code. This is followed by the *Intuit Quick-Books Certified User Exam Objectives,* where you'll find the full list of things you need to know to pass the QBCU exam, along with references to where the relevant content appears in the book – a handy reference for revision.

To get the most out of this book

This book is ideal for anyone who has accounting/bookkeeping knowledge as well as those that don't. Each chapter builds on the knowledge and information presented in the previous chapters. If you don't have any experience of using QuickBooks Online, we recommend you start with *Chapter 1, Getting Started with QuickBooks Online,* and complete the chapters in the order they are presented. If you have experience of using QuickBooks Online, feel free to advance to the chapters that cover the topics you need to brush up on.

Download additional files

The code bundle for the book is hosted on GitHub at `https://github.com/PacktPublishing/ Mastering-Quickbooks-2024-Fifth-Edition`. We also have other code bundles from our rich catalog of books and videos available at `https://github.com/PacktPublishing/`. Check them out!

Download the color images

We also provide a PDF file that has color images of the screenshots/diagrams used in this book. You can download it here: `https://packt.link/gbp/9781835469958`.

Conventions used

Bold: Indicates a new term, an important word, or words that you see on screen. For example, words in menus or dialog boxes appear in the text like this. Here is an example: "Click on the **Accounting** tab located in the left menu bar and select **Chart of Accounts**."

`CodeInText`: Indicates text that the user should type into a field or search bar. For example: "The email address in our example is `George_Jetson@thejetsons.com`."

 Warnings or important notes appear like this.

 Tips and tricks appear like this.

Get in touch

Errata: Although we have taken every care to ensure the accuracy of our content, mistakes do happen. If you have found a mistake in this book we would be grateful if you would report this to us. Please visit `http://www.packtpub.com/submit-errata`, selecting your book, clicking on the Errata Submission Form link, and entering the details.

Piracy: If you come across any illegal copies of our works in any form on the Internet, we would be grateful if you would provide us with the location address or website name. Please contact us at `copyright@packtpub.com` with a link to the material.

If you are interested in becoming an author: If there is a topic that you have expertise in and you are interested in either writing or contributing to a book, please visit `http://authors.packtpub.com`.

Share your thoughts

Once you've read *Mastering QuickBooks 2024*, we'd love to hear your thoughts! Scan the QR code below to go straight to the Amazon review page for this book and share your feedback.

https://packt.link/r/1835469957

Your review is important to us and the tech community and will help us make sure we're delivering excellent quality content.

Download a free PDF copy of this book

Thanks for purchasing this book!

Do you like to read on the go but are unable to carry your print books everywhere? Is your eBook purchase not compatible with the device of your choice?

Don't worry, now with every Packt book you get a DRM-free PDF version of that book at no cost.

Read anywhere, any place, on any device. Search, copy, and paste code from your favorite technical books directly into your application.

The perks don't stop there, you can get exclusive access to discounts, newsletters, and great free content in your inbox daily

Follow these simple steps to get the benefits:

1. Scan the QR code or visit the link below

https://packt.link/free-ebook/9781835469958

2. Submit your proof of purchase

3. That's it! We'll send your free PDF and other benefits to your email directly

Section 1

Setting Up Your Company File

1

Getting Started with QuickBooks Online

QuickBooks is the most popular accounting software for small businesses. The desktop version has been around for more than 25 years, and the online version for more than 10 years. It is affordable, easily accessible, and ideal for non-accountants. Before diving into the nuts and bolts of setting up QuickBooks for your business, you should understand what QuickBooks is and what your options are when it comes to using it. Once you know what your options are, you will be in a better position to choose the version of QuickBooks that will best suit your business needs. We will then show you how to create a **QuickBooks Online** (**QBO**) account and how to navigate in QBO.

If you don't have previous experience as a bookkeeper, then you will need to know a few bookkeeping basics before you get started. In the *Small-business bookkeeping 101* section, we will cover five key areas in terms of recording transactions in your business: money coming in, money going out, inventory purchases, fixed asset purchases, and liabilities. In this section, we will also cover the importance of the chart of accounts, accounting methods, and what double-entry bookkeeping is.

We will cover the following key concepts in this chapter:

- What is QuickBooks?
- Exploring QBO editions
- Choosing the right QBO edition
- Creating a QBO account
- Navigating in QBO
- Small-business bookkeeping 101

Once you've got these key concepts under your belt, you will be ready to dive into setting up your business in QBO.

 The US edition of QBO was used to create this book. If you are using a version that is outside of the United States, results may differ.

What is QuickBooks?

QuickBooks is an accounting software program that allows you to track your financial transactions such as income and expenses for your business. One of the benefits of using QuickBooks is having access to key financial reports (such as the balance sheet report) so that you can see the overall health of your business at any time. Having access to these reports makes filing your taxes a lot easier. QuickBooks has been around for almost three decades and is the accounting software used by millions of small businesses around the globe.

QuickBooks comes in two formats: software that you can install or download on a desktop computer, and a cloud-based program that is accessible from any mobile device or desktop computer with an internet connection.

The cloud-based version, **QuickBooks Online (QBO)**, is available in four editions: Simple Start, Essentials, Plus, and Advanced. The desktop version, **QuickBooks Desktop (QBD)**, also comes in four editions: QuickBooks Mac, Pro, Premier, and Enterprise. In this book, we will focus on QuickBooks Online, discussing each of its editions in detail next.

Exploring QBO editions

As described, QBO comes in four editions:

- Simple Start
- Essentials
- Plus
- Advanced

Each edition varies in terms of the price, the number of users to which you can give access, and the features included.

The following figure gives a summary of QBO pricing and features for each edition of QBO at the time of writing:

	Simple Start	Essentials	Plus	Advanced
Cost	$30	$60	$90	$200
Maximum number of users	1	3	5	25
Accountant users included	2	2	2	3
Income and expenses tracking	✓	✓	✓	✓
Invoice and payments (known as **accounts receivable**, or **A/R**)	✓	✓	✓	✓
Tax deductions	✓	✓	✓	✓
Reports	General	Enhanced	Comprehensive	Powerful
Receipt capture	✓	✓	✓	✓
Mileage tracking	✓	✓	✓	✓
Cash flow	✓	✓	✓	✓
Sales and sales tax tracking	✓	✓	✓	✓
Estimates	✓	✓	✓	✓
Pay 1099 contractors	✓	✓	✓	✓
Maximum number of sales channels	1	3	Unlimited	Unlimited
Bill management (accounts payable)		✓	✓	✓
Time tracking		✓	✓	✓
Inventory tracking			✓	✓
Project profitability			✓	✓

Data sync with Excel				✓
Track employee expenses				✓
Batch invoices and expenses				✓
Custom access controls				✓
Exclusive premium apps				✓ ✓
Workflow automation				✓
Data restoration				✓
24/7 support & training				✓
Revenue recognition				✓

Table 1.1: QBO edition comparison

As you can see from the preceding table, all four editions of QBO include the following features:

- **Maximum number of users**: Each plan includes a set number of users; Simple Start includes one user, Essentials includes three users, Plus comes with five users, and Advanced includes up to twenty-five users. In addition, each plan includes one or more accountant users. For example, you can give a bookkeeper or your certified public accountant access to your books.

- **Accountant users included**: Each plan includes two or more accountant users. Simple Start, Essentials, and Plus include two accountant users and Advanced includes three accountant users. Typically, you would give this level of access to a **Certified Public Accountant (CPA)** or tax preparer who has the authority to make changes to your books.

- **Track income and expenses**: Keep track of all sales to customers and expenses paid to vendors.

- **Invoice and payments (accounts receivable):** Invoice customers, enter payments, and stay on top of unpaid invoices.

- **Tax deductions:** Keeping track of all expenses will ensure you don't miss out on any tax deductions you may qualify for.

- **Reports:** QuickBooks includes pre-set reports so you don't have to create them from scratch. The number of reports available is based on your subscription plan. Simple Start includes the minimum number of reports, and Advanced includes the most reports.

- **Receipt capture:** Use your phone or mobile device to snap a photo of a receipt and upload it to QuickBooks. You can also link expense receipts to transactions.

- **Mileage tracking:** Automatically track miles with your phone's GPS and categorize them as business or personal trips.

- **Cash flow:** Stay on top of your cash flow by using the cash flow tools available in all QBO plans.

- **Track sales and sales tax:** Keep track of sales tax collected from customers, submit electronic payments to state and local authorities, and complete required sales tax forms and filings.

- **Estimates:** Create a quote or proposal and email it to prospective clients for approval.

- **Pay 1099 contractors:** You can keep track of payments made to independent contractors and generate 1099 forms at the end of the year.

- **Sales channels:** E-commerce businesses can connect QBO to their Amazon, Shopify, or eBay accounts to sync the sales with QBO.

The Simple Start plan is the most economical, at $30 per month, on sale currently with the first three months having 50% off, costing $15 per month. It includes one user and two accountant users.

The Essentials plan is the next tier and starts at $60 per month, on sale currently with the first three months having 50% off, costing $30 per month. It includes three users and two accountant users.

Unlike Simple Start, you can manage bills (also known as **accounts payable**, or **A/P**) with the Essentials plan. The Plus plan is $90 per month, on sale currently with the first three months having 50% off, costing $45 per month. It includes five users and two accountant users. Unlike the Simple Start and Essentials plans, you can track your inventory and project profitability with the Plus plan. The Advanced plan is the top-tier QBO plan. It starts at $200 per month (on sale currently with 50% off for the first three months, costing $100 per month) and includes up to twenty-five users and three accountant users.

Keep in mind that pricing is subject to change and that the pricing reflected in this book is based on what is reflected on the Intuit website at the time of writing.

We will discuss the features of each plan in more detail, and how to choose the right QBO edition for your business, in the next section.

Choosing the right QBO edition

Depending on the edition, QBO can be ideal for anyone from solopreneurs and freelancers all the way to mid- to large-sized businesses. If you tend to hire 1099 contractors, also known as independent contractors, QBO can help you keep track of payments made to contractors throughout the year. Since contractors are not employees of the business, you must provide a 1099 form at the end of the year to any contractor you have paid $600 or more to in the calendar year.

The needs of your business will determine which edition of QBO is ideal for you. The following provides some additional insight into the ideal edition of QBO for different types of businesses.

 When you purchase a QBO subscription, you can track business finances for one business entity. If you need to track more than one business, you will need to purchase a QBO subscription for each business entity that you have. In general, any business with a unique tax ID number will need their own set of books.

QBO Simple Start

QBO Simple Start is ideal for a freelancer or sole proprietor that sells services only, and no products. You may have employees that you need to pay, or 1099 contractors. The majority of your expenses are paid via online banking or wire transfer, so you don't need to write or print checks to pay bills.

QBO Essentials

QBO Essentials includes all of the features found in QBO Simple Start. QBO Essentials is ideal for freelancers and sole proprietors that only sell services and no products (or, those who sell "non-inventory" products, such as ebooks, other digital items, or subscription offerings). You have employees and/or contractors whose time you need to keep track of in order to bill back to clients. Unlike QBO Simple Start, you pay most of your bills by writing checks, and you need the ability to keep track of your unpaid bills. QBO Essentials is the next step for small businesses that may need more reporting options.

QBO Plus

QBO Plus includes all of the features found in Simple Start and Essentials. Unlike QBO Simple Start and QBO Essentials, QBO Plus is ideal for small businesses that sell products, since it includes inventory tracking. Similar to QBO Simple Start and QBO Essentials, you can pay employees. If you tend to work on a project basis, QBO Plus is ideal because you can track the profitability of all of your projects as well as create income and expense budgets.

QBO Advanced

QBO Advanced includes all of the features found in Simple Start, Essentials, and Plus. QBO Advanced is ideal for businesses that have more than five users needing access to their data. QBO Advanced is QBO Plus on steroids; it includes all of the features found in QBO Plus, along with some great bonus features, such as on-demand online training for your entire team, and business analytics with Excel.

The bonus features you will find in QBO Advanced are as follows:

- **Data sync with Excel**: Connect QBO to Excel to gain access to pre-made templates, and the ability to build consolidated reports for multiple companies and easily refresh your data.

- **Employee expenses tracking**: Employees can submit expenses directly to QuickBooks for easy tracking, review, and reimbursement.

- **Batch invoices and expenses**: Enter, edit, and email hundreds of invoices, checks, expenses, and bills instead of entering them one by one.

- **Custom access control**: Provides a deeper level of user permissions that allows you to manage access to sensitive data, such as bank accounts.

- **Exclusive premium apps**: Intuit has more than 600 best-in-class apps to customize Quick-Books for your business needs. For example, Amazon Marketplace Connector is available to automatically sync eCommerce sales to QuickBooks.

- **24/7 support & training**: With QBO Advanced, you get support 24 hours a day, 7 days a week at no additional cost. In addition, on-demand online training videos are available to help you and your staff get up to speed on how to use QBO. This training has an annual value of $3,000 but is included with your subscription to QBO Advanced at no additional cost.

- **Workflow automation**: Save time and minimize risk by implementing automation for repetitive tasks.

- **Data restoration**: Continuously back up changes to your company file or restore a specific version.

- **Revenue recognition**: This new feature allows you to automatically track and enter deferred revenue into your books so that you can stay compliant with standards that state how and when businesses should recognize their revenue.

For more in-depth information about the features and benefits of QBO Advanced, head over to *Chapter 17, QuickBooks Online Advanced*. In that chapter, we take a deep dive into the features available in this top-tier QBO plan.

Depending on your business and individual circumstances, you should now be able to determine whether you will need QBO Simple Start, Essentials, Plus, or Advanced. It is important to pick the right version for you so that you have access to the appropriate features you will need. However, you can upgrade or downgrade your QBO plan at any time. Now that you know about the QBO subscription plans, we will show you how to create a QBO account.

Creating a QBO account

The first step to setting up your business in QBO is to create a QBO account.

In this section, we will create a QBO account for **Small Business Builders, LLC**, a fictitious business we will use to demonstrate features and explain concepts taught throughout this book. Small Business Builders is owned by a partnership that provides consulting services in business plans, marketing plans, bookkeeping, tax planning, and website development to small businesses. Small Business Builders is in its first year of business and has no employees. However, the partners do hire a few contractors to help meet the demand during the peak months of the year.

To create a QBO account, go to the Intuit website and select a QBO subscription plan.

Follow these steps to create a QBO account:

1. Open your web browser and go to the Intuit website: `www.intuit.com`.
2. Click on **Products** and select **QuickBooks**, as shown in *Figure 1.1*:

Figure 1.1: Navigating to QuickBooks

3. Click on **Plans & Pricing**, as indicated in *Figure 1.2*:

Figure 1.2: Choosing Plans & Pricing

4. Choose from one of four pricing plans: **Simple Start**, **Essentials**, **Plus**, or **Advanced**, as indicated in *Figure 1.3*:

Figure 1.3: Choosing a pricing plan

The pricing shown here is correct as of the time of writing this book and is subject to change. To get a special discount on your QBO subscription, use my referral link: https://quickbooks.grsm.io/crystalynnshelton4264.

5. After selecting a plan, you will be asked if you want to continue without payroll. Select this option; in *Chapter 14, Managing Employees and 1099 Contractors in QuickBooks Online*, we will cover payroll in more detail.

 Pro Tip: Intuit has a service called QuickBooks Live that connects you with a bookkeeper, who can assist you in getting things set up properly and managing ongoing tasks.

6. Select **Off** for the **Live Bookkeeping** option.

7. Create an Intuit account by providing your business email address, mobile number, and password, as indicated in *Figure 1.4*:

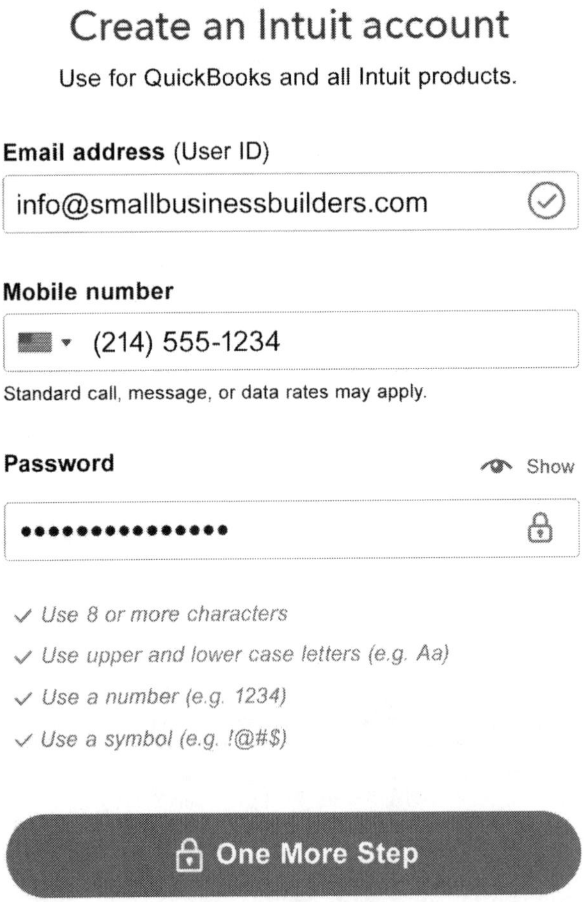

Create an Intuit account

Use for QuickBooks and all Intuit products.

Email address (User ID)

> info@smallbusinessbuilders.com   ⊘

Mobile number

> ▬ ▾ (214) 555-1234

Standard call, message, or data rates may apply.

Password   👁 Show

> ●●●●●●●●●●●●●●●●   🔓

✓ *Use 8 or more characters*
✓ *Use upper and lower case letters (e.g. Aa)*
✓ *Use a number (e.g. 1234)*
✓ *Use a symbol (e.g. !@#$)*

🔒 **One More Step**

Figure 1.4: Creating an Intuit account

8. After entering your credit card info, the following welcome screen will appear:

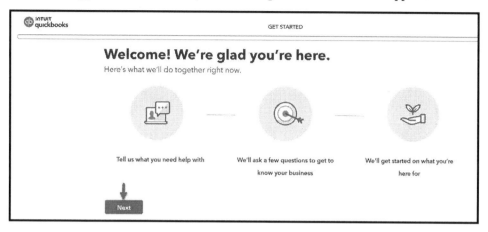

Figure 1.5: Welcome screen after account creation

9. Click **Next** as indicated in the screenshot above.

The following screen will appear:

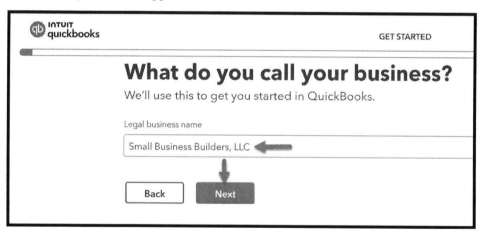

Figure 1.6: Entering your legal business name

10. Type your legal business name, as shown in the screenshot above, and click the **Next** button.

The following screen will appear:

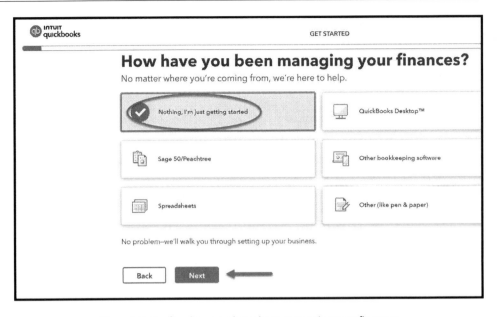

Figure 1.7: Confirm how you have been managing your finances

11. Select how you are currently keeping track of your finances. If you select **QuickBooks Desktop** or **Sage 50/Peachtree**, instructions for how you can convert that data into QBO will come up. For Small Business Builders, select **Nothing, I'm just getting started**. If you are migrating from another accounting software to QBO, refer to *Chapter 3, Migrating to QuickBooks Online* for step-by-step instructions.

On the next screen, indicate whether your business is your main source of income:

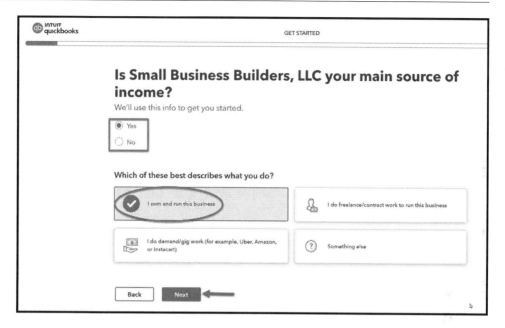

Figure 1.8: Confirm your main source of income

For Small Business Builders, choose **Yes** and **I own and run this business**, as indicated in *Figure 1.8*.

12. On the next screen, select how long you have been in business, as indicated below in *Figure 1.9*:

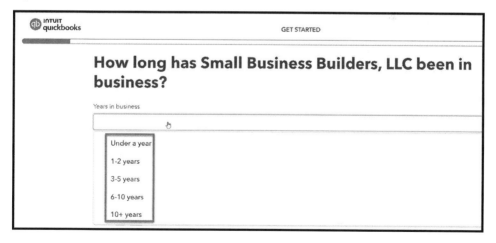

Figure 1.9: Selecting how long you have been in business

Small Business Builders, LLC has been in business for **under a year**.

13. On the next screen, indicate the structure of your business. Small Business Builders is an LLC with multiple partners that own the business.

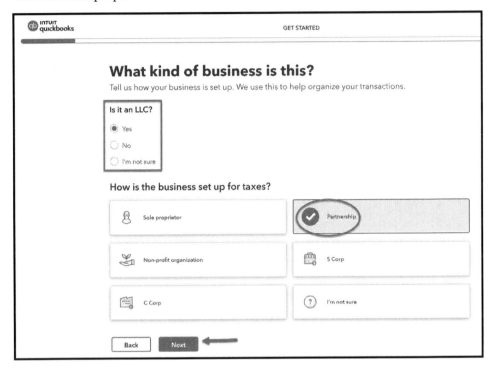

Figure 1.10: Selecting your business structure

14. Click the **Next** button.

Pro Tip: Most small businesses start out as sole proprietors. If you're not sure what your business structure is, talk to your accountant. You can always select **I'm not sure** and answer this question in the company settings section that we will explore in *Chapter 2, Company File Setup*. However, it's important that you select a business structure to customize QuickBooks for your business.

15. In the **Industry** field, type the industry that your business falls into and you will see a variety of options that you can choose from. Small Business Builders, LLC falls into the **Other management consulting services** industry:

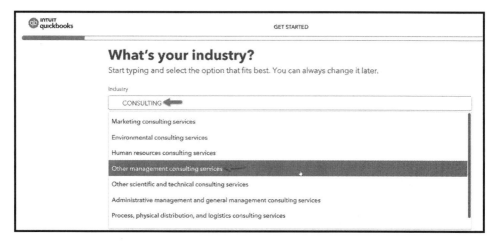

Figure 1.11: Selecting your industry

 Pro Tip: QuickBooks uses the industry selection to create a chart of accounts. Instead of having to create a chart of accounts list from scratch, QBO will provide you with a preset list of accounts that will include a few customized accounts commonly used by businesses in the industry that you select.

16. On the next screen, select your role in the business so that QuickBooks can customize your user experience to meet your specific needs. For Small Business Builders, choose **Owner or partner** and click the **Next** button, as shown in *Figure 1.12*:

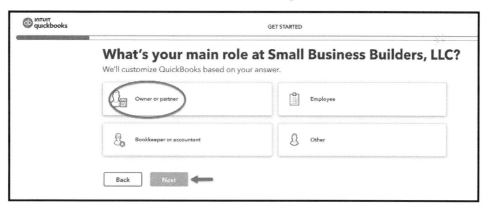

Figure 1.12: Selecting your role in the business

17. Click **Next**.

18. On the next screen, select the type of people that work at the business. Small Business Builders is a partnership with multiple owners who occasionally use contractors. Make the selections as indicated in *Figure 1.13*:

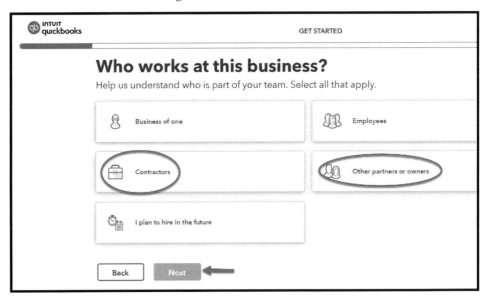

Figure 1.13: Selecting who works at the business

The purpose of this question is to determine whether or not you need to use the payroll features for employees or the contractor features for 1099 vendors. If you are a solopreneur, select **Business of one**. You can always turn on the payroll features when you are ready to hire employees.

19. Click **Next**.

20. On the next screen, you can indicate whether you have a bookkeeper that helps you manage your books.

Figure 1.14: Confirm whether you have a bookkeeper that needs to access QBO

21. Select **No** for Small Business Builders, LLC and click **Next**.

22. On the next screen, you can choose any apps you are currently using or would like to sync with QBO.

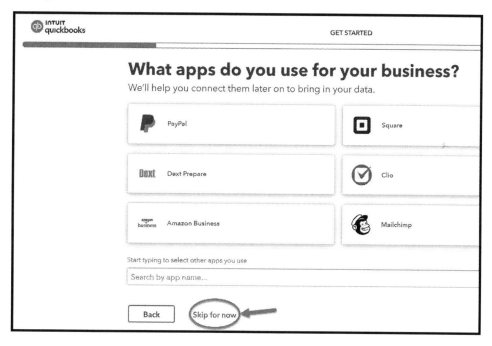

Figure 1.15: Selecting apps to sync with QBO

Pro Tip: One of the benefits of using QBO is the ability to connect it to more than 600 apps that are available in the Intuit App Store. The advantage of connecting apps to QBO is it allows you to share data from other programs with QBO, eliminating manual data entry altogether.

Choose **Skip for now** for Small Business Builders, as indicated in *Figure 1.15*.

23. QuickBooks allows you to link your bank and credit card accounts, so transactions are automatically downloaded. We will cover this in *Chapter 4, Customizing QuickBooks for Your Business*, so let's click **Skip for now**.

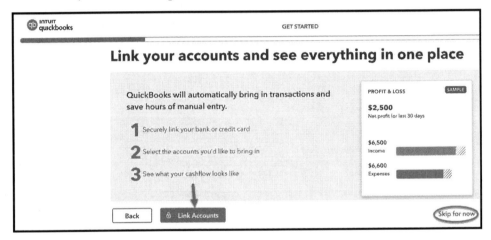

Figure 1.16: Option to link your bank and credit card accounts to QBO

24. On the next screen, indicate how you currently manage paper and digital receipts.

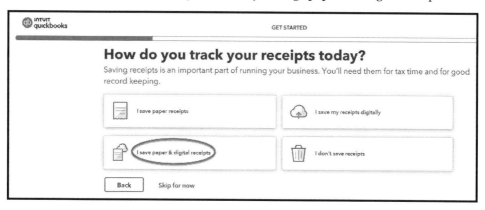

Figure 1.17: Confirm how you currently track your paper receipts

Small Business Builders currently keeps both paper and digital receipts, so click **I save paper & digital receipts**.

25. On the next screen, you can download the QBO app using your Apple or Android device using the QR code displayed.

Figure 1.18: Download the QuickBooks mobile app

26. On the next screen, you can select the features you plan to use in QuickBooks. This information will be used to further customize your user interface to meet your needs.

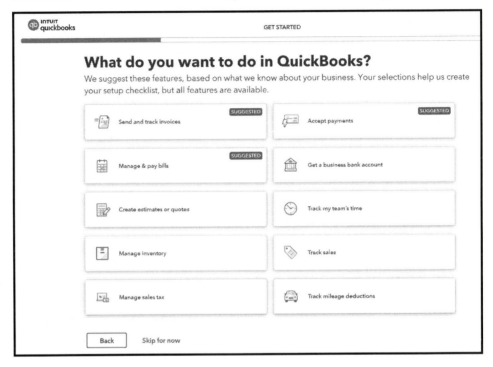

Figure 1.19: Selecting what you want to use QuickBooks for

27. After making your selections, click **Next**.

The following screen will appear:

Figure 1.20: Set up invoices and payment options

28. Click **Next** and the following screen will be displayed:

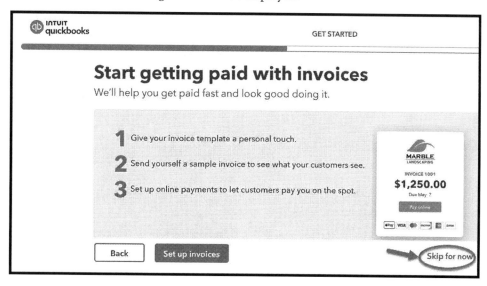

Figure 1.21: Set up invoices

If you choose **Set up invoices,** you can create custom invoice templates and set up your QuickBooks Payments account, which will allow you to accept online payments from customers. We will do this later on.

Choose **Skip for now** and the following screen will appear:

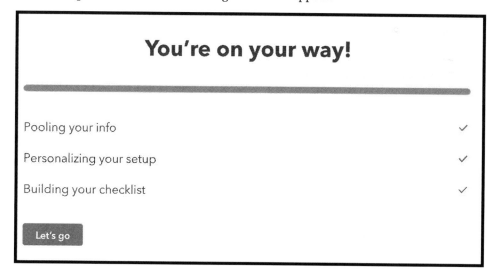

Figure 1.22: Completing the account setup

Congratulations! You have completed the initial QuickBooks setup, taking you one step closer to managing your books. Next, we will show you how to navigate through the program, which will help you locate what you need to complete your business set up.

Navigating in QBO

The QBO user interface is currently undergoing several changes as of the writing of this book. This means that screenshots in this section might vary slightly from what you see when you log in to your QBO account. There are a variety of ways you can navigate within the program, including via the following:

- Dashboards
- Left navigation menu
- The **Quick actions** section in the **Get things done** tab
- Gear menu
- **Quick Create** menu

Let's look at the dashboards and left navigation menu first.

QBO dashboards and left navigation menu

To explore what the QBO dashboards look like, we will use our sample company, Small Business Builders, LLC:

Figure 1.23: QBO dashboards

There are four dashboards that can be accessed from the **Dashboards** tab located on the left menu bar: **Get things done**, **Business overview**, **Cash flow**, and **Planner**. The following is a brief explanation of what you can find on each dashboard along with some snapshots:

- **Get things done**: When you access QBO for the first time, you will see a **Setup Checklist**. This checklist is designed to help you complete your QBO setup so that you can start managing your business finances. There is a **Bank Accounts** section, which gives you the option to link your bank and credit card accounts to QBO. The **Quick action**s section includes icons that allow you to quickly add customers, expenses, and vendors, and perform other tasks quickly, as indicated in *Figure 1.24*:

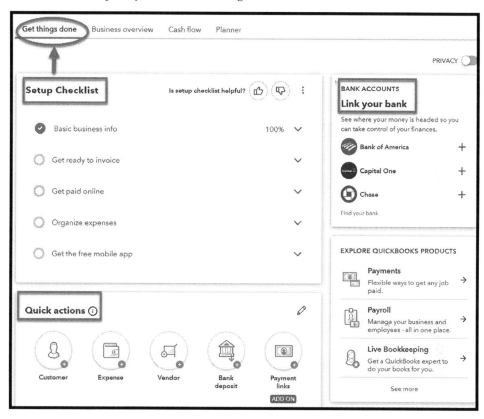

Figure 1.24: Get things done dashboard

- **Business overview**: Insights into your business are available on this dashboard. You can find your profit and loss, total expenses, outstanding invoices (paid and unpaid), and sales here. Similar to the **Get things done** tab, you can link your bank and credit card accounts from here as well, as shown in *Figure 1.25*:

Figure 1.25: Business overview dashboard

- **Cash flow**: This dashboard provides a way for you to track the money coming into and going out of your business. You can see how the **Money in** activities, such as customer payments compares to the **Money out** activities including payments to suppliers and creditors.

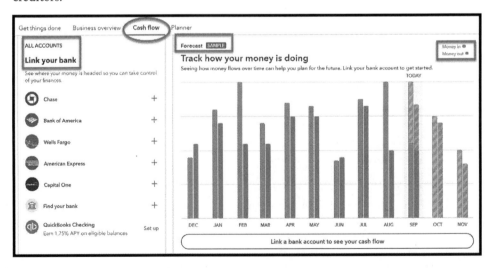

Figure 1.26: Cash flow dashboard

- **Cash flow outlook:** This dashboard provides insight into upcoming **MONEY IN** activities such as open/overdue customer invoices and customer payments that are coming up. In addition, you can view the **MONEY OUT** activities, which include unpaid/overdue bills and recent payments. Last but not least, at the very bottom of this screen, you can see an **Insights and ideas** section that includes upcoming invoices and expenses in the next few months, as indicated in *Figure 1.27*:

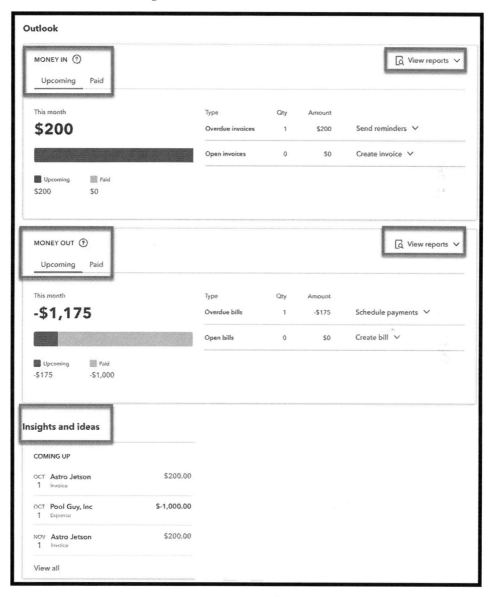

Figure 1.27: Cash flow outlook

- **Planner**: The cash flow planner pulls in the next 3 months of QuickBooks transactions for both money coming in to and going out of your business. This allows you to see what the overall impact on your cash flow will be. With this information, you can take the necessary steps to plan for any cash shortfalls or decide how you want to invest a cash surplus:

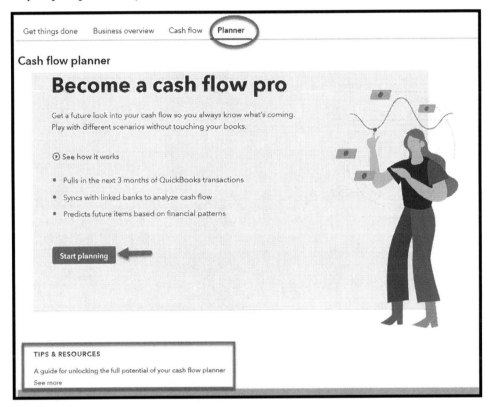

Figure 1.28: Cash flow planner dashboard

The left navigation menu is another way you can maneuver around QuickBooks. In the past, there was a business view and an accountant view that you could switch between. However, as of the writing of this book, both menus have been consolidated into one menu that works best for both accountants and business owners. The following is a snapshot of the new left navigation menu:

Figure 1.29: Left navigation menu

Within each menu, there are sub-menus. For example, if you hover your mouse over **Transactions**, you will see the following sub-menus:

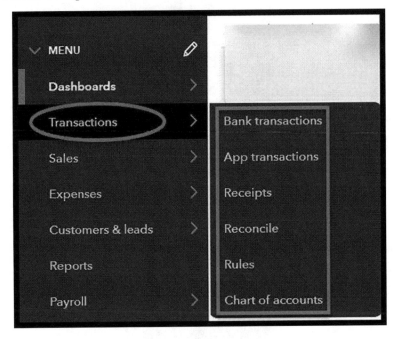

Figure 1.30: QBO sub-menus

Within the **Transactions** menu are **Bank transactions**, **App transactions**, **Receipts**, **Reconcile**, **Rules**, and **Chart of accounts** options. Within **Bank transactions**, you can manage all the transactions downloaded into QBO from the bank and credit card accounts you have linked to QuickBooks. **App transactions** is where you can manage transactions downloaded from the apps you have linked to QBO, such as PayPal, Shopify, Square, and so on. **Receipts** is where you can find any receipts you have uploaded using the QBO app. **Bank rules** allow you to create rules so that QBO can automatically categorize recurring transactions. Finally, **Chart of accounts** is a list of categories you can use to organize income and expense transactions.

Now that you have a better understanding of how to navigate QBO from the dashboards and the left navigation menu, along with how to customize it to fit your needs, let's look at the next navigation tool: icons.

QuickBooks Online icons

The following screenshot shows the common icons that can be found at the top of any screen in QBO:

Figure 1.31: Icons on the home page

The following are explanations of the options in the preceding screenshot:

- **My experts (1)**: Access to a live bookkeeper who can help you get your books set up is available through this link. You can also upgrade your QBO subscription or access a Quick-Books ProAdvisor through **My experts**.

- **Help (2)**: If you have a question or need to learn how to do something in QBO, you can click on this icon to launch the **Help** menu. You will find detailed support articles, video tutorials, and access to a sample company file in this section.

- **My apps (3)**: All sales channels and other apps you have connected with QBO will appear here so that you can easily manage them.

- **Search (4)**: If you need to locate an invoice, bill, or any transaction, you can do a global search of the program by typing an amount name, the name of a vendor, or any information in this field to search for it.

- **Notifications (5)**: Notifications about changes that have been made to your account or upgrades to your QBO subscription can be found here.

- **Gear (6)**: This icon will display a menu of tasks that you can perform in QBO. Tasks related to global company settings, lists, and tools such as reconciling and budgeting can be found here.

- **Account info (7)**: This button allows you to log out of QuickBooks or manage your Intuit account.

As we mentioned previously, the QBO icons allow you to navigate the program so that you can quickly get to the information you need. In addition to icons, the QBO menus allow you to access your overall company settings, lists, tools, and your company profile. We will cover QBO menus next.

QuickBooks Online menus

In addition to the left navigation menu, there are a couple more menus you can use to navigate QBO.

The first menu is accessible through the gear icon, located in the upper right-hand corner, next to the **Notifications** icon. The following screenshot shows the menu that will display when you click on the gear icon:

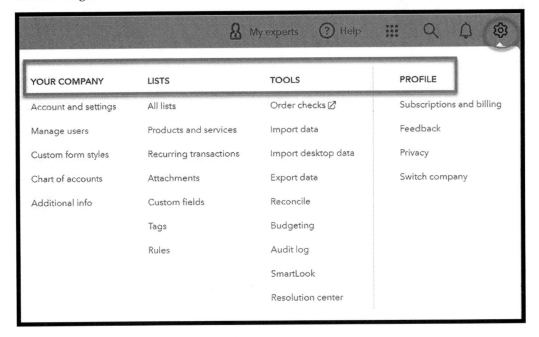

Figure 1.32: Menu options after clicking the gear icon

A brief description of the areas of QBO that you can access through the gear icon is as follows:

- **YOUR COMPANY**: This menu includes global company accounts and settings, which we will explore in detail in the next chapter. It also allows you to access **Manage users**, which is where you can give others access to your QuickBooks data. You can customize forms such as invoices and estimates, launch the chart of accounts, and access additional information, which shows you the keyboard shortcuts you can use to navigate QBO more efficiently.

- **LISTS**: The **Lists** menu includes several QuickBooks lists, such as products and services, recurring transactions, attachments, custom fields, tags, and rules. You can manage recurring transactions such as monthly rent or utility expenses from this menu. In addition, files or images that you have attached to QuickBooks transactions, such as receipts or signed contracts, are accessible in the form of attachments.

- **TOOLS**: If you need to order checks that you can print from QuickBooks, you can do so by selecting the **Order checks** option in this column. If you have customer, vendor, product, or service information that you need to import, you can select **Import data** and follow the on-screen instructions. If you are currently using QuickBooks Desktop, you can use the **Import desktop data** option to migrate your data from desktop to QBO. Also available are the bank and credit card reconciliation tool, the budgeting tool, and the audit log.

- **PROFILE**: You can manage your QBO subscription under the **Subscriptions and billing** section. There is also a **Feedback** section where you can submit recommendations or issues to the Intuit team. The **Privacy** option provides you with information about the built-in privacy features included in QBO. If you have multiple QBO companies, you can choose **Switch company** to navigate from one company to another.

Another menu that is available in QuickBooks is the **Quick Create** menu. You can access this menu by clicking on the **+ New** button located at the very top of the left navigation menu. The following screenshot shows the menu that you will see when you click on the **+ New** button:

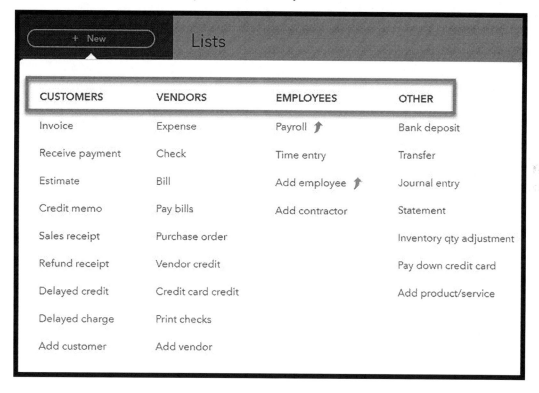

Figure 1.33: The Quick Create menu

Brief descriptions of the areas of QBO that you can access through the **Quick Create** menu are as follows:

- **CUSTOMERS**: Most of the transactions that pertain to customers can be found here, from creating invoices and sales receipts to accepting customer payments and adding new customers, to name a few.

- **VENDORS**: Tasks related to vendors can be found in this section. This includes recording expenses, writing checks, tracking unpaid bills, creating purchase orders, and adding new vendors.

- **EMPLOYEES**: If you sign up for a QuickBooks Payroll subscription, you can access all payroll-related tasks in this section. This includes adding new employees, setting up employee deductions, running payrolls, and making payroll tax payments.

- **OTHER**: This section includes making bank deposits, bank transfers, recording journal entries, generating customer statements, making inventory adjustments, paying down credit cards, and adding products and services.

In this section, we have learned how to access the menus of QBO, all of which give you access to your company information, lists, tools, and profile. In addition, the Quick Create menu allows you to access customers, vendors, employees, and other areas of QuickBooks. From *Chapter 2, Company File Setup*, onwards, we will show you how to navigate through these and customize QuickBooks for your business. To conclude this chapter, we will introduce you to a few important bookkeeping concepts to improve your use of QuickBooks.

Small-business bookkeeping 101

If you are an **Enrolled Agent (EA)**, **Certified Public Accountant (CPA)**, or aspiring bookkeeper or accountant, the concepts that we cover in this section will be familiar to you. However, if you are brand new to bookkeeping, make sure you grab a notepad to take notes, and a cup of coffee to stay alert.

One of the benefits of using QuickBooks to manage your books is that you don't need an accounting degree to learn how to use the software. However, you should have a basic understanding of how bookkeeping works and what's happening behind the scenes in QuickBooks when you record transactions.

The key aspects of small-business bookkeeping are the following:

- Money coming in to your business (sales)
- Money going out of your business (expenses)

- Inventory and fixed asset purchases
- Tracking the money you owe (liabilities)
- Using the chart of accounts to properly track everything
- Accounting methods – cash versus accrual
- Double-entry bookkeeping

Let's discuss each of these areas in more detail.

Recording sales

Every business generates sales by either selling products, services, or a combination of the two. For example, Small Business Builders generates sales by providing consulting services to their clients. Meanwhile, a retailer that sells custom T-shirts in various sizes and colors provides a product to generate sales.

In general, there are two types of sales: **cash sales** and **credit sales**. The primary difference between the two is when you receive payment from your customer. Cash sales are sales that require payment at the time a product is sold or services have been provided. For example, let's say a customer walks into a T-shirt shop and buys a T-shirt. This sale would be considered a cash sale because the sale of the T-shirt and payment by the customer take place at the same time.

Credit sales are the opposite of cash sales because the sale and the payment by the customer take place at separate times. For example, let's say Small Business Builders spends four hours consulting with a client and sends the client a sales invoice at the end of the week. This is considered a credit sale because payment will take place sometime in the future, depending on the payment terms. For bookkeeping purposes, credit sales are recorded as accounts receivable. **Accounts receivable**, also referred to as **A/R**, is the money that is owed to a business by its customers. We will talk more about how to keep track of your A/R balances later on.

Recording expenses

Most of the money that flows out of a business is used to pay for business expenses. Business expenses can be categorized as **recurring** or **non-recurring**. A recurring expense is one that repeats, such as rent, utilities, or insurance, which are typically paid on a monthly basis.

A non-recurring expense is one that is unexpected or takes place less frequently. For example, let's say the air conditioner goes on the blink at your office and you need a repairman to come out and fix it. This would be considered a non-recurring expense because it isn't likely to happen routinely.

QuickBooks is designed to help you easily track both recurring and non-recurring expenses. In this book, we will cover how to create recurring transactions in QuickBooks so that you don't have to manually enter them each time they occur. Plus, you will learn how to pay non-recurring transactions by writing a check, making online payments, or paying with a credit or debit card.

Recording inventory and fixed asset purchases

To keep track of all the costs and quantities for each item that you purchase, you create a purchase order and send it to your vendor supplier to place an order. When you receive the goods, you record them in your inventory. As you sell products to customers, you record the sales in QuickBooks so that your inventory, cost, and quantities can be adjusted in real time.

If you purchase computers, printers, or other equipment for your business, these items are called **fixed assets**. When you record these items in QuickBooks, they will be categorized as fixed assets. Fixed assets should be **depreciated** over their useful life. Depreciation is the reduction of the value of an asset due to wear and tear.

Pro Tip: Be sure to refer to current IRS guidelines or your tax preparer regarding thresholds for capitalizing assets versus expensing them at the time of purchase. Also, keep track of all receipts for fixed asset purchases so your tax preparer can calculate the amount of depreciation you are able to deduct on your tax return. Receipt capture can make it easy to upload receipts from your mobile device to QuickBooks. In *Chapter 8, Recording Expenses in QuickBooks Online*, we cover this in detail.

Recording liabilities

Many people think that liabilities are expenses, but they are not. A liability can be described as money that is owed to creditors, such as a loan you have with a financial institution or money that you owe to vendor suppliers, which is also called **accounts payable**. The primary difference between expenses and liabilities is that if you were to go out of business tomorrow, you would no longer have to pay expenses. Instead, you would stop making payments for utilities, and you would lay off employees to eliminate payroll expenses.

On the other hand, if you go out of business, you still have to pay your outstanding liabilities. They don't just disappear as expenses do. For example, if you have an outstanding loan with a bank, you still owe that money and will have to contact the financial institution to make payment arrangements. The same would apply to unpaid bills for products and/or services you received. This means you would have to contact the vendor/supplier and notify them you were going out of business in order to make payment arrangements.

Note: Money you borrow is not income, it is a liability that you will repay. Loan repayments are not expenses, they are a reduction of the liability that you owe.

The chart of accounts

The chart of accounts is a systematic way of categorizing financial business transactions. Every transaction for your business can be categorized into one of five primary categories: **Assets, Liabilities, Owner's Equity, Income, and Expenses**.

Here is a brief description of each category, with an example:

- **Assets**: Assets are items that your business owns. For example, the money in your business checking account is an asset, and the inventory that you have on hand is an asset until it is sold.
- **Liabilities**: As discussed, liabilities consist of money that you owe to creditors. This includes loans, lines of credit, and the money owed to vendor suppliers (for example, A/P).
- **Owner's equity**: Equity is everything the owner has invested in the business. For example, any money that you invest in your business is equity.
- **Income**: Proceeds from the sale of products, such as T-shirts, or services such as photography or consulting.
- **Expenses**: Payments made to maintain daily business operations. This includes, but is not limited to, rent, utilities, payroll, and office supplies.

When setting up your QuickBooks company account, you don't have to worry about creating a chart of accounts from scratch. Instead, QuickBooks will create a default chart of accounts based on the industry your business falls into. However, you can add and edit accounts to fit the needs of your business.

Choosing an accounting method

One of the key decisions a business will make when setting up their books is which accounting method to use. There are two accounting methods to choose from: **cash-basis accounting** and **accrual accounting**. The primary difference between the two accounting methods is the point when you record sales and purchase transactions as having occurred in your books.

Cash-basis accounting involves recording sales and purchases when cash changes hands. Going back to our previous example, where Small Business Builders invoices a client for consulting services provided, based on cash-basis accounting, Small Business Builders cannot count the consulting services as income until they receive payment in cash, by check, or by credit card.

Accrual accounting involves recording sales as soon as you have shipped the products to your customer or have provided services. Going back to our example, Small Business Builders would count the consulting services they provided as income once they completed the consultations, regardless of when the customer pays for the services.

In general, most small business owners will start out using the cash-basis accounting method. However, according to the **Internal Revenue Service (IRS)**, there are certain types of businesses that are not allowed to use this method of accounting.

The following businesses should never use cash-basis accounting:

- Businesses that carry an inventory
- C-corporations (regular corporations)
- Businesses with gross annual sales that exceed $5 million

One of the benefits of using QuickBooks, regardless of which accounting method you choose, is that it does not change how you record transactions. As a matter of fact, you can start recording transactions in QuickBooks and decide later on which method you will use. This is because, at any time, you can run reports for either method (cash or accrual). QuickBooks will determine which transactions belong in the report based on the accounting method chosen. In *Chapter 10, Report Center Overview*, we will cover in detail how to generate reports.

Double-entry bookkeeping

One of the key reasons why you don't need to have prior bookkeeping knowledge to use QBO is because the software records all debits and credits for you in the background. However, I thought it would be helpful to explain what is actually taking place when you record an invoice, a bill, or another transaction in QBO. You may have heard the term **double-entry accounting/bookkeeping**. This means that for every financial transaction you record, there are at least two entries—a debit and a credit. This ensures that both sides of the **accounting equation** always remain in balance.

The accounting equation is as follows:

```
Assets = Liabilities + Owner's Equity
```

Let's look at the following example. A T-shirt business owner goes out and purchases $100 of T-shirts from a supplier. They don't pay for the T-shirts right away, but the supplier will send a bill later on. For this transaction, inventory increases by $100 and accounts payable increase by $100. Since inventory is an **asset** and accounts payable is a **liability**, both **assets** and **liabilities** increased, which keeps our books in balance.

The impact of this transaction on the accounting equation is as follows:

```
Assets = Liabilities + Owner's Equity
$100 = $100 + $0
```

The left side of the equation (**Assets**) goes up by $100 and the right side of the equation (**Liabilities**) goes up by the same amount, $100. Therefore, the equation has been kept in balance.

Behind the scenes in QuickBooks, the following journal entry would be recorded for this transaction:

Financial impact	Account	Amount
Debit (Dr.)	Inventory (T-shirts)	$100
Credit (Cr.)	Accounts Payable	$100

Table 1.2: Example journal entry

We will discuss journal entries in more detail in *Chapter 15, Closing the Books in QuickBooks Online*.

In this section, we have covered the seven main areas of focus when managing the books for your business: money coming into a business in the form of sales to customers; money going out of a business for expenses such as office supplies and rent; inventory and fixed asset purchases, and how to record them in your books; money you owe to suppliers and creditors (liabilities); how to manage the chart of accounts; the two accounting methods (cash-basis versus accrual); and how double-entry bookkeeping works.

Summary

In this chapter, we explained what QuickBooks is and introduced you to the QBO product line. We covered setting up your QBO account and basic navigation using dashboards, icons, and online menus in QBO. We also provided tips on how to choose the right software for your business, and we provided you with some bookkeeping basics. Having a good understanding of the QuickBooks product line will help you to choose the best product for your business. In addition, having a basic knowledge of bookkeeping helps you understand the accounting that is taking place behind the scenes in QuickBooks when you enter an invoice or pay a bill.

In the next chapter, we will show you how to customize QuickBooks for your business. This will include setting up company preferences and other key information you will need in order to tailor QuickBooks to your business needs.

Join our community on Discord

Join our community's Discord space for discussions with the authors and other readers:

`https://packt.link/quickbooks`

2

Company File Setup

Picking up where we left off in *Chapter 1, Getting Started with QuickBooks Online*, we will show you how to customize your **QuickBooks Online (QBO)** account through the company preferences. Company preferences allow you to establish how sales and expenses are recorded, how payments are handled, and other advanced settings, such as selecting the start of your fiscal year and which accounting method to use.

Before we dive into company preferences, we will spend some time discussing key information and documents that you need to have handy. This will help you to include as much information as possible; otherwise, you will be missing key details that should appear on customer invoices, documents, and forms that can be produced in QuickBooks. In addition, we will show you how easy it is to edit information in this section whenever you need to.

In this chapter, we'll cover the following topics:

- Key information and documents required to complete the company file setup in QBO
- Setting up company preferences in QBO

 The US edition of QBO was used to create this book. If you are using a version that is outside of the United States, results may differ.

Key information and documents

Before we get into the mechanics of creating your company file, you will need to gather some key documents and answer a few questions first. This information is necessary so that you can customize QuickBooks for your business. Plus, having this information at your fingertips will help you to complete the company setup a lot faster.

The information you will need to know includes the following:

- **Company name**: This needs to be the legal name or the business name that should appear on all legal documents and payroll forms.

- **Company contact information**: This will include the mailing address, business telephone number, business email address, and website address of the company.

- **Industry**: In QuickBooks, you will select the industry that your business falls into. Using this information, a default chart of accounts list will be created for you.

- **Federal tax ID number**: A nine-digit number that identifies your business to the IRS. If you don't have a federal tax ID number, you can use your social security number.

- **Company organization type**: In QuickBooks, you will need to select from one of the following organization types: sole proprietor, partnership or LLC, nonprofit organization, C-Corp, or S-Corp.

 If you are a new business, this information can be found in the letter from the IRS that includes your **federal tax identification number (EIN)**. If you are an existing business, this information can be found on your most recently filed tax return for your business.

- **Fiscal year**: In QuickBooks, you will need to enter your company's fiscal year. For example, if you are on a calendar year, it will be January 1 to December 31.

- **List of products you sell**: If you have a lot of products, you should create an Excel or CSV spreadsheet that includes the product name, product description, cost, price, and quantity on hand. If you track inventory, we will show you how to import this information in *Chapter 5, Managing Customer, Vendor, and Products and Services Lists*.

- **List of services you sell**: Similar to products, you should create an Excel or CSV spreadsheet that includes the name of the service, a brief description, and the price. We will show you how to import this information in *Chapter 5, Managing Customer, Vendor, and Products and Services Lists*.

- **List of sales tax rates**: A list of each city, state, or jurisdiction for which you are required to collect sales tax, along with the name of the tax authority that you pay, is required to properly set up sales tax in QuickBooks.

- **List of customers**: Customer contact details, such as an address, email address, telephone number, Facebook handle, or other information you have on file, can be entered into an Excel or CSV file if you wish to import the information into QuickBooks.

Like products and services, we will show you how to import this information in *Chapter 5, Managing Customer, Vendor, and Products and Services Lists*.

- **List of vendor suppliers**: Vendor contact details, such as a remit-to address, email address, telephone number, primary contacts, and other information you have on file, can be entered into an Excel or CSV file if you wish to import it into QuickBooks. Similar to products, services, and customers, we will show you how to import this information in *Chapter 5, Managing Customer, Vendor, and Products and Services Lists*.

- **Chart of accounts list**: Your current list of accounts can be entered into an Excel spreadsheet if you wish to easily import it into QuickBooks. We show you how to import this information in *Chapter 5, Managing Customer, Vendor, and Products and Services Lists*.

 Pro Tip: Be sure to have copies of your most recent bank and credit card statements, along with the last bank reconciliations completed.

By taking the time to gather these documents, you will ensure that you are not missing key information when you create forms such as customer invoices. In addition, your financial statements will be more accurate and reliable.

QuickBooks includes default settings called **preferences**. You can edit preferences to customize them to your specific business needs.

Setting up company preferences in QBO

Before you start entering data into QuickBooks, you should spend some time going through the company preferences, which allow you to activate features that you would like to use and deactivate features that you don't plan on using. If you are not sure of what to select in this section, you can always update the settings later on. Click on the gear icon and select **Account and settings**, located below the **Your Company** column.

The company preferences are made up of eight key areas:

- Company settings
- Billing & subscription settings
- Usage settings
- Sales settings
- Expenses settings

- Payments settings
- Time settings
- Advanced settings

Let's look at each one of these in more detail.

Company settings

In your company preferences, you will provide basic information about your business, such as the contact email and telephone number, where customers can reach you, your company logo, and your mailing address. The contact information that's included in this section will appear on customer invoices and emails that are sent to them, ensuring that they know how to get in contact with you. You will also provide your company name and entity type (sole proprietor, partnership, LLC, C-Corp, or S-Corp). It is also a good idea to enter your **employer identification number** (**EIN**) or social security number in this section. This information will be used to file payroll tax returns and 1099 forms, and it can also be used by your tax preparer when filing your taxes.

A brief explanation of the entity types follows:

- **Sole proprietor**: A business that has one owner. Sole proprietors generally file a Schedule C to report their business income and expenses, along with IRS Form 1040.

- **Partnership**: A business with two or more owners. Partnerships generally file IRS Form 1065 to report their business income and expenses to the IRS.

- **Limited Liability Company** (**LLC**): A company with one or more owners who are not personally liable for the LLC's debts or lawsuits.

- **C-Corp**: A corporation that is taxed separately from its owners. Corporations typically file IRS Form 1020 to report business income and expenses.

- **S-Corp**: A closely held corporation that elects to be taxed under IRS Subchapter S. S-Corps typically file IRS Form 1020S to report business income and expenses.

Once you have filled in the **Company** settings, this page should resemble the one for our fictitious company, Small Business Builders, LLC, shown in *Figure 2.1*:

Figure 2.1: Company settings

The information provided in the **Company** preferences can impact several areas of QuickBooks, such as customer invoices, tax forms, and documents. Therefore, it's important to complete this information in its entirety before you begin using QuickBooks to track your business activity. Next, we will explain what information you will find in the **Billing & subscription** preferences.

Billing & subscription settings

The **Billing & subscription** settings provide details of the QBO plans and services you have subscribed to.

Your screen should resemble the one for our fictitious company, Small Business Builders, LLC, as shown in *Figure 2.2*:

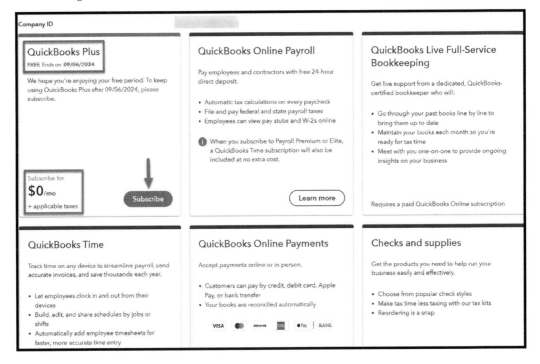

Figure 2.2: Billing & subscription settings

A brief description of the information you will find in the billing and subscription settings is as follows:

- **QuickBooks subscription**: Your subscription status will appear in this section. In our example, we are using QBO Plus. If you are currently using a trial version, it will show you the date the trial expires. After the trial period ends, you can click the **Subscribe** button to sign up for a paid account. If you are already signed up for QBO, you will see an upgrade and downgrade button should you decide to change your subscription plan. You can upgrade or downgrade your QBO subscription at any time.

- **QuickBooks Online Payroll**: If you have subscribed to Payroll, the details of your Payroll plan will be in this section. If you would like to sign up for a Payroll subscription, click on the **Learn more** link and follow the onscreen prompts to select a Payroll plan. Note that additional fees will apply.

- **QuickBooks Live Full-Service Bookkeeping**: QuickBooks provides bookkeeping services for those small businesses that need it. You can click on this tile to learn more about the plans available.

- **QuickBooks Time:** This is a time-tracking tool that integrates with QBO. If you have employees in the office or out in the field, they can clock in from any mobile device with an internet connection. Click on **Learn more** for additional information.

- **QuickBooks Online Payments**: If you would like to accept online payments from customers, sign up for QuickBooks Payments services. With this service, your customers can pay their invoices online via ACH bank transfer, debit card, credit card, or Apple Pay. Click on the **Learn more** link to sign up; note that additional fees will apply.

- **Checks and supplies:** If you write a lot of checks to pay bills, you should consider printing checks directly from QuickBooks. You can order checks from Intuit by clicking on the **Shop now** button. You can also order checks through your bank.

Now that you know how to review your subscription status and what services you are subscribed to, you need to know what your usage limits are. We will discuss what usage limits are and how they can affect your QBO subscription next.

Usage settings

A few years ago, Intuit implemented usage limits on all QBO plans. What this means is that each plan will have a maximum number of billable users, classes, locations, and accounts that you can add to the chart of accounts. The following is a brief description of these:

- **Billable users:** The total number of users you can give access to your QBO account. This includes bookkeepers, accountants, employees, and contractors.

- **Classes**: Depending on your business, a class can represent departments, office locations, or product lines. For example, our business management and consulting business could create a class for each type of service that they offer (for example, business plans, marketing plans, bookkeeping, tax planning, social media, etc). One of the benefits of using classes is the ability to generate reports you can filter by class.

- **Locations:** If you have multiple locations, you can turn on location tracking in QuickBooks. One of the benefits of using locations is you can generate reports and filter by location.

- **Chart of accounts:** We discussed the chart of accounts in the *Small business bookkeeping 101* section of *Chapter 1, Getting Started with QuickBooks Online*. The chart of accounts is used to classify your day-to-day business transactions. For example, office supplies and telephone expenses are two accounts that appear on the chart of accounts.

- **Tag groups:** Tags are customizable labels that let you track transactions in a variety of ways. You can tag invoices, expenses, and bills. You can also group tags together and run reports to see how specific areas of your business are doing.

The following is a summary table that includes the usage limits for each QBO plan:

	QBO Simple Start	QBO Essentials	QBO Plus	QBO Advanced
Classes and locations (combined)	0	0	40	Unlimited
Chart of accounts	250	250	250	Unlimited
Tag groups	10	20	40	Unlimited
Billable users	1	3	5	25

Table 2.1: QBO usage limits for each plan

Here is a brief explanation of the usage limits for each QBO plan:

- **QBO Simple Start:** QBO Simple Start does not have the ability to track classes or locations. You can have up to 250 accounts on the chart of accounts list. One billable user and two accountant users are included in this plan.

- **QBO Essentials:** Similar to Simple Start, QBO Essentials does not have the ability to track classes or locations. You can have up to 250 accounts on the chart of accounts list. Three billable users (that is, bookkeepers or employees) and two accountant users are included in this plan.

- **QBO Plus:** QBO Plus allows you to track classes and locations. You can add up to a total of 40 classes and/or locations combined. Five billable users and two accountant users are included in this plan.

- **QBO Advanced:** QBO Advanced allows you to track unlimited classes and locations. In addition, 25 billable users and 3 accountant users are included in this plan.

Your usage settings should resemble the ones for our fictitious company, Small Business Builders, LLC, as shown in *Figure 2.3*:

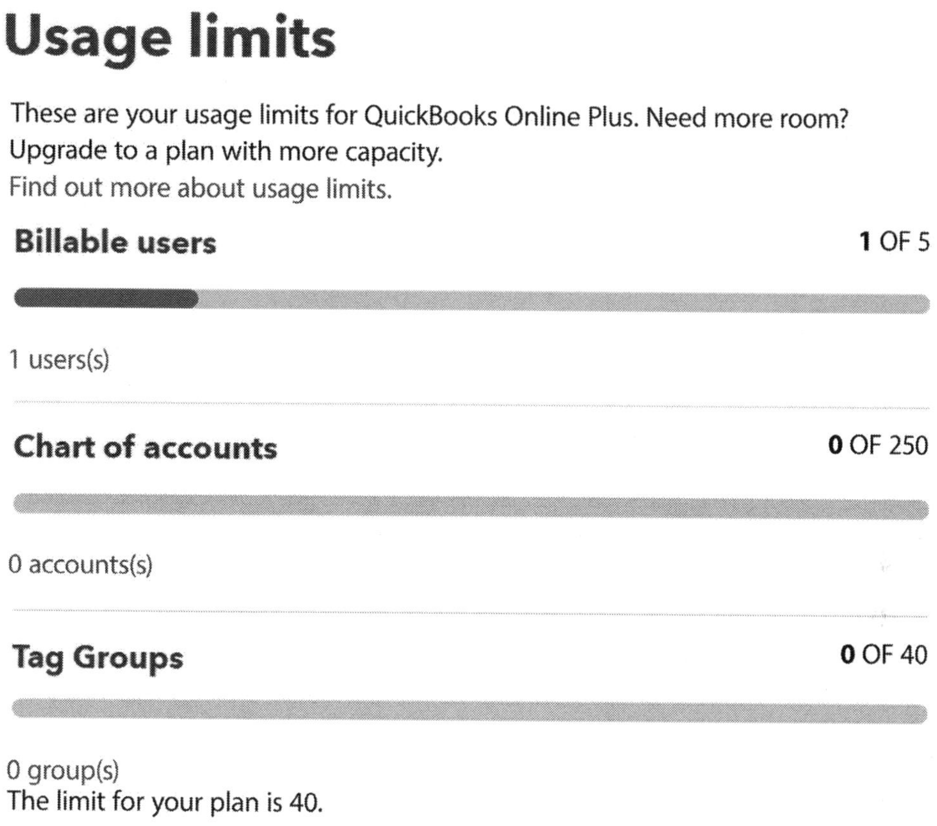

Usage limits

These are your usage limits for QuickBooks Online Plus. Need more room?
Upgrade to a plan with more capacity.
Find out more about usage limits.

Billable users   **1** OF 5

1 users(s)

Chart of accounts   **0** OF 250

0 accounts(s)

Tag Groups   **0** OF 40

0 group(s)
The limit for your plan is 40.

Figure 2.3: Usage settings

As we mentioned previously, usage limits can impact the number of users you can add to QBO and the classes, locations, and accounts you add to the chart of accounts. This can have a significant effect on how much you pay for your QBO subscription if you hit the maximum usage settings and need to upgrade.

Sales settings

The **Sales** settings allow you to select and customize invoices, estimates, and sales receipt templates. In this section, payment terms are set for customers. If you have a few customers whose payment terms differ, you can customize payment terms when you add a new customer. If you offer discounts to customers or require upfront deposits, you can turn these features on here.

The following is a screenshot of the settings for **Sales**:

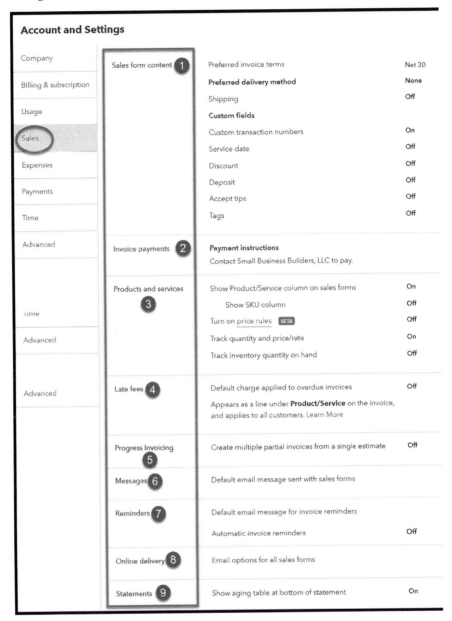

Figure 2.4: Sales settings

Here is a brief explanation of the information you can update/change in the **Sales** settings. You can click within each section or on the pencil icon to make the necessary changes:

1. **Sales form content (1)**: In this section, you can select the default payment terms for most customers. For example, if the invoice due date for most customers is Net 30 days, you will make that selection in the **Preferred invoice terms** field (shown in *Figure 2.4*). If you have customers that have different payment terms, you can select those terms when you add the customer to QuickBooks.

   If you offer customer discounts, accept deposits, or want to add custom fields, you will also turn these features on in this section. The main reason why you may want to offer customer discounts is to incentivize customers to order more, or use them as a way to reward customers who make frequent purchases. If you typically need to include a shipping address on your sales form, you can turn this feature on here. QuickBooks will automatically assign transaction numbers (invoice numbers), but if you prefer to generate custom transaction numbers, you can turn this feature on. Keep in mind that you can always return to the **Sales form content** section to activate any of these settings later on.

2. **Payment instructions (2)**: If you sign up for a QuickBooks Payments account, the payment methods that you accept will appear in this section. We will discuss how to apply for a Payments account in the *Payment settings* section later in this chapter.

3. **Products and services (3)**: The **Products and services** settings allow you to determine what information you would like to appear on the sales form. You can turn on **price rules**, which is a feature that allows you to set up automatic discounts for certain customers or on specific products and services. If you want to track inventory, you will need to turn on both the **Track quantity and price/rate** and **Track inventory quantity on hand** features.

4. **Late fees (4)**: Create a default charge that is automatically applied to delinquent invoices. Please note that when you turn this feature on, it applies to all customers. You are not able to pick and choose which customers you want this to apply to.

5. **Progress Invoicing (5)**: Progress invoicing allows you to bill a customer in installments. For example, imagine you have a job that is going to result in $100,000 in revenue but you are required to complete certain milestones before you can submit an invoice. Progress billing allows you to create multiple invoices for one estimate. QuickBooks allows you to run reports that will show you how much you have billed against the estimate and the remaining amount to be billed.

6. **Messages (6)**: When you email invoices, sales receipts, or estimates directly from QuickBooks, you can customize the message that is included in the body of the email. You can also select whether you want the invoice to be attached to the email as a PDF document or whether you prefer the invoice details to be included in the body of the email.

Below is a screenshot of the custom email message options you can choose from:

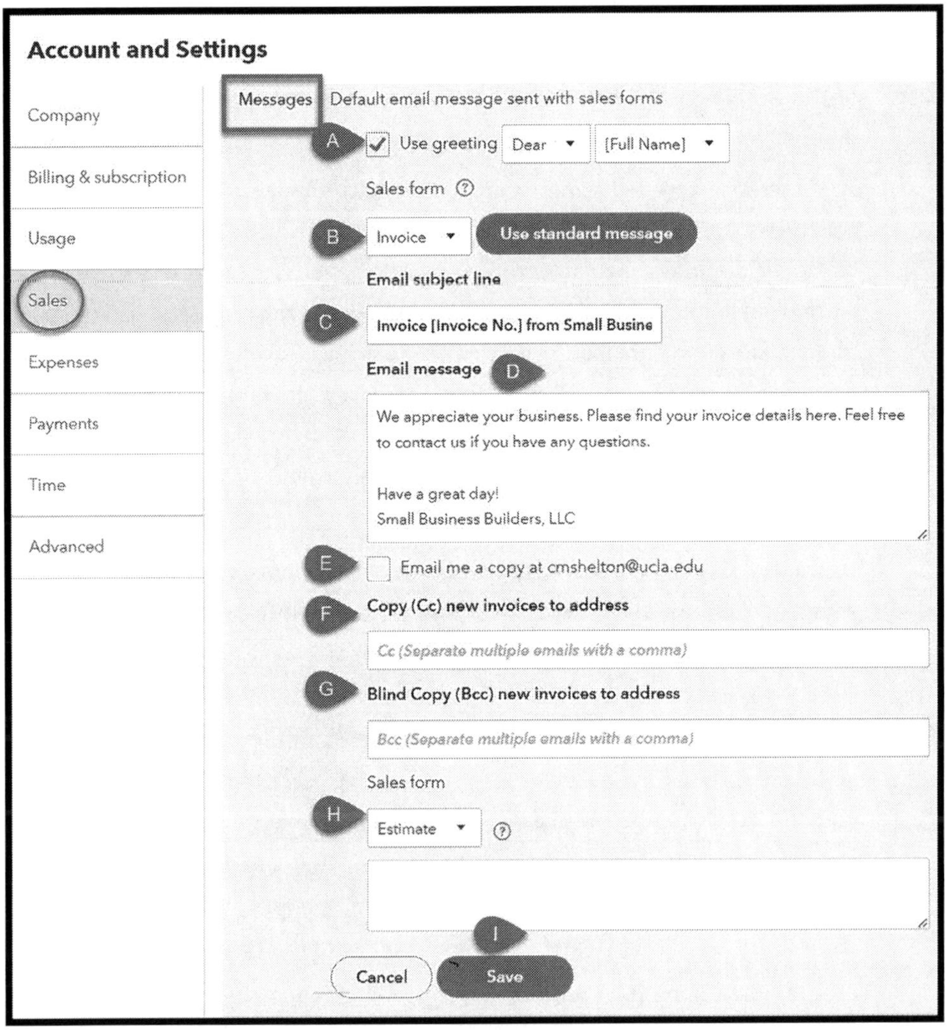

Figure 2.5: Customizing the email message for invoices, estimates, and sales receipts

To customize emails, you can choose to use a greeting (**A**), select the type of form (**B**), customize the email subject line (**C**), customize the email message (**D**), or choose to use the standard message shown. You can have a copy of the email sent to you (**E**), send a carbon copy to someone else (**F**), and **blind-copy** (Bcc) new invoices to multiple people (**G**). You can also customize emails for estimates and sales receipts by choosing the option from the drop-down (**H**).

After making your selections, be sure to click the **Save** button (I).

7. **Reminders (7)**: QuickBooks allows you to send payment reminder emails to customers. You can customize the message that goes out to your customers in this section.

8. **Online delivery (8)**: Online delivery allows you to select the format of all the sales forms that will go out to customers. The options are PDF, HTML, or a link to the online invoice. The selections that are made here will affect all invoices, sales receipts, and estimates that are emailed directly from QuickBooks.

9. **Statements (9)**: If you prefer to send statements to customers, you can select from two types of formats. You can have each transaction listed as a single line on the statement, or you can list each transaction and the details on the statement.

Now that you know how to customize sales forms, set payment terms for customers, and turn on discounts and deposits, it's time to learn how to manage expenses. We will discuss **Expense** settings next.

Expense settings

The settings in the **Expense** section include preferences for managing bills, expenses, and purchase orders. In this section, you will determine what information you want to appear on expense and purchase forms, whether you want to track expenses and items by customer, and default payment terms.

The following is a screenshot of the **Expense** settings:

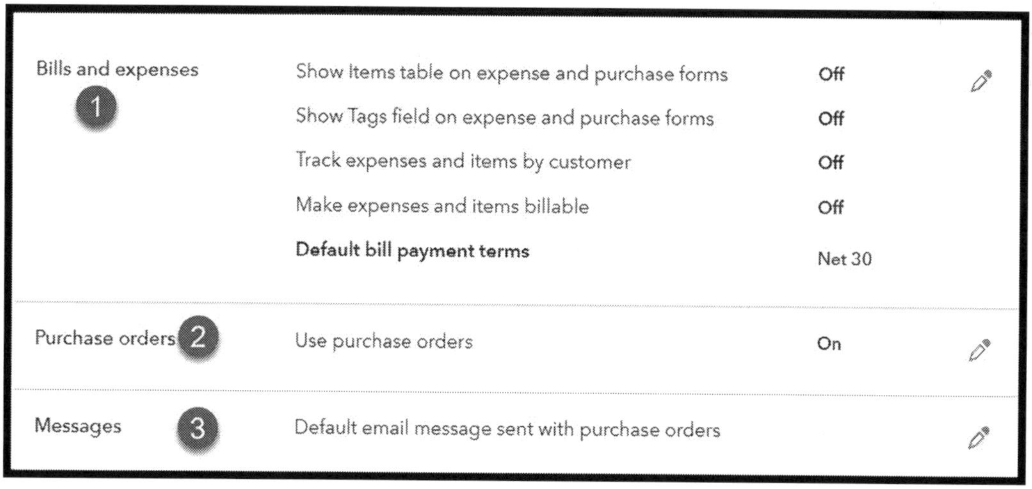

Bills and expenses ①	Show Items table on expense and purchase forms	Off	
	Show Tags field on expense and purchase forms	Off	
	Track expenses and items by customer	Off	
	Make expenses and items billable	Off	
	Default bill payment terms	Net 30	
Purchase orders ②	Use purchase orders	On	
Messages ③	Default email message sent with purchase orders		

Figure 2.6: Expense settings

The following is a brief explanation of what you can find in the **Expense** preferences:

1. **Bills and expenses (1)**: This section includes the following five options for tracking expenses:

   - **Show Items table on expense and purchase forms**: This feature is automatically turned on, and it will add a *products and services* table to your expense and purchase forms so that you can itemize your products and services. You will learn more about products and services lists in *Chapter 5, Managing Customer, Vendor, and Products and Services Lists.*

   - **Show Tags field on expense and purchase forms**: This feature is automatically turned on. If you don't use tags to track expenses, you can turn this feature off.

   - **Track expenses and items by customer**: This feature allows you to tag expenses with a specific customer. This is ideal for reporting purposes if you want to keep track of specific items that have been purchased but may or may not be billable to customers. For example, let's say we want to keep track of the hours worked by contractors for each client. If Small Business Builders, LLC bill their customers a flat rate, then there is no need to bill the client back for those hours worked, but they need to keep track of them to ensure the flat rate is accurate.

   - **Make expenses and items billable**: This feature adds a billable column on all expense and purchase forms so that you can bill customers for items you've purchased on their behalf. Using our previous example, if Small Business Builders, LLC did bill their customers by the hour, they could easily select the client and mark the billable column to bill their clients for the hours worked by contactors, as opposed to billing them a flat fee.

   - To see a list of unbilled expenses, you can run the *Unbilled Charges* report, which is located in the **Who Owes You** report group.

   - **Default bill payment terms**: If most of the bills you receive have similar payment terms (for instance, **Net 30**), you can set payment terms for all vendors here and then change the vendor profile for those vendors whose payment terms may differ. In *Chapter 5, Managing Customer, Vendor, and Products and Services Lists*, we cover this in detail.

2. **Purchase orders (2)**: If you plan to create purchase orders, be sure to turn this feature on. If you don't need to create purchase orders, you can leave it turned off.

3. **Messages (3)**: You can email purchase orders directly from QuickBooks to vendor suppliers. This section allows you to customize the email message that your vendor supplier will receive along with the purchase orders.

Now that you are familiar with the **Expense** settings that affect bills, purchase orders, and expenses, you can set up QuickBooks the way you need in order to track expenses that are incurred by your business. Next, we will discuss a way for you to get paid faster by your customers using QuickBooks Payments.

Payments settings

QuickBooks Payments allows you to accept online payments from customers in the form of bank transfers, debit cards, and credit cards. Once approved, all the invoices that you email to customers (directly from QuickBooks) will include a payment link. Your customers can click on the link, enter their payment details, and submit a payment in just a few minutes.

To apply for a **QuickBooks Payments** account, click on the **Learn more** button shown in *Figure 2.7*:

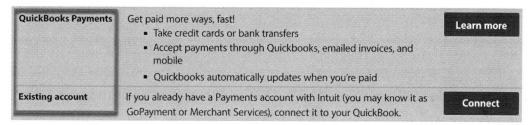

Figure 2.7: Payments settings

If you have an existing Payments account, you can connect it by clicking the **Connect** button and following the onscreen instructions.

As we mentioned previously, QuickBooks Payments makes it easier to get paid by customers in a timely manner. This will allow you to maintain a positive cash flow, which is important for your business.

Time settings

Basic time tracking is included in all QBO subscription plans. Time tracking allows your team to keep track of the hours they work, using a mobile app with GPS. With GPS, you are able to see the location that a worker clocked in from. In addition, workers can keep track of their mileage. As a business owner, you can schedule workers, manage time off, and review reports in real time. To learn more about the time tracking plans available, click on the **See plans** button, as shown in *Figure 2.8*:

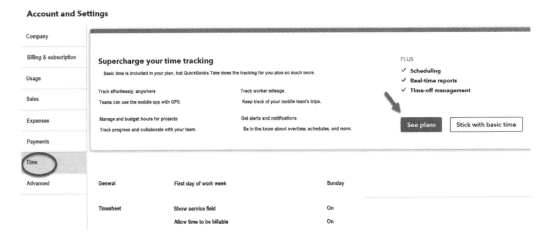

Figure 2.8: See plans button on the Time settings page

Advanced settings

The **Advanced settings** page includes eight key settings: **Accounting**, **Company type**, **Chart of accounts**, **Categories**, **Automation**, **Projects**, **Currency**, and **Other preferences**.

The following is a screenshot of the **Advanced** settings section:

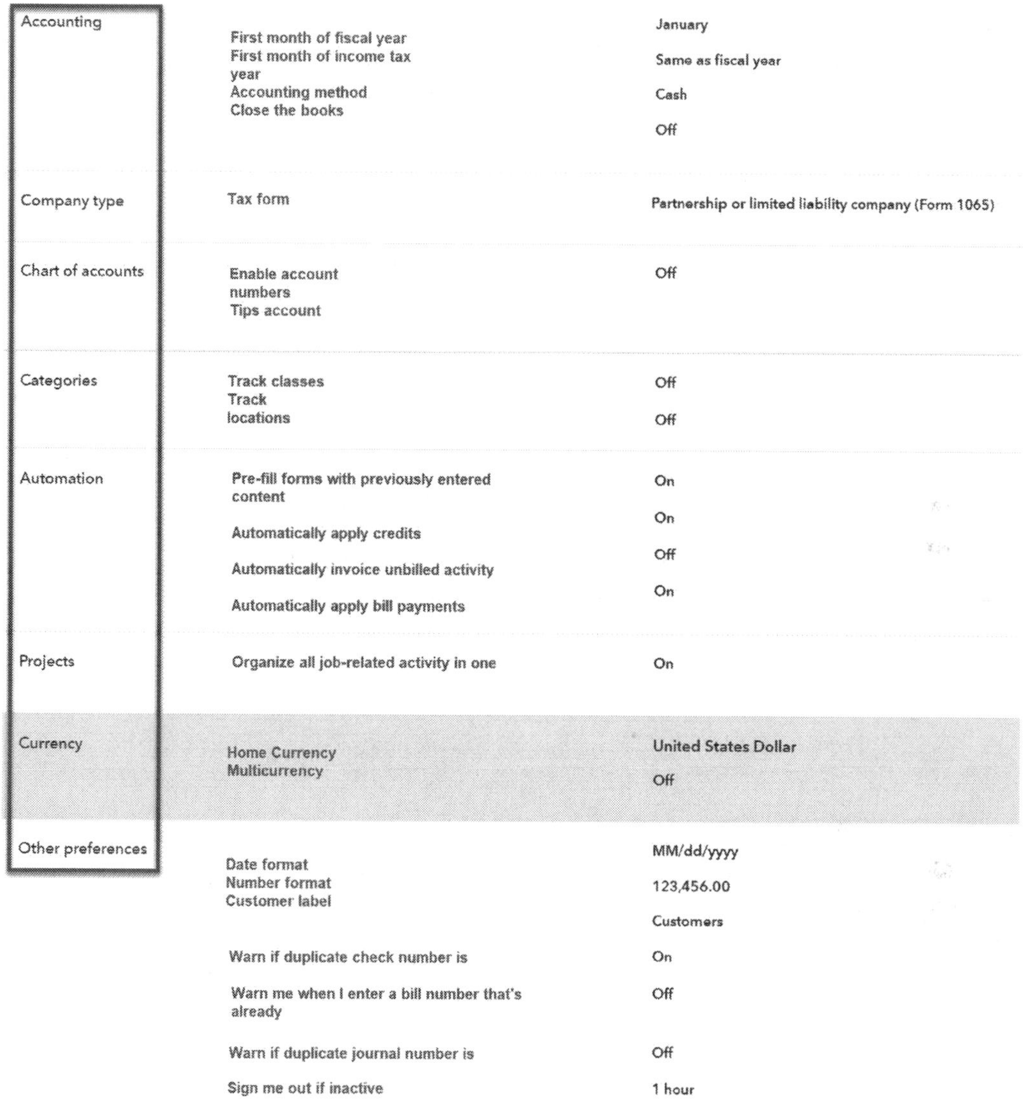

Accounting	First month of fiscal year	January
	First month of income tax year	Same as fiscal year
	Accounting method	Cash
	Close the books	Off
Company type	Tax form	Partnership or limited liability company (Form 1065)
Chart of accounts	Enable account numbers	Off
	Tips account	
Categories	Track classes	Off
	Track locations	Off
Automation	Pre-fill forms with previously entered content	On
	Automatically apply credits	On
	Automatically invoice unbilled activity	Off
	Automatically apply bill payments	On
Projects	Organize all job-related activity in one	On
Currency	Home Currency	United States Dollar
	Multicurrency	Off
Other preferences	Date format	MM/dd/yyyy
	Number format	123,456.00
	Customer label	Customers
	Warn if duplicate check number is	On
	Warn me when I enter a bill number that's already	Off
	Warn if duplicate journal number is	Off
	Sign me out if inactive	1 hour

Figure 2.9: Advanced settings

A brief description of what information is included in the **Advanced** settings section is as follows:

- **Accounting**: In the accounting settings, you will select the first month of your fiscal year and income tax year, which may be the same. You will indicate your accounting method (for example, cash or accrual), and there is an option to close the books. Closing the books allows you to prevent any changes from being made to your financial data after a certain date. For example, once you have filed your tax returns for the year, you should enter the last day of the previous year as your closing date (for example, 12/31/2023). This will ensure that information dated 12/31/2023 and prior cannot be changed. A password will be assigned to prevent changes to closed periods.

- **Company type**: In this field, you will select the structure of your business. The common business structures are sole proprietor, partnership, limited liability, C-Corp, and S-Corp. In our example, Small Business Builders is a **limited liability company (LLC)**.

 Pro Tip: The company type is helpful in assigning your chart of accounts to specific line items on the tax return. This is beneficial for linking to tax software or for your tax preparer. For example, if you are a sole proprietor, then you will complete *Schedule C* to report your business income and expenses to the IRS. When adding a new account to the chart of accounts list, the field named **Tax Form Section** will list the categories on *Schedule C* so that you can assign an account to the specific line item on the tax form.

- **Chart of accounts**: As we discussed in *Chapter 1, Getting Started with QuickBooks Online*, the chart of accounts is a way to categorize your day-to-day business transactions. You have the option to assign account numbers to your chart of accounts list by turning on the **Enable account numbers** preference. If your business allows customers to leave tips, you can keep track of these tips in a separate account.

- **Categories**: There are two types of categories in QuickBooks: classes and locations. Classes are generally used to track income and expenses for departments or product lines. Locations are used to track income and expenses for multiple locations of your business. These preferences must be turned on for you to use them.

- **Automation**: You can save time by automating certain tasks. QuickBooks will automatically pre-fill forms based on the information you have provided in a previous transaction for a customer or vendor. You can also allow QuickBooks to automatically apply credit that's been received from vendor suppliers and bill payments.

- **Projects**: The **Projects** feature allows you to keep track of all income and expenses for jobs/projects that you are working on. To view all projects, click on the **Projects** tab, which is located on the left navigation bar.

- **Currency**: QuickBooks allows you to create invoices and pay bills in multiple currencies. You can do business with vendor suppliers and customers across the globe by providing invoices in their native currency. All of your financial reports can be generated in your home currency or any currency that you choose.

 Pro Tip: Once you turn on the multi-currency feature, it cannot be turned off. This is because several conversion tables are activated in the background once you turn this feature on and start using it.

- **Other preferences**: The **Other preferences** section involves general formatting preferences for the dates and numbers that appear throughout the program. You can also select the type of label for your customers. For example, if you are a nonprofit organization, you can select **Donors**, and if you are a real estate investor, you can select **Tenants**. This nomenclature will appear throughout the program. This preference also includes a warning if you use a duplicate check number or vendor invoice number. You should turn both of these features on to help prevent duplicate payments. A similar warning is also included when recording journal entries. A journal entry is an adjustment made to the books for transactions that are only recorded prior to closing the books, like depreciation. For security reasons, QBO will automatically sign you out after you have been inactive for 1 hour. However, you can change this setting to a maximum of 3 hours.

You now know that accounting settings affect several areas of QuickBooks. You can determine your chart of accounts structure, turn on time tracking, set your home currency, and turn on the multi-currency feature if you do business in other countries. In addition, you can turn on the projects and categories feature for additional tracking of income and expenses.

Summary

In this chapter, we have covered key information and documents required to set up a QBO account. We have also shown you how to customize the company settings, which include billing and subscription, usage limits, sales, expenses, payments, time, and advanced settings. Taking the time to set up your company file will help you save time in the long run because you won't have to do it later on. Plus, you won't have to worry about customer invoices or vendor bills missing key information because your company file wasn't set up properly.

Remember, you can always edit these settings whenever you need to. While it is ideal to complete this setup now so that when you are ready to start recording transactions in QBO, many of the fields on invoices and bills will automatically populate for you, at some point, if your contact information or business entity changes, you can always make any necessary updates.

In the next chapter, we will take a look at what information you will need to convert from your existing accounting software to QBO.

This will include choosing your QuickBooks start date, the order you need to follow when importing historical data into QuickBooks, and various options when it comes to converting from another system to QBO.

Join our community on Discord

Join our community's Discord space for discussions with the authors and other readers:

`https://packt.link/quickbooks`

3

Migrating to QuickBooks Online

In this chapter, we have provided the information that you need to migrate from one form of accounting software (like QuickBooks Desktop) to QuickBooks Online. While you can certainly migrate the data on your own, I recommend that you consult with a QuickBooks expert or the Intuit support team who can provide guidance every step of the way. Whether you are currently using another form of accounting software or spreadsheets to manage the books for your business, you will need to gather a few key documents and bits of information to migrate over to **QuickBooks Online (QBO)**, a list of which we gave you at the start of the previous chapter. In addition, the date on which you decide to start implementing QuickBooks will also determine what information is required for a smooth migration. Providing all of the information required will ensure that QuickBooks is properly set up prior to you using it to track your business income and expenses. Otherwise, you could encounter inaccurate and unreliable financial statements, which will make it hard to know your business's overall health and make filing taxes difficult.

In this chapter, we will help you determine if QBO is right for your business and discuss questions you need to answer before conversion regarding how you will run your business. Then, we will cover the steps of converting your **QuickBooks Desktop (QBD)** data to QBO. If you are unable to convert your data, you can choose one of the alternatives to converting QBD data. The final section of this chapter will cover how to convert from Excel spreadsheets or pen and paper to QBO.

In this chapter, we will cover the following five key concepts:

- Deciding whether QuickBooks Online is right for your business
- Questions to ask yourself in preparation for data conversion
- Converting QBD data to QBO

- Alternatives to converting QBD data to QBO
- Converting from Excel spreadsheets or pen and paper to QBO

 The US edition of QBO was used to create this book. If you are using a version that is outside of the United States, results may differ.

Deciding whether QuickBooks Online is right for your business

It's important to make sure that moving your business to QBO is the right thing to do. While QuickBooks Online is ideal for many businesses, if one or more of the following is true about your business, you may want to contact the Intuit support team or consult a QuickBooks ProAdvisor to assist you with making the decision:

- **Multiple businesses:** If you have more than one business to manage, you need to know that you will need to purchase a separate QBO subscription plan for each business that has its own federal tax identification number. For example, let's say I have a tax preparation business and I have a few luxury properties that I rent on Airbnb. These are two separate businesses, which means I would need to purchase two QBO plans. The good news is you can create a new QBO account using the same user ID and password as an existing QBO account. This will ensure that you are able to sign in once and select the business you wish to access.

- **Comprehensive inventory accounting requirements:** If your business manufactures products that require the tracking of multiple items using a bill of materials, you may want to consider using QuickBooks Desktop. In addition, QBO uses the **first in, first out (FIFO)** method to track inventory. That means if you use **last in, first out (LIFO)** or average cost to keep track of your inventory, you will need to convert to FIFO if you plan to convert to QBO.

- **Specialized industries:** If you are a general contractor, manufacturing and wholesale, retail, non-profit, or professional services business, you may want to consider using QuickBooks Desktop instead of QBO. QuickBooks Desktop has customized software that includes a custom chart of accounts and reports for businesses in these industries. While QBO can be customized to meet the needs of these industries, you will have to invest the time to make the necessary adjustments.

If you decide that QBO is the right move for your business and you are currently using QBD, you need to review the list of key features that you may currently use in QBD that are not available in QBO. Finally, you need to review the data that will not convert from QBD to QBO.

This is important because there may be features that are not available in QBO that you need to run your business. You also need to determine whether you actually need the information that does not convert over to QBO. If you are not currently using QBD, you can skip to the *Questions to ask yourself in preparation for data conversion* section.

Functionality not available in QBO

QBO does not include the ability to create sales orders. Therefore, we do not recommend that you convert from QBD to QBO unless you have a workaround for sales orders.

 Sales orders: A form used to record and track customer orders. A sales order will commit the quantity ordered or trigger a backorder if the product is out of stock.

If you currently use sales orders in QBD, you should either find a workaround in QBO or postpone converting over to QBO if they are critical to your business.

QuickBooks Desktop data that will not convert to QBO

As we mentioned previously, QBD and QBO are two completely different products. QBD is available for Windows and iOS platforms, whereas QBO is a cloud-based software, which means you simply need internet access and it can be used on any platform. With that said, there are several data points that will not convert to QBO.

The following table provides a summary of the data that will not convert to QBO, along with a workaround in QBO. For the complete list of Desktop features and how they will (or will not) convert to QBO, read *What to expect when you switch from QBD to QBO*, an article by Intuit: https://quickbooks.intuit.com/learn-support/en-us/convert-data-files/what-to-expect-when-you-switch-from-quickbooks-desktop-to/00/186758.

QBD data that will not convert to QBO	Workaround in QBO
Attachments	Attachments in QBD will not convert to QBO; you will need to manually attach documents in QBO after the data is converted.

Audit trail report with historical activity	Print and save the audit trail report from QBD. Refer to the backup QBD file (covered later in this chapter).
Banking	Downloaded bank/credit card activity pending review will not convert to QBO. You will need to re-establish the connection in QBO for all bank and credit card accounts.
Budgets	Balance sheet budgets will not convert to QBO and you cannot create a balance sheet budget in QBO. However, you can create profit and loss budgets if you have the QBO Plus or Advanced plan.
Chart of accounts	For security reasons, bank account numbers and internal notes in QBD will not convert to QBO. You will need to add this information after converting the data.
Closing date exceptions	Closing date exceptions in QBD will not transfer over to QBO but new exceptions from the date of the conversion will be tracked.
Custom fields	Custom fields in QBD do not convert to QBO. You will need to recreate any custom fields in QBO after converting the data.
Custom templates	Custom templates such as invoices, estimates, and sales receipts do not convert to QBO. You will need to create new templates using the built-in template layout designer in QBO.
Customer/jobs	The following customer/job fields in QBD *do not* convert to QBO: **contact, alt contact, customer type, rep, price level, custom fields, account, credit limit, job status, start date, project end date, end date, job description, job type, job bill to address, job ship to address,** and **job email.**
Inventory	QBO does not support units of measure. If you need to convert inventory, it will be valued using the FIFO inventory method. In order to track inventory quantity and cost, you need to sign up for a QBO Plus or Advanced plan.
Memorized reports	Memorized reports will not move to QBO. In QBO, recreate reports that you run often and save them in **Favorites.**
Mileage tracking	Mileage tracking is available in all QBO subscription plans. However, you will need to manually add any previous mileage recorded in QBD into QBO.

Multi-currency	Multi-currency is only available in QBO Plus and Advanced subscriptions. However, transactions with three different currency types won't copy to QBO.
Payroll	Payroll history does not convert to QBO. This includes payroll item breakdown and employee **year-to-date (YTD)** numbers. You will need to manually enter this information into QBO after converting the data.
Pending sales (sales orders)	Pending sales orders will not convert to QBO. Currently, you cannot create sales orders in QBO.
Price levels	While price levels will not convert to QBO, if you have QBO Plus or Advanced, you can recreate the price levels.
Reconciliation reports	Reconciliation reports for all bank and credit card accounts will not convert. However, all transactions with the reconciled status, **R**, will convert. Therefore, after converting the data, do one big reconciliation, or redo them individually to recreate the reports in QBO.
Transactions	Subtotals on invoices do not convert. Progress invoices and their extra fields do not convert. Recurring customer payments do not convert. The link between bills and purchase orders is removed when converted to QBO. Open purchase orders will not reflect items received.
Users and permissions	Existing users in QBD don't automatically have access to QBO. They need to be invited to QBO to gain access. We cover how to give other users access in *Chapter 4, Customizing QuickBooks for Your Business*.
Vendors	The following vendor fields in QBD *do not* convert to QBO: **contact, alt contact, note, status, vendor type, credit limit, custom fields, alt. phone**, and **1099 ID**.

Table 3.1: Workarounds in QBO for QBD data that will not convert

You should determine whether the workaround is an ideal solution, or if you can run your business without bringing over certain data. After you have compiled key information, asked yourself a few questions, and familiarized yourself with the data that will not convert, you are ready to convert your data. Next, we will cover the questions you need to answer in order to determine the type of setup you will need.

Questions to ask yourself in preparation for data conversion

When setting up your QuickBooks company, you will need to determine whether you want to bring over any data from your existing accounting program. Additionally, you need to know what features you want to use in QuickBooks. Answering the following questions will help determine what type of setup you need to manage your day-to-day business activities:

1. **How much historical data do you want to bring over to QuickBooks?**

    If you are converting in the middle of the year, you need to determine whether you will bring over all the transactions that have occurred thus far, or just start from the current month you are in. The benefit of bringing over transactions that go back to the beginning of the year is that it will allow you to run financial statements in QuickBooks for the entire year, as opposed to only part of the year. Keep in mind that it could be more time-consuming to do this, so you will need to weigh the cost versus the benefit to determine whether it is worth it.

     Pro Tip: The best practice is to start tracking your data in QuickBooks at the beginning of a year, quarter, or month. For example, let's say after filing your taxes, you decide you want to start using QBO. If it's not feasible or cost-effective to go back to January 1st, then go back to April 1st (the beginning of a month and the 2nd quarter) and start using QuickBooks from that date forward. At least you will have 9 months' worth of data in QBO and only 3 months (January to March) of doing it the "old way."

2. **How much detailed information do you want to bring over to QuickBooks?**

    If you do decide to bring over the historical information for an entire year, you've got two options. First, you can enter each transaction individually into QuickBooks. Depending on how much data you have, this could be quite labor-intensive and expensive if you have to pay someone else to do it. Second, you can create a summary journal entry, which is a lot faster than entering each individual transaction, but you will not have the details of each transaction in QuickBooks. If you have a ton of transactions, then using a summary journal entry is going to be the best option for you. However, if you don't have a lot of activity, then enter transactions individually.

Pro Tip: While it can be time-consuming, entering historical transactions is a great way to learn how to use QBO.

3. **Do you create estimates or proposals for existing or prospective customers?**

   There are several benefits of creating estimates/proposals in QBO. First, you can easily email estimates to customers and track the status of when the estimates are approved, or not approved, by the customer. After an estimate is approved, you can create an invoice with just a click of a button and all of the information that is on the estimate will automatically be copied to the invoice. From there, you can bill the customer for the entire estimate or a portion of it.

4. **Do you plan to create account statements for customers?**

   Depending on the type of business you own, you may want to generate account statements that cover multiple transactions for customers. This is common for doctors' offices and for companies that provide services to customers on a recurring basis (for example, monthly, quarterly, or annually).

5. **Do you want to use invoices to bill customers?**

   If you choose to create billing statements for some customers but want to create invoices for others, you can do that in QuickBooks. Invoices are commonly used to bill customers to whom you have extended credit terms. This means that payment is not due when you provide goods and/or services. Instead, you send these customers an invoice that includes a due date, and they are expected to remit payment before or by the due date. For example, Net 30 payment terms mean that the bill is due 30 days after the date on the invoice.

6. **Do you want to keep track of your bills through QuickBooks?**

   During the QBO account setup process, you will choose whether or not you want to track and pay bills in QuickBooks. If you have a lot of bills to keep track of, you should consider entering all bills into QuickBooks. Once you enter a bill into QuickBooks, it will alert you when the bill is getting close to the due date. You can pay the bill through online banking, or you can pay the bill by writing a check directly from QuickBooks. If you don't receive a lot of paper bills, then it may not be ideal to track unpaid bills through QuickBooks. Instead, you can track expenses as they are paid from your bank/credit card account.

7. **Do you want to keep track of inventory through QuickBooks?**

   If you need to keep track of inventory purchases by tracking quantities and costs, then you need to track the inventory in QuickBooks. QBO Plus and QBO Advanced are the only plans that include inventory tracking. Inventory must be activated during the QBO account setup process. However, if you prefer to keep track of sales only, you do not need inventory tracking, which means the QBO Simple Start or Essentials plans will work for you.

8. **Do you have employees or 1099 contractors?**

   Payroll is not automatically activated when you set up your QBO account. You will need to purchase a payroll subscription in order to activate this feature and complete the set-up. If you have employees or 1099 contractors that you need to track in QuickBooks, see *Chapter 14, Managing Employees and 1099 Contractors in QuickBooks Online*, to learn how to set up and track payments to 1099 contractors and your options for paying employees.

9. **Do you need to track income and expenses by department, business segment, or location?**

   If you need to track income and expenses by department or business segment, you will need to turn on class tracking in the QBO account setup process. You can also turn on location tracking if you have more than one store or office location you need to keep track of. Class tracking and location tracking are only available in the QBO Plus and QBO Advanced plans.

Similar to the key information and documents discussed in the previous section, it's important for you to think about how you want to use QuickBooks. Answering a few simple questions can help you determine what features you need to turn on in QBO to manage your books.

Converting QuickBooks Desktop data to QBO

Now that you are familiar with most of the limitations of converting data from QBD to QBO, we will walk through the steps for doing this. There are seven primary steps involved with converting data from QBD to QBO:

1. Checking the target count
2. Creating a QuickBooks Online account
3. Backing up your QuickBooks Desktop file
4. Checking for updates
5. Running the QuickBooks Desktop conversion tool
6. Logging in to QuickBooks Online
7. Verifying that all of your data was converted

Let's look at each of these steps, one by one.

Checking the target count

In order to convert your Desktop data to Online, your target count must not exceed 750,000.

To check your target count, open your QuickBooks Desktop file. From the home page, press *Ctrl + 1* on your keyboard, which will open the **Product Information** screen. On this screen, you will find your product license number, the location of your company file, and other key data points, such as the target count.

Figure 3.1 includes an example of the target count on the **Product Information** screen. For this company file, the target count is 5,937, which is well below the 750,000 limit:

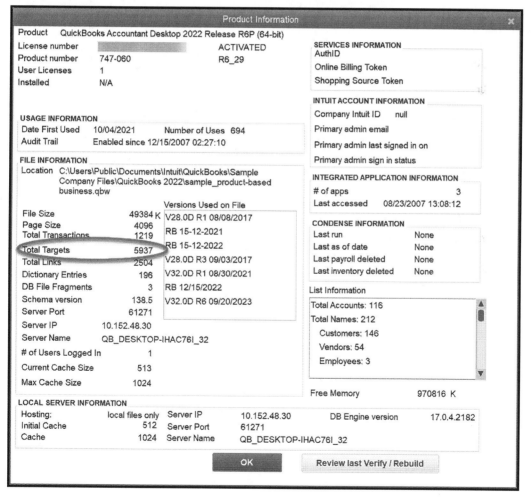

Figure 3.1: Checking the total targets

Pro Tip: If your file exceeds the maximum 750,000 targets, you can try to reduce the targets by condensing your QuickBooks file. Read this article by Intuit, *Condense your QBD file for import to QBO* (`https://quickbooks.intuit.com/learn-support/en-us/migrate-services/condense-your-quickbooks-desktop-file-for-import-to-quickbooks/00/186240`), to learn how this works.

CAUTION: If this process does not reduce the targets, you cannot convert your file to QBO. Instead, you will need to choose one of the alternatives that we will cover later in this chapter.

If your QuickBooks Desktop file is below the 750,000 limit, you can proceed to create a QBO account.

Creating a QBO account

Prior to converting your data, you must already have a QBO account. If you don't have a QBO account, refer back to *Chapter 1, Getting Started with QuickBooks Online*, to learn how to set one up. If you have an existing account, you must convert your QBD data within the first 60 days of your QBO subscription date. If you are past the 60 days, you will need to cancel your account and create a new QBO subscription.

To recap, follow these steps to create a QBO account:

1. Go to `www.intuit.com`.
2. Click on **Products** and choose **QuickBooks**.
3. Click on **Plans & Pricing**.
4. Choose one of the following QBO subscription plans:

   - **Simple Start**
   - **Essentials**
   - **Plus**
   - **Advanced**

5. Refer to *Chapter 1, Getting Started with QuickBooks Online*, for a detailed guide to setting up your account.

The final step is to **log out of your account**. As we go through the *Logging in to QBO* section later in this chapter, the system will prompt you to log back in when appropriate.

After creating your QBO account, you are ready to convert your data. Before converting your Desktop data, it's important to save a backup of your QuickBooks Desktop file. If there is an error when converting your data, you can always refer to the backup file if you need to. Let's walk through backing up your QBD file.

Backing up your QuickBooks Desktop file

Converting your data does not change it. However, you should always have a backup copy of your data prior to conversion.

Follow these steps to create a backup copy of your QuickBooks file:

1. Click on the **File** menu.
2. Select **Create Copy**.
3. Select **Backup copy**, as indicated in *Figure 3.2*:

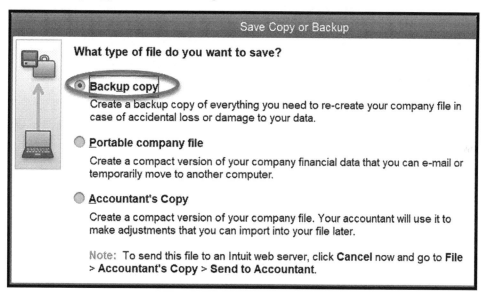

Figure 3.2: Creating a backup copy

4. Follow the onscreen instructions to save your file to a local drive.

   Now that you have a backup copy of your QuickBooks Desktop data, you can proceed with the conversion. To avoid errors when converting your data, you need to ensure that you are working with the latest version of QuickBooks Desktop.

Pro Tip: In addition to having a backup copy of your QuickBooks desktop data, you should also save a yearly balance sheet report, income statement (profit and loss), and a current accounts receivable and accounts payable report. In addition to using this information to verify the data once it converts to QBO, you will need it in order to file your tax returns.

Checking for updates

Before using the conversion tool, you need to make sure you have the most recent version of the tool. For QuickBooks Pro, Premier, and Enterprise users, follow these instructions to check for updates:

1. From the **Help** menu at the very top of the home page, select **Update QuickBooks Desktop…**:

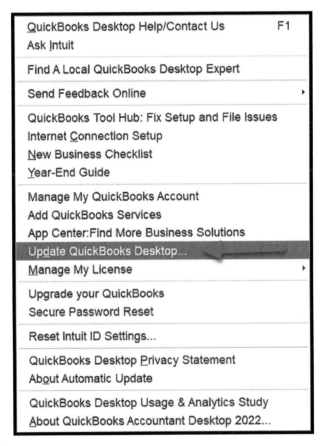

Figure 3.3: The Update QuickBooks Desktop setting

2. Next, click on the **Update Now** tab, select all the updates by putting a checkmark in the first column to select the available updates, and click **Get Updates**, as indicated in *Figure 3.4*:

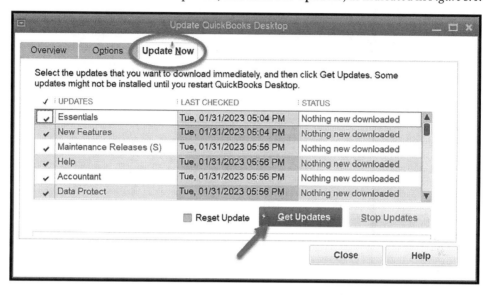

Figure 3.4: Getting all updates

Once your QuickBooks software has been updated to the most recent version, you are ready to run the QBD conversion-to-QBO tool. We will cover this in detail next.

Running the QBD conversion-to-QBO tool

There is a QBD conversion tool within QuickBooks Desktop. To access it, from the **Company** menu, select **Export Your Company File to QuickBooks Online**, as indicated in *Figure 3.5*:

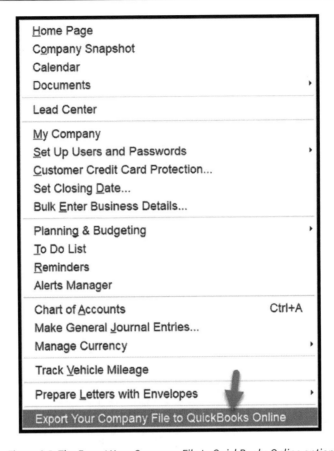

Figure 3.5: The Export Your Company File to QuickBooks Online option

Select **Start your export**. The next screen will allow you to log in to the QBO account that you set up in the *Creating a QBO account* section. To complete the QBD data conversion, log in to your QBO account.

 Pro Tip: You must log in as an administrator to import your data into QBO. If you are the only user, you are automatically the administrator.

Logging in to QBO

After exporting your QuickBooks data file, the login screen for QBO will appear. Follow the steps outlined here:

1. Enter your secure email or user ID and password for your QBO account:

Figure 3.6: Signing in to QBO

2. Follow the onscreen instructions to complete the upload.

 Pro Tip: If you track inventory in QBD, select **yes** to bring the inventory into QBO and enter the **as of date** value. Select **no** if you don't want to bring the inventory into QBO and plan to set up new items later on.

3. Once the upload is complete, you will see an onscreen notification that your data has been successfully uploaded. The length of time this will take will depend on how large your company file is. In general, this takes place within 1 to 24 hours, at the most. When your data is ready, you will receive an email from the Intuit support team.

Once you have received an email from the Intuit support team confirming your data has been uploaded, the final step in converting your data is to verify that the data in your QBO file is correct.

Verifying that all of your data was converted

The final step in the conversion process is to verify that all your data was successfully imported into QuickBooks Online. To do this, you need to run a profit and loss report and a balance sheet report in both QuickBooks Online and QuickBooks Desktop. For instructions on how to run these reports in QBO, head over to *Chapter 11, Business Overview Reports*. Be sure to use the following report parameters:

- All dates
- Accrual accounting method

Compare the reports to see if they match. If they don't, contact the Intuit support team by clicking on the **Help** menu in your QBO file and then selecting the option to chat with a support representative, or you can contact them by telephone. A support representative will assist you with troubleshooting any out-of-balance issues.

Once you have verified that your data was successfully converted to QBO, you are ready to start using QBO to manage your bookkeeping. You should keep the backup file created in the previous section, in case you discover an issue later on.

Alternatives to converting a QuickBooks Desktop file to QBO

If you are unable to convert your existing QuickBooks Desktop data to QBO, you have a few other options to choose from:

- *Option 1* is to export all of your lists (vendors, customers, chart of accounts, products and services, etc.) to Excel and then import that data into QBO. From there, you can connect your bank and credit card accounts and start using QBO to manage your business without bringing over historical data. The good news is that you can always refer back to the backup file for QBD if you need to.

- *Option 2* is to import all of your lists and record a summary journal entry of historical data in QBO. This option is ideal if you need to have the historical data in QBO but you don't have a lot of time to enter all of the details or you don't want to pay someone to do it.

- *Option 3* is to import all of your lists and record the details of historical data into QBO. This option would be ideal if you are converting in the middle of the year and want to have a full year's worth of data in QBO for year-end reports. Depending on how much data you have, this option will also be the most time-consuming and costly if you hire someone to do it.

In this section, we will show you how to import your list data into QBO (option 1), record a summary journal entry of historical data (option 2), and record the details of historical data into QBO (option 3).

Importing list data into QBO

Organize your data into an Excel or CSV file so that you can easily import that data into QBO. Currently, you can import data from your bank data, customer lists, vendor lists, chart of accounts, products and services, and invoices. Follow the steps below to import this data into QBO:

1.   Click on the gear icon and select **Import data**, as shown in *Figure 3.7*:

Figure 3.7: The Import data option

2. The following screen will appear:

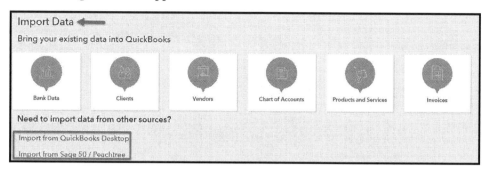

Figure 3.8: The Import Data screen

3. Click on the icon that represents the type of data you would like to import and follow the onscreen instructions to import the data into QBO.

 Pro Tip: If you are migrating from QuickBooks Desktop, Sage 50, or Peachtree, you can click on the respective link shown at the bottom of *Figure 3.8* and follow the on-screen instructions to convert your data into QBO.

For step-by-step instructions on importing bank data and a chart of accounts, refer to *Chapter 4, Customizing QuickBooks for Your Business*. To learn how to import customers, vendors, and products and services data, refer to *Chapter 5, Managing Customer, Vendor, and Products and Services Lists*.

If you don't have the time to enter individual transactions, you can opt for recording a summary journal entry.

Recording a summary journal entry of historical data in QBO

A summary journal entry will only include lump sum total amounts. To enter balances for balance sheet accounts, you should run a balance sheet report in your current accounting system for the last day of the year for which you are bringing over data. If you would like to also bring over income and expense data, you need to print an income statement from your existing accounting system, as of the last day of the fiscal year (i.e., 12/31/20XX) for which you are bringing over data. Enter the totals for each account into QuickBooks.

Pro Tip: Make sure the accounts that appear on both the balance sheet and income statement reports have been added to the chart of accounts list in QuickBooks *before* you create the journal entry. In *Chapter 4, Customizing QuickBooks for Your Business*, we show you how to create new accounts.

Follow these steps to create a journal entry in QBO:

1. Navigate to the **Journal entry** screen by clicking on the **+ New** button on the left navigation bar, as indicated here:

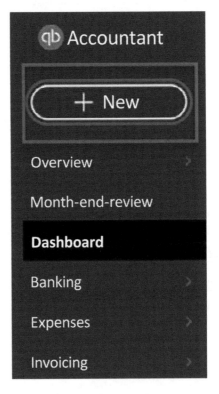

Figure 3.9: The + New button

2. In the **OTHER** column, click on **Journal entry**, as follows:

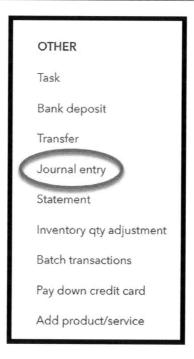

Figure 3.10: Navigating to the journal entry form

3. Complete the fields in the **Journal entry** form:

Figure 3.11: The journal entry form

4. You will need to complete 7 fields. Here is a brief explanation of what information to include in each field:

   - **Journal date** (1): Enter the effective date of the journal entry. For example, you would enter the last date of the fiscal year for which you are bringing data over (for example, December 31, 20XX).

- **Journal no.** (2): QuickBooks will automatically assign a journal entry number, beginning with **1**. However, you can start with a different number, such as **1000**, and QuickBooks will automatically increment each journal number thereafter.

- **ACCOUNT** (3): From the drop-down menu, select the account(s) that requires a debit. After all debits have been entered, you can enter the accounts that will be credited right after.

- **DEBITS** (4): Enter all debit amounts in this field.

- **CREDITS** (5): Enter all credit amounts in this field.

- **DESCRIPTION** (6): Enter a brief description of the purpose of the journal entry (for example, to bring over existing balances as of December 31, 2023).

- **NAME** (7): If a line item is for a specific customer, you can select the appropriate customer from the drop-down menu.

 Pro Tip: The **NAME** field is used in those instances when you are making an adjustment to the accounts receivable balance for a specific customer.

So far, we've covered two of the three options for converting QBD data to QBO: importing lists and recording a summary journal entry. The final option (and the best option, in my opinion) is to record all details of historical data in QBO. To clarify, there is no need to bring over data if you have already filed your tax returns for that year. However, you do need to keep your backup for those prior years in case you are ever audited.

If you are in the middle of a year, or even the end of the year, it is ideal to record details of historical data for the current year if you have the resources to do so. We will cover how to do this next.

Recording details of historical data in QBO

As mentioned previously, the ideal method of entering historical data into QBO is to enter individual transactions. While this is more time-consuming than completing a summary journal entry, it includes all the details of each transaction.

Individual transactions must be entered in the correct order to avoid any issues. The order in which to enter historical transactions into QBO is as follows:

1. Purchase orders, bills and payments, credits from vendors, credit card charges, checks, and inventory on hand

2. Employee timesheets and billable hours

3. Invoices, sales receipts, credit memos, and returns

4. Customer payments and bank deposits

5. Sales taxes paid and payroll transactions

6. All banking transactions (not previously entered) and credit card transactions (not previously entered), and reconcile all bank and credit card accounts

It's important that you follow these steps to avoid issues later on.

Converting from Excel spreadsheets or pen and paper to QBO

There are four primary steps for converting from Excel spreadsheets to QBO:

1. Complete the initial company file setup.

2. Make sure that you have a separate Excel spreadsheet for each type of list: customers, vendors, and products and services.

3. Import all list information for customers, vendors, and products and services. Refer to the *Importing list data into QBO* section above for detailed instructions.

4. Import your chart of accounts list or update the default listing in QuickBooks to match your current list.

5. Verify the accuracy of the data that has been converted.

In *Chapter 2, Company File Setup*, we covered in detail how to complete the initial company file setup. Refer to *Chapter 4, Customizing QuickBooks for Your Business*, to learn how to import all of your list data.

Summary

We have covered what you need to consider when deciding if QBO is right for your business, what questions to ask yourself, the steps needed to convert your QBD data to QBO, alternatives to converting your QBD data if you are unable to do so, and how to convert from Excel spreadsheets or pen and paper to QuickBooks Online. Once all of your data has been converted and verified, you are ready to customize QuickBooks Online for your business.

In the next chapter, we will show you how to customize QuickBooks Online for your business

Join our community on Discord

Join our community's Discord space for discussions with the authors and other readers:

https://packt.link/quickbooks

4

Customizing QuickBooks for Your Business

Whether you created your **QuickBooks Online (QBO)** account from scratch or transferred your details from another accounting software program, there are some additional areas that you need to set up to further customize QBO for your business.

In this chapter, we will show you how to add, edit, and delete accounts to customize the chart of accounts for your business. We will walk through the process of connecting your bank and credit card accounts to QBO so that transactions will automatically be downloaded. By connecting your bank accounts to QuickBooks, you will reduce, if not eliminate, the need to manually enter these transactions into QuickBooks.

Please note that uploading bank and credit card transactions to QBO does not record them in your books. You will need to review and record these transactions after they are uploaded. In *Chapter 9, Reconciling Uploaded Bank and Credit Card Transactions*, we will cover this in detail.

If you need to give other users access to your QuickBooks data, you can easily do so; we will show you how to give your bookkeeper, accountant, and other users access.

We will wrap this chapter up with showing you how to navigate the QuickBooks Apps Center. Apps are a great way to help you streamline day-to-day business tasks that can be time-consuming.

The following are the key topics that will be covered in this chapter:

- Customizing the chart of accounts list
- Connecting bank accounts to QBO

- Connecting credit card accounts to QBO

- Giving other users access to your QuickBooks data

- Using apps in QuickBooks Online

 The US edition of QBO was used to create this book. If you are using a version that is outside of the US, results may differ.

Customizing the chart of accounts list

As we saw in *Chapter 1, Getting Started with QuickBooks Online*, the chart of accounts is a list of accounts that is used to categorize your day-to-day business transactions. It is the backbone of every accounting system, and if it is not set up properly, it can result in inaccurate financial statements. One of the benefits of using QuickBooks is that you don't have to create a chart of accounts from scratch. Based on the industry that you selected when you created your QBO account, QuickBooks will include a preset chart of accounts list. You can customize the chart of accounts by adding, editing, or deleting accounts to fit your business needs. In this section, we will show you how to add, edit, delete (inactivate), and merge accounts on the chart of accounts list.

Adding a new account to the chart of accounts list

The default chart of accounts list will include a generic list of accounts used by most businesses, with a few custom accounts related to your industry. However, you will most likely need to customize the list based on your accountant's preferences or your own. For example, if you sell products and services, you may want to create an income account for each, as opposed to lumping sales for both into one account.

Go through the following three steps to add a new account to the chart of accounts list:

1. Click on the **Transactions** tab located on the left menu bar and select **Chart of accounts**, as shown in *Figure 4.1*:

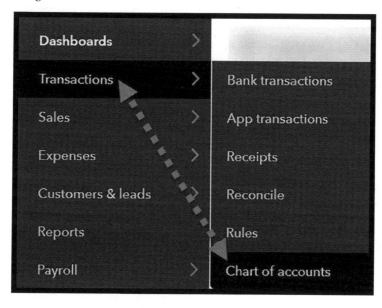

Figure 4.1: Navigating to the Chart of accounts option

2. Click on the **New** button located in the upper-right corner of the screen, directly to the right of the **Run Report** button, as shown in *Figure 4.2*:

Figure 4.2: The New button

3. To create a new account, you will need to provide the type of account, the section of the tax form it belongs to, the account name, and a description of the account, as shown in *Figure 4.3*:

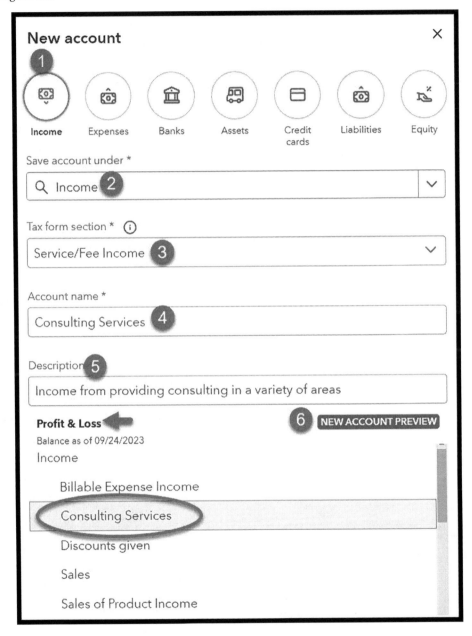

Figure 4.3: New account creation page

The following is a brief description of what information should be included in the fields that are labeled:

- **Account type (1)**: From the menu, select the account type that the new account should be categorized as. As we saw in *Chapter 1, Getting Started with QuickBooks Online,* the five main account types are assets, liabilities, equity, income, and expenses. You will also find other account types in this list, such as fixed assets, banks, and credit cards, and they should be used when appropriate.

- **Save account under (2)**: From the drop-down menu, select the category that most accurately describes the type of account you are setting up. The options in the drop-down menu will differ based on the account type selected.

- **Tax form section (3)**: The options in this field will be based on the entity that you chose when you set up your QBO account (i.e., LLC, Sole proprietor, C-Corp, S-Corp). QuickBooks will provide you with categories from the tax form applicable to your entity. Select the section that most accurately describes the account.

- **Account name (4)**: Type the name of the account in this field. In our example, it is **Consulting Services**.

- **Description (5)**: This field is self-explanatory, and should include a brief description of the types of transactions that should be posted to this account.

> **Pro Tip:** While you may be tempted to leave the **Description** field blank, we recommend that you don't. It can be useful to include a detailed description so that a bookkeeper or someone who you have hired to manage your books will know what type of transactions belong in this account. If you don't think a description is needed, copy and paste the account name into this field. That way, this field will not appear blank on reports. You can also use this field to enter more details about the accounts, such as account numbers or other useful information.

- **NEW ACCOUNT PREVIEW (6)**: This section informs you of the financial report the account will show up on (**Profit & Loss,** in our example). In addition, it shows that **Consulting Services** will be grouped with the **Income** accounts on the profit and loss report.

4. Once you have completed all the fields for the new account and saved it, the new account will appear on your chart of accounts list, as shown in *Figure 4.4*:

Bank transactions	App transactions	Receipts	Reconcile	Rules	**Chart of accounts**

	NAME ↑	ACCOUNT TYPE ⇕	DETAIL TYPE ⇕
☐	Commissions & fees	Expenses	Commissions & fees
☐	Consulting Services	Income	Service/Fee Income

Figure 4.4: The Chart of accounts list

As you can see, adding a new account to the chart of accounts list is pretty straightforward. If you need to add more than five accounts, you may want to consider importing new accounts instead of manually entering them. I recommend that you set up accounts that will be useful for you in managing your business.

> **Pro Tip: Sub-accounts** are used to provide a more detailed breakdown of an account that is used for multiple types of transactions. For example, it is a good idea to create a main account for car expenses and sub-accounts for repairs, registration, and gasoline. Having a detailed breakdown of each type of expense will allow you to easily run a report to see how much you have spent on each account.

In the next section, we will show you how to import a chart of accounts list from an Excel file.

Importing a chart of accounts list

If your accountant has given you a chart of accounts list that they prefer you to use, you can import that list into QBO. Go through the following steps to import a chart of accounts list. The template can be found at `https://github.com/PacktPublishing/Mastering-QuickBooks-2024-Fifth-Edition/tree/main/Chapter04`.

1. Format your Excel spreadsheet to include the following columns (**Account Number, Account Name, Type**, and **Detail Type**) and save it in `.csv` format:

Account Number	Account Name	Type	Detail Type
112720	Checking Account - Bank of America	Bank	Checking
112721	Money Market - First National Bank	Bank	Money Market
410790	Product Sales Revenue	Income	Sales of Product Income
500780	Cost of materials	Cost of Goods Sold	Supplies & Materials

Figure 4.5: Chart of accounts import template

2. Navigate to **Chart of accounts,** as indicated below:

Figure 4.6: Navigating to Chart of accounts

3. Click on the arrow to the right of the **New** button and select **Import,** as shown in *Figure 4.7:*

Figure 4.7: Clicking Import

4. The **Import Accounts** screen displays:

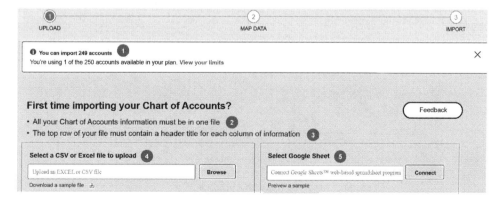

Figure 4.8: Import Accounts screen with highlighted items

A brief description of the highlighted items above is as follows:

- **Import limit (1)**: Depending on the QBO plan you have purchased; you will be limited to a certain number of accounts you can import. In our example, the limit is 250, but we can only import 249 accounts after adding the **Consulting Services** account in the previous example.

- **All of your Chart of Accounts information must be in one file (2)**: Be sure to organize all of your accounts into a single spreadsheet.

- **Include header information (3)**: When formatting your spreadsheet, be sure that the first row is a header row that contains a description of the info included in each column. Refer to *Figure 4.5*.

- **CSV or Excel file upload (4)**: You can upload a CSV or Excel (.xls) file format; no other file format is allowed.

- **Google Sheet (5)**: If you have your data in a Google Sheet, it is also compatible with QBO. Simply click the **Connect** button shown above and follow the onscreen instructions.

Follow the onscreen prompts to complete the import.

Next, we will show you how to edit the chart of accounts list.

Editing accounts on the chart of accounts list

On occasion, you may want to make changes to an existing account on the chart of accounts list. You can change the account name and description at any time; however, you can only make changes to the account type and detail type if you have *not* used the account in a transaction. If you have used the account and then realize that you selected the wrong account type, you will not be able to change it.

Instead, you will need to create the account again from scratch with the correct account or detail type. Once the new account has been created, you'll need to transfer the transactions that were coded to the wrong account to the new account. After transferring all the recorded transactions to the new account, you can inactivate the old account.

You can edit accounts on the chart of accounts list by going through the following steps:

1. Click on the **Transactions** tab located on the left menu bar and select **Chart of accounts**, as shown in *Figure 4.9*:

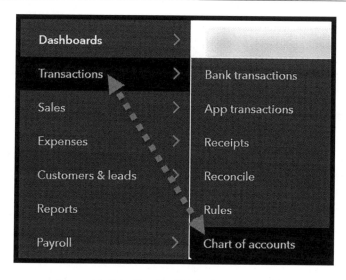

Figure 4.9: Selecting the Chart of accounts option

2. Scroll through the chart of accounts list to find the account you want to edit. *Figure 4.10* shows the **ACTION** column on the far right. Click on the arrow located to the right of **Run Report**, as shown in *Figure 4.10*:

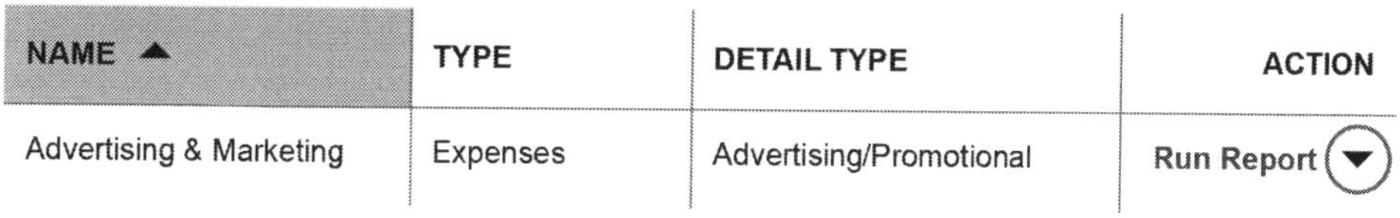

NAME ▲	TYPE	DETAIL TYPE	ACTION
Advertising & Marketing	Expenses	Advertising/Promotional	Run Report ▼

Figure 4.10: Editing an account

3. On the next screen, you will see two options: **Edit** and **Make inactive**, as shown in *Figure 4.11*:

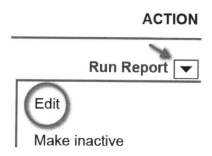

Figure 4.11: Choosing the Edit option

The following is a brief explanation of when you should edit an account and when you should make an account inactive:

- **Edit**: To make changes to the account name, account description, or sub-account, click on the **Edit** button. As we mentioned previously, the only time you can edit the account type and detail type is if you have not used the account in any transactions that you have recorded in QuickBooks. However, you can edit the name of the account and description even if an account has been used in a transaction.

- **Make inactive**: Once you have created an account in QuickBooks, there is no way to delete it. Instead, you will need to inactivate the account. When you inactivate an account in QuickBooks, it will still exist, but it will disappear from the chart of accounts list and will not appear in any drop-down lists. The primary reason for this is that if you have recorded transactions to an account that you decide to stop using, then your transactions will remain in QuickBooks. This is very important in order to maintain accurate financial records. If you need to review accounts that have been made inactive or reactivate an account, you can easily do so. We will cover this in the *Reactivating an account on the chart of accounts list* section.

4. When you click **Edit**, the current account setup will be displayed. Make the necessary changes, as shown in *Figure 4.12*:

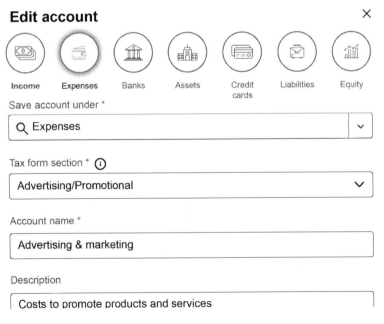

Figure 4.12: Editing the account details

If you have not used the account in a transaction, the account type (**Income, Expenses, Banks, Assets, Credit cards, Liabilities,** or **Equity**) and the **Save account under** category fields will also be editable.

In this section, we covered how to make changes to an existing account on your chart of accounts list. We also explained the difference between editing an account and making an account inactive. As previously mentioned, you cannot delete an account, but you can make it inactive. In the next section, we will show you how to inactivate an existing account.

Inactivating an account on the chart of accounts list

Once you add an account to the chart of accounts list, you cannot delete it; however, if you decide that you no longer want to use an account, you can inactivate the account. Inactivating an account will remove the account from the chart of accounts list and the drop-down menus, but it will still exist in the program. This will ensure that any transactions that have been recorded will remain intact, which will also ensure that you have accurate financial statements.

To inactivate an account, go through the following steps:

1. Click on the **Transactions** tab located on the left menu bar and select **Chart of accounts**, as shown in *Figure 4.13*:

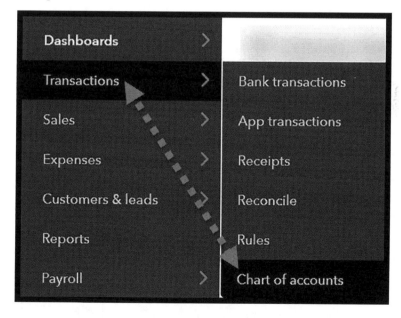

Figure 4.13: Navigating to the Chart of accounts option

2. Scroll through the chart of accounts list to find the account you want to edit. In the **AC-TION** column on the far right, click on the arrow located to the right of **Run Report**, as shown in *Figure 4.14*:

NAME ▲	TYPE	DETAIL TYPE	ACTION
Advertising & Marketing	Expenses	Advertising/Promotional	Run Report ▼

Figure 4.14: Editing an account

3. Select **Make inactive** from the drop-down arrow, as shown in *Figure 4.15*:

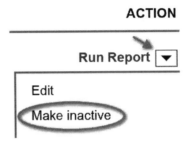

Figure 4.15: Making an account inactive

4. You will then receive a message similar to the one shown in the following screenshot, asking you to confirm that you would like to inactivate the account:

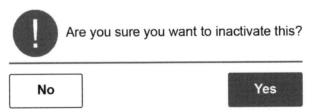

Figure 4.16: Inactivation confirmation message

5. Click **Yes** to proceed with the inactivation or **No** to leave the account active.

Pro Tip: All accounts that appear on the **Balance Sheet** report will show a **View register** link in the **Action** column. This is because all balance sheet accounts keep a running balance from one period to the next, whereas income and expense accounts do not keep a running balance because they are closed at the end of each fiscal period (i.e., month). Therefore, income and expense accounts will show a **Run Report** link in the **Action** column.

Reactivating an account on the chart of accounts list

If you decide to reactivate an account that was previously made inactive, you can easily do this:

1. From the chart of accounts list, click on the gear icon located directly above the **ACTION** column, as indicated below:

Figure 4.17: The gear icon

2. Put a checkmark in the box that says **Include inactive** so that all inactive accounts appear on the chart of accounts list, as indicated below:

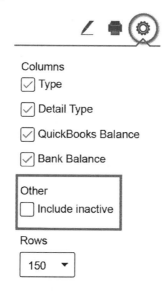

Figure 4.18: The Include inactive option

3. Next to the inactive accounts, click the link that says **Make active** to the right of the account, as shown in *Figure 4.19*:

NAME ▲	TYPE	DETAIL TYPE	ACTION
Advertising & Marketing (deleted)	Expenses	Advertising/Promotional	➡ Make active ▼

Figure 4.19: The Make active option

As mentioned previously, you cannot delete accounts in QBO. However, when an account is made inactive, you will see **deleted** in parentheses next to the account name. While this may be confusing, the account has not been deleted.

Merging accounts in QBO

An issue that you may encounter at some point is duplicate accounts. For example, you may end up having accounts with similar names, like *office supplies* and *office supplies expense*. This can happen if you have more than one person adding accounts to the chart of accounts, or if you have not documented a procedure for creating new accounts. However, you can easily fix this issue by merging the accounts, which will combine all of the data from both accounts into one.

Follow the steps below to merge accounts:

1. Navigate to the account list and identify the duplicate accounts:

NAME	TYPE ▲	DETAIL TYPE
Office Supplies	Expenses	Office/General Administrative Expenses
Office Supplies & Software	Expenses	Office/General Administrative Expenses

Figure 4.20: Identifying duplicate accounts in the chart of accounts

In the image above, **Office Supplies** and **Office Supplies & Software** are the same accounts.

2. Click once on the account you plan to remove and choose **Edit** from the **Run report** drop-down in the far-right column. In our example, we will remove **Office Supplies**.

The following account information will appear:

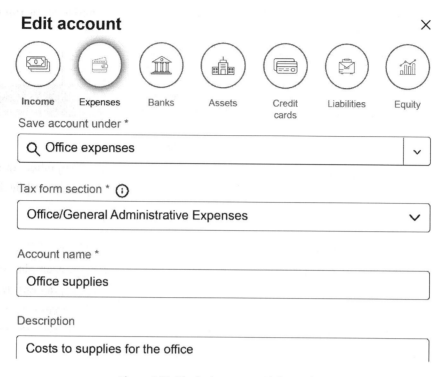

Figure 4.21: Displaying account information

3. Type the name of the account you wish to keep in the **Account name** field. In our example, this would be **Office Supplies & Software**.

4. Click the **Save** button.

 Pro Tip: You must type the name of the account you would like to keep (**Office Supplies & Software**) exactly as it appears in QuickBooks. To ensure accuracy, I recommend that you use your keyboard to copy and paste the name so that it is correct.

The following message will appear:

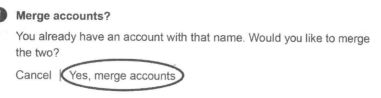

Figure 4.22: Confirm that you would like to merge the duplicate accounts

5. Choose **Yes, merge accounts** and then click the **Save** button, and the two accounts will be consolidated into one:

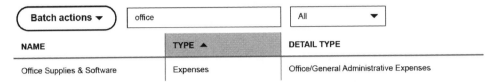

Figure 4.23: Chart of accounts list with the duplicate account removed

As you can see, the duplicate account (**Office Supplies**) is no longer on the chart of accounts list. All transactions recorded for this account have been transferred to the **Office Supplies & Software** account.

You now know how to add an account, import a chart of accounts list, edit an account, inactivate and reactivate an account, and merge accounts on the chart of accounts list. The chart of accounts is the backbone of the system. Now that you know how to manage your chart of accounts list, you can be confident that your financial statements will be accurate.

In the next section, we will show you how to reduce the number of transactions entered manually by connecting your bank accounts to QuickBooks. In the long run, this will save you a lot of time.

Connecting bank accounts to QBO

One of the best features of using cloud accounting software such as QBO is the ability to connect your bank account to the software so that your books are always up to date with the most recent deposits and withdrawals that have been made to your bank accounts.

There are two ways in which you can update QuickBooks with your banking activity. You can connect your bank account to QuickBooks so that transactions are imported automatically into QuickBooks, or you can upload transactions from an Excel spreadsheet. We will walk you through each of these processes in more detail now.

Importing banking transactions automatically

There are several benefits to importing your banking transactions automatically. First, you will save a ton of time because you won't have to enter transactions manually. Second, QuickBooks will be updated on a *daily* basis with the most recent banking activity on your account. And finally, it will be a breeze to reconcile your bank account on a daily, weekly, or monthly basis.

Go through the following steps to import banking transactions automatically into QBO:

1. Select **Transactions** and **Bank transactions** from the left menu bar, as shown in *Figure 4.24*:

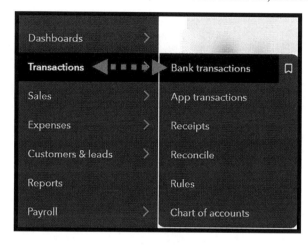

Figure 4.24: Selecting Bank transactions

2. If this is your first time connecting to a bank/credit card account, you will get the following screen. Click on the **Connect account** button, as shown in *Figure 4.25*:

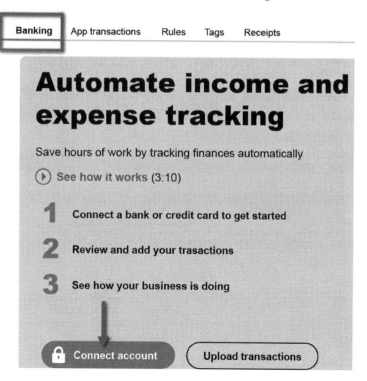

Figure 4.25: Clicking on Connect account

3. If you have connected to a bank/credit card account previously, you will see the **Link account** option. Click on it:

Figure 4.26: The Link account button

4. To connect your bank account, select your bank by clicking on the icon or typing the name of the bank in the search box, as shown in *Figure 4.27*:

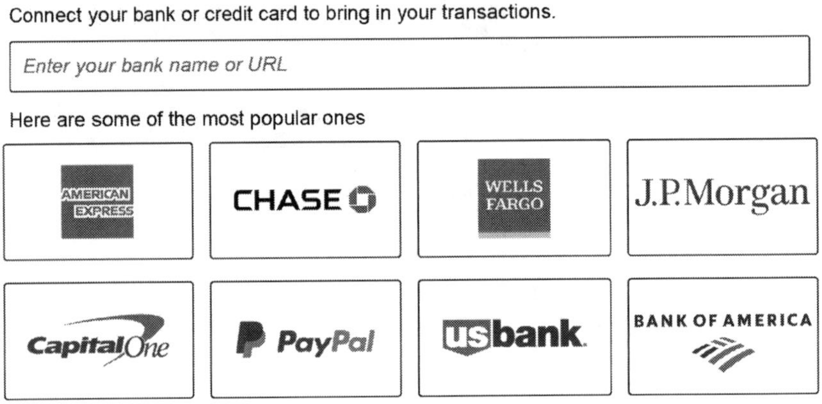

Connect your bank or credit card to bring in your transactions.

> *Enter your bank name or URL*

Here are some of the most popular ones

AMERICAN EXPRESS	CHASE ◐	WELLS FARGO	J.P.Morgan
CapitalOne	P PayPal	USbank.	BANK OF AMERICA

Figure 4.27: Selecting your bank

If you cannot locate your bank, you will not be able to connect your account to QuickBooks; however, you can still download your banking information into QuickBooks, which we will cover in the next section.

5. Sign in to your bank account using the secure user ID and password issued by your bank:

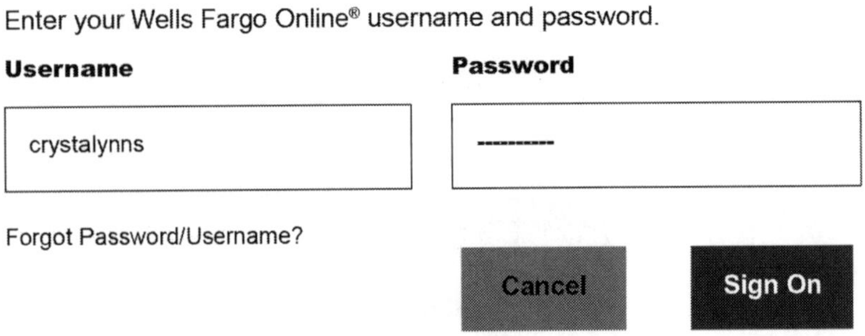

Enter your Wells Fargo Online® username and password.

Username

crystalynns

Password

Forgot Password/Username?

Cancel   Sign On

Figure 4.28: Signing into your bank account

6. Before connecting your bank account to QBO, you will be required to consent to the terms and conditions set by your bank. This consent confirmation is documentation that proves you agree to share your financial data with QuickBooks:

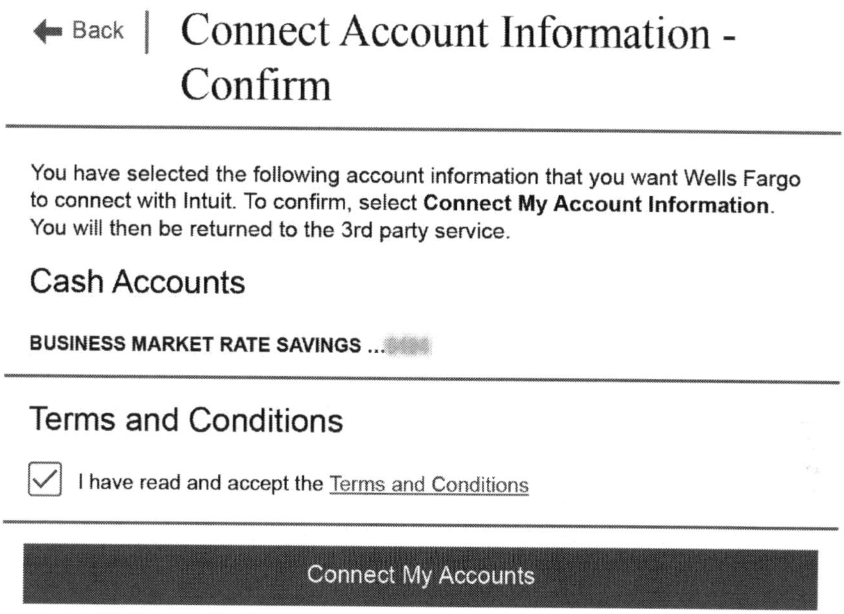

← Back | # Connect Account Information - Confirm

You have selected the following account information that you want Wells Fargo to connect with Intuit. To confirm, select **Connect My Account Information**. You will then be returned to the 3rd party service.

Cash Accounts

BUSINESS MARKET RATE SAVINGS ...

Terms and Conditions

 I have read and accept the <u>Terms and Conditions</u>

> Connect My Accounts

Figure 4.29: Consenting to your bank's terms and conditions

7. Follow the remaining onscreen instructions to connect your bank account to QuickBooks. If you have more than one account with the same financial institution, you will have the option to connect all bank accounts or select specific bank accounts to connect with QuickBooks.

 Pro Tip: Make sure that you only connect *business* bank accounts to QuickBooks and not personal bank accounts; otherwise, you will have personal banking activity co-mingled with business transactions, which is not a best practice.

 Pro Tip #2: Some financial institutions limit how far back in time you are able to pull data from. Let's say you need to import data for the last 12 months, but your bank only allows you to go back 90 days; go ahead and import that last 90 days. For the data that it did not allow you to access, you can either request a CSV (Excel) file from your online banking department so you can import it or enter the data manually from your bank statement.

You can save yourself a lot of time by connecting your bank account to QuickBooks so that your transactions automatically download. However, if your bank does not allow you to connect your account, you can still save time by obtaining an Excel (.xls) or CSV file from your bank so that you can upload the transactions to your QuickBooks file.

Uploading banking transactions from an Excel or CSV file

If your financial institution does not integrate with QuickBooks, then you need to upload your banking transactions as an Excel or CSV file. Most banks allow you to download your transactions as a PDF or CSV file. Log in to your bank account and look for the **Download Transactions** option, or other data download options. If you don't see this option, contact your bank and inform them that you need your banking transactions in a CSV file so that you can upload them into QuickBooks.

To upload banking transactions from an Excel or CSV file to QuickBooks, go through the following instructions:

1. At the beginning of this chapter, we showed you how to add a new account to the chart of accounts list. Follow those step-by-step instructions and add your bank account to QuickBooks.

2. Your bank account setup screen should resemble the one in *Figure 4.30*:

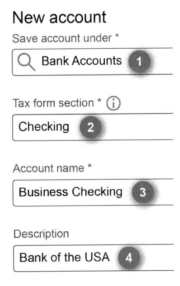

Figure 4.30: Bank account setup screen

3. Here is a brief explanation of how to fill in the new bank account fields:

    - **Save account under (1):** The account type will be **Bank Accounts** for all checking, savings, and money market accounts.

    - **Tax form section (2):** The options in this field will be based on the entity that you chose when you set up your QBO account (for example, **LLC**, **Sole proprietor**, **C-Corp**, **S-Corp**). QuickBooks will provide you with categories from the tax form applicable to your entity. Select the section that most accurately describes the account.

    - **Account name (3):** The name of the bank account belongs in this field. In our example, we have created a business checking account and named it accordingly. This will work if all of your bank accounts are at the same financial institution; however, if you have multiple bank accounts set up at different financial institutions, you should include the name of the bank along with the type of account in this field – for example, Wells Fargo Business Checking, Bank of America Business Savings, and so on.

       Pro Tip: If you have several accounts, it might be helpful to include the last four digits of each account number as part of the account name (such as Chase Business Checking, x1234). This will help you to quickly determine which account you are in.

    - **Description (4):** You can include a brief description of the account that you are adding in this field such as the name of the bank or financial institution and account number.

4. The bottom part of the setup screen includes the date to start tracking, the opening balance, and the preview of the account on the balance sheet shown in *Figure 4.31*:

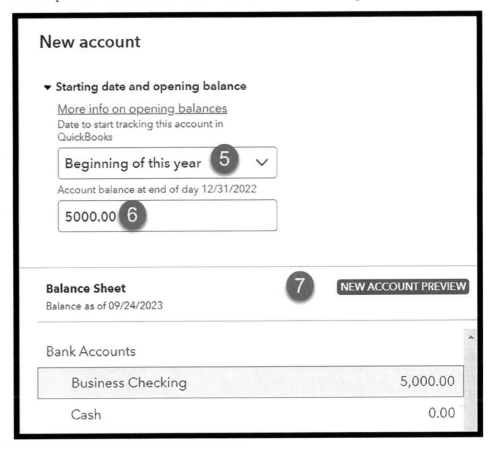

Figure 4.31: Scrolling down the setup screen to see more fields

Here is a brief explanation of what information to include in these fields:

-   **Date to start tracking in QuickBooks (5):** From the drop-down, select the date you want to begin tracking your finances for this account.

-   **Account balance at end of day (6):** Enter the current balance in your bank account as of your QuickBooks start date from *the previous bullet*. For example, if you are starting to use QuickBooks as of January 1, enter the balance of your bank account as of the last day of the previous period, which would be December 31 of the previous year.

- **NEW ACCOUNT PREVIEW (7)**: In this section, you will see a preview of where on the financial statements this account will appear. In our example, it will appear on the **Balance Sheet** report as a sub-account below **Bank Accounts**.

Pro Tip: It's important to have your bank statements handy as you are adding bank accounts to QuickBooks. This is to ensure that you enter the correct balance and effective dates. It will also help you to balance later on when you are ready to reconcile the account.

5. From the gear icon, select **Import Data**, which is located in the **Tools** column, as shown in *Figure 4.32*:

Figure 4.32: The Import Data option

6. The **Import Data** screen is where you can import banking transactions, customers, vendors, a chart of accounts list, products and services, and invoices. Select the **Bank Data** option to display the setup screen, as shown in *Figure 4.33*:

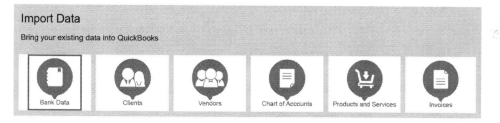

Figure 4.33: The Import Data screen

The following screen appears. Click on **select files** to select the file that includes your bank data, as indicated below:

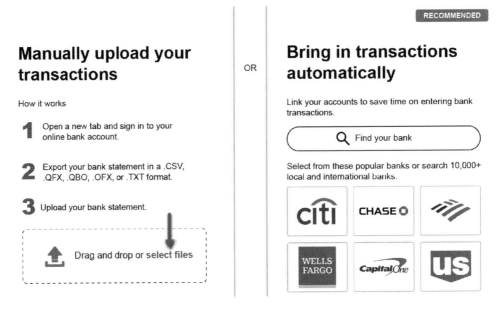

Figure 4.34: Clicking select files

The selected filename will appear in the field, as shown below:

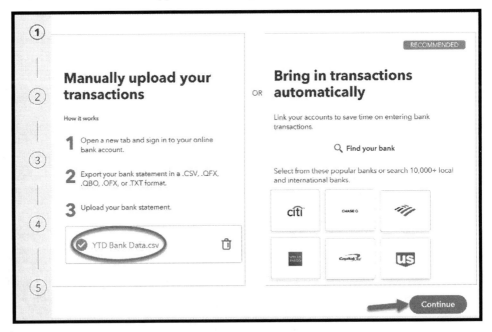

Figure 4.35: Checking the filename

7. Click the **Continue** button to proceed to the next step.

8. In this step, you will select the bank account from which you want the transactions to be uploaded to QuickBooks. Select the **Business Checking** account from the drop-down menu, as shown in *Figure 4.36*:

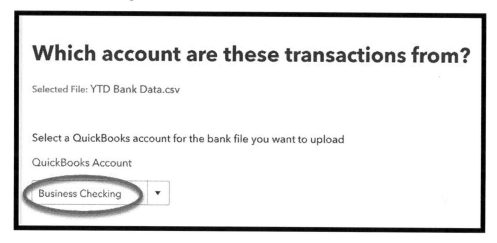

Figure 4.36: Selecting the bank account

9. Click **Continue**.

 Pro Tip: If you have more than one bank account, you will need to set up an account on the chart of accounts for each bank account and link them.

The following setup screen will appear:

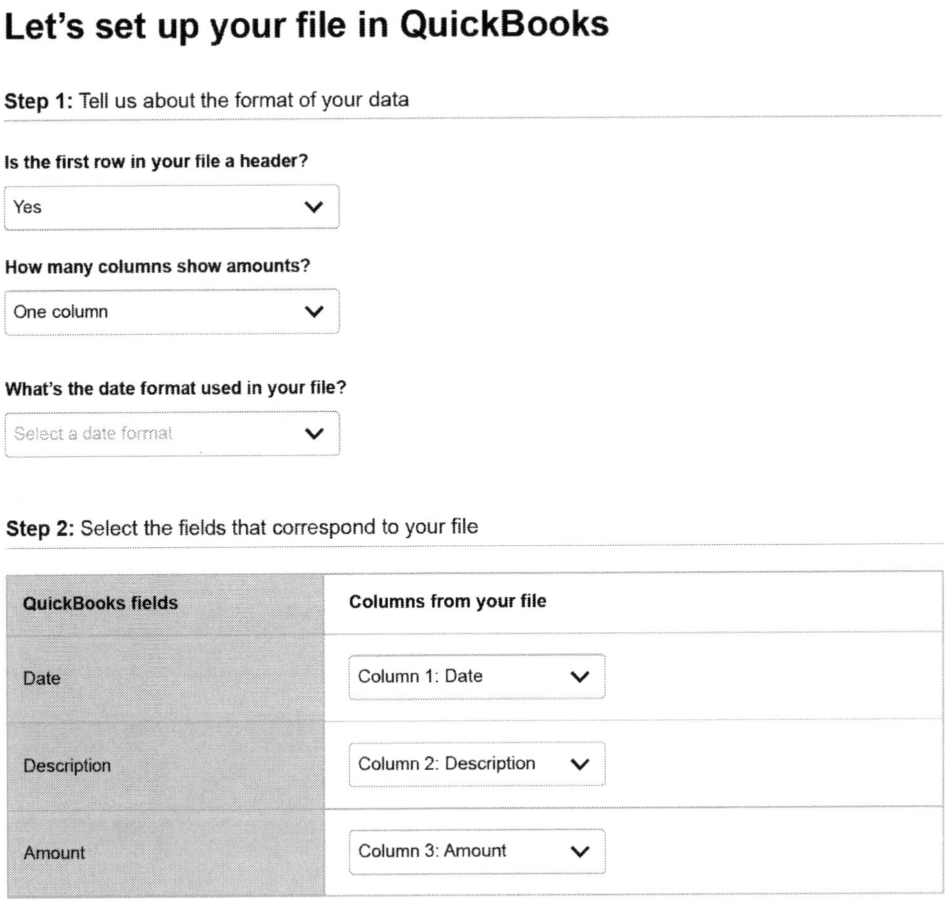

Let's set up your file in QuickBooks

Step 1: Tell us about the format of your data

Is the first row in your file a header?

Yes ⌄

How many columns show amounts?

One column ⌄

What's the date format used in your file?

Select a date format ⌄

Step 2: Select the fields that correspond to your file

QuickBooks fields	Columns from your file
Date	Column 1: Date ⌄
Description	Column 2: Description ⌄
Amount	Column 3: Amount ⌄

Figure 4.37: Setup screen

On this screen, you will provide responses to the three questions in step 1, and in step 2 you will map the columns in your CSV file to a field in QuickBooks. This is a very important step to ensure that the information is entered into the correct fields in QuickBooks.

For each QBO field located on the left, select the column from your import file that includes the corresponding data, as shown in *Figure 4.37* above. There are three fields that need to be populated in QuickBooks: the transaction date, a brief description, and the transaction amount. You will need to indicate what column in your CSV file includes this information:

- **Date:** From the drop-down, select the column in the CSV file that includes the date of the banking transactions. You can also select the format that the date is in (for example, mm/dd/yyyy).

- **Description:** Select the column in the CSV file that includes descriptions of the transactions.

- **Amount:** From the drop-down, select the column in the CSV file that includes the transaction amounts. Amounts can be formatted into one column that includes both positive and negative numbers, or into two separate columns, one for positive numbers (deposits) and one for negative numbers (withdrawals). In our example, both positive and negative numbers are formatted into one column.

10. Click **Continue**.

A preview of how your data will be uploaded to QuickBooks will appear. It's important to review the data to ensure that the correct fields are populated:

Figure 4.38: A preview of your data before importing to QBO

11. To select all transactions for import, put a checkmark in the box highlighted in the above screenshot. Alternatively, you can put a checkmark next to each individual transaction you wish to import into QBO.

12. Click the **Next** button in the lower-right corner to proceed to the next screen.

13. On the next screen, QuickBooks will provide you with the number of transactions to be uploaded. This is your final opportunity to confirm that the data is correct. Once you confirm this, there will be no option to undo it. To proceed with the upload, click the **Yes** button, as shown in *Figure 4.39*:

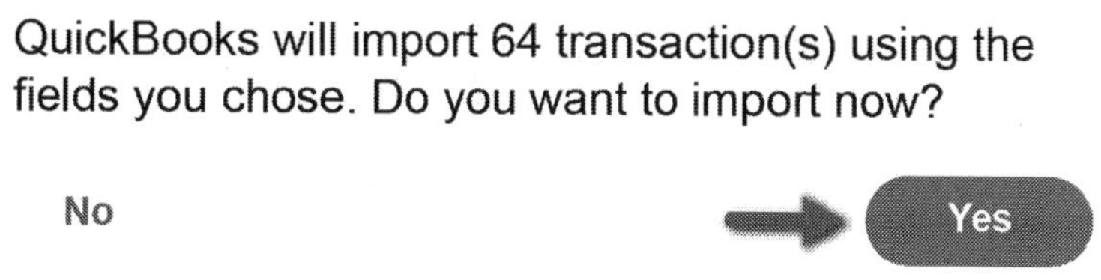

QuickBooks will import 64 transaction(s) using the fields you chose. Do you want to import now?

No ➡ Yes

Figure 4.39: Confirming the import

14. After confirming the number of transactions to import, your transactions will be added to QuickBooks. To verify the data was imported correctly, head over to the banking center where you can see the number of transactions that were successfully imported from your CSV file, along with their dates, descriptions, and dollar amounts. In *Chapter 9, Reconciling Uploaded Bank and Credit Card Transactions*, we will show you what to do with this data after it has been imported.

Now that we know how to connect our bank accounts to QBO, let's learn how to connect our credit card accounts in the next section.

Connecting credit card accounts to QBO

Similar to bank accounts, you can connect your credit card accounts to QBO. There are two ways that you can update QuickBooks with your credit card activity. You can connect your credit card account to QuickBooks so that transactions are imported automatically into QuickBooks. The other option is to upload transactions from an Excel spreadsheet. We will walk you through each process in more detail in the following sections.

Importing credit card transactions automatically

There are several benefits to importing your credit card transactions automatically. First, you will save a lot of time because you won't have to manually enter transactions. Second, QuickBooks will be updated on a daily basis with the most recent credit card activity on your account. Third, it will be much easier to reconcile your credit card accounts.

Listed below are the steps required to import credit card transactions automatically into QBO:

1. Select **Transactions** and **Bank transactions** from the left menu bar, as shown in *Figure 4.40*:

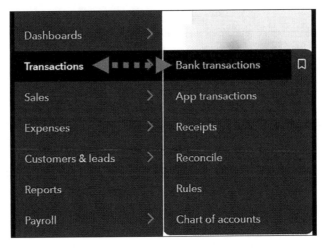

Figure 4.40: The Bank transactions option

2. On the following screen, you will see a link to a short video tutorial, which is a demo of how the banking center works. Click on the **Connect account** button, or the **Link account** button if you have previously connected a bank/credit card account:

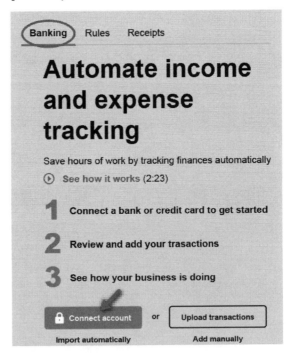

Figure 4.41: Connecting an account

3. To connect your credit card account, select your credit card company by clicking on the icon or typing the name of the financial institution in the search box, as shown in *Figure 4.42*:

Connect your bank or credit card to bring in your transactions.

Enter your bank name or URL

Here are some of the most popular ones

Figure 4.42: Selecting your bank

If you cannot locate your financial institution, you will not be able to connect your account to QuickBooks. Skip to the next section, *Uploading credit card transactions from an Excel or CSV file.*

4. Sign in to your credit card account using the secure user ID and password issued by your bank.

5. Before connecting your credit card account to QBO, you will be required to consent to the terms and conditions set by your bank. This consent is used as documentation, proving that you agree to share your financial data with QuickBooks.

6. Follow the remaining onscreen instructions to connect your credit card account to QuickBooks. If you have more than one account with the same financial institution, you will have the option to connect all credit card accounts or just select specific credit card accounts.

 Pro Tip: Make sure that you only connect *business* credit card accounts to QuickBooks and not personal credit card accounts; otherwise, you will have personal credit card activity co-mingled with business transactions, which is not ideal.

After connecting your credit card accounts to QuickBooks, they will appear in the banking center. From the banking center, you can see the date of the most recent download along with a description and the amount of each transaction downloaded. If your financial institution does not allow you to connect your credit card account to QuickBooks, you will need to upload credit card transactions from an Excel or CSV file.

Uploading credit card transactions from an Excel or CSV file

If your financial institution does not integrate with QuickBooks, you need to download your credit card transactions to an Excel or CSV file. Most banks allow you to download your transactions as a PDF or CSV file. Log in to your credit card account and look for a **Download Transactions** option. If you don't see this option, contact the credit card company and inform them that you need your transactions in a CSV file so you can upload them to QuickBooks.

 Pro Tip: While you cannot use a PDF file to upload transactions to QBO, there are programs that will extract transactions from bank and credit card PDF statements into QBO. **MoneyThumb** is one of many programs that will do this: `https://www.moneythumb.com/quickbooks-converters-benefits/`.

To upload credit card transactions from an Excel or CSV file to QuickBooks, follow these instructions:

1. At the beginning of this chapter, we showed you how to add a new account to the chart of accounts list. Follow those step-by-step instructions and add your credit card account to QuickBooks.

2. Your credit card account setup screen should resemble the one in *Figure 4.43*:

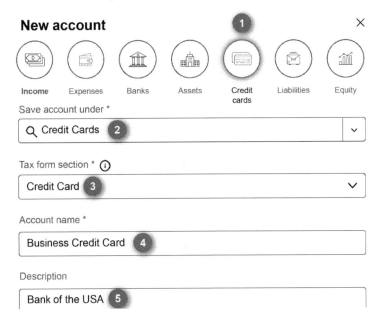

Figure 4.43: Adding account details for a credit card

The following is a brief explanation of the new credit card account fields:

- **Account type (1):** The account type will be a **credit card**.

- **Save account under (2):** This field will automatically be populated with your selection for the account type.

- **Tax form section (3):** The options in this field will be based on the entity that you chose when you set up your QBO account (i.e., **LLC**, **Sole proprietor**, **C-Corp**, **S-Corp**). QuickBooks will provide you with categories from the tax form applicable to your entity. Select the section that most accurately describes the account.

- **Account name (4):** The name of the credit card belongs in this field. If you have multiple credit card accounts at the same financial institution, you may want to consider entering the last four digits of each account in this field. This will make it easier when you are entering transactions and reconciling accounts.

- **Description (5):** You can include a brief description of the account that you are adding in this field or enter the name of the account.

The bottom part of the setup screen includes the date to start tracking, the opening balance, and the preview of the account on the balance sheet, as shown in *Figure 4.44*:

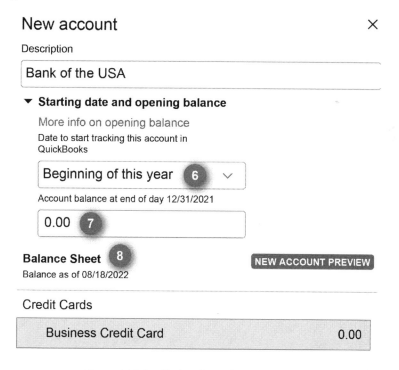

Figure 4.44: Continuing down the setup screen

- **Date to start tracking in this account QuickBooks (6)**: From the drop-down, select the date you want to begin tracking your finances for this account.

- **Account balance (7)**: Enter the current outstanding balance due on your credit card account as of your QuickBooks start date (see *step 5*). For example, if you began to use QuickBooks as of January 1, enter the balance owed on your credit card as of the last day of the previous period, which would be December 31 of the previous year.

- **NEW ACCOUNT PREVIEW (8)**: In this section, you will see a preview of where on the financial statements this account will appear. In our example, it will appear on the **Balance Sheet** report as a sub-account below **Credit Cards**.

> **Pro Tip**: It's important to have your credit card statements handy as you are adding credit card accounts to QuickBooks. This is to ensure that you enter the correct balance and effective dates. If you leave this field blank, you will not be able to access this field later on; instead, you will have to make a balance adjustment directly in the credit card register.

3. From the gear icon, select **Import data** in the **Tools** column, as shown in *Figure 4.45*:

TOOLS

Order checks

Import desktop

Figure 4.45: The Import data option

4. The **Import Data** screen is where you can import bank and credit card transactions, customers, vendors, a chart of accounts list, a products and services list, and invoices. Select the **Bank Data** option to display the setup screen, as shown in *Figure 4.46*:

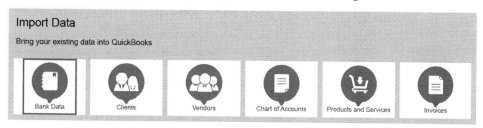

Figure 4.46: The Import Data screen

The following screen appears. Click on **select files** to choose the file that includes your bank data, as indicated below:

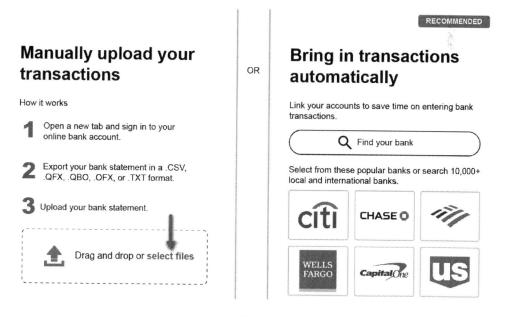

Figure 4.47: Clicking select files

The filename will appear in the field as shown below:

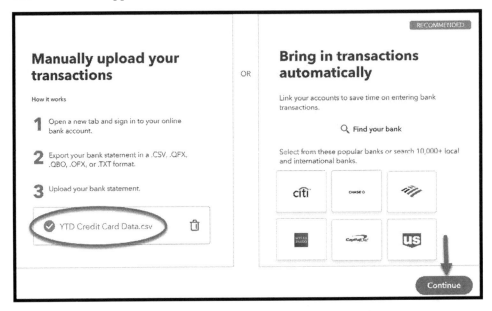

Figure 4.48: Checking the filename

5.   Click the **Continue** button to proceed to the next step.

6.   In this step, you will select the credit card account for which you want the transactions to be uploaded to QuickBooks. Select the **Business Credit Card** account from the drop-down menu, as shown in *Figure 4.49*:

Which account are these transactions from?

Selected File: **January 2021 Credit Card Data.csv**

Select a QuickBooks account for the bank file you want to upload

QuickBooks Account

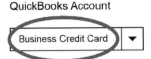

Figure 4.49: Selecting the account

7.   Click **Continue**.

The following screen appears:

Let's set up your file in QuickBooks

Step 1: Tell us about the format of your data

Is the first row in your file a header?

Yes ⌄

How many columns show amounts?

One column ⌄

What's the date format used in your file?

Select a date format ⌄

Step 2: Select the fields that correspond to your file

QuickBooks fields	Columns from your file
Date	Column 1: Date ⌄
Description	Column 2: Description ⌄
Amount	Column 3: Amount ⌄

Figure 4.50: Setting up your file in QuickBooks

On this screen, you will respond to the three questions in *Step 1*, and in *Step 2* you will map the columns in your CSV file to a field in QuickBooks. This is a very important step to ensure that the information is populated into the correct fields in QuickBooks.

Pro Tip: If you have additional columns of information in your Excel or CSV file, that is OK. QuickBooks is only going to pick up the information in the three required fields: **Date**, **Description**, and **Amount**.

8. For each QBO field located on the left, select the column from your import file that in-cludes the corresponding data, as shown in the screenshot above. There are three fields that need to be populated in QuickBooks: the transaction date, a brief description, and the transaction amount. You will need to indicate what column in your CSV file includes this information:

    - **Date**: From the drop-down, select the column in the CSV file that includes the dates of the credit card transactions. You can also select the format that the date is in (for example, mm/dd/yyyy).

    - **Description**: Select the column in the CSV file that includes descriptions of the transactions.

    - **Amount**: From the drop-down, select the column in the CSV file that includes the transaction amounts. Amounts can be formatted into one column that includes both positive and negative numbers or into two separate columns, one for pos-itive numbers (credit card charges) and one for negative numbers (credit card payments and credits).

9. Click **Continue**.

    On the next screen is a preview of how your data will upload to QuickBooks. It's important to review the data to ensure that the correct fields are populated:

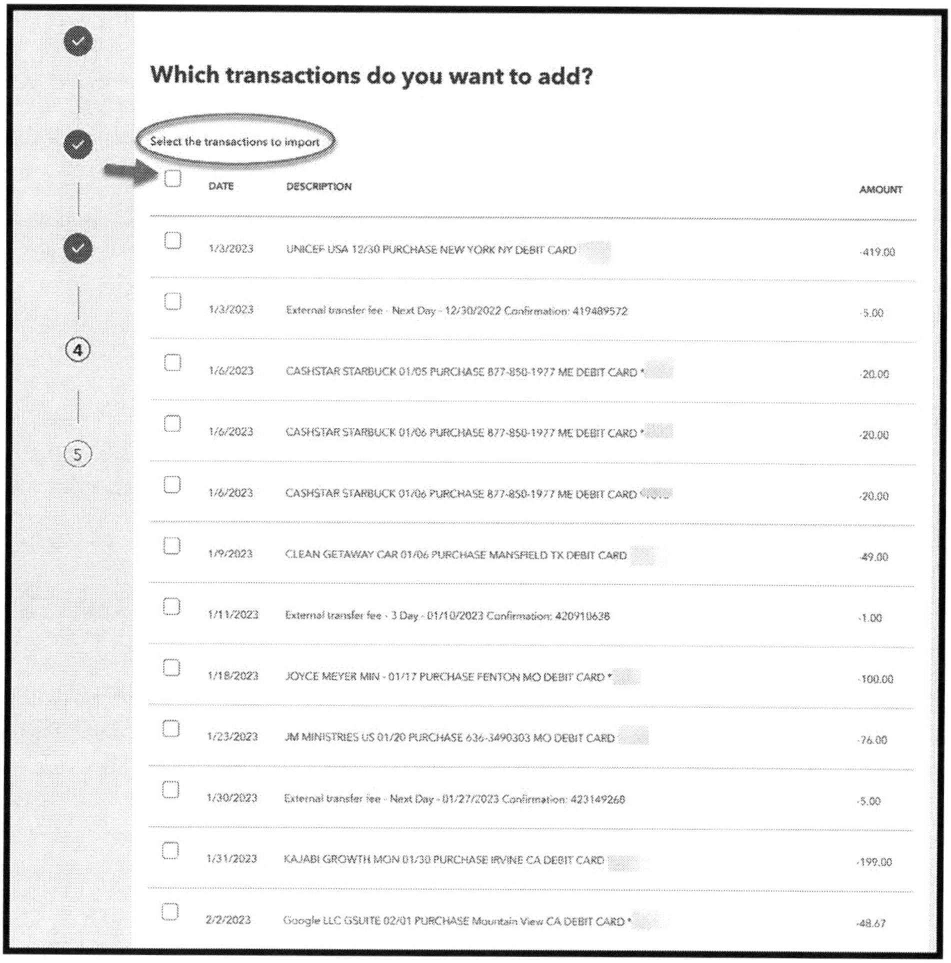

Figure 4.51: Checking your data

10. Click the **Next** button to proceed.

On the following screen, QuickBooks will provide you with the number of transactions to be uploaded. This is your final opportunity to confirm that the data is correct. Once you confirm this, there will be no option to undo it. To proceed with the upload, click the **Yes** button, as shown in the following screenshot:

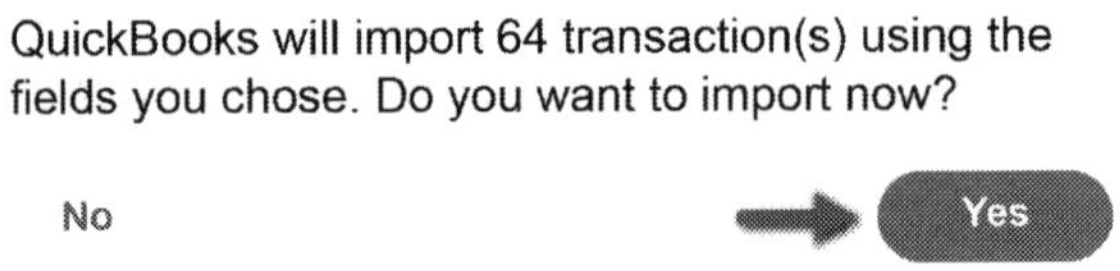

QuickBooks will import 64 transaction(s) using the fields you chose. Do you want to import now?

No   ➡   Yes

Figure 4.52: Confirming the import

After confirming the number of transactions to import, your transactions will be added to Quick-Books. To verify the data was imported correctly, head over to the banking center where you should see the dates, descriptions, and number of transactions that were successfully imported from your CSV file.

Pro Tip: Many financial institutions have different ways to connect your bank accounts to QuickBooks. I recommend that you contact the small business banking department at your bank and ask them what your options are for connecting your business bank accounts to QBO. By default, most banks allow you to import the last 90 days. However, if you need to go back further than that, be sure to inform them so that they can provide you with the best solution.

Giving other users access to your QuickBooks data

The ability to give other users access to your data is one of the many benefits of using QBO. With the exception of QBO Advanced, which includes three accountant users, the other QBO subscriptions include access for two accountant users and access for one or more additional users. There are two main groups that users fall into: billable roles and non-billable roles. Billable roles count towards your user limit. For example, QBO Plus is limited to 5 users. Billable roles count toward this limit. Non-billable roles do not count toward your user limit. For example, if you give a contractor track time only access, that access would not count toward your user limit because it is a non-billable role.

There are six *billable* roles that you can create in QBO:

- Company administrator
- Standard all access
- Standard limited customers and vendors

- Standard limited customers only
- Standard limited vendors only
- Standard no access

There are two *non-billable* roles that you can create in QBO:

- Track time only
- View company reports

We will discuss each of these in more detail in the following subsections.

Company administrator

The company administrator role includes access to every aspect of QuickBooks. This includes adding new users, changing passwords, and having control of your QBO subscription. Because there are no limitations to what this user can do, we recommend that you limit this role to owners of the business, IT personnel, or an officer of the company.

Go through the following steps to assign the administrative role:

1. From the gear icon, select **Manage users** in the **YOUR COMPANY** column, as shown in *Figure 4.53*:

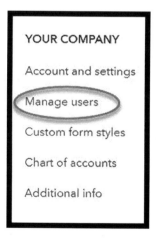

Figure 4.53: The Manage users option

Pro Tip: Since the company administrator has access to everything, you will just enter their name and email address to send them an invite to your QBO file. Once they accept, they will have full access to your QBO file.

Standard all access user

The standard all access user has full access to QBO without admin privileges, plus access to payroll. This user has partial access to bills and company information. This user does not have the ability to change your QBO subscription, nor are they able to add, edit, or delete new users. Go through the following steps to assign the standard all access role to a new user:

1. From the gear icon, select **Manage users** in the **YOUR COMPANY** column, as shown in *Figure 4.54*:

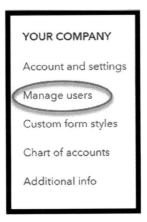

Figure 4.54: The Manage users option

2. Click on the **Add user** button:

Figure 4.55: The Add user button

3. Enter the first name, last name, and email address of the new user as indicated in *Figure 4.56*:

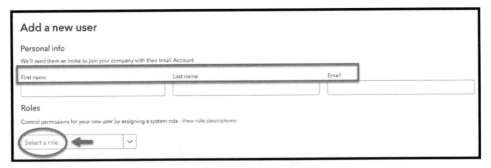

Figure 4.56: Choosing a user type

A standard all access user will count toward the total number of users included in your QBO subscription. To recap, the following is a summary of the number of users that are included in each plan:

- QuickBooks Online Simple Start: 2 accountants and 1 user
- QuickBooks Online Essentials: 2 accountants and 3 users
- QuickBooks Online Plus: 2 accountants and 5 users
- QuickBooks Online Advanced: 3 accountants and 25 users

4. From the drop-down, select **Standard all access** as indicated in *Figure 4.57*:

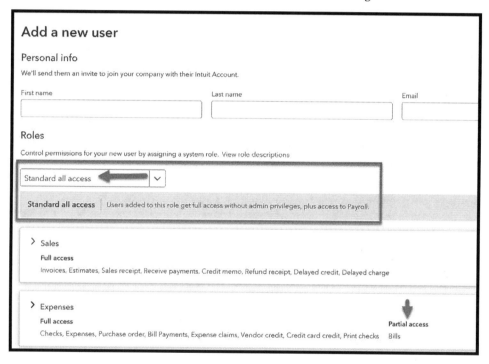

Figure 4.57: Selecting access rights for the user

Users who are assigned to the standard limited customers and vendors role have the ability to manage customers and vendor activities. This includes but is not limited to adding new customers and vendors and managing all aspects of accounts receivable (invoices and payments) and accounts payable (bills, checks, and expenses).

The following is a snapshot of the access rights for **Standard limited customers and vendors**:

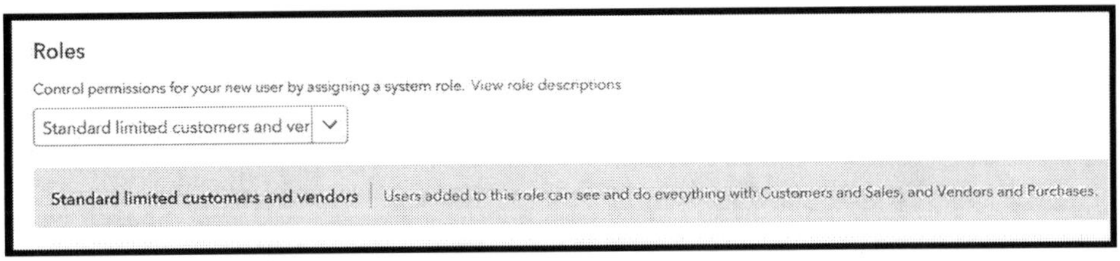

Figure 4.58: Access rights for standard limited customers and vendors

The **Standard limited customers only** role gives the user the ability to manage all customers and sales transactions. This level of access would be ideal for an accounts receivable clerk who only needs access to customers and sales.

The following is a snapshot of the access rights for **Standard limited customers only**:

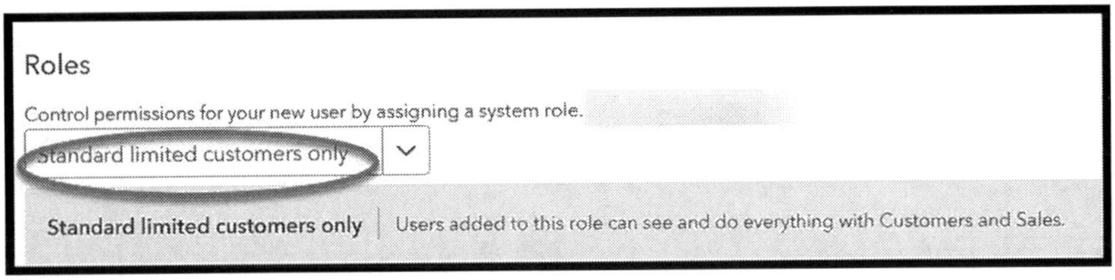

Figure 4.59: Access rights for customers only

The following is a snapshot of the access rights for **Standard limited vendors only**:

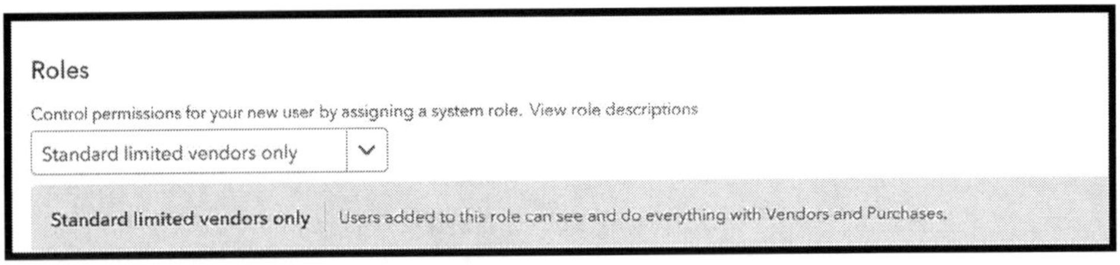

Figure 4.60: Access rights for Standard limited vendors role

The **Standard limited vendors only** role gives the user the ability to manage all vendor and purchasing transactions. This level of access would be ideal for an accounts payable clerk who needs access to vendors and purchasing transactions.

The following is a snapshot of the access rights for **Standard no access**:

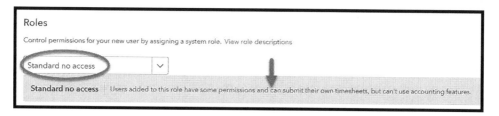

Figure 4.61: Access rights for Standard no access role

Standard no access gives the user some permissions, like submitting their own timesheet, but they have no access to accounting features.

5. Once you have specified how much access you want the user to have, click the **Send invite** button in the lower-right corner of the screen to send the email invitation to the new user.

Reports-only user

The **View company reports only** role is very limited. This role can generate just about any report in QuickBooks except payroll or vendor and customer contact information; however, the reports-only user cannot add, edit, or change any QuickBooks data. They also do not have the ability to view anything outside of reports. This role is ideal for a business partner who wants to periodically review reports but has no day-to-day responsibilities. Unlike the standard and company admin roles, the reports-only role does not count toward your user limit, which means you can give reports-only access to an unlimited number of users, at no additional charge. To add a reports-only user, follow *Steps 1* and *2* in the *Standard all access user* section. In *Step 3*, select **View Company Reports** and follow the onscreen prompts to complete the setup.

Time tracking user

Similar to the **View company reports only** role, the **Track time only** role is also very limited. This role is limited to entering timesheets. It is ideal for employees and contractors who don't need access to any other areas of QuickBooks. Like the reports-only role, the time tracking user does not count toward your user limit. This means that you can add an unlimited number of time tracking users at no additional charge. To add a time tracking user, follow *Steps 1* and *2* in the *Standard all access user* section. In *Step 3*, select **Time tracking only** and follow the onscreen prompts to complete the setup.

Accountant user

Each QBO plan includes at least two accountant users, at no additional cost. The level of access the accountant user has is identical to that of the company administrator. Accountant users can access all areas of QuickBooks.

This includes adding users, editing passwords, and managing your QuickBooks subscription. You should be extremely careful who you give this level of access to; ideally, it should be limited to your **Certified Public Accountant (CPA)**, tax preparer, or bookkeeper.

Go through the following steps to invite an accountant to access your QuickBooks data:

1. Click on the gear icon and select **Manage users** from the company info column, as shown in *Figure 4.62*:

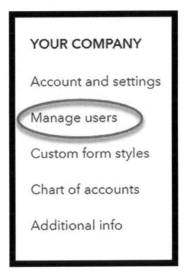

Figure 4.62: The Manage users option

2. On the **Manage users** page, click on **Accountants**, as shown in *Figure 4.63*:

Figure 4.63: The Accountants tab

3. The following screen appears. Type your accountant's email address in the field and click the **Invite** button, as shown in *Figure 4.64*:

Figure 4.64: Inviting your accountant to your QBO account

4. Your accountant will receive an email inviting them to access your QBO account. They will need to accept the invitation and create a secure password. Their user ID will be the email address that you entered in the screenshot above.

Editing user privileges

You can remove access for any user at any time. Follow the steps below to delete a user from access to your QuickBooks file:

1. Navigate to the **Users** page, as shown in the upper-left of *Figure 4.65*:

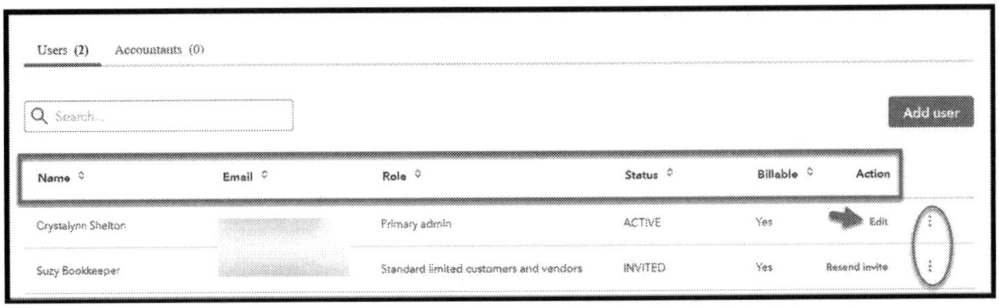

Name ◇	Email ◇	Role ◇	Status ◇	Billable ◇	Action
Crystalynn Shelton		Primary admin	ACTIVE	Yes	Edit
Suzy Bookkeeper		Standard limited customers and vendors	INVITED	Yes	Resend invite

Figure 4.65: Users page in a QuickBooks file

2. Next to the appropriate user, click on **Edit** to change the user's role, or click on the three dots to the right of **Edit** and select **Delete** to remove the user's access altogether, as shown in *Figure 4.65*.

> **Pro Tip**: If a user has the **Primary admin** role (as Crystalynn Shelton does in *Figure 4.65*), you will not be able to delete that user. First, you will need to transfer the **Primary admin** access to another user. Once this is complete, you will be able to delete the previous **Primary admin** user.

You should now have a better understanding of the five types of users you can set up in QuickBooks (standard, company admin, reports-only, time tracking, and accountant). Using the detailed information we have provided on the level of access each user has, you can start inviting your accountant, bookkeeper, and other users to access your QuickBooks data.

We will wrap this chapter up with showing you how to navigate the QuickBooks Apps Center. Apps are a great way to help you streamline day-to-day business tasks that can be time-consuming.

Using apps in QuickBooks Online

There are many benefits and a few risks of extending functionality through apps. Some of the **benefits** of using apps in QBO are:

-   The ability to expand the functionality of the software so you can have what you need to run all aspects of your business

- Access to more than 700 apps that integrate seamlessly with QBO, allowing you to manage your inventory, accept online payments, pay your bills, and manage your eCommerce transactions

- The companies featured in the QuickBooks Apps Center have gone through an extensive vetting process and were approved by Intuit to create apps that will help you simplify tasks, streamline data entry, and sync with QuickBooks

A couple of the **risks** involved with using apps are:

- The apps are not free, which means the fees charged to use an app will be in addition to what you pay for your monthly QBO subscription, so be sure to do a cost/benefit analysis to ensure you can take on the additional cost.

- You will need to give permission for your data in QBO to be shared with any company whose app you wish to use. You can be confident that your data is secure, since that is also a requirement to become a partner with Intuit.

The app store is organized into categories based on app functionality. Customer reviews are included, along with short video demonstrations to show you how the app works and customer service information if you have additional questions. In this section, we will provide you with an overview of the Apps Center, show you how to find apps that are relevant to your business needs, and show you how to connect apps to QuickBooks Online.

 Pro Tip: Because of the large number of apps that are available, it's impossible for ProAdvisors and accountants to be familiar with all apps. Therefore, you will need to reach out to the technical support team for the app that you choose for assistance with setup, implementation, and training needs.

Overview of the QuickBooks App Center

The layout of the App Center is very simple. You can easily search for apps, see a list of the apps you have added, and check out apps that have been recommended based on the type of business you have. Let's take a look at the layout of the App Center:

1. On the left menu bar, click on **Apps** to navigate to the App Center, as follows:

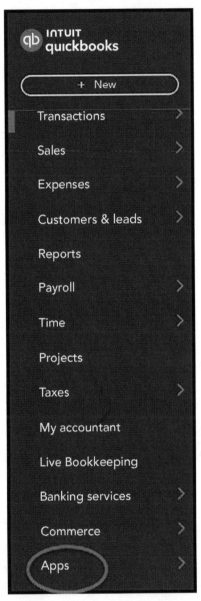

Figure 4.66: Navigating to the QuickBooks App Center

The screen displays as shown in *Figure 4.67*:

Save time and streamline your business

Connect your favorite business apps to see more and do more, all in one place.

 Find apps

Figure 4.67: The Find apps window displays

2. To start your search, click on the **Find apps** tab next to the **Overview** tab or click the **Find apps** button shown at the bottom of the screen.

3. The App Center will be displayed, as shown in *Figure 4.68*:

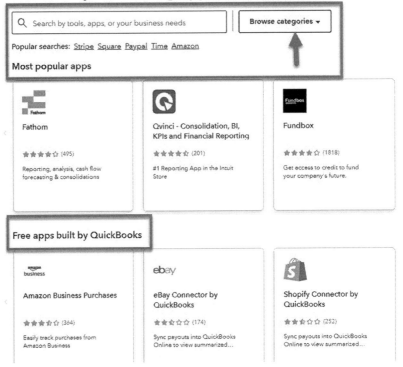

Figure 4.68: QuickBooks App Center

The three key areas of the QuickBooks App Center are as follows:

- **Search options:** If you know the name of the app you are searching for, you can simply type the name of the app into the search box shown in the preceding screenshot. However, if you don't know the name of the app and simply want to search by category, you can do so by clicking on the **Browse categories** button.

- **Browse categories:** There are several categories you can search by, such as **Get customers**, **Get paid**, **Get capital**, **Manage workforce**, **Access advice**, **Be compliant and organized**, **Manage business**, **Manage sales**, and **Manage data**. This will help to narrow down the search so that you can quickly find the apps that you are looking for.

- **Free apps built by QuickBooks:** In this section, you will find apps that were created by QuickBooks.

If you're not sure which app to choose, I recommend that you schedule a live demo with the app company so that you can see how the app works and get your questions answered. Many companies offer a trial period of 14 days or more so that you can try the app before you buy it. Like QBO, there are no contracts, so you can cancel your subscription at any time. Let's now walk through an example of how to find apps for your business.

Finding apps for your business

As we mentioned previously, there are more than 700 apps in the QuickBooks App Center. While it can be overwhelming at first, you should focus on the needs of your business. There is a lot of information in the center about each app, which will save you the time you would have normally spent doing research. Let's take a look at an app to see what kind of information you can expect to find here.

Scroll down to the **Most Popular** category and click on the **Fathom** app. You will be greeted with the following screen:

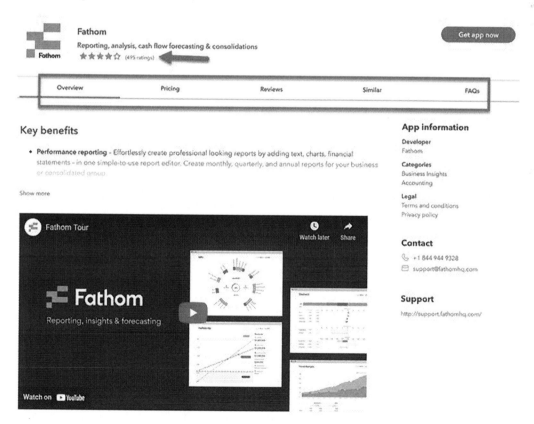

Figure 4.69: The app profile for the Fathom app

The following is a brief description of the information you will find in the app profile:

- **Overview**: The **Overview** tab includes a list of the key benefits the app has, how the app works with QuickBooks Online, and additional details. Like Fathom, most apps will include a short video to demonstrate how the app works, along with additional screenshots of the user interface.

- **Pricing**: Unfortunately, these apps are not free. Pricing will vary and is usually subscription-based, like QuickBooks Online. However, you will be billed by the third-party company (in this case, Fathom), not QuickBooks. The good news is that most apps will offer a free trial period of at least 14 days.

- **Reviews**: Like most products, you will see a rating of the app based on customer reviews. Click on the link to see what customers are saying about the app. The more reviews an app has, the better the chance of getting a broad perspective.

- **Similar**: The **Similar** tab shows a list of apps that have similar functionality to the one you are looking at.

- **FAQs**: A list of the most frequently asked questions and answers can be found on this tab.

Once you have decided which app(s) to go with, it's easy to get started. Simply click on the **Get app now** button located on each app profile. Follow the onscreen instructions to complete the app's setup.

 Pro Tip: Reaching out to an industry-specific professional organization is a great way to find out the most popular apps used for your industry. This may help narrow down your search for the right fit.

There are several apps that allow you to accept credit card payments from customers. If you sign up for one of these apps, it will make managing credit card payments that much easier in QuickBooks. Next, we will explain how to manage credit card payments.

Summary

In this chapter, we showed you how to customize the chart of accounts by adding, editing, deleting, and merging accounts. We covered how to connect your bank and credit card accounts to QuickBooks so that transactions are automatically downloaded into QuickBooks. We also covered how to import banking transactions into QuickBooks from a CSV file. Keep in mind that the bank and credit card transactions are not yet recorded on your books.

After importing the transactions, they are sitting in the banking center and will require you to review and categorize them. In *Chapter 9, Reconciling Uploaded Bank and Credit Card Transactions*, we will show you how to do this.

We showed you how to give other users, such as a bookkeeper, business partner, or CPA, full or limited access to your QuickBooks data. Finally, we showed you how to search the QuickBooks App Center for apps that can help to streamline your business processes. By now, you should know how to manage your chart of accounts, bank, and credit card accounts, how to add additional users as well as how to delete users, and how to navigate the QBO App Center.

In the next chapter, we will show you how to manage customers, vendors, and products and services in QBO. This will include how to add, edit, and inactivate customers, vendors, and products and services.

Join our community on Discord

Join our community's Discord space for discussions with the authors and other readers:

```
https://packt.link/quickbooks
```

5

Managing Customer, Vendor, and Products and Services Lists

Now that you've created your company files, it's time to add the people you do business with on a regular basis. This includes the customers to whom you sell your products and services and the vendors from whom you purchase services and supplies. We will also cover how to create a products and services list in QuickBooks Online so that you can keep track of your sales.

In this chapter, we will cover the following key concepts:

- Managing customer lists in QuickBooks Online
- Managing vendor lists in QuickBooks Online
- Managing products and services lists in QuickBooks Online

By the end of this chapter, you will understand how to add, edit, delete, and merge customers, vendors, and products and services that you sell.

 The US edition of QBO was used to create this book. If you are using a version that is outside of the US, results may differ.

Managing customer lists in QuickBooks Online

A customer is anyone that you sell products or services to. A customer can be an individual or a business.

Some of the information QuickBooks Online allows you to keep track of related to customers includes contact information, such as their telephone number and email address, payment terms, invoicing, and payment history. You can enter customer information manually or import it from an Excel spreadsheet. If you need to make changes to the contact information for a customer, you can do so easily. If you stop doing business with a customer, you can make customers inactive so that they no longer appear in the customer listing. You can also merge customers if you have duplicates. In this section, we will show you how each of these works, beginning with manually adding customers.

Manually adding customers in QuickBooks Online

In order to add new customers to **QuickBooks Online (QBO)**, you need to have the basic contact details of your customer. This includes their company name, billing address, business telephone number, and the first and last name of the primary contact. You should also know what payment terms you will extend to customers (for example, net 30 days or net 60 days).

Follow these steps to add a new customer in QBO:

1. Navigate to **Customers** by selecting **Sales** from the left menu bar and then **Customers**, as shown in *Figure 5.1*:

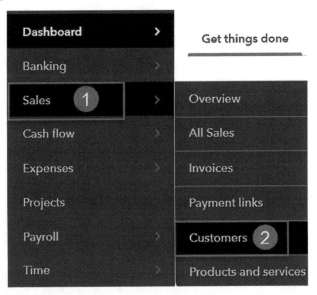

Figure 5.1: Navigating to Customers

The following screen will appear:

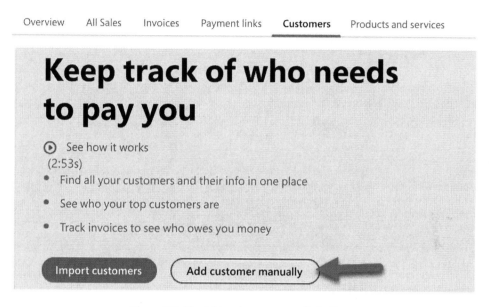

Figure 5.2: The Add customer manually button

2.   Click on the **Add customer manually** button. Note that this button will not appear if you have added customers previously to QuickBooks.

3. Fill in the fields on the **Customer** information screen, as shown in *Figure 5.3*:

Figure 5.3: Filling in customer information

4. When adding a new customer, there are five key areas that need to be completed: name and contact, addresses, notes and attachments, payments, and additional information. You can navigate to each area using the icons located in the top-right corner of the screen, as indicated in *Figure 5.3*.

5. The following is a brief description of the 11 fields of information you can enter in the **Name and contact** section. While the only required field is the **Customer display name** field, I recommend that you take the time to add as much information as you can about your customers:

- **First name** and **Last name** (1): If the customer is an individual, enter their first and last names in these fields. If the customer is a business, leave these fields blank. Note that if a business is a sole proprietorship or a single-member LLC and you want to keep track of the name of the business owner and the legal business name, complete both fields.

- **Company name** (2): If the customer is a business, enter the business name in this field. If the customer is an individual, leave this field blank.

- **Customer display name** (3): There is no need to input anything in this field; it will automatically populate with the information you entered in the **Company name** or **First name** and **Last name** fields. This field is important because the information will be displayed in the customer list found in the customer center.

- **Email** (4): Enter the business email address for customers in this field.

- **Phone number** (5): Enter the business telephone number for customers in this field.

- **Mobile number** (6): Enter the mobile number for customers in this field.

- **Fax** (7): Enter the fax number (if applicable) for customers in this field.

- **Other** (8): Enter an additional contact phone number in the **Other** field.

- **Website** (9): Enter the website address for the business if you have one.

- **Name to print on checks** (10): Similar to the **Customer display name** field, this field will automatically populate with the information that you entered in the **Company name** or **First name** and **Last name** fields. If you need to change the payee name, enter the name you would like to appear on checks. Typically, you would issue a check to a customer in the case of a refund, so it is important to have the correct payee name in this field.

- **Is a sub-customer** (11): If you have more than one job or project you are working on for the same customer, you can create sub-customers to keep track of the income and expenses for each job separately. For example, if a contractor is working on a kitchen remodel and a bathroom remodel for the same customer, each of these jobs can be set up as a sub-customer so that you can track income and expenses for each job (sub-customer) separately. This will allow you to easily run reports by sub-customer (job, project) so that you can see the profitability of each one.

Pro Tip: Before you can create a sub-customer, the main customer must be added to QuickBooks first. Going back to our contractor example, the customer must be added to QuickBooks first before adding kitchen remodel and bathroom remodel as sub-customers.

6. Complete the following fields in the **Addresses** section:

Figure 5.4: Addresses section of the Customer information screen

The following is a brief description of the fields of information you can enter in the **Addresses** section:

- **Billing address** (1): Enter the address where your customers would like their invoices to be mailed to and/or where correspondence should be sent. Even if you plan to email all the invoices and other correspondence, we recommend that you keep an address on file for all customers.

- **Shipping address** (2): The address entered in the **Billing address** field will automatically be copied to the **Shipping address** field. This can be edited if necessary. The billing address will be used to mail invoices to customers, and the shipping address is where products are shipped, if applicable.

7. Complete the following fields in the **Notes and attachments** section:

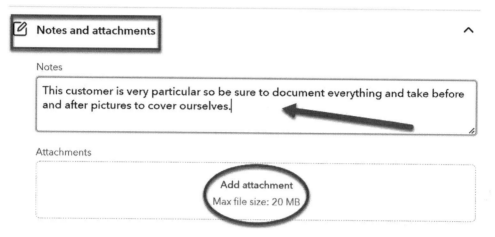

Figure 5.5: Descriptive note and button to add an attachment

- **Notes:** This field can be used to enter additional information about your customers, such as any preferences they have, or even to document previous incidents or issues. This information is for internal use only and is not visible to the customer.

- **Attachments:** You can store important documents such as contracts, engagement letters, or proposals in QuickBooks. Simply scan the document into your computer and attach it to the customer with whom it is associated.

8. Complete the following fields in the **Payments** section:

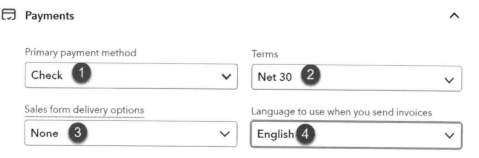

Figure 5.6: Payments section of the Customer information screen

There are four fields in the **Payments section** – **Primary payment method, Terms, Sales form delivery options**, and **Language to use when you send invoices**:

- **Primary payment method** (1): Choose from the drop-down the payment method used most often by the customer. Cash, check, and credit card are the options available, but you can also add new payment methods, such as Cash App or Zelle.

- **Terms** (2): Select the payment terms for customers in this field. For example, **Net 30** means the customer has 30 days from the invoice date to remit payment. If payment is not received by the due date, QuickBooks will flag the invoice as past due. You can set QuickBooks up to automatically send a reminder email to customers when invoices are coming due or past due. Refer to *Chapter 2, Company File Setup*, to learn how to do this.

- **Sales form delivery options** (3): From the drop-down, you can select the method that typically provides customers their invoices (**Email, Printed copy, Default method**, or **None** are the options).

- **Language to use when you send invoices** (4): From the drop-down, you can select the language you would like to invoice customers in. Currently, the choices are **English, French, Spanish, Italian, Chinese (Traditional)**, and **Portuguese (Brazil)**.

9. Complete the following fields in the **Additional info** section:

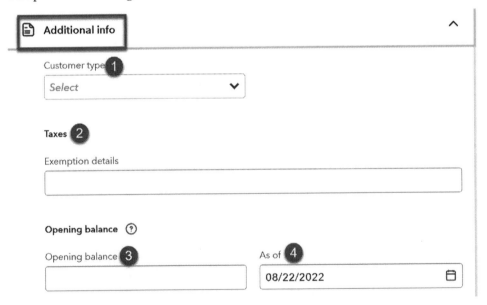

Figure 5.7: Additional info screen of the Customer information screen

- **Customer type** (1): If you need to categorize your customers into different types (for example, wholesaler or retailer), you can create custom types and assign each customer to a type. This will allow you to run reports and filter by customer type to get detailed information, such as sales by customer type.

- **Taxes** (2): Enter the details for tax-exempt customers such as their resale certificate number. In addition, you should request a copy of the certificate and attach it in the **Notes and Attachments** section. This will cover you if you ever have a sales tax audit and need to provide supporting information on why you did not charge a customer sales tax.

- **Opening balance** (3): Generally, you wouldn't use this field unless converting from other accounting software. This field is useful to record the existing accounts receivable balance that customers have with you at the time of converting from your old accounting system to QuickBooks. However, if you plan to enter unpaid invoices into QuickBooks, leave this field blank.

- **As of** (4): If you entered an opening **accounts recievable (A/R)** balance in *step 3*, enter the effective date in this field. This would typically be the date you start using QuickBooks to track your business finances.

10. Be sure to click the **Save** button at the very bottom of the screen to save the customer information in QuickBooks.

If you have more than a handful of customers to add to QuickBooks, I recommend you put the customer information into an Excel spreadsheet and import the data into QuickBooks.

Importing customers into QuickBooks Online

You can import all of your customer details from a CSV file into QuickBooks. A template can be found here: `https://github.com/PacktPublishing/Mastering-QuickBooks-2024-Fifth-Edition/tree/main/Chapter05`.

Follow these steps to import customers into QuickBooks Online:

1. Navigate to **Customers** by selecting **Sales** from the left-hand menu bar and then **Customers**, as shown in *Figure 5.8*:

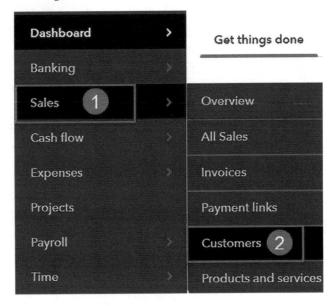

Figure 5.8: Navigating to Customers

2. Click the drop-down arrow next to the **New customer** button, located in the upper-right corner, and select **Import customers**, as shown in *Figure 5.9*:

Figure 5.9: The Import customers option

3. On the **Import customers** screen, click the **Browse** button to upload the Excel or CSV file from your computer, as shown in *Figure 5.10*:

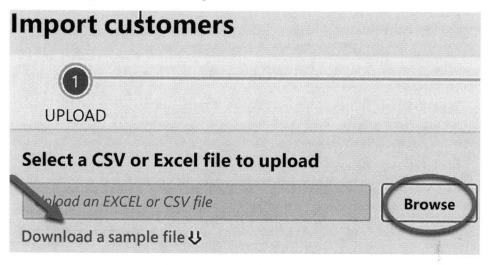

Figure 5.10: Uploading a CSV or Excel file

4. You can click on the blue link to download the sample file (shown in the preceding screenshot). This file includes all of the fields of information you can upload for customers. Save this file and use it as your template.

5. Follow the onscreen instructions to import your customer data into QBO.

Pro Tip: A common error made when importing data is the use of special characters. QuickBooks will not accept the use of special characters (for example, &, !, and $), so be sure to avoid doing this. For additional tips on troubleshooting errors during importing, you can download the troubleshooting guide using this link: https://github.com/PacktPublishing/Mastering-QuickBooks-2024-Fifth-Edition/tree/main/Chapter05.

Making changes to existing customers in QuickBooks Online

There may be times when you need to correct or update a customer's information. For example, if a customer's address changes or their primary contact changes, you will need to update your records with the new information. Updating customer information is easy to do in QuickBooks – all you need to do is navigate to the Customer Center and select the customer that you need to make changes to.

Follow these steps to edit an existing customer in QuickBooks Online:

1. Navigate to **Customers** by selecting **Sales** from the left-hand menu bar and then **Customers**, as shown in *Figure 5.11*:

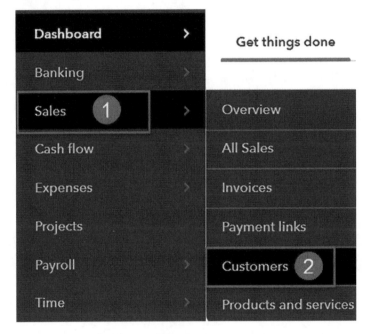

Figure 5.11: Navigating to Customers

2. The Customer Center will appear on the next screen. Click on the customer name, as indicated in *Figure 5.12*:

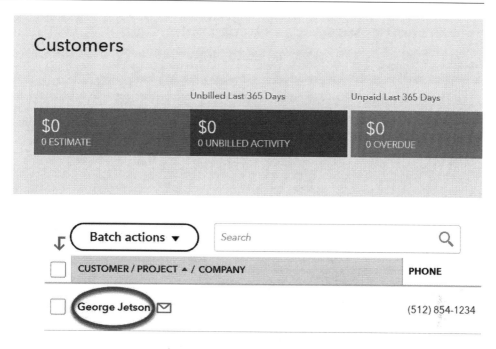

Figure 5.12: Editing customer details

3. The following screen appears. Click the **Edit** button shown in *Figure 5.13* and make the necessary changes:

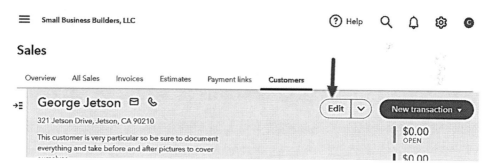

Figure 5.13: Edit button for a customer listed in the Customer Center

You can update the information you have on file for your customers at any time. Having up-to-date information will ensure that invoices, sales receipts, and other documents contain the most recent contact information, such as billing and shipping address information, on file.

Inactivating customers in QuickBooks Online

Unlike QuickBooks Desktop, which allows you to delete customers, vendors, or products as long as you have not used them in a transaction, you cannot delete customers, vendors, or products in QBO. However, similar to accounts on the chart of accounts, you can inactivate customers, vendors, and products, which will keep the existing transactions recorded in QuickBooks but "hide" the customer, vendor, or item from the drop-down list.

Follow these steps to inactivate customers in QuickBooks Online:

1. Navigate to **Customers** by selecting **Sales** from the left-hand menu bar and then **Customers**, as shown in *Figure 5.14*:

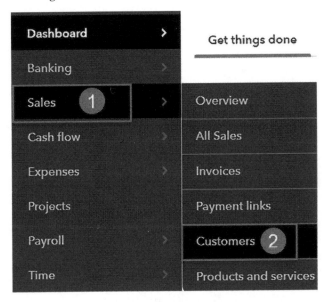

Figure 5.14: Navigating to Customers

2. Put a checkmark next to the customer you want to inactivate, click the arrow next to **Batch actions**, and select **Make inactive**, as shown in *Figure 5.15*:

Figure 5.15: The Make inactive option

Similar to accounts and customers, you can inactivate vendors and items that have been used in a transaction from their drop-down lists. This action is called **Make inactive**, and it will prevent someone from selecting customers, vendors, and items you no longer wish to use, while preserving the historical transactions that have been recorded for each customer, vendor, and item at the same time. We will cover how to make vendors and items inactive later on in this chapter.

 Pro Tip: To review the steps we have covered in this section, watch this Intuit video tutorial, *Adding your Customers in QuickBooks Online*: `https://youtu.be/DWOZZ6kcL6c`.

Merging customers in QuickBooks Online

A common issue that you may encounter is duplicate customers. If you have more than one person setting up customers in QuickBooks or you don't have an established way of adding new customers, you will have this issue. The best way to avoid having duplicate customers is to establish a specific process to add new customers. For example, have only one person who is responsible for adding customers in QuickBooks, and establish whether you will enter customers by first name, last name, or last name, first name.

If you do encounter duplicate customers, you can combine the information entered for the duplicate customers to create one customer profile.

Follow the steps below to merge customers:

1. Navigate to the Customer Center and identify the duplicate customers:

Figure 5.16: Identifying duplicate customers in the Customer Center

2. In *Figure 5.16*, **Astro Jetson** and **Jetson, Astro** are the same customer. Since the owner would like all customer information entered as first name, last name, the customer profile we want to keep is the one at the top of the list, **Astro Jetson**.

3. Click once on the customer profile you plan to remove. In our example, this is **Jetson, Astro**.

    The following appears once we click on **Jetson, Astro**:

Figure 5.17: Viewing customer information

4. Click the **Edit** button.

    The **Customer** information screen will appear:

Figure 5.18: Editing information for an existing customer

5. Click once in the **Customer display name** field, and type the name exactly as it appears in the customer profile that you wish to keep. In our example, this would be **Astro Jetson**, as shown below:

Figure 5.19: Editing the Customer display name field

6. Click the **Save** button in the lower-right corner.

The following message will appear:

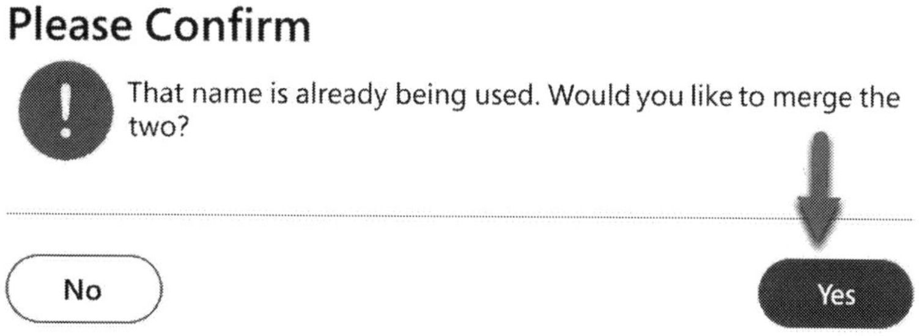

Please Confirm

That name is already being used. Would you like to merge the two?

No   Yes

Figure 5.20: Confirming the merging of customers

7. Click **Yes** and the customer profiles will be combined into one:

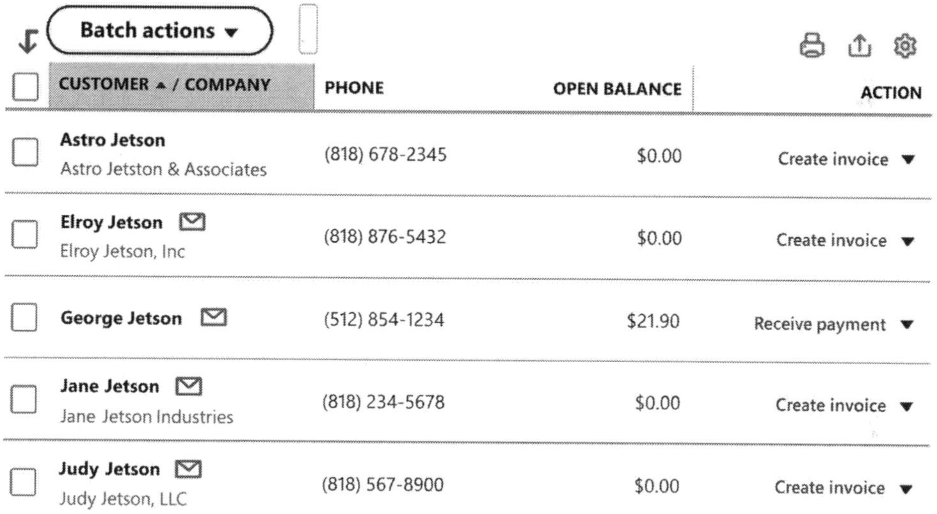

	CUSTOMER ▲ / COMPANY	PHONE	OPEN BALANCE	ACTION
☐	**Astro Jetson** Astro Jetston & Associates	(818) 678-2345	$0.00	Create invoice ▼
☐	**Elroy Jetson** ✉ Elroy Jetson, Inc	(818) 876-5432	$0.00	Create invoice ▼
☐	**George Jetson** ✉	(512) 854-1234	$21.90	Receive payment ▼
☐	**Jane Jetson** ✉ Jane Jetson Industries	(818) 234-5678	$0.00	Create invoice ▼
☐	**Judy Jetson** ✉ Judy Jetson, LLC	(818) 567-8900	$0.00	Create invoice ▼

Batch actions ▼

Figure 5.21: The Customer Center with both profiles combined

8. As you can see, the duplicate profile (**Jetson, Astro**) is no longer on the customer list. All of the transactions recorded for that customer have been moved to the **Astro Jetson** profile.

In this section, we have shown you how to manually add, import, edit, inactivate, and merge customers. In the next section, we will show you how to add, import, edit, inactivate, and merge vendors.

Managing vendor lists in QuickBooks Online

A vendor is an individual or a business that you pay. Vendors can be 1099 contractors, which are independent contractors whom you pay $600 or more in a calendar year, utility companies, or businesses you purchase products from. Similar to customers, you can keep track of all vendor information, such as the company's address, telephone number, email address, and federal tax ID number for 1099 reporting. 1099 reporting is required for contractors that you have paid $600 or more to within a calendar year.

In this section, we will show you how to add new vendors, edit existing vendors, inactivate vendors, and merge vendors in QuickBooks.

Manually adding vendors in QuickBooks Online

To add new vendors to QBO, you need to have each vendor's contact details. This includes a business telephone number, remit to address, email address, and tax ID number (or social security number) for 1099 vendors You can also enter the payment terms your vendor has extended to you. Entering these payment terms will allow QuickBooks to remind you when bills are due or past due.

Follow these steps to manually add vendors in QuickBooks Online:

1. Navigate to **Vendors** by clicking on **Expenses** on the left-hand menu bar and selecting **Vendors**, as shown in *Figure 5.22*:

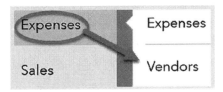

Figure 5.22: Selecting Vendors

2. Click the **New Vendor** button located in the upper-right corner, as shown in *Figure 5.23*:

Figure 5.23: The New Vendor button

3. If this is the first time you are accessing the Vendors Center, you will see the option **Add vendor manually** instead of the **New Vendor** button.

4. Fill in the fields in the **Vendor** window, as shown in *Figure 5.24*:

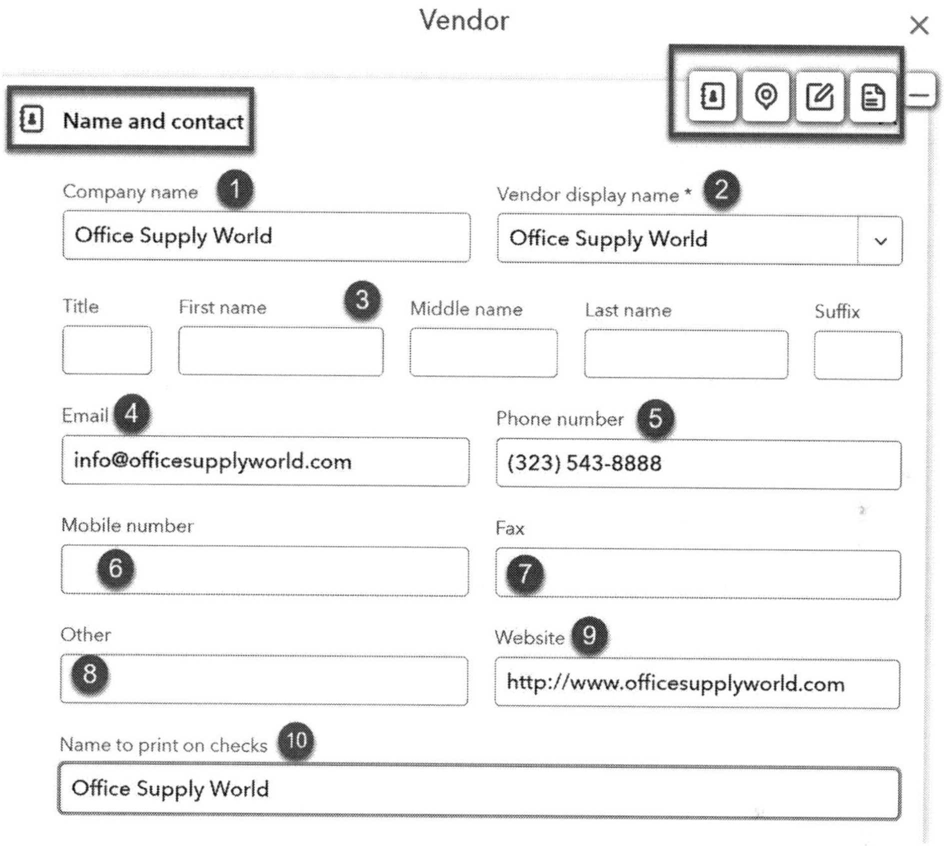

Figure 5.24: Filling in the Vendor window

The following is a brief description of the 10 fields of information you can enter for new vendors:

- **Company name** (1): Enter the name of the business that you are purchasing from. If the vendor is an individual, such as a 1099 contractor, leave this field blank and complete the **First name** and **Last name** fields instead.

Pro Tip: If you have an existing customer who is also a vendor, you will need to set them up as a vendor in QuickBooks. Since QuickBooks does not allow you to use duplicate names, we recommend you add additional verbiage after the name, such as V or Vend, to differentiate between the customer profile and the vendor profile. For example, if Cameras-R-Us is already set up in QuickBooks, we would set it up as a vendor as Cameras-R-Us-V or Cameras-R-Us-Vend.

- **Vendor display name** (2): This field will automatically populate with the company name that was entered in *step 1*.

- **First name** and **Last name** (3): If purchasing from an individual and not a business, enter the name of the individual you are purchasing goods or services from. If the vendor is a sole proprietorship or LLC and you want to keep the name of the business owner, enter both.

- **Email** (4): Enter the primary email address for the vendor in this field. This email address will be used to send purchase orders and other vendor-related documents directly from QuickBooks.

- **Phone number** (5): Enter the vendor's telephone number in this field.

- **Mobile number** (6): Enter the vendor's cell phone number in this field.

- **Fax** (7): Enter the vendor's fax number in this field.

- **Other** (8): Enter any additional contact information in this field.

- **Website** (9): Enter the vendor's website information in this field.

- **Name to print on checks** (10): The information entered for the company name (1) or the first and last name (3) will automatically appear in this field. If necessary, you can edit this information.

5. Enter the address where you mail your payments. If you don't mail payments, you still want to complete these fields if you have the info:

Figure 5.25: Adding vendor address details

> 💡 **Pro Tip:** If you make your payments online or via credit card, it's still a good idea to keep an address on file for each vendor. This is especially important to do for 1099 contractors because you are required to mail a 1099 form to them at the end of the year for tax reporting purposes.

6. Complete the **Notes and attachments** section, as shown in *Figure 5.26*:

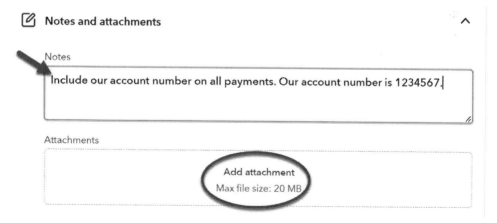

Figure 5.26: Notes and attachments section of the Vendor information screen

7. Like customers, you can add notes about your vendors and suppliers that are for *internal purposes only*. Any information added to this section is not visible to vendors. In addition, you can attach contracts, files, emails, and other pertinent documents in the section labeled **Add attachment**, as shown in *Figure 5.26*.

8. Complete the fields in the **Additional info** section:

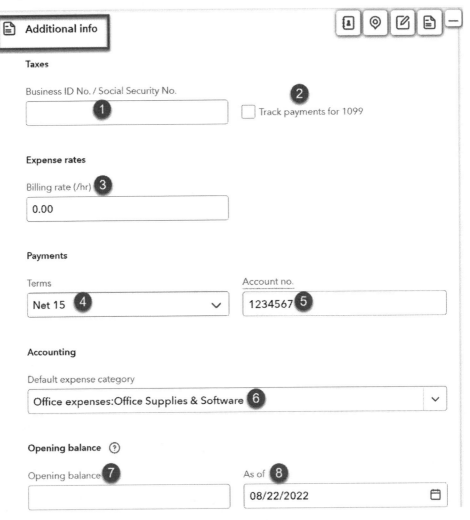

Figure 5.27: Additional info section of the Vendor information screen

- **Business ID No.** (1): Enter the social security number or federal tax ID number for all 1099 vendors in this field. If a business is incorporated, there is no need to obtain this information.

Pro Tip: It's good practice to request a W9 form from all 1099 contractors before you remit payment. A W9 form includes an individual's first and last names, **Doing Business As (DBA)** company name, mailing address, business entity (for example, sole proprietor or LLC), and social security or federal tax ID number. In *Chapter 14, Managing Employees and 1099 Contractors in QuickBooks Online*, we cover how to invite a new contractor to complete an electronic W9 form.

- **Track payments for 1099** (2): Select this checkbox for any individuals you purchase goods and services from that are not incorporated. By marking this box, QuickBooks will flag these vendors so that they appear on the 1099 report at the end of the year.

Pro Tip: In the US, if you pay $600 or more to a 1099 contractor during the year, you are required to provide that contractor with a 1099 form at the end of the year. If total payments during the year do not equal $600 or more, you are not required to provide a 1099 form. In *Chapter 14, Managing Employees and 1099 Contractors in QuickBooks Online*, we will introduce you to the Contractors Center. In the Contractors Center, you can add, edit, and pay 1099 contractors. In addition, you can also complete your annual 1099 report filings.

- **Billing rate** (3): If you have an agreed-upon billing rate that does not change, enter that information in this field. However, if the billing rate varies, leave this field blank.

- **Terms** (4): Select the payment terms the vendor has extended to you (for example, net 30 days, net 15 days, or due upon receipt). It's important to select payment terms so that QuickBooks can use this information to remind you when bills are due or past due.

- **Account no.** (5): If your vendor has given you an account number, enter it in this field. Otherwise, you can leave this field blank.

- **Default expense category** (6): If you use the same category for all payments to a vendor, you can select the category from the drop-down. This will allow QuickBooks to automatically populate the category field each time you record a new transaction for this vendor. If the category varies, leave this field blank.

- **Opening balance** (7): If you are converting from other accounting software to QuickBooks, you can enter the outstanding accounts payable balance for suppliers in this field. However, if you plan to manually enter unpaid bills into QuickBooks, leave this field blank.

- **As of** (8): If you entered an opening balance in *step 7*, enter an effective date in this field. In general, this date will be the same as the date you start tracking your income and expenses in QuickBooks.

Similar to customers, you can include a wealth of information in QuickBooks pertaining to your vendors. By including this information in QuickBooks, you can easily create purchase orders, bills, and other forms and documents without needing to enter this information over and over.

Importing vendors into QuickBooks Online

If you have more than a few vendors to add to QuickBooks, you may want to consider importing the information instead of manually inputting it into QuickBooks. Similar to customers, you can import your vendor details from a CSV file. This template can be found here: `https://packt.link/MQ23chapter5`.

Follow these steps to import vendors into QuickBooks Online:

1. Navigate to **Vendors** by clicking on **Expenses** on the left-hand menu bar and selecting **Vendors**, as shown in *Figure 5.28*:

Figure 5.28: Selecting Vendors

2. Click on the arrow to the right of the **New vendor** button, located in the upper-right corner, and select **Import vendors**, as shown in *Figure 5.29*:

Figure 5.29: The Import vendors option

3. On the **Import vendors** screen, click the **Browse** button to upload the Excel or CSV file from your computer, as shown in *Figure 5.30*:

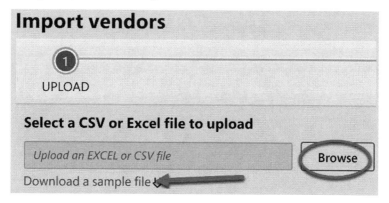

Figure 5.30: Uploading a CSV or Excel file

4. You can click on the blue link to download the sample file (shown in the preceding screenshot). This file includes all of the fields of information you can upload for vendors. Save this file, and use it as your template.

5. Follow the onscreen prompts to import your vendors into QBO.

Review the vendor information to ensure accuracy. If you do find errors, you can easily fix them.

Making changes to existing vendors in QuickBooks Online

Similar to customers, the information that you have on file for vendors can change. For example, the remit address where payments are mailed could change, or the telephone number may need to be updated. When it does, you can quickly update your records in QuickBooks. You will need to navigate to the Vendors Center and select the vendor that you need to make changes to.

Follow these steps to edit an existing vendor in QuickBooks Online:

1. Navigate to **Vendors** by clicking on **Expenses** on the left-hand menu bar and selecting **Vendors**, as shown in *Figure 5.31*:

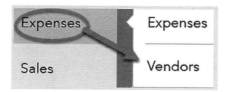

Figure 5.31: Selecting Vendors

2. Select the vendor you want to edit by clicking on the vendor's name, as shown in *Figure 5.32*:

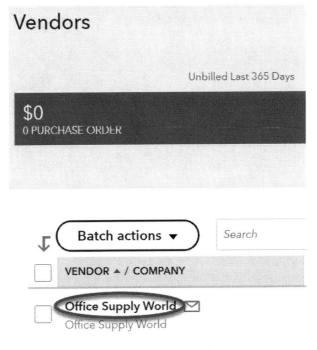

Figure 5.32: Clicking on a vendor name

3. The Vendors Center will be displayed on the next screen. Click on the **Edit** button to make changes:

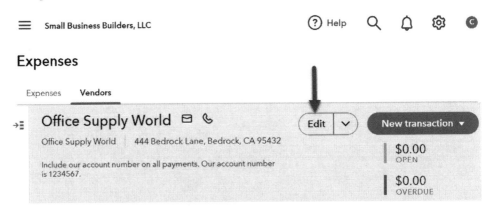

Figure 5.33: Editing a vendor

QuickBooks makes it easy to update vendor contact information. Having up-to-date vendor information will ensure that all purchase orders, bills, and reports are accurate. If you decide you no longer want to do business with a vendor, but you have existing transactions in QuickBooks, you can inactivate vendors. We will look at this next.

Inactivating vendors in QuickBooks Online

Similar to customers, you cannot delete vendors, but you can inactivate any vendors you no longer do business with. This will maintain your existing vendor transactions that were previously recorded but remove the vendor from the Vendors Center.

Follow these steps to inactivate vendors in QuickBooks Online:

1. Navigate to **Vendors** by clicking on **Expenses** on the left-hand menu bar and selecting **Vendors**, as shown in *Figure 5.34*:

Figure 5.34: Selecting Vendors

2. Put a checkmark in the box next to the vendor you want to inactivate and select **Make inactive**, as shown in *Figure 5.35*:

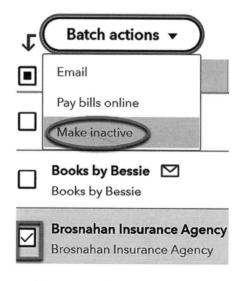

Figure 5.35: Making a vendor inactive

When you inactivate a vendor, QuickBooks will preserve the existing historical transactions but remove the vendor from the drop-down list so that it cannot be used in future transactions, such as purchase orders and bills.

 Pro Tip: To review the information covered in this section, watch this Intuit video tutorial, *Adding vendors to QuickBooks Online*: https://youtu.be/HGLgzJjcxrA.

Merging vendors in QuickBooks Online

Similar to customers, you could run into an issue where you have inadvertently added a vendor twice. Like customers, you can easily merge duplicate vendors. Follow the steps below to merge two vendor profiles:

1.   Navigate to the Vendors Center and identify the duplicate vendors:

Figure 5.36: Duplicate vendors in the Vendors Center

2.   Notice we have one vendor that includes a period after each letter in U.S.A. and another vendor without the periods in between. These are duplicate vendors, and we will keep the vendor that does not include the periods, **Bank of the USA.**

3. Click once on the vendor you do not wish to keep. In our example, that would be **Bank of the U.S.A.**.

The following appears after clicking once on **Bank of the U.S.A.**:

Figure 5.37: Viewing vendor information

4. Click on the **Edit** button, as indicated above.

The **Vendor** information window will appear:

Figure 5.38: Editing information for an existing vendor

5. Click once in the **Company name** field, and type the name exactly as it appears in the vendor profile that you wish to keep. In our example, this would be **Bank of the USA**. Repeat these steps for the **Vendor display name** field, as shown below:

Figure 5.39: Editing the Company name and Vendor display name fields

6. Click the **Save** button in the lower-right corner.

The following message will appear:

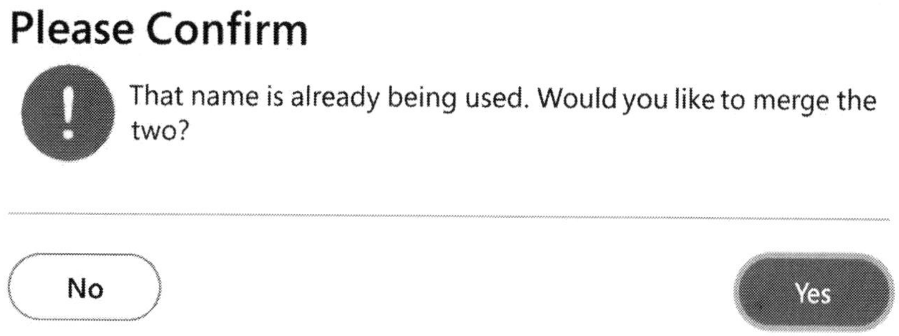

Please Confirm

That name is already being used. Would you like to merge the two?

No   Yes

Figure 5.40: Confirming the merge of duplicate vendors

7. Click **Yes**, and the two vendor profiles will be combined into one:

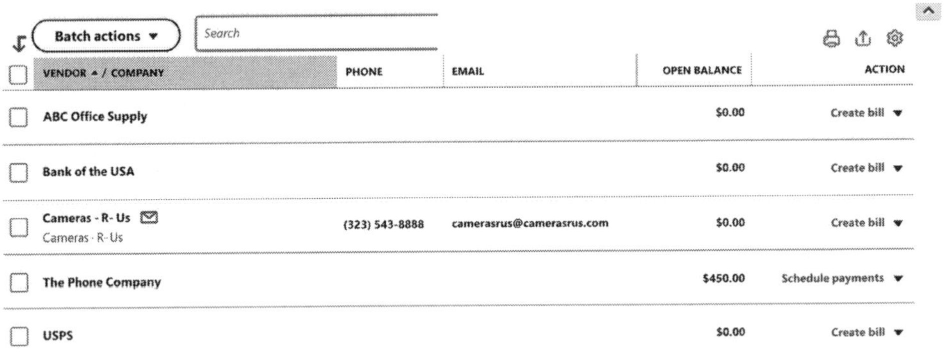

Figure 5.41: The Vendors Center with the vendors merged

As you can see, the duplicate profile (**Bank of the U.S.A.**) is no longer on the vendor list. All of the transactions recorded for that vendor have been moved to the **Bank of the USA** profile.

In this section, we have covered how to manually add vendors, how to import vendors, how to make changes to vendors, and how to inactivate and merge vendors. Next, we will cover how to add, import, edit, inactivate, and merge products and services that you sell.

Managing products and services lists in QuickBooks Online

The products and services that you sell are referred to as **items** in QuickBooks. You can track all of the products and services that you sell in QuickBooks Online. This includes the product name, product (item) number, product description, cost, selling price, and quantity on hand. It's important to set up products and/or services so that you can easily invoice customers for their purchases. In addition, these items are linked to an account on the chart of accounts so that QuickBooks can do the accounting behind the scenes for you. Once you have added products and services to QuickBooks, you will be able to run detailed reports on the products and services you sell.

In this section, we will cover how to manually add items, import items, modify existing items, inactivate items, and merge items in QuickBooks Online. You will need to create items in order to invoice customers.

Pro Tip: Keep in mind that you must have a QuickBooks Plus or QuickBooks Advanced subscription to track inventory items.

Manually adding products and services in QuickBooks Online

In order to add products and services in QuickBooks, you need to have a list of the products or services you plan to sell, along with the cost, sales price, and a brief description that you want to appear on invoices.

Follow these steps to add a new item in QuickBooks Online:

1. Navigate to the **Products and Services** list by clicking on the gear icon and selecting **Products and Services**, as shown in *Figure 5.42*:

Figure 5.42: Selecting Products and Services

2. Click on the **New** button, as indicated here:

Figure 5.43: The New button

3. If this is your first time adding a product/service, you will see the **Add an item** button instead, as shown in *Figure 5.44*:

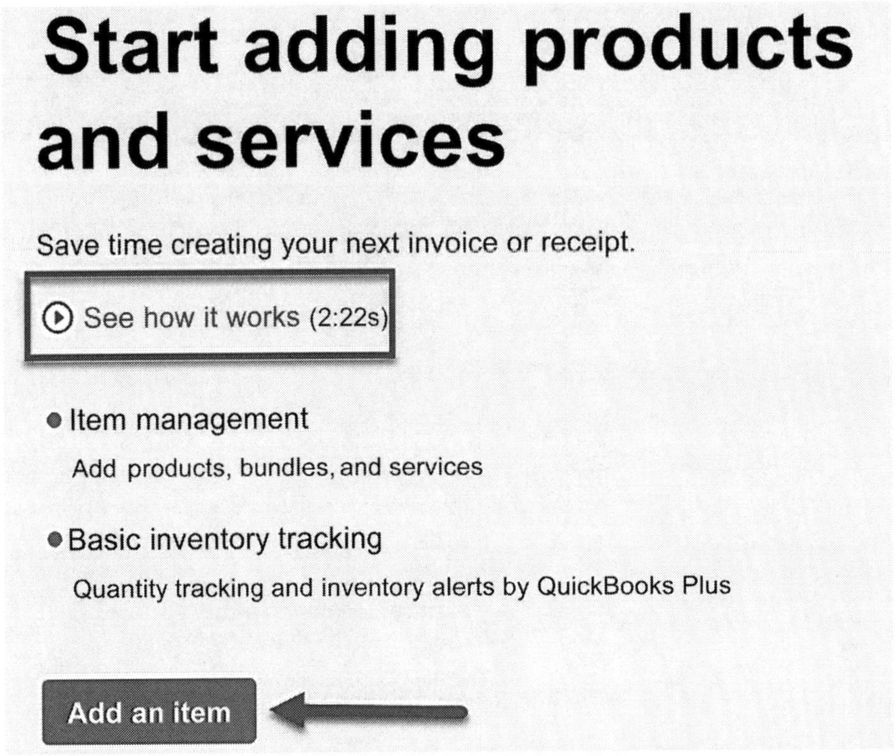

Start adding products and services

Save time creating your next invoice or receipt.

⊙ See how it works (2:22s)

● Item management

     Add products, bundles, and services

● Basic inventory tracking

     Quantity tracking and inventory alerts by QuickBooks Plus

Add an item ⬅

Figure 5.44: Button to add an item for the first time

4. On the next screen, select the appropriate item type, as shown in *Figure 5.45*:

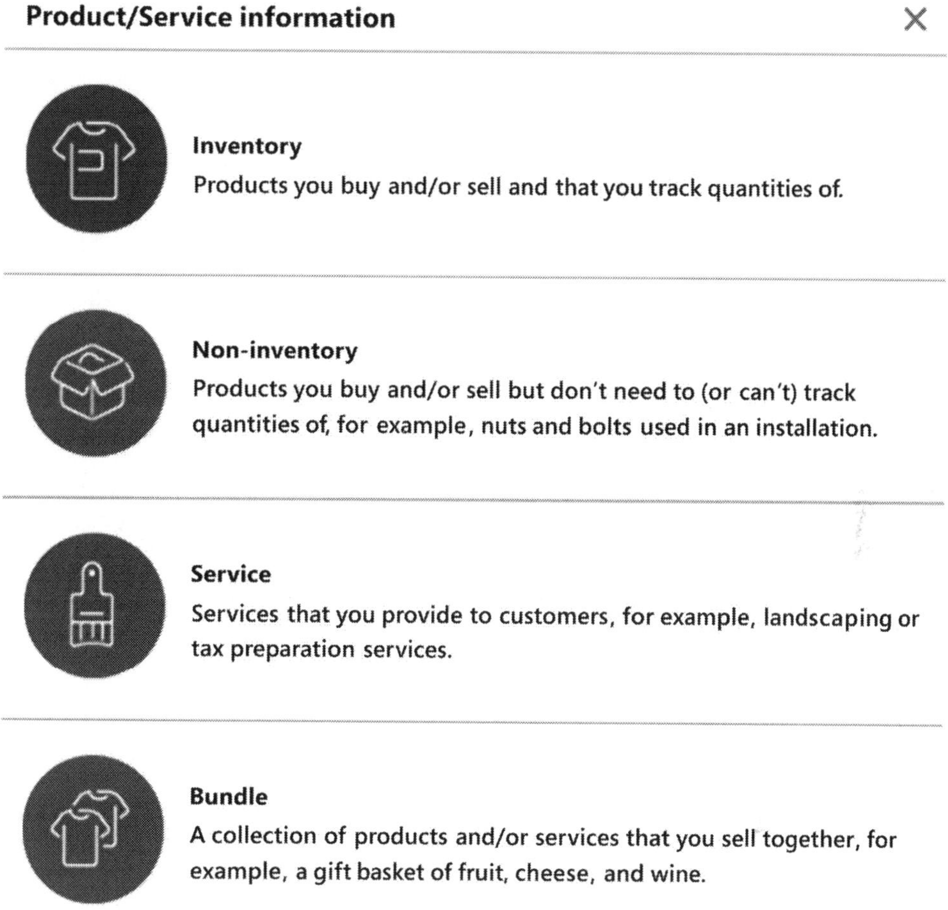

Product/Service information

Inventory
Products you buy and/or sell and that you track quantities of.

Non-inventory
Products you buy and/or sell but don't need to (or can't) track quantities of, for example, nuts and bolts used in an installation.

Service
Services that you provide to customers, for example, landscaping or tax preparation services.

Bundle
A collection of products and/or services that you sell together, for example, a gift basket of fruit, cheese, and wine.

Figure 5.45: Selecting an item type

There are four item types to choose from. A brief description of each item type follows:

- **Inventory**: Products that you buy and sell and want to track in inventory should be set up as **Inventory** items – for example, a retail T-shirt store that purchases T-shirts and resells them, or a grocery store that needs to keep track of the items they've purchased and sold.

- **Non-inventory**: The **Non-inventory** type is used to track items you sell but don't keep in inventory. For example, a photographer may purchase photo paper to print pictures but does not keep track of the quantity of photo paper they've purchased.

- **Service**: This is typically used for services that you sell – for example, bookkeeping services, photography services, or landscaping services.

- **Bundle**: A **bundle** is a collection of products that are sold together – for example, a gift set that includes all the James Bond movies.

5. Fill in the following fields to add a new **Service** item:

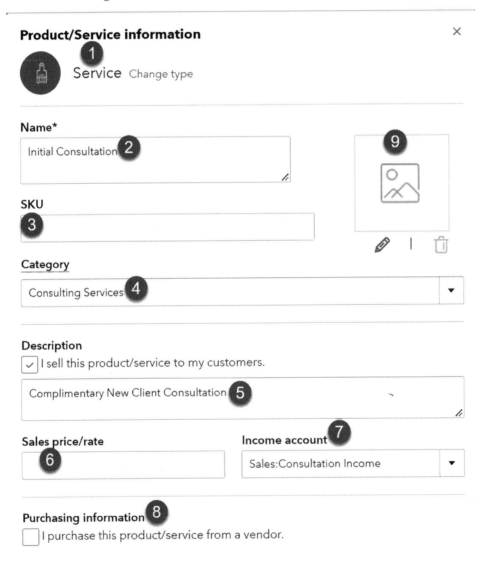

Figure 5.46: Adding a new product or service

A brief description of the eight fields you will complete in order to add a new service item in QuickBooks Online follows:

- **Item type** (1): This is the item type selected in the previous screen. In our example, **Service** is selected.

- **Name** (2): Enter the name of the service you will be selling to customers.

- **SKU** (3): A **stock-keeping unit (SKU)** is a scannable bar code printed on product labels in a retail store. If applicable, enter the SKU for the product you are selling. In general, an SKU applies to products and not service items.

- **Category** (4): This field is *optional*. If you want to categorize the products and services you sell, you can do so by creating categories. For example, in addition to general consulting, Small Business Builders offers a variety of coaching services such as business plans, marketing plans, bookkeeping, and tax planning. They would like to track their sales by each category. In our example, the initial consultation is a complimentary service that will be tracked in the **Consulting Services** category. To create a category, just type the name of the category in the field and save it.

- **Description** (5): Enter a brief description of the item in this field. In our example, it is `Complimentary Initial Consultation`. This description will appear on all customer invoices and sales receipts. However, you can always change the information directly on the invoice/sales receipt if needed.

- **Sales price/rate** (6): Enter the sales price for the item if it is generally the same for all customers. However, if the price varies by customer, you can leave this field blank and complete it when you create an invoice to bill your customers. Since the service we are setting up is complimentary, there is no charge, so we will leave this field blank.

- **Income account** (7): This is a required field. From the drop-down, select the appropriate income account where you want sales for this item to be recorded on the financial statements. In our example, we have selected **Consultation Income**.

 Pro Tip: Every item you create in QuickBooks will be mapped to an account. Using this information, QuickBooks will record the debits and credits for you in the background so that you don't have to.

- **Purchasing information** (8): If you are setting up an item that you purchase from a vendor/supplier, you will need to enter this information to track the cost of each item.

6. Fill in the following fields to set up an **Inventory** item:

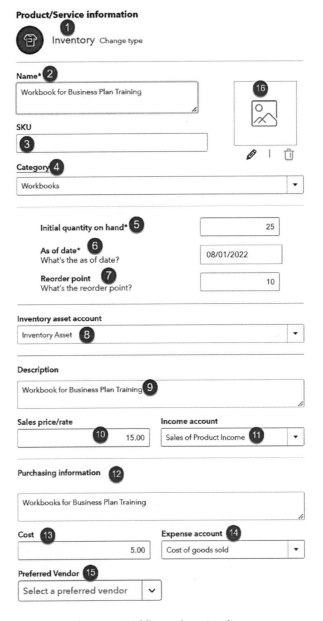

Figure 5.47: Adding an inventory item

Here are some brief descriptions of the fields you will fill in when setting up an **Inventory** item:

- **Item type** (1): Select the type of item you are setting up. In our example, it is an inventory item.

- **Name** (2): Enter the name of the product or item.

- **SKU** (3): In general, an SKU applies to products and not service items, so it is more likely to be relevant here than when we covered service items previously.

- **Category** (4): This field is *optional*. If you want to categorize the products and services you sell, you can do so by creating categories. In our example, we have created a category called **Workbooks**. You can easily create a category by simply typing the name of that category in this field and clicking **Save**.

- **Initial quantity on hand** (5): This should represent the total quantity for each item you have in your inventory as of the date the inventory was counted.

> **Pro Tip:** You need to perform a physical inventory count before setting up inventory items in QBO. If you don't have the inventory quantity when setting up the item, you won't be able to add it to this screen later on. Instead, you will have to create an inventory adjustment journal to record the inventory. You will learn how to record inventory adjustments in *Chapter 15, Closing the Books in QuickBooks Online.*

- **As of date** (6): Enter the date when the inventory was counted.

- **Reorder point** (7): The reorder point is the minimum you want your inventory count to go down to before QuickBooks alerts you to place an order. In our example, when the inventory goes down to 10 workbooks, QuickBooks will alert us to place an order.

- **Inventory asset account** (8): All inventory is recorded as an asset and the default account is **Inventory Asset**, as indicated in our example.

- **Description** (9): Enter the description that you want to appear on customer sales receipts and invoices. In our example, it is Workbook for Business Plan Training.

- **Sales price/rate** (10): Enter the price you sell the item for. If it varies, leave it blank, and you can complete it when you create the customer invoice. In our example, the sales price is **15.00** per workbook.

- **Income account** (11): Enter the account you want to track all sales of for this product. In our example, we are going to use the **Sales of Product Income** account.

- **Purchasing information** (12): Enter the description that you want to appear on purchase orders when placing an order with your supplier. In our example, that is `Workbooks for Business Plan Training`.

- **Cost** (13): Enter the amount that you pay your vendor/supplier for this item. *The cost reflected here is for information purposes only and will be determined by QuickBooks after bills are entered.* In our example, the cost of each workbook is **5.00**.

- **Expense account** (14): The default expense account is the **cost of goods sold** for products. However, if you prefer to track these costs in a different account, you can click on the drop-down and add a new account.

- **Preferred Vendor** (15): This field is *optional*. If you choose to use it, you can add the vendor that you purchase this item from most often. If the vendor is not in the drop-down menu, you can select **Add** to set up the vendor in QuickBooks.

- **Product image** (16): You can add a picture of the product for easy reference by clicking on the pencil icon and selecting the image saved on your computer.

If you don't have the time to enter your products and services manually, you can import this data into QuickBooks, as we have demonstrated already for accounts, customers, and vendors.

Importing products and services in QuickBooks Online

Similar to customers and vendors, you can import a products and services list in QuickBooks. This can save you a lot of time if you have a sizeable list of products or services that you sell. You can import this information from a CSV file into QBO. This template can be found here: `https://github.com/PacktPublishing/Mastering-QuickBooks-2024-Fifth-Edition/tree/main/Chapter05`.

Follow these steps to import products and services into QuickBooks Online:

1. Navigate to the **Products and Services** list by clicking on the gear icon and selecting **Products and Services**, as shown in *Figure 5.48*:

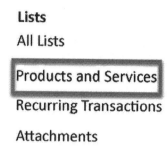

Figure 5.48: Selecting Products and Services

2. Click on the arrow next to the **New** item button located in the upper-right corner and then click on **Import**, as shown in *Figure 5.49*:

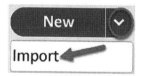

Figure 5.49: The Import option

3. Click the **Browse** button to upload the Excel or CSV file from your computer, as shown in *Figure 5.50*:

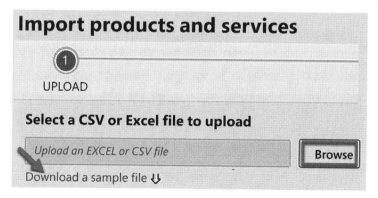

Figure 5.50: Uploading a CSV or Excel file

4.   You can click on the blue link to download the sample file (shown in the preceding screen-shot). This file includes all of the fields of information you can upload for items. Save this file and use it as your template.

5.   Follow the onscreen prompts to import your products and services into QuickBooks Online.

Be sure to review the data imported to ensure accuracy. If you do find that corrections are needed, you can easily make them.

Making changes to existing products and services in QuickBooks Online

You can change any fields in existing products and services except the item type. If you have already used an item in a transaction, QuickBooks will not allow you to change the item type. Instead, you will need to inactivate the old item and add a brand-new item with the correct item type.

Follow these steps to make changes to existing products and services in QBO:

1.   Navigate to the **Products and Services** list by clicking on the gear icon and selecting **Products and Services**, as shown in *Figure 5.51*:

Figure 5.51: Selecting Products and Services

2.   Select the product or service you would like to make changes to by clicking on the **Edit** button in the far-right column, as shown in *Figure 5.52*:

NAME ▲	TYPE	SALES DESCRIPTION	SALES PRICE	COST	ACTION
Hours	Service				Edit ▾
Photography Services	Service	Photography Services	150		Edit ▾
Picture Frame - 8X10	Inventory	8X10 Picture Frame	20	10	Edit ▾
Sales	Service				Edit ▾

Figure 5.52: Editing a product or service

As we mentioned previously, you can change an item type if you haven't used it in a transaction in QuickBooks. However, if you have used an item in a transaction and the item type is incorrect, you will need to create a new item with the correct item type and inactivate the old item.

Inactivating products and services in QuickBooks Online

As we discussed when we talked about customers and vendors, you cannot delete products and services in QBO once you have created them; however, you can inactivate them. This will preserve the existing transactions and remove the product or service from the items list so that it cannot be used in new transactions.

Follow these steps to inactivate a product or service in QuickBooks Online:

1. Navigate to the **Products and Services** list by clicking on the gear icon and selecting **Products and Services**, as shown in *Figure 5.53*:

Figure 5.53: Selecting Products and Services

2. Scroll down the items list to the product (or service), click on the **Edit** button, and select **Make inactive**, as shown in *Figure 5.54*:

Figure 5.54: Making a product or service inactive

Similar to customers and vendors, inactivating a product or service will remove it from selection for future transactions. However, the existing data will remain intact to ensure reports are accurate for tax and other reporting purposes.

Pro Tip: To recap the steps covered in this section, watch this Intuit video tutorial, *Creating inventory products in QuickBooks Online:* `https://youtu.be/aE_vWm5KasI`.

Merging products and services in QuickBooks Online

Like vendors and customers, you can also merge duplicate services that have been entered into QuickBooks by mistake. Unfortunately, you cannot merge duplicate inventory items because of the complexity of inventory tracking. Instead, you will need to inactivate one of the duplicate inventory items and record inventory adjustments to manage the transactions that have been recorded. Consult your accountant before making any inventory adjustments.

Follow the steps below to merge duplicate services:

1. Navigate to the **Products and Services** list and identify the duplicate items:

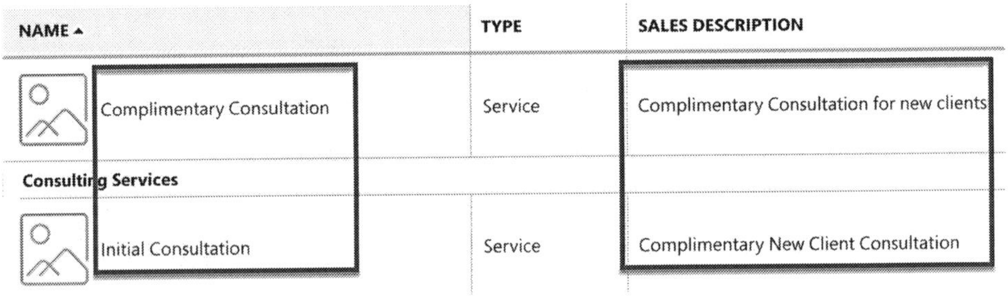

NAME ▲	TYPE	SALES DESCRIPTION
Complimentary Consultation	Service	Complimentary Consultation for new clients
Consulting Services		
Initial Consultation	Service	Complimentary New Client Consultation

Figure 5.55: Identifying duplicate services in the Products and Services list

2. As you can see in the image above, there is an item called **Complimentary Consultation** and a duplicate item called **Initial Consultation**. To maintain accurate records, we must merge them into one. The item we will keep in our example is **Initial Consultation**.

3. Click on the item that you wish to remove – **Complimentary Consultation** in our example.

4. After you click on **Complimentary Consultation**, the **Product/Service information** window will appear:

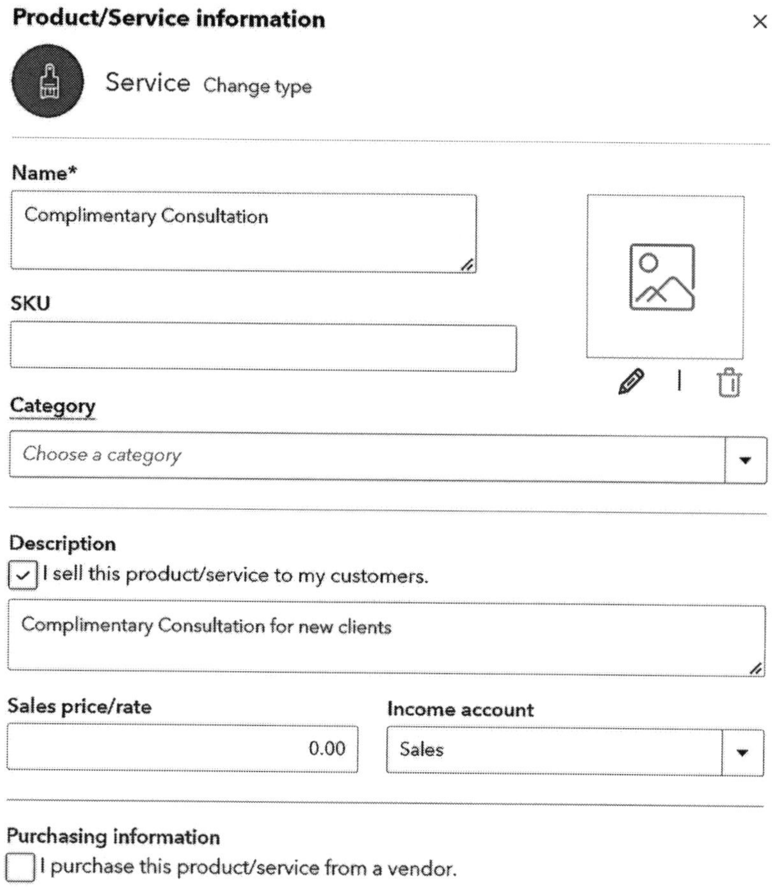

Product/Service information ✕

Service Change type

Name*

Complimentary Consultation

SKU

Category

Choose a category ▼

Description

☑ I sell this product/service to my customers.

Complimentary Consultation for new clients

Sales price/rate   **Income account**

0.00   Sales ▼

Purchasing information

☐ I purchase this product/service from a vendor.

Figure 5.56: Displaying products and services information

5. Click once in the **Name** field and type in the item name you want to merge with – `Initial Consultation` in our case. Select **Consulting Services** in the **Category** field. Type `Complimentary New Client Consultation` in the **Description** field, as shown below:

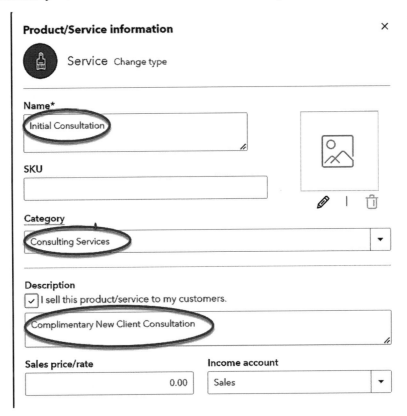

Figure 5.57: Editing product and services information

6. Click the **Save and Close** button in the lower-right corner.

The following message will appear:

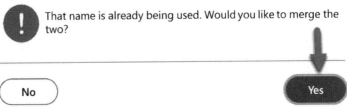

Figure 5.58: Confirming the merging of duplicate service items

7. Click **Yes**, and the two service items will be combined:

NAME ▲	TYPE	SALES DESCRIPTION	SALES PRICE	COST	QTY ON HAI	REORDER
Consulting Services						
Initial Consultation	Service	Complimentary New Client Consultation				
Hours	Service					
Sales	Service					
Workbooks						
Workbook for Business Plan Training	Inventory	Workbook for Business Plan Training	15	5	25	10

Figure 5.59: The Products and Services list with the merged item

Notice the **Complimentary Consultation** item is no longer shown because it has been merged with **Initial Consultation**.

We have now covered how to manually add products and services, import products and services, make changes to existing products and services, inactivate products and services (also known as items), and merge items.

Summary

In this chapter, we covered how to manage customer data by manually adding and importing the information, editing existing customers, and inactivating customers you no longer do business with.

In addition, we covered how to manage vendor data by manually adding and importing the information, editing existing vendors, inactivating vendors you no longer do business with, and merging duplicate customer and vendor records.

Finally, we showed you how to manage products and services, also referred to as items, including how to add and import data, how to edit existing products and services, how to inactivate products and services, and how to merge service items in QuickBooks Online.

Keep in mind that you will need to update customer, vendor, and products and services lists when the information changes. For example, if customers and vendors move, you will need to update your records with their new mailing address. In addition, if you start selling new products and services, you will need to add them to the list. By the same token, if you discontinue a product or service, you should inactivate these items to keep your records current.

Now that you understand how to manage your customers, it's time to learn how to set up and manage sales tax. In the next chapter, we will show you how to set up sales tax, create an invoice that includes sales tax, and run sales tax reports.

Join our community on Discord

Join our community's Discord space for discussions with the authors and other readers:

`https://packt.link/quickbooks`

Section 2

Recording Transactions in QuickBooks Online

6

Managing Sales Tax

In this chapter, we will cover how to manage sales tax in **QuickBooks Online (QBO)**. In the United States, sales tax is typically applied to the sale of products. However, some states and local tax jurisdictions also apply sales tax to certain types of services. You need to consult with your CPA or tax professional to determine which laws apply in your geographical location. While you cannot pay sales tax directly from QBO, we will cover how to record the payment in QBO after you have paid your tax authority.

We will cover the following topics in this chapter:

- Setting up sales tax in QuickBooks Online
- Creating an invoice that includes sales tax
- Sales tax reports
- Paying sales tax when it comes due

 The US edition of QuickBooks Online was used to create this book. If you are using a version that is outside of the United States, results may differ.

Do you need to charge sales tax?

Before we dive into the mechanics of setting up sales tax, you may be wondering whether you need to charge sales tax or not. The short answer is *yes* if you sell any type of product, such as T-shirts, books, a cup of coffee, and so on. If you don't sell a product but you do sell services, such as bookkeeping, legal, or consulting, then the answer is *maybe*. Because the answer is dependent on the rules and regulations of your state/local jurisdiction, it's important that you seek the advice of a CPA or tax preparer.

However, there are a couple of resources that we recommend you check out. First, this article from the QuickBooks blog *Do I need to charge sales tax?*: `https://quickbooks.intuit.com/r/taxes/need-collect-sales-tax-much/`. Another great resource is **Avalara**. Avalara is a company that specializes in sales tax compliance. Not only do they offer sales tax compliance services but they are also a great resource for any questions you may have regarding whether or not you need to charge sales tax and how to go about making sure you are in compliance.

Setting up sales tax in QuickBooks Online

If you are required to collect sales tax from customers, it is important to complete the sales tax setup in QuickBooks prior to invoicing customers. If you create an invoice without sales tax, you will ultimately underpay the sales tax you are required to submit to your local tax authority. This could lead to additional taxes and penalties, which can add up quickly. Setting up sales tax in QuickBooks from the start allows QuickBooks to automatically calculate and keep track of the amount of sales tax that you owe.

Perform the following steps to set up sales tax:

1. Click **Taxes** and select **Sales Tax** on the left menu bar, as indicated in *Figure 6.1*, to navigate to the Sales Tax Center:

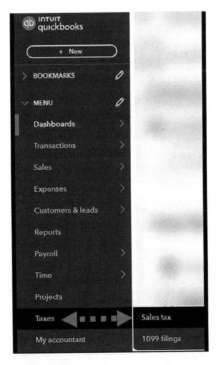

Figure 6.1: Navigating to the Sales Tax Center

2. The following message will appear. Click the **Use Automatic Sales Tax** button, as indicated in *Figure 6.2*:

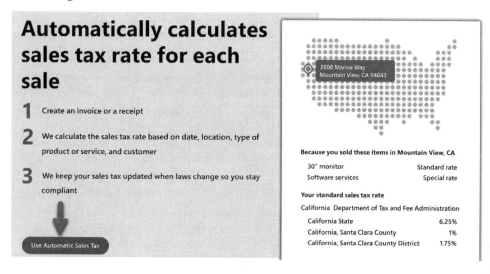

Figure 6.2: Sales Tax Center welcome page

The following window will appear:

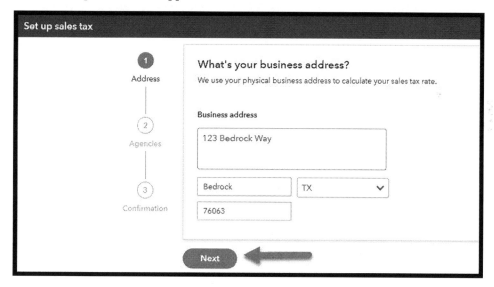

Figure 6.3: Entering the business address used to calculate sales tax

3.   Your business address should automatically populate the fields (as indicated in *Figure 6.3*). If it does not, complete any missing fields.

4.   Click **Next**.

The following screen will appear:

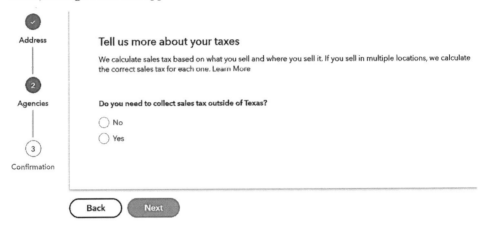

Figure 6.4: Sales tax information outside of your state

5.   If you are not required to collect sales tax outside of your state, select **No**, and the tax agency that you should remit payment to will be listed, as indicated in *Figure 6.5*; click **Next**:

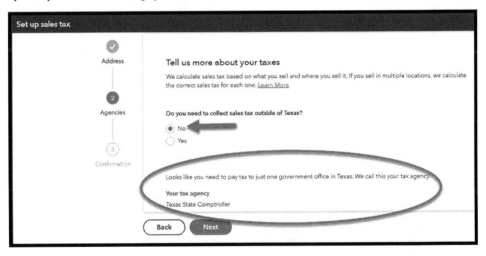

Figure 6.5: Sales tax information within your state only

6. If you are required to collect sales tax outside of your state, select **Yes** and click on the drop-down arrow below the **Your tax agency** field to select all of the jurisdictions you are required to collect sales tax from, as indicated in *Figure 6.6*.

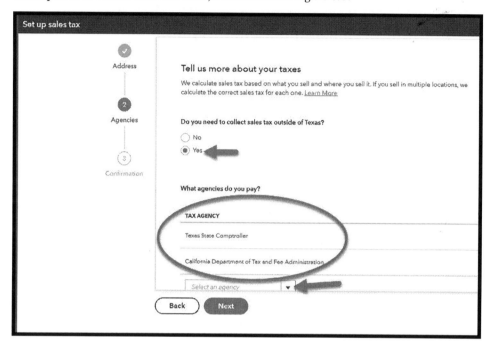

Figure 6.6: Sales tax information in other jurisdictions

 Pro Tip: Most businesses are not required to collect sales tax outside their state. If you are not sure, you need to consult with your tax professional or CPA on this matter.

7. Click **Next** and the following screen will appear, indicating that the automatic sales tax setup is complete:

Automatic sales tax is all set up

Give it a spin by creating your first invoice.

Figure 6.7: Confirmation that automatic sales tax is set up

8. Click **X** in the upper-right corner of the screen to bypass the preceding message and navigate to the **How often do you file sales tax?** screen:

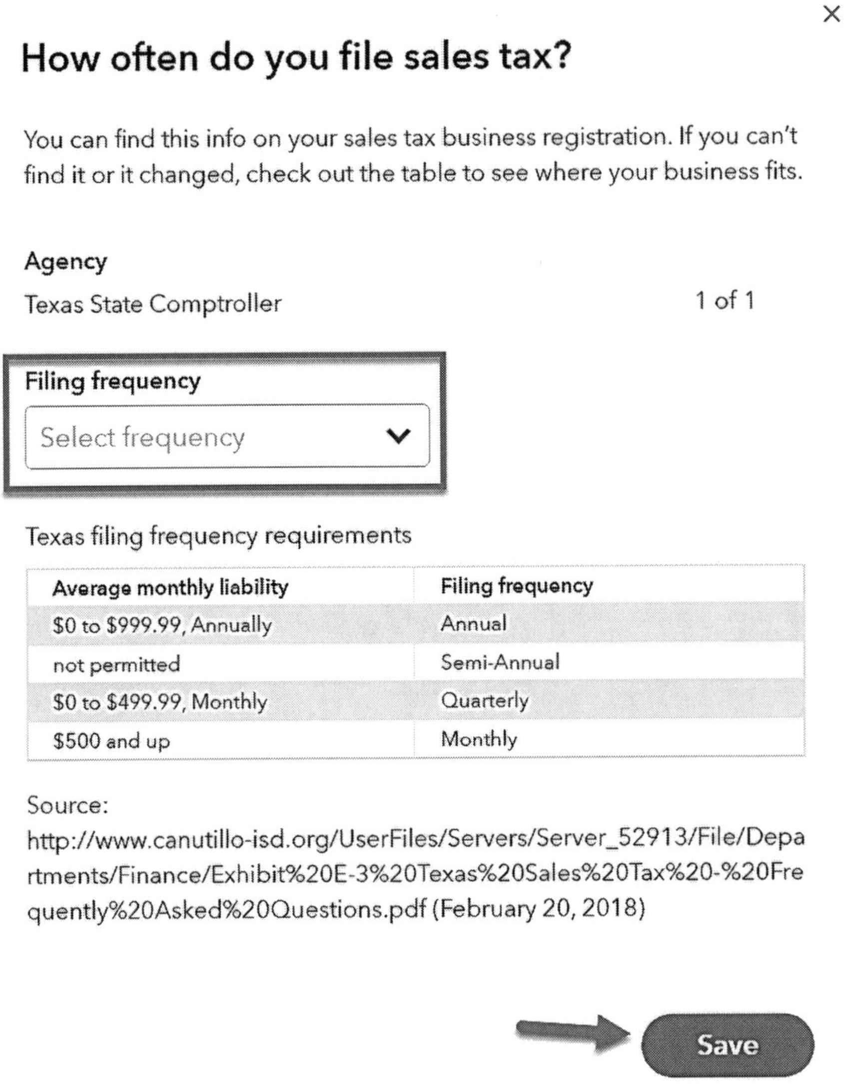

✕

How often do you file sales tax?

You can find this info on your sales tax business registration. If you can't find it or it changed, check out the table to see where your business fits.

Agency

Texas State Comptroller   1 of 1

Filing frequency

Select frequency   ⌄

Texas filing frequency requirements

Average monthly liability	Filing frequency
$0 to $999.99, Annually	Annual
not permitted	Semi-Annual
$0 to $499.99, Monthly	Quarterly
$500 and up	Monthly

Source:
http://www.canutillo-isd.org/UserFiles/Servers/Server_52913/File/Depa
rtments/Finance/Exhibit%20E-3%20Texas%20Sales%20Tax%20-%20Fre
quently%20Asked%20Questions.pdf (February 20, 2018)

Save

Figure 6.8: Filing frequency for sales tax

Based on the state where your business is located, the **Agency** field will automatically be populated.

9. From the **Filing frequency** drop-down menu, select the frequency with which you file sales tax. The options are **Monthly**, **Quarterly**, and **Yearly**.

> **Pro Tip**: If you are not sure how often you need to submit sales tax, refer to the chart that appears below the **Filing frequency** field or contact the tax agency directly.

10. Click the **Save** button to keep your changes.

The Sales Tax Center will appear:

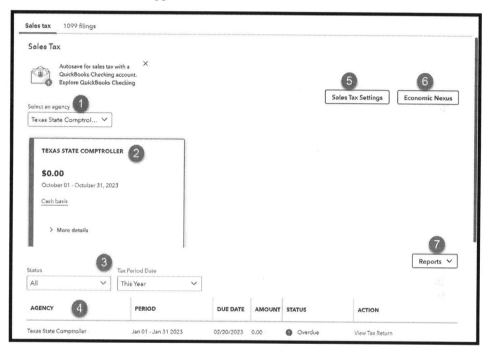

Figure 6.9: Sales Tax Center

11. Within the sales tax center, you can see the amount of tax due for each agency that you collect sales tax for:

-   (1) Select the agency from the drop-down menu and it will appear as shown in *Figure 6.9*.

-   (2) The agency (**Texas State Comptroller**), in our example appears in this section, along with the tax period due and the accounting method.

-   (3) Select the status and tax period date using the drop-down menus.

- (4) In this section, you will see a summary of your selections for **Agency**, **Tax Period**, **Due Date**, **Amount**, **Status**, and **Action** items.

- (5) Review your **Sales Tax Settings** and make any necessary changes.

- (6) Review your **Economic Nexus**.

- (7) Generate sales tax reports. Since we don't currently have any taxable sales recorded, we will create an invoice with sales tax next.

Creating an invoice that includes sales tax

After completing the setup for sales tax, you are ready to create invoices and sales receipts with sales tax. In this section, we will create an invoice and show you how to include sales tax.

Perform the following steps to create an invoice with sales tax:

1.   From the left menu bar, click on **Sales** and then select **Invoices**, as indicated in *Figure 6.10*:

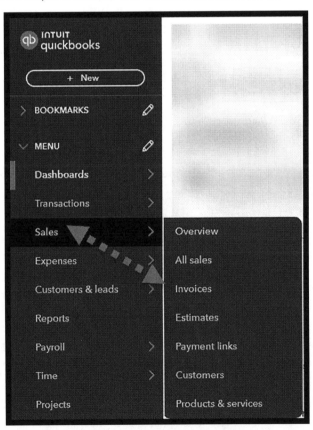

Figure 6.10: Navigating to Invoices

2. Click the **Create invoice** button, as indicated in *Figure 6.11*:

Figure 6.11: Creating an invoice

3. A blank invoice template will appear. Complete the fields as follows:

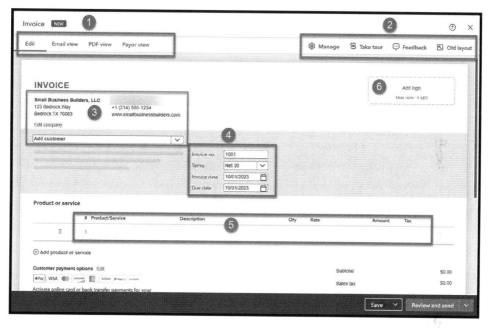

Figure 6.12: Invoice template

4. There are six key areas within the invoice template:

- **Invoice view** (1): There are four different views for the invoice template. The default mode is **Edit**, which is the mode you want to be in when making changes to the invoice; **Email view** is the view that your customers will see when they receive the invoice via email; **PDF view** is the appearance of the invoice as a PDF document, and Payor view is the preview of the invoice when the customer receives it.

- **Other options** (2): In this section, you can manage invoice settings, take a tour of the features available for invoicing, provide feedback to Intuit about your experience using the invoice template, and revert to the old layout of the invoice template if you prefer to use that instead.

- **Your company information and customer info** (3): Your company mailing address, telephone number, and website info will appear in this section. This is the information that was entered when you set up the company preferences in *Chapter 2, Company File Setup*. Below this info is a drop-down field where you can select the customer you wish to create an invoice for.

- **Invoice details** (4): Within this section of the invoice, you will find the invoice number, which is automatically generated by QBO, and the payment terms, which you set up back in *Chapter 2, Company File Setup*. The invoice date and the due date will also appear in this section. All of these fields can be edited as needed.

- **Billing details** (5): From the drop-down menu, you will select the item(s) you are billing your customer for. In *Chapter 5, Managing Customer, Vendor, and Products and Services Lists,* we covered how to add your products and services to QBO.

- **Add a logo** (6): If you added your company logo in *Chapter 2, Company File Setup*, it would appear in this section. If you did not add it, you can add it by clicking **Add logo** and following the on-screen prompt.

5. Based on the city/state for your business, the sales tax rate for that geographical location will be applied. In the bottom-right corner, you can see that sales tax of **$18.56** was calculated on this sale of **$225.00**. The total amount due with tax is **$243.56**.

Pro Tip: QuickBooks will automatically use your business address as the sales location. Be sure to confirm the location of the sale is correct. If necessary, you may need to charge a different sales tax based on the city/county/tax jurisdiction for each sale. If necessary, you can update your business address if needed within the account and settings. In *Chapter 2, Company File Setup*, we show you how to do this. Be sure to consult with your tax preparer or accountant for additional guidance.

6. Click the **Save** button to save the invoice and click **X** in the upper-right corner to close the invoice.

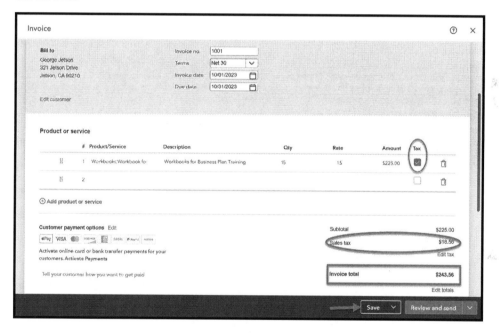

Figure 6.13: Completed invoice with sales tax

7. Navigate back to the Sales Tax Center by clicking on **Taxes** from the left menu bar. The following window will appear:

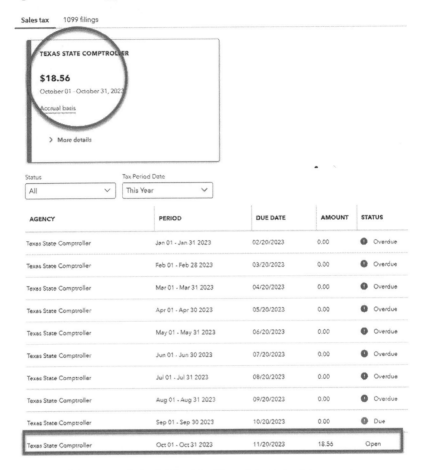

Figure 6.14: Sales Tax Center with updated sales tax amount

As you can see, the tax of **$18.56** now shows up as upcoming sales tax that will be due sometime in the future. Once the sales tax becomes due, the status will change to **Due**. Next, we will cover the sales tax reports you can generate to determine how much sales tax you owe and when it is due. Sales tax reports are also used to complete the sales tax return.

Sales tax reports

QuickBooks makes it easy to stay on top of the sales tax collected, which will ensure that you pay the correct amount when it comes due. There are three reports available to help you stay on top of the sales tax you owe: a tax liability report, a taxable customer report, and a non-taxable transaction review report.

Within the Sales Tax Center, click on the **Reports** link to access the sales tax reports, as indicated in *Figure 6.15*:

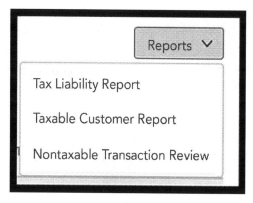

Figure 6.15: Sales tax reports

The first report is the **Tax liability** report. This report will show you the sales tax collected for a specific period of time. The report will show gross sales, taxable sales, non-taxable sales, and the tax amount.

In the report shown below, there are four columns: **GROSS TOTAL, NON-TAXABLE, TAXABLE AMOUNT**, and **TAX AMOUNT**. The gross total amount is **$225.00**, the non-taxable amount is **$0**, the taxable amount is **$225.00**, and the total tax amount is **$18.56**:

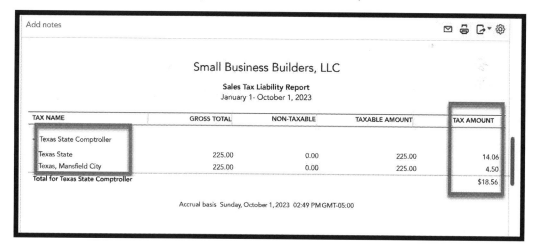

Figure 6.16: Sales tax liability report

The second option is the **Taxable customer** report. This report will list all customers who are subject to sales tax, along with their billing address, shipping address, taxable sales, and tax rate. Below is a snapshot of what this report looks like:

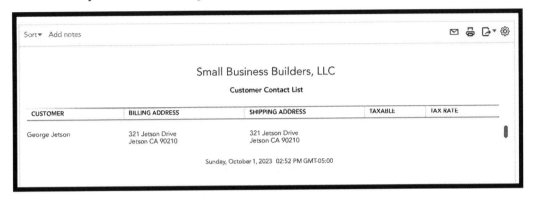

Figure 6.17: Taxable customer report

As you can see, it is easy to keep track of sales tax in QuickBooks. You can use the tax liability report and the taxable customer report to prepare your sales tax return. In addition, you will use these reports to determine the amount owed.

 Pro Tip: Be sure to select the correct accounting method (cash or accrual) before running your reports. Refer to the *Small Business Bookkeeping 101* section of *Chapter 1, Getting Started with QuickBooks Online*, to learn the difference between cash and accrual accounting.

Paying sales tax when it comes due

Unfortunately, you cannot pay sales tax within QuickBooks Online. You must visit the website of your state tax authority and submit payment online or mail a check before the due date. The following Intuit video tutorial provides a recap of what we have covered in this chapter, plus the steps you need to take to make a payment and record it in QuickBooks Online: `https://youtu.be/Rns_R4fRros`.

Summary

In this chapter, we have discussed the importance of setting up sales tax in QuickBooks so it can automatically calculate sales tax for you. We have shown you how to create an invoice and include sales tax, and we have covered the key reports available to help you stay on top of your sales tax liability.

Since you cannot make sales tax payments in QuickBooks, we have also included a video that explains how to make your sales tax payments outside of QuickBooks. It's important to make sure you set up sales tax and use the correct sales tax rate. This will help you to avoid penalties or fees for under-reporting and underpaying sales tax to your state tax office. In the next chapter, we will cover how to record invoices and sales receipts in QuickBooks Online.

Join our community on Discord

Join our community's Discord space for discussions with the authors and other readers:

`https://packt.link/quickbooks`

7

Recording Sales Transactions in QuickBooks Online

In *Chapter 5, Managing Customer, Vendor, and Products and Services Lists,* you learned how to customize QuickBooks by adding customers, vendors, and the products and services you sell to QuickBooks. Now that you have completed your QuickBooks setup, it's time to learn how to record transactions. Recording sales transactions will allow you to keep track of how much money your business is making. This information is important and will help you to determine whether or not your business is profitable.

In this chapter, we will focus on recording sales transactions in **QuickBooks Online (QBO)** as well as how to customize sales templates. We will cover the three types of sales transactions, when you should use them, how to record each transaction, and the behind-the-scenes accounting that QuickBooks does for you. We will also show you how to record customer payments, how to manage credit card payments, and how to issue credit memos and refunds to customers.

In this chapter, we will cover the following key concepts:

- Entering sales forms—sales receipts, deposits, and sales invoices
- Customizing sales templates
- Recording payments received from customers
- Managing credit card payments
- Recording payments to the payments to deposit account
- Issuing credit memos and refunds to customers

The US edition of QBO was used to create this book. If you are using a version that is outside of the United States, results may differ.

Entering sales forms

Recording income for a business can be accomplished in a variety of ways. There are three primary ways to record income in QBO. First, a **sales receipt** is used when you receive payment at the same time as you provide products and/or services to your customers. Second, you can use a **deposit** to record income for a specific customer or to record income from multiple customers at any one time. Third, you can use a **sales invoice**, which allows you to bill a specific customer, who will pay you based on payment terms that are agreed upon upfront.

In the following sections, we will cover when and how to record income using a sales receipt, a deposit, and a sales invoice. We will also show you the accounting that takes place behind the scenes for each transaction. This will include the debits and credits recorded for each transaction.

Recording income using a sales receipt

A sales receipt is used when the sale of a product or service and the receipt of the customer payment take place simultaneously. For example, retail businesses such as restaurants or clothing stores will receive payment at the same time as they provide their service (for example, serving food to customers) or products (for example, clothing items for purchase). In general, you would record a sales receipt immediately upon making the sale so that you can either give a copy to your customer or send it via email. For a restaurant or coffee shop, you may only record sales receipts on a daily or weekly basis, especially if you have a **point of sale** (**POS**) system that you can use to keep track of your daily sales. You can record a sales receipt in QuickBooks by completing a couple of simple steps.

Follow these steps to record a sales receipt:

1. From the **+ New** menu, select **Sales receipt**, as indicated in *Figure 7.1*:

Figure 7.1: Navigating to the Sales Receipt form

Figure 7.2 shows a completed sales receipt:

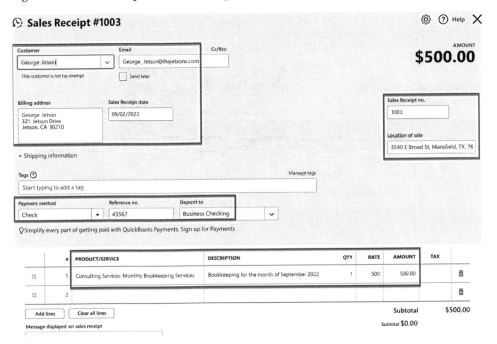

Figure 7.2: Completing the Sales Receipt form

There are several fields of information that need to be completed on the **Sales Receipt** form. The following is a brief description of the information you need to include in each field:

- **Customer**: Select the customer you sold the product or service to by clicking on the drop-down arrow in this field. **George Jetson** is the customer in our example. If you have not added any customers yet, you can add a new customer by typing the customer's name in this field.

> **Pro Tip**: If you need to record sales for an event for multiple customers at once, you can enter the event name and date or the week instead of a specific customer; for example, Sales for the week of 2/1/23 to 2/7/23.

- **Email**: This field will automatically be populated with the email address you have on file for the customer. The email address in our example is George_Jetson@ thejetsons.com. If the field is blank, you can type an email address directly in this field.

QuickBooks will email the sales receipt to the email address you include in this field.

- **Billing address:** This field will automatically be populated with the billing address you have on file for this customer. The billing address in our example is **321 Jetson Dr., Jetson, CA 90210**. If you don't have an address on file, you can enter one directly in this field.

- **Sales Receipt date:** Enter the date of the sale in this field, which is 09/02/22 in our example.

- **Payment method:** Select the payment method by clicking the drop-down arrow. We have selected **Check** in our example.

- **Reference no.:** If your customer paid by check, enter the check number in this field. If payment was made by cash or credit card, you can enter a reference number, or leave this field blank. The reference no. is 43567 in our example.

- **Deposit to:** From the drop-down menu, select the bank account to which you will deposit this payment. In our example, the funds will be deposited into the **Business Checking** account.

> **Pro Tip:** If you plan to deposit payments for multiple customers on the same day, select the **Payments to deposit** account (formerly **Undeposited funds**), instead of the **Business Checking** account as the **Deposit to** account. Later on, you will be able to select the specific deposits made on each day. This will make it much easier to reconcile the bank account.

- **Sales Receipt no.:** QuickBooks will automatically generate this number, which is **1003** in our example.

- **Location of sale:** For sales tax purposes, this field will automatically be populated with the business address of our sample company. The business address in our example is **3540 E Broad St, Mansfield, Tx 76063**.

- **PRODUCT/SERVICE:** From the drop-down menu, select the type of service (or product) sold to the customer. In our example, it is a bookkeeping service. **Monthly Bookkeeping Services** has not been added, so you will need to select **Add New** and complete the following fields to add it to the list:

  - **Name:** Monthly Bookkeeping Services

- **Description:** Bookkeeping for the month of September 2022
- **Rate:** $500.00
- **Account:** Consultation Income

- **DESCRIPTION:** This field will automatically be populated based on the product/service selected. In our example, the description is **Bookkeeping for the month of September 2022**.

- **QTY:** Enter the quantity of items sold or the total hours of service provided. In our example, the quantity is 1.

- **RATE:** Enter the hourly rate for your services or the unit cost of the product sold. This field should automatically populate with the rate that was set. In our example, the rate is $500.

- **AMOUNT:** You don't need to enter anything in this field. QuickBooks will multiply the quantity by the rate to automatically calculate the total amount of the sales receipt. In our example, the total amount is **$500**.

- **TAX:** This box may automatically be turned on. Remove **X** from this field since this service is not taxable.

 Pro Tip: This Intuit video tutorial summarizes the steps we have covered on how to create a sales receipt: https://quickbooks.intuit.com/learn-support/en-us/sales-receipts/how-to-record-a-sales-receipt/00/344860.

As mentioned in *Chapter 1, Getting Started with QuickBooks Online*, one of the benefits of using QuickBooks is that you don't need to have knowledge of debits and credits to use the software. QuickBooks will automatically debit and credit the appropriate accounts for you. However, it is important for you to understand the impact of recording transactions in QuickBooks.

The following table shows the journal entry that is recorded behind the scenes in QuickBooks for the sales receipt displayed previously in *Figure 7.2*:

Date	Account Name	Debit	Credit
9/2/2022	Business Checking	500	
	Consultation Income		500

Figure 7.3: Automatic journal entry recorded for a sales receipt

When you create a sales receipt in QuickBooks, it has an impact on the balance sheet and the income statement. You can find both of these reports in the Report Center.

In *Chapter 11, Business Overview and Cash Flow Reports*, we show you how to generate these reports. In our example, the checking account is increased by **$500**, which increases the total assets on the balance sheet report. **Consultation Income** has also increased by **$500**, which increases the total income on the profit and loss (income statement).

Now that you know how to use a sales receipt to record income, we will show you how to record income using a deposit, and the impact deposits have on financial statements.

Recording income using a deposit

Another method used to record income in QuickBooks is that of a deposit. The downside to using this method is that you won't have a detailed record of the type of service that was performed, since there is no field to select the service or product provided. This method should be used if you don't need to record your sales by the type of product or service that was sold. An example of a business that might use this method is a real estate agent recording commission income. You can record a lump-sum deposit amount for multiple checks, or you can record deposits for a specific customer. Recording a deposit in QuickBooks can be done in just a couple of steps.

Follow these steps to record income in QuickBooks using a deposit:

1. From the **+ New** menu, select **Bank deposit** in the **OTHER** column, as indicated in *Figure 7.4:*

Figure 7.4: Navigating to Bank Deposit

Figure 7.5 shows a completed **Bank Deposit** form:

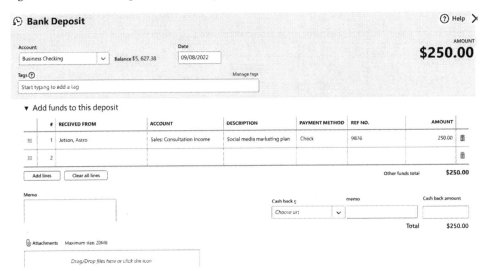

Figure 7.5: Bank Deposit form

Brief descriptions of the fields that need to be completed in a deposit slip are given here. All fields are required except for the **DESCRIPTION, PAYMENT METHOD**, and **REF NO.** fields:

- **Account**: Use the drop-down arrow to select the bank account to which the deposit will be made. In our example, we have selected the **Business Checking** account.

- **Date**: Enter the date on which you will make the deposit with your bank. This deposit was made on **09/08/2022**.

- **RECEIVED FROM**: Click in this field and select the customer from whom you received the payment. If you prefer not to track income according to the customer, you can leave this field blank. Our deposit was received from **Astro Jetson**.

- **ACCOUNT**: From the drop-down menu, select the appropriate account to which this income should be categorized. This should be based on the type of product or service provided. The account in our example is **Sales: Consultation Income**.

- **DESCRIPTION**: This field is optional. You can type a brief description of the product or service provided. The description in our example is **Social media marketing plan**.

- **PAYMENT METHOD**: In this field, you can indicate the method of payment received (that is, by credit card, cash, or check). The payment method in our example is **Check**.

- **REF NO.:** If the payment method was **Check**, enter the check number in this field. For all other payment methods, you can leave this field blank. The reference number is **9876** in our example.

- **AMOUNT:** Enter the amount of the sale in this field. The total amount of the above deposit is **$250**.

When you create a deposit transaction in QuickBooks, it affects the balance sheet and profit and loss (income statement) reports. The bank account where the deposit will be made goes up, which increases the assets section of the balance sheet report. The profit and loss report is increased by the product or service that was sold.

The following table shows the journal entry recorded for the deposit transaction displayed in *Figure 7.5*:

Date	Account Name	Debit	Credit
9/8/2022	Business Checking	250	
	Consultation Income		250

Figure 7.6: Automatic journal entry to record a bank deposit

In our example, the **Business Checking** account increased by **$250**, which will increase the total assets on the balance sheet report. **Consultation Income** also increased by **$250**, which will increase the total income on the profit and loss report? (income statement).

Pro Tip: This method can also be used to record miscellaneous deposits, such as a refund check from a vendor or the IRS. In addition, if you receive a rewards check from a credit card company, that can be recorded as a deposit.

Now that you know how to record income using a deposit, we will show you how to record income using a sales invoice.

Recording income using a sales invoice

A sales invoice is used to record income from customers who have been given extended payment terms. This means the customer does not pay at the time the product is sold or services are rendered; instead, they pay you sometime in the future. The most common payment term is **net 30**, which means the invoice is due 30 days from the sales date or the invoice date.

Unlike the sales receipt and deposit forms, which record both the sale and the receipt of payment in a single transaction, recording a sales invoice and payment is done in two steps. In this section, we will cover the first step: recording a sales invoice. We will cover recording customer payments in the next section.

To record a sales invoice in QBO, follow these steps:

1. Navigate to the **+ New** menu and select **Invoice** under **CUSTOMERS**, as indicated here:

Figure 7.7: Navigating to the Invoice form

In *Figure 7.8*, we have an example of a complete sales invoice form:

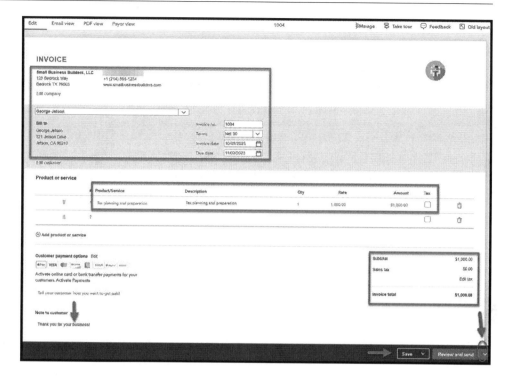

Figure 7.8: The Invoice form

Here are brief descriptions of the fields that need to be completed in a sales invoice. All fields are required except for the **Description, Qty,** and **Note to customer** fields:

- **Customer**: Select the customer from the drop-down menu. **George Jetson** is the customer selected in our example.

- **Bill to**: This field will automatically be populated with the address information you have on file for your customer. If you have not set up the address information, you can type it directly in this field. The billing address in this field is **321 Jetson Drive, Jetson, CA 90210**.

- **Terms**: This field will automatically be populated with the payment terms you have set up for your customer. In our example, we have set payment terms of **Net 30**, which means the invoice is due 30 days from the invoice date. If you have not set up payment terms, you can select these from the drop-down menu.

- **Invoice date**: Enter the date of the sale in this field. The invoice date is **10/03/2023** in our example.

- **Due date:** This field is automatically calculated by QuickBooks. Since the payment terms are **Net 30**, it adds 30 days to the invoice date in order to compute the date payment is due. The due date is **11/02/2023** in our example.

- **Invoice no.:** QuickBooks will automatically populate this field with the next available invoice number. In our example, the invoice number is **1004**.

- **Product/Service:** From the drop-down menu, select the product and/or services provided to the customer. In our example, the product sold is **Tax planning and preparation**. Select **Add new** from the drop-down menu to add this service to the list.

- **Description:** This field will automatically be populated based on the product/service selected in the previous field. The description of the product sold in our example is **Tax planning and preparation**.

- **Qty:** Enter the quantity of the product or the total hours to bill the customer. In our example, the fee is a flat amount, so the **Qty** field will automatically populate with **1**.

- **Rate:** This field will automatically be populated based on the product/service selected. However, if you don't have a rate set up, you can enter the price per unit or the hourly rate in this field. In our example, the rate for tax planning and preparation is **$1,000.00**.

- **Amount:** QuickBooks will automatically calculate the total invoice amount by taking the quantity and multiplying it by the rate. In our example, the total amount due is **$1,000.00**.

- **Note to customer:** This field is optional. You can type a personal thank you message to your customer and it will appear on the invoice. In our example, we have entered the following message: **Thank you for your business!**

You have the option to print the sales invoice, email it, or save it as a PDF document. If you would like to allow customers to pay their invoices online, you can sign up for the Intuit Payments service. This service allows you to accept payments from customers via eight payment methods: Apple Pay, Visa, Mastercard, Discover Card, Amex, ACH, PayPal, and Venmo. Using Intuit Payments is a fast and efficient way to get paid.

Pro Tip: You can now send invoices in one of six languages: English, French, Spanish, Italian, Portuguese (Brazil), and Chinese (traditional). To select the preferred language for a customer, navigate to the customer profile and click on the **Language** tab.

This Intuit video tutorial summarizes the steps we have covered on how to create an invoice in QuickBooks Online: https://www.youtube.com/watch?v=o56z20jLzas.

When you create a sales invoice in QuickBooks, it has an impact on the balance sheet as well as the profit and loss statement. The accounts receivable account will increase, which will result in an increase in the total assets on the balance sheet report. Income will also increase the profit and loss statement.

Figure 7.9 shows the journal entry that will be recorded in QuickBooks for our sample sales invoice shown in *Figure 7.8*:

Date	Account Name	Debit	Credit
10/3/2023	Accounts Receivable	1000	
	Consultation Income		1000

Figure 7.9: Automatic journal entry recorded for the invoice

The amount owed by customers—also known as accounts receivable—goes up by **$1,000.00**, and consultation income is increased by **$1,000.00**. In the next section, we will show you how to apply payments to open accounts receivable balances.

Now that you know how to record income using a sales invoice, we will cover how to customize sales templates. Understanding how to customize sales templates with your company name and logo will allow you to make your brand style consistent across different forms.

Customizing sales templates

QuickBooks allows you to create custom sales forms to match your brand and style. Taking the time to customize sales templates will allow you to create professional-looking forms so your customers can easily see what they owe and make payments online in just a few minutes. You can customize invoices, estimates, and sales receipt templates. Follow these steps to learn how to customize these sales templates:

1. Click on the gear icon and select **Custom form styles** from the **YOUR COMPANY** column, as shown in *Figure 7.10*:

Figure 7.10: Navigating to Custom form styles

2. Click on the **New style** button and select a sales template to customize:

Figure 7.11: Clicking the New style button

3. The following window will display three areas you can customize for sales templates:

Figure 7.12: Three customization options for sales templates

The following is a brief explanation of the information you can customize in each of these areas:

-   **Design:** The **Design** section allows you to create your template style and format. You will select a template design, add your company logo, add your brand colors, and choose the font size and style.

- **Content:** For **Content**, you can select what information you would like to appear on the sales template, including your basic contact information, such as business telephone number and mailing address. You can also add your website and email address to the form. In the billing section, you can determine how much detail you would like to include in the sales form. For example, an invoice should include a list of each product or service you are billing the customer for.

- **Emails:** QuickBooks allows you to email a sales form directly to customers. In this section, you can decide whether you want any details of the form to be included in the body of the email. Also, you can choose to have a PDF document attached to the email.

4. After completing each section, click the **Done** button at the bottom of the screen to save your changes. A preview of your customized sales form should appear, as shown in *Figure 7.13*:

Small Business Builders, LLC
3540 E Broad St
Mansfield, TX 76063
US

www.smallbusinessbuilders.com

INVOICE

BILL TO			INVOICE	12345
Smith Co.			DATE	01/12/2016
123 Main Street			TERMS	Net 30
City, CA 12345			DUE DATE	02/12/2016

DATE		DESCRIPTION	QTY	RATE	AMOUNT
12/01/2016	Item name	Description of the item	2	$225.00	$450.00
01/12/2016	Item name	Description of the item	1	$225.00	$225.00

SUBTOTAL		$675.00
TAX		$101.00
TOTAL		$776.00
BALANCE DUE		**$776.25**

Figure 7.13: Sample custom invoice for Small Business Builders, LLC

You can create an unlimited number of templates for various types of sales and customers. It is easy to make changes to them anytime. The best part is that you don't have to create any templates from scratch.

 Pro Tip: Learn how to customize sales forms with this Intuit video tutorial with tips and tricks on customizing sales forms in QBO: `https://www.youtube.com/watch?v=b51wvS-4g1w`.

Now that you know how to record income using a sales invoice and customize sales templates, we will cover the second step, which is receiving customer payments. You must correctly apply customer payments to outstanding sales invoices to ensure that your accounts receivable balance is always up to date.

Recording customer payments

If you record income using a sales invoice, you will receive payment based on the terms you have agreed with your customer. When customer payments are received, you must apply payments to an outstanding sales invoice to reduce the accounts receivable balance. As mentioned previously, you can accept multiple payment methods in QuickBooks, including check, cash, Apple Pay, Visa, Mastercard, Discover Card, Amex, ACH, PayPal, and Venmo. To learn more about managing credit card payments, refer to *Chapter 16, Handling Special Transactions in QuickBooks Online*.

Follow these steps to receive payment from a customer:

1. Click on the **+ New** menu.

2. Navigate to **Receive payment**, located below **CUSTOMERS**, as indicated in *Figure 7.14*:

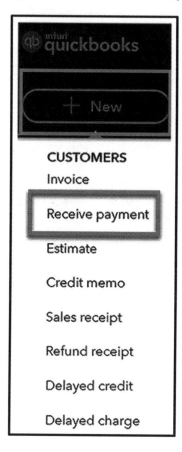

Figure 7.14: Navigating to Receive payment

3.   Complete the fields, as indicated in *Figure 7.15*, to record the customer payment:

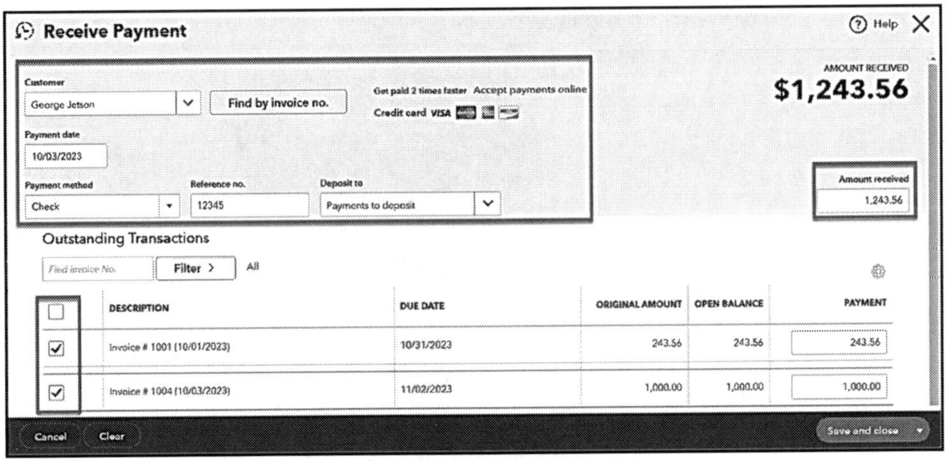

Figure 7.15: The Receive Payment window

The following are brief descriptions of the key fields for receiving customer payments:

- **Customer**: Select the customer by clicking the drop-down arrow. **George Jetson** is the customer selected in our example.

- **Payment date**: Enter the date payment was received. The payment date is **10/03/2023** in our example.

- **Payment method**: From the drop-down menu, select the payment method received (that is, by credit card, check, or cash). The payment method is **Check** in our example.

- **Reference no.**: If payment was made by check, enter the check number in this field. If another payment method was used, you can leave this field blank. The reference number is 12345 in our example.

- **Deposit to**: Select the bank account to which you will deposit this payment. **Payments to deposit** (formerly "undeposited funds") is the **Deposit to** account in our example.

- **Amount received**: Enter the amount of the payment received. The amount received in our example is **$1243.56**.

- **Outstanding Transactions**: A list of unpaid invoices will appear in this section. Based on the amount entered in the **Amount received** field, QuickBooks will select the invoice that matches that amount and is closest to the date of the transaction. In our example, **Invoice # 1001** for **$243.56** and **Invoice # 1004** for **$1,000.00** are the invoices that payment has been received for. If QuickBooks selects the wrong invoice, you can remove the checkmark and manually select the invoices to apply the payment to.

Recording customer payments affects the balance sheet report but not the income statement. Since income was recorded at the time the invoice was created, there is no impact on profit and loss (income statement).

The following table shows the journal entry that will automatically be recorded in QuickBooks for a customer payment of **$1243.56**:

Date	Account Name	Debit	Credit
10/3/2023	Business Checking	1243.56	
	Accounts Receivable		1243.56

Figure 7.16: Automatic journal entry recorded for customer payment received

The payments to deposit account is increased by **$1,243.56**, which will result in an increase in the assets section of the balance sheet report. **Accounts Receivable** will decrease by **$1,243.56**, which will result in a decrease in the **Assets** section of the balance sheet report.

The **Receive payments** method should be used when an invoice has previously been issued. Using **Receive payments** without an invoice will result in a credit balance on the customer account.

The **Accounts receivable aging summary** report shows all open invoices and credits for each customer. It should be reviewed periodically to capture any credits on customer accounts. We will review this report in detail in *Chapter 12, Customer Sales Reports in QuickBooks Online*.

Managing credit card payments

In addition to traditional payments such as cash and checks, you can accept credit cards as another form of payment from your customers. QBO has a built-in credit card processor called QuickBooks Payments. QuickBooks Payments is a merchant account that allows you to accept credit cards, PayPal, Venmo, Apple Pay, and ACH (bank transfers) from your customers. While there are fees associated with accepting credit card payments, there are several benefits. First, you can get paid faster with a credit card than waiting to receive a check in the mail.

Second, if you sign up for a QuickBooks Payments account (`https://quickbooks.intuit.com/payments/?sc=seq_intuit_pay_click_ft`), you can email customers their invoice, which includes a payment link. They can click on the link, enter their payment information, and pay their invoice in a matter of minutes, which is much faster than waiting to receive a check in the mail. Best of all, QuickBooks will mark the invoice as paid, which automatically reduces your accounts receivable balance. As we discussed in *Chapter 7, Recording Sales Transactions in QuickBooks Online*, you can send your customers payment reminder emails, which will include a copy of the open invoices, along with a payment link.

In this section, we will show you how to record credit card payments that have been received from customers via QuickBooks Payments and a third-party credit card processing company.

Before you can perform the steps, you will need to have an active QuickBooks Payments account that is connected to your QBO account. Visit QuickBooks Payments (`https://quickbooks.intuit.com/payments/?sc=seq_intuit_pay_click_ft`) to apply for a QuickBooks Payments account and learn more about how this works.

If you are using a third-party processor, you may be able to connect your account to QuickBooks. For example, PayPal and Square have apps within the QBO App Center. In *Chapter 4, Customizing QuickBooks for Your Business*, we cover how the integration between apps works. If you are not sure if your credit card processor works similar to this, contact your credit card processor to find out if they are compatible with QuickBooks Online.

Follow these steps to record a credit card sale if you have a QuickBooks Payments account:

1. Click on the **+ New** button and select **Sales receipt** from the **Customers** column, as shown in *Figure 7.17*:

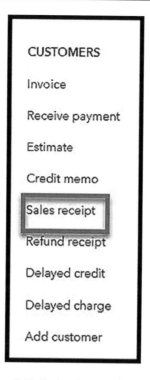

Figure 7.17: Navigating to Sales receipt

2. Fill in the fields in the sales receipt form, as shown in *Figure 7.18*:

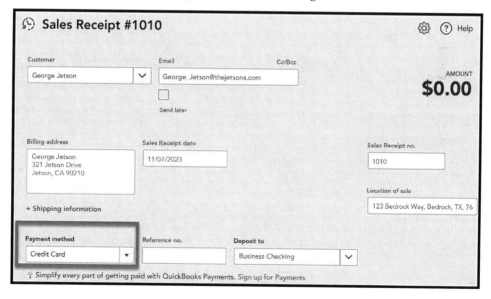

Figure 7.18: Completing the sales receipt form

After selecting the customer from the drop-down menu, the **Email** and **Billing address** fields will automatically be populated with the information you have on file.

3. Next, select a payment method from the drop-down menu. When you select **Credit Card** as the payment method and you have a QuickBooks Payments account, you will see an option to enter credit card details directly below the **Payment method** field.

The following screen will appear so that you can enter the required credit card information, as shown in *Figure 7.19*:

Figure 7.19: Completing the credit card payment information

In *Figure 7.19*, the credit card number has been removed for security reasons. Be sure to complete all the necessary fields and click the **Use this info** button to save the information.

 Pro Tip: After entering the customer's credit card information, QuickBooks will keep this information on file. You won't have to enter it again unless your customer would like to use a different payment method or the credit card expires.

4. This will take you back to the sales receipt form, where you can fill in the details of the services/products provided and the amount. When you click the **Save** button, the credit card payment will be processed and an email with the sales receipt attached will be sent to the customer.

> **Pro Tip:** If you don't have a QuickBooks Payments account, you can still enter the credit card information and save it. However, you will need to process the credit card payment outside of QuickBooks using your third-party merchant company. When the payment is deposited into your bank account, you will need to match it up with the sales receipt in the Banking Center. To learn more about matching transactions, read *Chapter 9, Reconciling Uploaded Bank and Credit Card Transactions.*

You now know the benefits of accepting credit card payments from customers and how to manage these payments in QuickBooks.

Recording payments to the payments to deposit account

In the previous examples, each of the payments that have been recorded from customers, whether on a sales receipt, deposit slip, or invoice, were all deposited to the business checking account. This is ideal if you don't deposit more than one check (customer payment) at a time.

However, like most businesses, you will probably wait until you have multiple checks before you head to the bank to make a deposit. In that case, you will need to record all customer payments to an account called **payments to deposit** (formerly "undeposited funds").

The payments to deposit account is an account that is automatically created by QuickBooks. It acts like a cash drawer, where all customer payments are held until you record a deposit in QuickBooks.

After you make a deposit with the bank, you need to record that deposit in QuickBooks. Follow the steps below to record a deposit that includes multiple checks (customer payments):

1. Click on the **+ New** button and select **Bank deposit**, as shown below:

Figure 7.20: Navigating to Bank deposit

2. The **Bank Deposit** form will appear:

Figure 7.21: The Bank Deposit form

3. Select the bank account to which the deposit will be made. **Business Checking** is the account selected in our example. In the **Date** field, select the date of the deposit; in our example, it is **10/03/2022**.

4. Below the **Select the payments included in this deposit** heading, put a checkmark next to each payment included in this deposit. In our example, there are two payments from two different customers (**Jenny Jetson** and **Judy Jetson**), which total **$1500.00**.

5. Click the **Save** button to record the deposit.

When this deposit is recorded in QuickBooks, the following journal entry is created behind the scenes:

Date	Account Name	Debit	Credit
9/12/2022	Business checking	1500	
	Payments to deposit		1500

Figure 7.22: Journal entry to transfer payments from payments to deposit to the checking account

Pro Tip: You can also print a deposit slip from the screen shown in *Figure 7.14*, which you can take to your bank along with the checks you are depositing.

When this deposit is recorded in QuickBooks, it only affects the balance sheet report. The business checking account (an asset) increases by the total deposit amount, and the payments to deposit account (also an asset) decreases by the total deposit amount. To ensure you are in balance when you reconcile your bank accounts, always make sure that you have recorded all deposits in QuickBooks. If you have any payments sitting in the payments to deposit account (and they were actually deposited), you will be out of balance. To learn more about how to reconcile bank accounts, head over to *Chapter 9, Reconciling Uploaded Bank and Credit Card Transactions*.

Now that you know how to record income and apply payments to outstanding customer invoices, we will show you how to handle customer returns and refunds in the next section.

Issuing credit memos and refunds to customers

There may be times when a customer returns merchandise, or you need to refund a customer due to an issue with the services or products you have provided.

When that happens, you can create a credit memo in QuickBooks that can be applied to a future invoice, or you can refund the customer instead by clicking on + **New**, selecting **Refund receipt**, and following the onscreen instructions.

Follow these steps to create a credit memo in QuickBooks Online:

1. Click on the + **New** menu and select **Credit memo** below **CUSTOMERS**, as indicated in *Figure 7.23*:

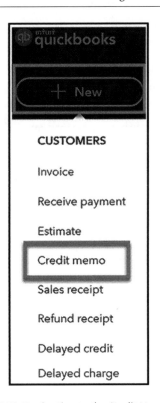

Figure 7.23: Navigating to the Credit Memo form

2.   Complete the key fields indicated here for the credit memo:

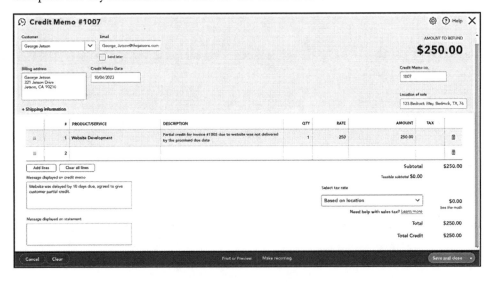

Figure 7.24: Credit Memo form

The following are brief descriptions of the key fields to complete for a credit memo. All fields are required except for the **QTY, DESCRIPTION**, and **Message displayed on credit memo** fields:

- **Customer**: From the drop-down menu, select the customer you need to refund. **George Jetson** is the customer selected in our example.

- **Email**: This field will automatically be populated with the email address you have on file. If you don't have an email address on file, you can enter the email address in this field if you would like to email the credit memo to the customer. The email address for George Jetson is George_Jetson@thejetsons.com.

- **Billing address**: This field will automatically be populated with the billing address you have on file. If you don't have a billing address on file, you can enter it directly in this field. The billing address for George Jetson is **321 Jetson Drive, Jetson, CA 90210**.

- **Credit Memo Date**: Enter the date for which you are creating this credit memo. The credit memo is dated **10/03/2023**.

- **PRODUCT/SERVICE**: From the drop-down menu, select the product or service for which you are providing a refund. The product in our example is **Website Development**.

- **DESCRIPTION**: This field will be populated automatically, but you should edit this to specify the reason for the credit as well as the original invoice number used to bill the customer. In our example, the description is: **Partial credit for invoice #1005 due to website was not delivered by the promised due date**.

- **QTY**: Enter the number of items or hours for which you are refunding the customer. The quantity in our example is 1.

- **RATE**: This field will automatically be populated based on the product/service selected. However, if there is no rate set up, you can enter the rate in this field. The rate is **$250** in our example.

- **AMOUNT**: This field is automatically calculated by multiplying the quantity by the rate. You do not have to enter anything in this field. The total amount to be credited to the customer is **$250.00** in our example. Since the customer has not paid the invoice yet, we will apply this credit to the open invoice. However, if the invoice had already been paid, you would have issued a refund to the customer.

- **Message displayed on credit memo:** In this field, you can add the original invoice number for which you are providing a full or partial credit, or a brief description of the reason for the credit. The message on our credit memo is: **Website was delayed by 10 days due, agreed to give customer partial credit.**

Recording a credit memo in QuickBooks will have an impact on the balance sheet and income statement reports. The income account (sales) will decrease, which will reduce the total income on the profit and loss report. If the original invoice has not been paid, the credit memo can be applied to that invoice to reduce the total amount due from the customer. The accounts receivable account will decrease since the amount due from the customer has been reduced.

The journal entry for the preceding credit memo will automatically be recorded in QuickBooks as follows:

Date	Account Name	Debit	Credit
10/3/2023	Consultation Income	250	
	Accounts Receivable		250

Figure 7.25: Automatic journal entry recorded for the credit memo

 Pro Tip: This Intuit video tutorial recaps the steps we've covered: *How to give customers credit in QuickBooks Online*: `https://youtu.be/UmnAMGvTamY`.

Applying a credit memo to an open invoice

After recording a credit memo for a customer, the credit will immediately be applied to the open balance for that customer. Let's assume that George Jetson has sent a payment in for invoice #1005. Navigate to the **Receive Payment** window, select **George Jetson** from the **Customer** drop-down, and the following screen will display:

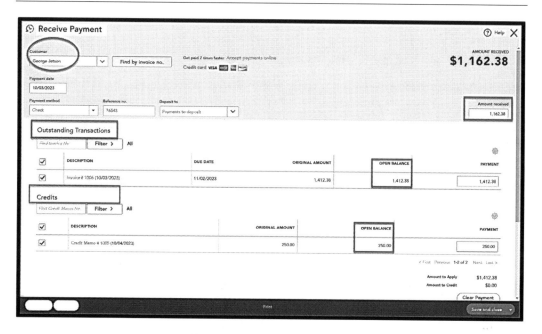

Figure 7.26: George Jetson invoice

As you can see in *Figure 7.26*, the original invoice amount was **$1,412.38**, and now that the credit has been recorded, the open balance has been reduced by the **$250** credit amount (shown in *Figure 7.18*) to **$1,162.38**.

Pro Tip: If you do not invoice customers through QuickBooks, you can issue a refund check by going to **+ New** and selecting **Check**, listed below the **Vendors** column. This will allow you to refund a customer instead of creating a credit memo since you will never have an invoice to apply it to.

Summary

In this chapter, you have learned how to record sales transactions for the sale of products and services using a sales receipt, a deposit, and a sales invoice. You now know when to use each sales transaction and how to record them in QuickBooks Online. We have also covered the journal entry that is recorded behind the scenes by QuickBooks for each transaction. To put your best foot forward, we have shown you how to create professional-looking invoices, sales receipts, and estimates by adding your brand colors and logo. In addition, you have learned how to record customer payments so that they are correctly applied to open invoices. We have also covered how to manage credit card payments by signing up for a QuickBooks Payments account. Finally, we covered how to issue credit memos and refunds to customers. Recording sales transactions will allow you to keep track of how much money your business is making. This is important so that you can determine whether your business is profitable or not. In the next chapter, we will look at how to record the money that flows out of your business to cover expenses.

Join our community on Discord

Join our community's Discord space for discussions with the authors and other readers:

`https://packt.link/quickbooks`

8

Recording Expenses in QuickBooks Online

Managing expenses incurred by a business is one of the primary reasons why many businesses decide to use QuickBooks. Most businesses know when they are generating income, but when it comes to where their money is going, it's a whole different story. For a business to be profitable, it must be able to control expenses that directly affect the bottom line.

In this chapter, we will show you four ways to record expenses, also known as **money-out** transactions: (1) entering and paying bills, (2) managing recurring expenses, (3) writing and printing checks, and (4) capturing and categorizing receipts and bills.

Entering a bill is ideal for suppliers who have extended credit to you. You receive your purchases immediately and payment is due sometime in the future. However, expenses that require immediate payment should be paid via check, debit card, or credit card. In *Chapter 9, Reconciling Uploaded Bank and Credit Card Transactions*, we will show you how to record payments made with a debit or credit card. Entering a check allows you to record both the expense and the payment at the same time.

Using one or more of these methods will give you access to detailed reports that will give you insight into all of your money-out transactions. This is a key component in having the ability to control expenses.

In this chapter, we will cover the following topics:

- Entering and paying bills
- Managing recurring expenses

- Writing checks

- Printing checks

- Editing, voiding, and deleting expenses

- Capturing and categorizing receipts and bills

By the end of this chapter, you will know how to enter and pay your bills, and how to create recurring expenses for rent, utilities, and other recurring costs. Plus, you will understand how to write a check and print it directly from QuickBooks, and you will become familiar with the various ways in which you can upload receipts and bills in QuickBooks.

 The US edition of QBO was used to create this book. If you are using a version that is outside of the United States, results may differ.

Entering and paying bills

For purchases made on account, entering bills into QuickBooks and paying them a few days before they become due is the best way to manage your cash flow. If you enter bills into QuickBooks as you receive them, you can run reports that will show you which bills are due or are nearly due, so that you can plan ahead and ensure you have sufficient cash on hand to pay them. Unpaid bills are also referred to as **accounts payable**, or **A/P** for short. In the following sections, we will first cover how to enter bills, and then we will discuss how to pay a bill in **QuickBooks Online (QBO)**.

 Pro Tip: There are a number of apps available to help automate the bill entry process. From the left navigation bar, select **Apps**. In the search box, type the keywords bill pay, and several options such as **Bill Pay for QuickBooks Online** and **bill.com** will display. To learn more about the Intuit Apps marketplace, refer to *Chapter 16, Handling Special Transactions in QuickBooks Online*.

Entering bills into QuickBooks Online

Entering your bills into QuickBooks before they come due will help you to manage your cash flow. You can easily run reports, such as the **Unpaid Bills** report or the **A/P Aging** report, to see which bills are coming due or are past due.

To enter bills into QuickBooks Online, you will need to complete the following steps:

1. Click on the **+ New** button and select **Bill** in the **Vendors** column, as indicated in *Figure 8.1*:

Figure 8.1: Navigating to Bill from the Vendors menu

2. Complete the key fields in the **Bill** form, as indicated in *Figure 8.2*:

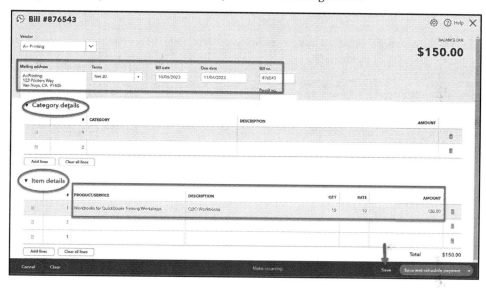

Figure 8.2: Completing the Bill form for a vendor

3. The following is a brief description of the key fields in the **Bill** form. All fields must be completed:

   - **Vendor:** Select a vendor from the drop-down menu, or add a new vendor if they have not been previously set up in QuickBooks. You can do this by selecting **Add New** from the drop-down menu. In our example, **A+ Printing** is the vendor.

   - **Mailing address:** This field will automatically be populated for vendors you have previously created in QuickBooks. If this is a new vendor, you can enter the address in this field. In our example, the address is **123 Printers Way, Van Nuys, CA 91405**.

- **Terms:** This field will automatically be populated with the vendor terms you have set up. If you have not previously set up vendor terms, you can select the appropriate payment terms from the drop-down menu. The payment terms should be **Net 30** for **A+ Printing**.

- **Bill date:** Enter the date that appears on the vendor bill. Our bill date is **10/05/2023**.

- **Due date:** The due date will be calculated automatically based on the payment terms selected. If payment terms were not selected, you can also enter the due date directly in this field. The due date in our example is **11/04/2023**.

- **Bill no.:** The bill number is the invoice number assigned by the vendor supplier. If the bill does not include a unique number, create one. Having a unique bill number is very important so that QuickBooks can track bills and alert you if there is a duplicate bill number used. If a bill does not include a bill number, utilize the bill date, or something unique, for each bill. The bill number in our example is **876543**.

- **Category details:** Complete this section if you have purchased services from the vendor. Since we have purchased workbooks that are tracked in our inventory, we will complete the **Item details** section right below **Category details**.

- **Item details:** Complete this section if you have purchased a product that you need to keep in inventory so that you can track the quantity and/or costs. From the drop-down menu, select the product/service purchased. If the item has not been added to QuickBooks, you can do so on this screen by selecting the **Add new** option. The **New item** window will display so that you can complete the item setup. For more information on adding a new item to the products and services list, see *Chapter 5, Managing Customer, Vendor, and Products and Services Lists*.

- **DESCRIPTION:** Enter a brief description of what was purchased in this field. For this example, the description is **QBO Workbooks**.

- **QTY:** Enter the quantity of the item purchased. In our example, **15** workbooks were purchased.

- **RATE:** This field should automatically populate with the rate entered when setting up the item. If no rate was added, you can enter it directly in this form. The rate is **10** in our example.

- **AMOUNT**: QuickBooks will automatically calculate the total amount by multiplying the quantity entered by the rate. In our example, the total amount calculated is **$150.00**.

- **Save** or **Save and schedule payment**: You have the option to save the bill and schedule payment at a later date, or schedule payment now. We will save the bill for now and cover how to schedule payment later in this chapter.

In our example, this bill only has an impact on the balance sheet. There is no impact on the profit and loss (income statement) reports. Inventory (which is an asset) increases by $150.00, and A/P also increases, which, in turn, increases current liabilities on the balance sheet report.

The journal entry that is recorded in QuickBooks for the preceding bill is shown in *Figure 8.3*:

Date	Account Name	Debit	Credit
10/5/2023	Inventory	150	
	Accounts Payable		150

Figure 8.3: Journal entry to record a vendor bill

In our example, we have used the **Item details** section, because the product is placed in inventory. If you are recording the purchase of an expense (such as consultation services or office supplies), instead of inventory, an expense account such as **Consulting expense** or **Office supplies** can be used in the **Category details** section. This would increase expenses on the profit and loss report. Accounts payable would still increase by the amount that was purchased.

In order to stay on top of your bills, it's a good idea to enter them as soon as you receive them. Be sure to enter the date of the bill and the due date; this will ensure that QuickBooks will calculate the correct due date and alert you when a bill is coming due.

Paying bills in QuickBooks Online

After you enter a bill in QuickBooks, you will need to pay it before the due date. Paying bills in QuickBooks will ensure that the A/P balance is always up to date. It will also allow you to run reports, and to see which bills have been paid or need to be paid.

Follow these steps to pay bills in QuickBooks Online:

1. Click on the **+ New** button and select **Pay Bills** in the **Vendors** column, as indicated in *Figure 8.4*:

Figure 8.4: Navigating to Pay Bills from the Vendors menu

2. The **Pay Bills** form displays, as indicated in *Figure 8.5*:

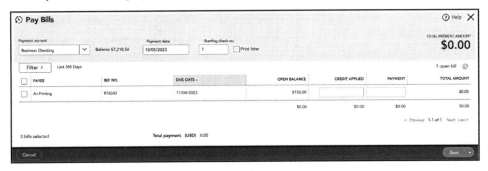

Figure 8.5: The Pay Bills form displays

3. Complete the fields as indicated in *Figure 8.6* to record the bill payment:

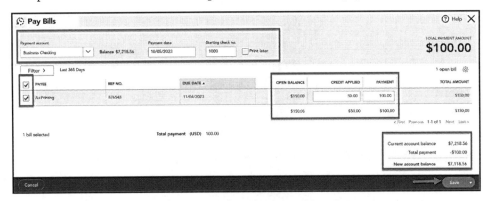

Figure 8.6: Completing the Pay Bills form

4. The following is a brief description of the fields in the **Pay Bills** form; all fields must be completed:

- **Payment account**: Select the bank or credit card account from which you want to deduct this bill payment. **Business Checking** is the account selected in our example.

- **Balance**: The amount next to the payment account is the current balance per QuickBooks. *Please note, if you have banking transactions that have not been reviewed and added to QuickBooks, this balance will not match your actual bank account. Be sure to double-check your actual bank balance before making payments.*

- **Payment date**: Select the date on which you will pay this bill. If writing a check, this will be the check date. The payment date is **10/05/2023** in our example.

- **Starting check no.**: If you are writing a check, make sure the check number is the next available number. The starting check number is **1000** in our example.

- **Print later**: Put a checkmark in this box if you don't plan to print the check now, but will print it later on. We will show you how to print checks later in this chapter.

- PAYEE: This field will include a list of the payees with open bills. To select a bill for payment, put a checkmark in the box to the left of the **PAYEE** field. In our example, we have one payee with an open bill: **A+ Printing**.

Pro Tip: If you have more than one invoice for a vendor and your vendor prefers separate checks for each invoice, select the first invoice and save it, and then select each invoice one at a time, clicking **Save** in between each. Then, when you print checks, there will be separate checks for each invoice. An example where this might be useful is paying utility bills. Many utility companies prefer separate checks per account for which you are paying a bill.

- **REF NO.**: This field will include the invoice number (or bill number) that was entered when the bill was saved in QuickBooks. In our example, **876543** is the reference number for the **A+ Printing** bill.

- **DUE DATE**: This field will automatically be populated with the due date that was entered when the bill was saved in QuickBooks. In our example, the due date for the **A+ Printing** bill is **11/04/2023**.

- **OPEN BALANCE**: This field will automatically be populated with the unpaid amount of the bill. The open balance for the **A+ Printing** bill is **$150.00**.

- **CREDIT APPLIED:** If you have open credits for a vendor, you will see them listed in this column. In our example, **A+ Printing** has an open credit of **$50.00**. This will reduce the total amount due from **$150.00** to **$100.00**.

- **PAYMENT:** Enter the amount you would like to pay in this field. You can pay the bill in full or make a partial payment. If you make a partial payment, QuickBooks will keep the remaining balance due on file for you to pay in the future. The payment amount is **$100.00** for the **A+ Printing** bill. However, if you wish to pay less than the bill amount, you can do so by entering the amount you want to pay in this field.

- **TOTAL AMOUNT:** This column is automatically calculated for you. You cannot edit this field.

- **New account balance:** In the lower-right corner, QuickBooks calculates the new balance in the business checking account after deducting the amount of the total bill payment. In our example, the new balance in the business checking account is **$7,118.56**.

5. You have the option to pay your bills online using your bank account or debit/credit card information. To do so, you would select the **Schedule Payments Online** button and follow the on-screen prompts to sign up for bill payment services. However, if you prefer to manually write checks or print them from QuickBooks, click on the arrow to the right of **Schedule Payments Online** and select **Save**. We will cover how to write checks in QuickBooks later in this chapter.

 Pro Tip: To reinforce the steps covered for entering and paying bills in QuickBooks, watch this Intuit video tutorial, *How to manage your bills in QuickBooks Online*: `https://youtu.be/p4FPKQ8Bf5M`.

When you pay a bill in QuickBooks, it only has an impact on the balance sheet report. The A/P balance goes down because you no longer owe your vendor for the bill, and the business checking account goes down because a payment has been made. If you pay the bill with a credit card, the credit card balance goes up, which increases liabilities.

The following table shows the journal entry recorded for the preceding bills:

Date	Account Name	Debit	Credit
10/5/2023	Accounts Payable	100	
	Business Checking		100

Figure 8.7: Journal entry to pay bills

In our example, the debit to A/P decreases total liabilities on the balance sheet report by **$100**. In addition, the credit to the business checking account decreases the total assets on the balance sheet report by **$100**. Paying bills in QuickBooks will give you access to detailed information about your expenses. You can run reports to show how much you are spending, which vendors you purchase from, and how often. These reports will help you to control what you are spending your money on, which allows you to properly manage your expenses. In *Chapter 13, Vendor and Expenses Reports*, we cover reports in detail.

Creating recurring expenses in QuickBooks can save you a lot of time. We will cover how to manage recurring expenses next.

Entering vendor credits into QuickBooks Online

If you overpay a vendor or receive a credit for damaged or returned merchandise, you can enter the credit memo into QuickBooks. By entering the credit memo into QBO, you can easily apply it to future purchases from the vendor. However, if you don't plan to order from that vendor again, you should request a refund. In our example, we received a credit on the order for the workbooks because the shipment was short by 5 workbooks, and we can apply the vendor credit to future purchases.

To enter vendor credits into QuickBooks Online, you will need to complete the following steps:

1. Click on the **+ New** button and select **Vendor credit** in the **Vendors** column, as indicated in *Figure 8.8*:

Figure 8.8: Navigating to the Vendor Credit form

2. The **Vendor Credit** form will appear. Complete the fields in this form as shown in *Figure 8.9*:

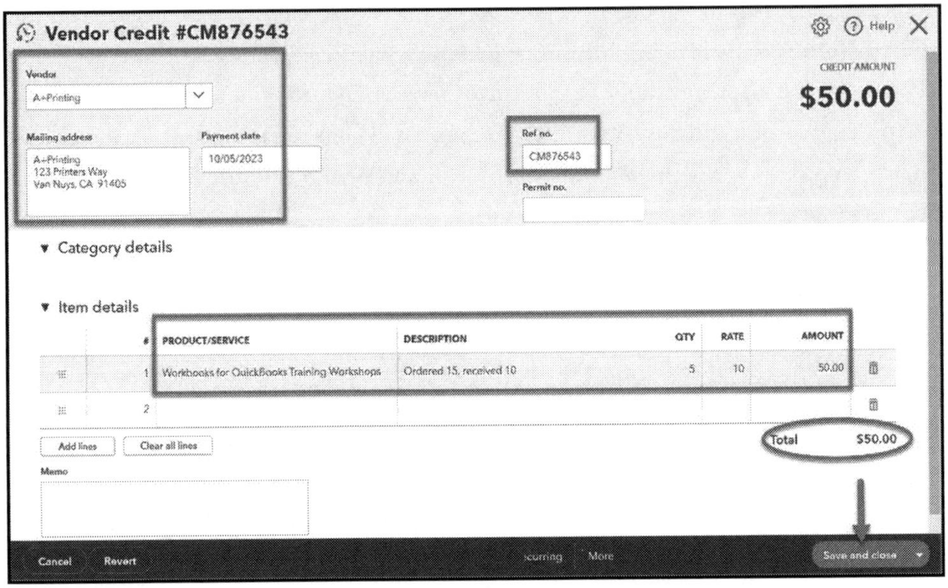

Figure 8.9: Completing the Vendor Credit form

3. The following is a brief description of the key fields in the **Vendor Credit** form. All fields must be completed, except for the **DESCRIPTION** field:

- **Vendor**: Select a vendor from the drop-down menu. In our example, **A+ Printing** is the vendor.

- **Mailing address**: This field will automatically be populated for vendors you have previously created in QuickBooks. If this is a new vendor, you can enter the address in this field. In our example, the address is **123 Printers Way, Van Nuys, CA 91405**.

- **Payment date**: Enter the date that appears on the vendor credit memo. Our payment date is **10/05/2023**.

- **Ref no.:** The reference number is the vendor credit memo number assigned by the vendor supplier. If the vendor credit memo does not include a unique number, create one. Having a unique vendor credit memo number allows QuickBooks to track vendor credits and alert you if there is a duplicate number used. If a vendor credit memo does not include a number, I typically use the letters **CM**, short for credit memo, and the original bill number paid. The vendor credit memo number in our example is **CM876543**.

- **Category details**: Complete this section if you have purchased services or non-inventory expenses from the vendor. Since we have purchased workbooks that are tracked in our inventory, we will complete the **Item details** section right below **Category details**.

- **Item details**: Complete this section if you have purchased an item added on QuickBooks that you need to keep track of quantity and/or costs for. From the drop-down menu, select the product/service purchased. If the item has not been added to QuickBooks, you can do so on this screen by selecting the **Add new** option. The new item window will display so that you can complete the item setup. For more information on adding a new item to the products and services list, see *Chapter 5, Managing Customer, Vendor, and Products and Services Lists*.

- **DESCRIPTION**: Enter a brief description of what was purchased in this field. In our example, the description is **Ordered 15, received 10**.

- **QTY**: Enter the total number of items the credit is for. In our example, the quantity is **5**.

- **RATE**: This field should automatically populate with the rate that was set for the item. If not, enter the rate in this field. In our example, the rate is 10.

- **AMOUNT**: QuickBooks will multiply the **QTY** field by the **RATE** field to get the total amount of the credit. The total amount is **$50** for the vendor credit from **A+ Printing**.

If you receive the credit before paying the original bill, when you enter the vendor credit into QBO, the A/P account will be reduced by the credit, and the inventory will be reduced by the same amount. Both of these accounts will only impact the balance sheet report. There is no impact on the income statement.

The journal entry that is recorded in QuickBooks for the preceding vendor credit is shown in *Figure 8.10*:

Date	Account Name	Debit	Credit
10/5/2023	Accounts Payable	100	
	Inventory		100

Figure 8.10: Journal entry to record a vendor credit

In our example, the debit to **Accounts Payable** decreases the current liabilities on the balance sheet report by **$50**, and the credit to **Inventory** decreases the total inventory on the balance sheet by **$50**.

Managing recurring expenses

In this section, we will show you how to create a template for recurring (repeat) expenses. Most businesses purchase goods and services from the same vendors. For example, rent and utilities are examples of recurring expenses that are generally paid monthly. Instead of creating these expenses from scratch each month, you can create a recurring expense, which is a template you can save with the vendor, amount, account, and other pertinent information.

When you are ready to pay a recurring expense, you can schedule the expense to be recorded automatically on a certain day. You can manually generate the expense when you need to pay it or have QuickBooks send you an alert when it's time to make a payment. Using recurring expense templates will save you time and will reduce the amount of manual data entry required.

Follow these steps to create a recurring expense in QuickBooks:

1. Navigate to the gear icon and select **Recurring Transactions** from the **Lists** column, as indicated in *Figure 8.11*:

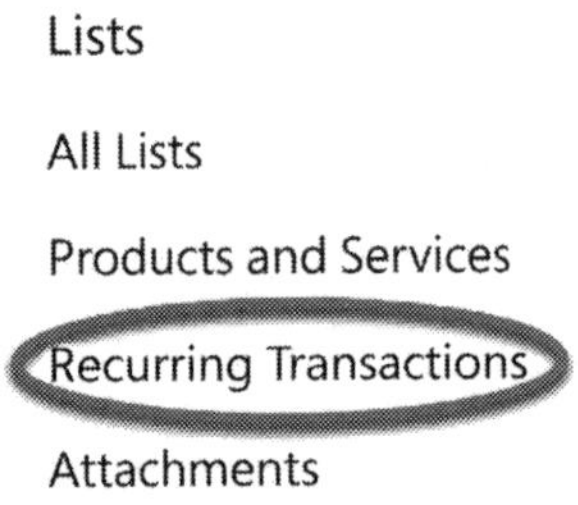

    Lists

    All Lists

    Products and Services

    Recurring Transactions

    Attachments

    Figure 8.11: Selecting Recurring Transactions from the Lists menu

2. Click the **New** button in the upper-right corner, as indicated in *Figure 8.12*:

    Figure 8.12: Clicking New to create a new recurring transactions template

3. Select the transaction type from the drop-down menu, as indicated in *Figure 8.13*, and click the **OK** button:

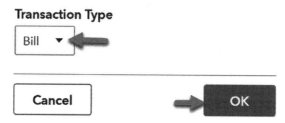

Figure 8.13: Selecting the transaction type for a recurring transactions template

4. You can create a recurring transaction for several different types of transactions besides a bill. The other options available from the drop-down include **Check**, **Credit card credit**, **Credit memo**, **Deposit**, **Estimate**, **Expense**, **Invoice**, **Journal entry**, and a few others. While the screens may differ slightly, they will be very similar to what you see in this example.

5. Click **OK** to select **Bill** and a blank recurring transactions template will appear, called **Recurring Bill**. Complete the fields as indicated in *Figure 8.14*:

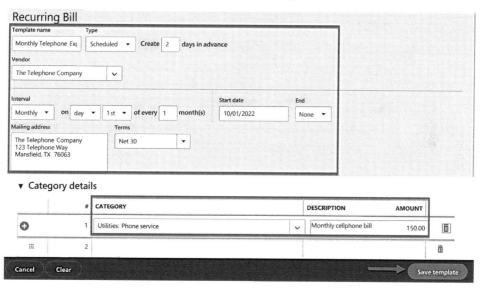

Figure 8.14: Completing the recurring transactions template

6.   The following is a brief description of the information required to complete the recurring transactions template:

- **Template name:** This field should include the type of expense or the payee's name. **Monthly Telephone Expense** is the template name in our example.

- **Type:** From the drop-down menu, you can select **Scheduled, Reminder,** or **Unscheduled. Scheduled** is the type of template we are setting up.

- **Create X days in advance:** QuickBooks will create the transaction in advance of the due date. 2 days in advance is selected in our example.

- **Vendor:** Select the payee from the drop-down menu. If you have not added vendors to QuickBooks, you can add a new vendor by selecting **Add new** in the drop-down field. **The Telephone Company** is the vendor in our example.

- **Interval:** This field refers to how often you would like to create this recurring transaction. The options are **Daily, Weekly, Monthly,** or **Yearly. Monthly** is the interval selected in our example.

- **Start date/End:** Select the date on which you would like to start using the recurring transaction and, if applicable, you can select an end date, or select **None.** The start date is **10/01/2022** and the end date is **None** in our example.

- **Mailing address:** If you plan to mail your payment, you need to add a mailing address to this field. However, if the payment is automatically deducted from your business checking account or made using a credit card, you can leave this field blank. The mailing address for The Telephone Company is **123 Telephone Way, Mansfield, TX 76063.**

- **Terms:** Include the payment terms for the vendor in this field. Payment terms are **Net 30** in our example.

- **CATEGORY:** From the drop-down menu, select the account that accurately describes the type of purchase made. The category is **Utilities: Phone service** for our example.

- **DESCRIPTION:** Include a brief description of the expense in this field. **Monthly cellphone bill** is the description in our case.

- **AMOUNT:** Enter the amount of the expense in this field. The amount is **$150.00** in our example.

7. Be sure to click **Save template** when you are done. After saving the template, the **Recurring Transactions** template list will appear, as indicated in *Figure 8.15*:

TEMPLATE NAME ▼	TYPE	TXN TYPE	INTERVAL	NEXT DATE	CUSTOMER/VENDOR	AMOUNT	ACTION
Monthly Telepho…	Scheduled	Bill	Every Month	10/01/2022	The Telephone Co…	150.00	Edit ▾

Figure 8.15: Recurring transactions template (expense)

8. In the **Recurring Transactions** template list, you will see the information previously entered in the template. The following info appears in *Figure 8.15* above:

- **TEMPLATE NAME: Monthly Telephone Expense**
- **TYPE: Scheduled**
- **TXN TYPE: Bill**
- **INTERVAL: Every Month**
- **NEXT DATE: 10/01/2022**
- **CUSTOMER/VENDOR: The Telephone Company**
- **AMOUNT: 150.00**
- **ACTION:** From the drop-down menu in this column, you can choose **Edit, Use, Duplicate, Pause, Skip**, or **Delete. Edit** simply allows you to make changes to the template; **Duplicate** allows you to create a template with the same information; **Pause** allows you to stop the recurring transaction temporarily; **Skip** allows you to skip a recurring transaction; and **Delete** allows you to delete the template.

9. In addition to creating recurring transactions such as bills to pay expenses, you can also create the following types of recurring transactions:

- **Check:** Payments made via check for products or services purchased.
- **Credit card credit:** Credit card credit is money that was refunded to you from a previous credit card charge. This could also be a cashback rebate given to you by your credit card merchant for meeting a certain spending threshold.
- **Credit memo:** A credit memo is issued to customers for a product they have returned or for services that were not provided.
- **Deposit:** A deposit is money received from customers, which is then deposited into your bank account. If you have customers who pay via wire transfer or **Automated Clearing House (ACH)** bank transfer on a periodic basis, you could set these deposits up as recurring.

- **Estimate:** An estimate is a bid or quote, created to provide customers with an approximate cost of your products or services.

- **Expense:** An expense is a payment for services received from a vendor/supplier.

- **Invoice:** An invoice is a sales form, used to record the sale of products or services provided on credit.

- **Journal entry:** A journal entry form is used to make adjustments to the financial statements before closing the books.

- **Refund:** A product returned by you or your customer will result in a refund of the payment that was made for the returned goods or unfulfilled services.

- **Sales receipt:** A sales receipt is used to record sales whereby payment is made immediately by the customer (for example, businesses such as clothing stores or restaurants).

- **Transfer:** A transfer is used to move money between bank accounts, such as business checking and savings accounts.

- **Vendor credit:** A vendor credit is a refund issued to you by a vendor supplier for a product you have returned or for services that were not performed.

Pro Tip: Recurring transactions are ideal for loan payments or other cash disbursements for which you may not receive a monthly bill.

Pro Tip #2: If you need to pay a bill that was unexpected or past due, *you don't need to enter it as a bill and then pay it.* Instead, you can pay it with a debit or credit card and categorize it when it comes into the banking center OR you can go directly to the check register and write a check. We will cover writing checks in the next section.

Writing checks

So far, we have discussed how to pay expenses by entering them as bills and paying them at a later date, and how to set up recurring expenses. A third way in which you can record expenses for your business is by writing checks. The benefit of writing checks directly in QuickBooks is that you don't have to waste time manually writing a check. Instead, you can create checks and print them directly from QuickBooks. This is ideal for vendors that typically don't accept debit or credit card payments.

Follow these steps to write checks in QuickBooks Online:

1. Click on the **+ New** button and select **Check** in the **Vendors** column, as indicated in *Figure 8.16*:

Figure 8.16: Navigating to Check

2. The following screenshot shows the fields of information to be completed in the **Check** form:

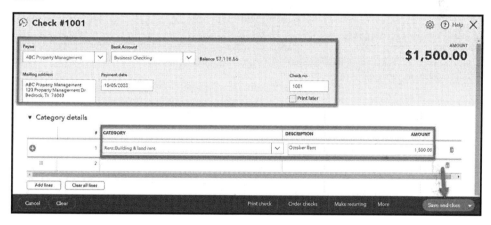

Figure 8.17: Completing the Check form

3. The following is a brief description of the information in the **Check** form:

    *   **Payee**: From the drop-down menu, select the vendor to whom you are making a payment. If you have not added vendors, you can do so by selecting **Add new** from the drop-down menu. **ABC Property Management** is the payee in our example.

    *   **Bank Account**: This field will automatically be populated with your business checking account. However, if you have more than one checking account, be sure to select the correct account from the drop-down menu. **Business Checking** is the bank account in our example.

- **Balance:** Based on the bank account selected, you will see the current balance (per QuickBooks) of the business checking account you have selected. The current balance in the business checking account is **$7,118.56** in our case.

- **Mailing address:** This field will automatically be populated with the information on file for the payee. In our case, the mailing address is **123 Property Management Rd, Bedrock, TX 76063.**

- **Payment date:** This date should reflect the check date. In our example, the payment date is **10/05/2023**

- **Check no.:** The check number will automatically be populated with the next available check number. The check number is **1001** in our example.

> **Pro Tip:** You can also use the **Check** form to record expenses paid with a debit card. Instead of entering a check number in the **Check no.** field, you would use **DB** or **Debit**, indicating the expense was paid with a debit card. To record ACH transactions, you would put **ACH** in the check number field.

- **CATEGORY:** Select the category (account) that best describes the items purchased. In our example, the category is **Rent: Building & land rent**.

- **DESCRIPTION:** Enter a detailed description of the items purchased. **October Rent** is the description in our example.

- **AMOUNT:** Enter the amount of the purchase. The amount in our example is **1,500.00**.

When entering a check into QuickBooks, it can have an impact on accounts that appear on both the balance sheet and the profit and loss (income statement). The balance sheet will always be affected because the bank account is included in the assets section of the balance sheet. However, the profit and loss will only be affected if you purchase an expense. Otherwise, if you purchase a product for resale (inventory), it will only have an impact on the balance sheet.

Figure 8.18 shows the journal entry recorded for the check in *Figure 8.17*:

Date	Account Name	Debit	Credit
10/5/2023	Rent Expense	1500	
	Business Checking		1500

Figure 8.18: Journal entry to record payment of a bill by check

In our example, **Rent Expense** increased by **$1,500**, which increases expenses on the profit and loss (income statement). The **Business Checking** account decreased by **$1,500**, which means assets have gone down on the balance sheet report.

After entering a check, you can choose to print the check immediately, or wait and print a batch of checks later on. In the next section, we will show you how to print checks.

Printing checks

In order to print checks, you must purchase check stock that is compatible with QuickBooks Online. You can order checks from a variety of places, such as your financial institution, or directly from Intuit. Visit the *Intuit Checks and Supplies* (`https://intuitmarket.intuit.com/checks`) website to learn more.

Follow these steps to print checks:

1. Click on the **+ New** button and select **Print Checks** in the **Vendors** column, as indicated in *Figure 8.19*:

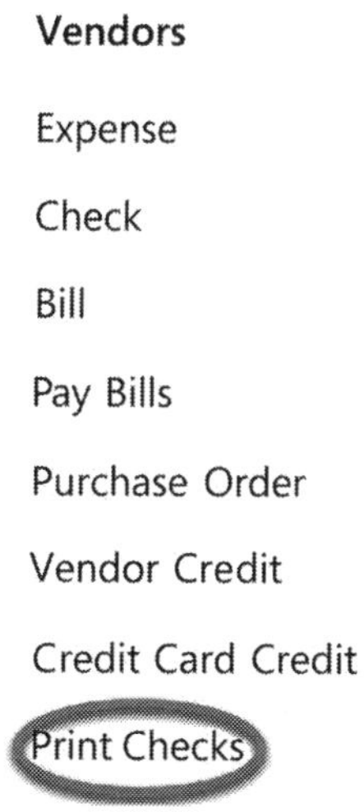

Vendors

Expense

Check

Bill

Pay Bills

Purchase Order

Vendor Credit

Credit Card Credit

Print Checks

Figure 8.19: Navigating to Print Checks

2. Follow the steps on the next screen to ensure that your printer is set up properly:

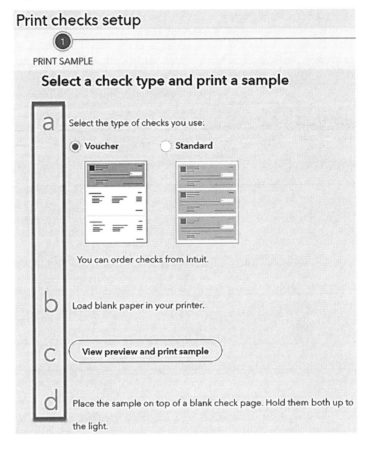

Figure 8.20: Selecting the check type for printing checks

The following is a brief description of the steps:

a. **Select the type of checks you use**: There are two types of checks, **Voucher** and **Standard**. The **Voucher** check includes one check per page and two printed vouchers (one for you and one for the payee). The **Standard** check has three checks per page and no voucher.

Pro Tip: A voucher is a printout of the payment details, including bill number, amount, and check number.

b. **Load blank paper in your printer**: Before loading real check stock, run a test using blank paper. Draw an arrow on the top of the first sheet of paper to see how the information will print so that you know how to load the check stock in your printer.

c. **View preview and print sample**: You can preview a sample check to see whether it is aligned properly. If not, follow the on-screen instructions to fix any issues before using real check stock. Checks will print to a preview screen where you can select your printer.

 Pro Tip: To recap the steps on writing and printing checks in QuickBooks, watch this Intuit video tutorial: `https://quickbooks.intuit.com/learn-support/en-us/write-checks/how-to-record-print-checks/00/344866`.

As discussed, printing checks directly from QuickBooks will save you time when you reconcile your bank account. Since expenses paid with a check are automatically recorded in QuickBooks when you save the check, you won't have to worry about manually entering them later on. One way to have quick access to source documents is to attach receipts and bills to transactions by using the capture and categorize receipts feature. We will discuss this shortly.

 Pro Tip: Let's say you have pizza delivered to the office and you need to quickly print one check. Click the **+ New** button, select **Check**, enter the payment details, and select **Print check** at the bottom of the screen.

Editing, voiding, and deleting expenses

Like most transactions in QuickBooks, you can edit bills up until they are paid. However, after you have paid a bill, you will need to either record a credit memo if you overpaid or request a new bill if you underpaid. To edit a bill, you need to go to the Vendor Center, select the vendor, and then click on the bill you wish to make changes to. After making the necessary changes, save the bill and close it.

You can also edit checks in a similar manner. As long as you have not printed the check, you can make any changes necessary. Navigate to the check register, locate the check, and make the necessary changes. After you have printed a check, you will need to void it if it is incorrect. From the check register, select the check that needs to be voided. Click the **Edit** option and the check will display on your screen.

At the very bottom of the page, you will see a tab that says **More**; click on it and the following menu will appear:

Figure 8.21: Reaching the option for voiding an expense from the More button

For expenses in general, if you have not closed the books or reconciled the bank account for the period, you can make changes to expenses that were previously recorded.

If you have closed the books or reconciled the bank account for the period, you *cannot* make changes to the transaction date or amount. If a correction to the books is required, you will need to consult with your accountant to discuss recording a journal entry. See *Chapter 15, Closing the Books in QuickBooks Online*, to learn more about journal entries.

Capturing and categorizing receipts and bills

Receipt capture allows you to attach receipts and bills to transactions in QuickBooks. As a result, you will be able to quickly access source documents when needed. This feature works in two different ways. First, you can attach receipts and bills to transactions previously entered into QuickBooks Online. Second, you can use receipt capture to record a transaction for the first time. Of course, you can use both methods interchangeably.

Perform the following steps to capture a receipt or bill:

1. Navigate to **Transactions** and select **Receipts**.

2. The following screen will appear (make sure you are on the **Receipts** tab, as indicated here):

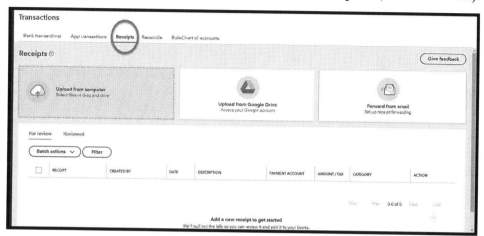

Figure 8.22: Uploading receipts to QBO

3. There are three options available to capture receipts:

    -   **Upload from computer**: If the bill or receipt is saved to your computer, select this option and navigate to where the receipt or bill is located on your computer.

    -   **Upload from Google Drive**: If the receipt/bill is located in your Google Drive account, you can access it by clicking on this icon and following the on-screen instructions to locate the file in Google Drive.

    -   **Forward from email**: By selecting this option, QuickBooks will take you through a few setup screens to create a custom email address that can be used to forward receipts and bills to QuickBooks.

 Pro Tip: Keep in mind that for each of the receipt capture options, there should only be *one receipt per file*. If you try to include more than one receipt in a file, QuickBooks will not be able to process the receipt capture.

4. Once you add receipts to QuickBooks, they will show up in the **For review** section just below the receipt capture options, as follows:

Figure 8.23: Reviewing receipts uploaded in QBO

5. You can click on the review link in the **ACTION** column located on the far right and the following info will display:

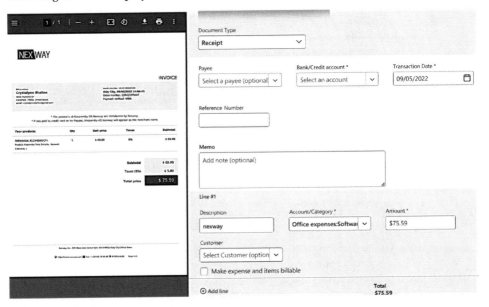

Figure 8.24: Reviewing a selected receipt in QBO

6. Complete any empty fields and review the information for accuracy in the fields that QuickBooks has automatically completed. Once you are satisfied with the information, you can save it and it will be recorded in your books.

Pro Tip: You can also add receipts to transactions using the paperclip (**Attachments**) feature located at the bottom of the screen when you have an individual transaction open such as a bill:

Figure 8.25: Button for attaching a receipt to a transaction

To summarize, we have covered how to use the capture and categorize receipts and bills feature, which allows you to attach source documents such as bills to existing transactions. In addition, you can create new transactions using this feature, which will save you the time you normally would have spent entering the data manually.

Summary

In this chapter, we have shown you how to enter and pay your bills, how to enter vendor credits, how to manage recurring expenses, how to write checks, and how to print checks. We also covered the three ways in which you can upload bills and receipts to QuickBooks.

Having a good understanding of the various options you have to record your expenses will ensure that you have recorded them properly. By recording your expenses in a timely manner, you have a good idea of what your obligations are, which helps you to stay on top of your cash outflow.

In the next chapter, we will show you how to reduce or eliminate the need to manually enter bank and credit card transactions by uploading transactions automatically into QuickBooks using bank feeds.

The primary difference between expense transactions and bank feed transactions is that expense transactions are typically entered manually through bills, checks, recurring expenses, and receipt capture, whereas bank feeds do not require manual data entry. Instead, your bank account is connected to QuickBooks and bank transactions automatically "feed" into the Banking Center in QuickBooks, saving you time.

Join our community on Discord

Join our community's Discord space for discussions with the authors and other readers:

`https://packt.link/quickbooks`

9

Reconciling Uploaded Bank and Credit Card Transactions

In *Chapter 4, Customizing QuickBooks for Your Business*, we showed you how to connect bank and credit card accounts to **QuickBooks Online (QBO)** to reduce the amount of time you spend manually entering data. Reviewing these transactions will give you important insight into where you are spending your money. While many business owners can tell you who their top 5 customers are, they typically don't know what their top 5 expenses are.

In this chapter, we will show you how to manage bank and credit card transactions that have been uploaded to QuickBooks. Dealing with fraudulent transactions has become a reality for many people. On more than one occasion, I received a call from my financial institution asking me to verify purchases that, for one reason or another, sent a red flag to my bank because they were "out of the norm" for me or made internationally. Reconciling your bank and credit card accounts often will help you to identify unauthorized purchases that your financial institution does not catch. Since there is a time limit on when you can dispute these charges, it's important to be aware of them as soon as possible.

When bank and credit card transactions are uploaded, they are organized in the **Banking Center**. This area serves as a holding place where transactions can be reviewed before they are recorded in your books. Before these transactions can be recorded in QuickBooks, you must review them. This includes matching them with transactions that have already been entered into QuickBooks, adding payee or category information, and providing any additional details to help identify each transaction. We will also show you how bank rules can help to reduce the number of transactions requiring manual review. Last but not least, we will show you how to reconcile your accounts.

Reconciling is the process of making sure your QuickBooks data matches the monthly statements provided by your financial institution. By reconciling often, you can catch errors made by the bank or credit card company and catch fraudulent transactions a lot sooner.

In this chapter, we will cover the following topics:

- Overview of the Banking Center
- Matching transactions
- Editing banking transactions
- Creating and using bank rules
- Reconciling accounts
- Troubleshooting tips

By the end of this chapter, you will have a solid understanding of how the Banking Center works. You will know how to match transactions, and how to edit transactions by adding a memo or changing the category. You will be more efficient with managing banking transactions by using bank rules. Finally, you will be confident in reconciling your accounts with the statements received from your financial institution. We will start by giving you an overview of the Banking Center, which is where you will find uploaded bank and credit card transactions.

 The US edition of QBO was used to create this book. If you are using a version that is outside of the United States, results may differ.

Overview of the Banking Center

The Banking Center is where you can manage bank and credit card transactions that have been uploaded into QuickBooks from your financial institution. These transactions require your review before they are recorded in your books.

At the very top of the page, you will see tiles that represent bank and credit card accounts you have added to QuickBooks. On each tile, you will find the name of the account, the current balance (per your financial institution), the current balance (per QuickBooks), and the number of transactions that require review before they can be recorded in a QuickBooks account register.

Follow these steps to navigate to the Banking Center:

1. Click on the **Transactions** tab, located on the left menu bar, and select **Bank transactions**, as indicated in *Figure 9.1*:

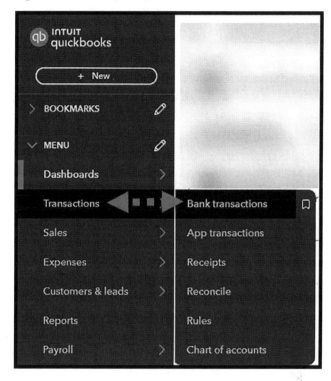

Figure 9.1: Navigating to the Banking Center

2. The Banking Center will appear, as indicated in *Figure 9.2*:

Figure 9.2: Bank and credit card accounts in the Banking Center

Pro Tip: If you have not connected a bank or credit card account to Quick-Books, your screen will not appear as it does in *Figure 9.2*. Instead, you will be given the option to **Connect account** or **Upload transactions**, as shown in *Figure 9.3* below:

Banking

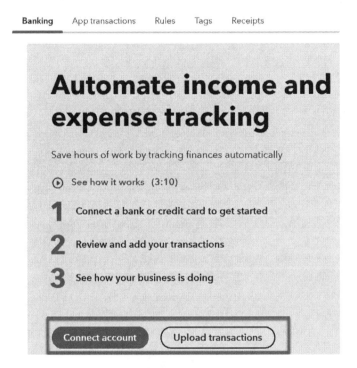

Figure 9.3: Option to connect accounts in the Banking Center

3. The following is a brief description of the information you will find in the Banking Center:

    -   **Bank account name:** At the very top of each tile, you will find the name of the account (for example, **Checking**, **Savings**, or **Mastercard**).

    -   **BANK BALANCE:** The balance of the account, per your financial institution, will be displayed below the bank account name.

- **IN QUICKBOOKS**: The balance of the account, per QuickBooks, will be displayed right below the bank balance.

- **Transactions for review**: Transactions that have been uploaded from your financial institution and are pending your review will be indicated in the lower-right corner of each tile. In the screenshot in *Figure 9.2*, these numbers are **25**, **1**, and **7**.

Pro Tip: If the bank balance and the balance in QuickBooks match, this means all uploaded transactions have been reviewed. As a result, you will not see a number in the lower-right corner of the tile. If the balances do not match and you don't have any transactions in the **For review** tab, that does not necessarily mean that you are missing something. A difference in the two balances can be from outstanding items that have not yet cleared the bank due to timing differences, or transactions that have not yet been uploaded to QBO.

If you imported your transactions into QuickBooks from a CSV file instead of connecting your bank and credit card accounts to QuickBooks, you will only see a QuickBooks balance (not a bank balance) for each account. I recommend reviewing transactions on a daily or weekly basis so that you don't get too far behind.

Now that we have shown you how to navigate the Banking Center so you can review and manage bank and credit card transactions, you are ready to take action on the uploaded transactions. In the next section, we will show you how QuickBooks can save you time by matching uploaded transactions with transactions previously entered into QuickBooks.

Matching transactions

In this section, we will cover a process called **matching transactions**. QuickBooks will automatically attempt to match transactions that have been uploaded into QuickBooks with transactions that have already been recorded in QuickBooks. This process can help you save the time you would normally have spent trying to match transactions manually. We will show you how this process works by going through examples.

In the **For review** tab, we can see that QuickBooks has attempted to match three transactions that were previously entered into QuickBooks:

Figure 9.4: Banking transactions in the For review tab

The following is a brief explanation of the preceding three transactions for which QuickBooks has found a match:

- **Deposit** for **$868.15**: QuickBooks has found a deposit in the file for **$868.15** (dated **09/03/21**), which matches a deposit the bank has uploaded to the Banking Center for **$868.15**. If these transactions are one and the same, simply click **Match** in the far-right column. This item will be recorded in QuickBooks and moved from the **For review** tab to the **Categorized** tab.

- **Check** for **$228.75**: QuickBooks has identified Check 75 for **$228.75**, which matches a withdrawal uploaded from the bank for the same amount. If these transactions are one and the same, simply click **Match** in the far-right column. This item will be recorded in QuickBooks and moved from the **For review** tab to the **Categorized** tab.

- **Bill Payment** for **$114.09**: QuickBooks has found a bill payment for **$114.09**, which matches a withdrawal uploaded from the bank for the same amount. If these transactions are one and the same, simply click **Match** in the far-right column. This item will be recorded in QuickBooks and moved from the **For review** tab to the **Categorized** tab.

Keep in mind that if you don't match transactions that are truly one and the same, you will duplicate them in your books by adding them again. In the three examples above, if we did not match these transactions and instead added them, they would be recorded in QBO twice. This will result in you being unable to reconcile your accounts to the bank/credit card statements.

Pro Tip: Transfers between bank accounts are also very common. If both bank accounts are connected to QuickBooks, it will most likely automatically match these bank transfers for you. Be sure to verify the accounts are correct before recording in QuickBooks.

As mentioned previously, when you click **Match**, these items will move from the **For review** tab to the **Categorized** tab in the Banking Center. These items will also be marked as cleared in QuickBooks, which will be important when we get ready to reconcile these accounts later on. If QuickBooks has not found the right match, you can replace it with the correct match.

To change the match recommended by QuickBooks, click on the transaction, and then click on the **Find other matches** button, as indicated in *Figure 9.5*:

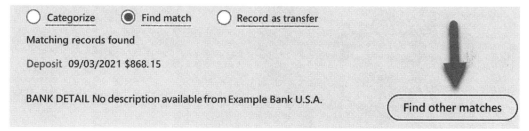

Figure 9.5: Matching transactions in the Banking Center

In addition to matching transactions, you will need to provide additional information, such as the payee and category (the account), before the transaction can be recorded in QuickBooks. Banking transactions that have not been matched will remain in the Banking Center to be categorized and added to your books. Some examples are debit card and **Automated Clearing House (ACH)** transactions, and manual or handwritten checks.

Now that we have shown you how matching transactions works and how you can post a matching transaction with just a few clicks, we will cover how to make any necessary changes to recorded transactions. In the next section, we will cover how to edit banking transactions.

Editing banking transactions

When you first start adding banking transactions to QuickBooks, you will need to review each transaction to ensure it has a proper payee (vendor) or customer and account category assigned to it. As you begin to repeat transactions, QuickBooks will remember how a transaction was recorded previously, and it will automatically assign the payee (vendor) and account category for expenses. Be sure to verify that everything is correct before recording the transaction in QuickBooks.

Follow these steps to edit banking transactions in the Banking Center:

1. From the left menu bar, select **Transactions** and then **Bank transactions**, as indicated in *Figure 9.6*:

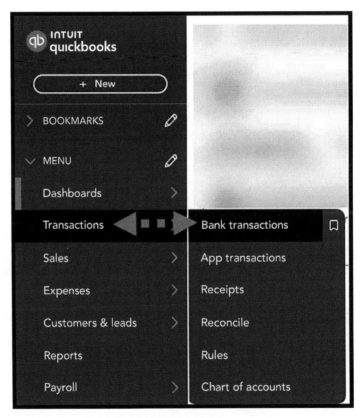

Figure 9.6: Navigating to the Banking Center

2. Click on the **For review** tab, as indicated in *Figure 9.7*:

Figure 9.7: The For review tab in the Banking Center

3. Click anywhere within any of the banking transactions listed to make any necessary changes, as indicated in *Figure 9.8*:

Transactions

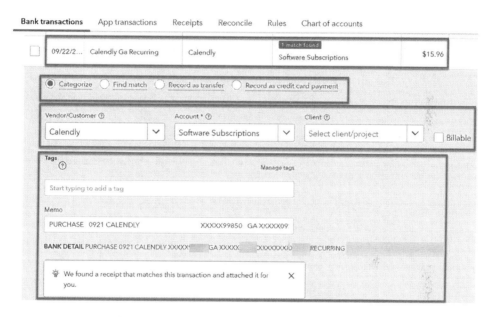

Figure 9.8: Editing a transaction in the Banking Center

4. You will find the following information in the editing a banking transaction window:

    - **Vendor/Customer**: For withdrawals, select the payee (vendor) from the drop-down menu. For deposits/receipt of customer payments, select the customer. If it is a new vendor or customer, you can click **Add new** from the drop-down menu and add them here. It is important to complete this field for reporting purposes, such as 1099 preparation.

    - **Account** (category): From the drop-down menu, select the account (category) that best describes the transaction you are recording (that is, **Fuel**, **Software Subscriptions**, **Office Supplies**, or something else).

- **Client**: From the drop-down menu, select a client/project that the transaction is associated with, if applicable. To the right of this field is a box to mark the transaction as billable. If this is something you need to bill a client back for, be sure to click the **Billable** box.

- **Tags**: Use tags to earmark or flag specific types of income or expenses you choose to keep tabs on. In *Chapter 2, Company File Setup*, we discussed how tags can be used.

- **Memo**: The bank details will generally appear in this field. This could be the name of the merchant. You can edit this information as needed, so be sure to do so since this information will appear on reports.

- **BANK DETAIL**: This information comes directly from the financial institution. It is used to help you identify what the transaction is for. You will not be able to edit this information.

- **Receipt notification**: Below the bank detail information, you may see a notification similar to the one in *Figure 9.8*: **We found a receipt that matches this transaction and attached it for you**. If you use the receipt capture feature, when the corresponding transaction is uploaded from the bank, it will match the two together. This will allow you to link the actual receipt to the transaction. To ensure QBO has correctly identified a match, click on the attachment to view the receipt. If it is not a match, you can remove the receipt by clicking the **X** at the end of the filename, as shown in *Figure 9.8*. You can learn more about how receipt capture works in *Chapter 8, Recording Expenses in QuickBooks Online*.

- **Split**: To the left of the **Add** button is a **Split** transaction button. A split transaction allows you to assign more than one category (account) to a transaction. For example, let's say you purchased an office chair that cost $300. The total bill was $325, which includes a shipping charge. You can split this bill by putting $300 into the **office expenses** category and $25 into the **shipping/freight expenses** category.

- **Add**: Once all fields are complete, click on the **Add** button to record this transaction in the check or credit card register in QuickBooks. When you add this transaction to QBO, it will move over to the **Categorized** tab within the Banking Center.

5. Watch this Intuit video tutorial for a recap of how to categorize banking transactions: `https://quickbooks.intuit.com/learn-support/en-us/bank-transactions/adding-transactions-from-your-bank-credit-card/00/344865`.

As discussed, QuickBooks will automatically recall the vendor or customer and category (account) that was previously used.

If you realize that a transaction that you previously accepted and moved over to the **Categorized** tab needs to be adjusted, you can easily edit this transaction as follows:

1. Click on the **Categorized** tab, locate the transaction, and click on the **Undo** option in the far-right column, as indicated in *Figure 9.9*:

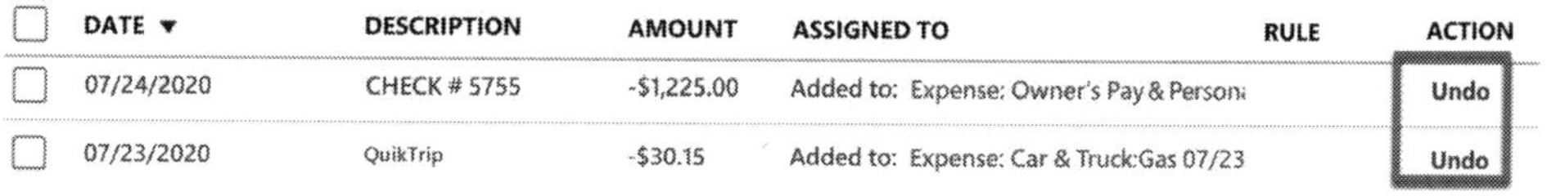

DATE ▼	DESCRIPTION	AMOUNT	ASSIGNED TO	RULE	ACTION
07/24/2020	CHECK # 5755	-$1,225.00	Added to: Expense: Owner's Pay & Person:		Undo
07/23/2020	QuikTrip	-$30.15	Added to: Expense: Car & Truck:Gas 07/23		Undo

Figure 9.9: Editing a transaction previously accepted in the Banking Center

2. The transaction will move back to the **For review** tab as follows:

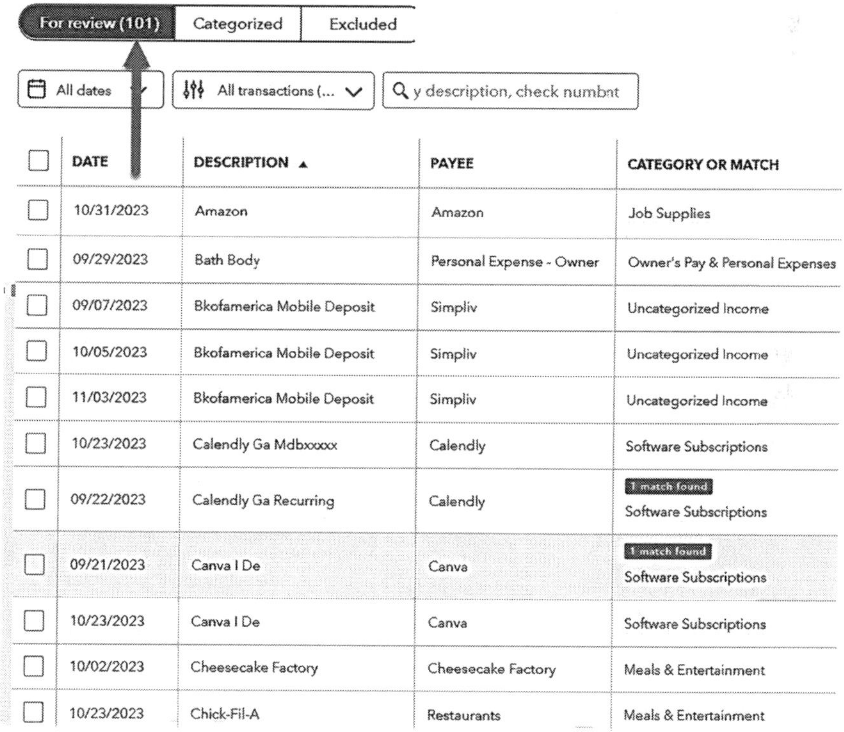

	For review (101)	Categorized	Excluded

📅 All dates ▾   ⫶↓↑⫶ All transactions (... ▾   🔍 y description, check numbt

	DATE	DESCRIPTION ▲	PAYEE	CATEGORY OR MATCH
☐	10/31/2023	Amazon	Amazon	Job Supplies
☐	09/29/2023	Bath Body	Personal Expense - Owner	Owner's Pay & Personal Expenses
☐	09/07/2023	Bkofamerica Mobile Deposit	Simpliv	Uncategorized Income
☐	10/05/2023	Bkofamerica Mobile Deposit	Simpliv	Uncategorized Income
☐	11/03/2023	Bkofamerica Mobile Deposit	Simpliv	Uncategorized Income
☐	10/23/2023	Calendly Ga Mdbxxxxx	Calendly	Software Subscriptions
☐	09/22/2023	Calendly Ga Recurring	Calendly	1 match found Software Subscriptions
☐	09/21/2023	Canva I De	Canva	1 match found Software Subscriptions
☐	10/23/2023	Canva I De	Canva	Software Subscriptions
☐	10/02/2023	Cheesecake Factory	Cheesecake Factory	Meals & Entertainment
☐	10/23/2023	Chick-Fil-A	Restaurants	Meals & Entertainment

Figure 9.10: The For review tab in the Banking Center

3. You can click once on any transaction to change the category or match as well as editing other fields in the transaction, as indicated in *Figure 9.10*.

Pro Tip: Next to the **Categorized** tab is the **Excluded** tab. This tab is used to handle transactions you do not want posted in QuickBooks. For example, if a duplicate transaction was uploaded into QuickBooks (which is rare, but does happen), you would only want to post one of the transactions that were uploaded. Since you are not able to delete uploaded transactions, simply mark it as excluded and it will move from the **For review** tab to the **Excluded** tab. Please note that transactions that appear in the **Excluded** tab are *not recorded* in your books and, therefore, have no impact on the financial statements.

Now that we have shown you how to modify banking transactions and utilize the auto-recall feature, we will introduce you to bank rules in the next section. Using bank rules is the best way to ensure the accuracy of transactions recorded. We will discuss how to create and use bank rules in the next section.

Understanding bank rules

Bank rules are a list of conditions that must be met in order for QuickBooks to automatically assign a payee, account (category), class, and location to upload banking transactions to. Bank rules will apply only to bank or credit card transactions in the **For review** tab of the Banking Center. Since most businesses have the same transactions that take place month after month, using bank rules can save you the time you would have spent reviewing transactions in the Banking Center before they can be recorded in QuickBooks.

Follow these steps to create a bank rule:

1. Click on **Transactions** from the left menu and select **Rules**, as indicated in *Figure 9.11*:

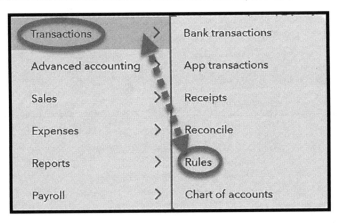

Figure 9.11: Navigating to bank rules

2. Click on the **New rule** button, as indicated in *Figure 9.12*:

Figure 9.12: Creating a new bank rule

3. The following screen will appear:

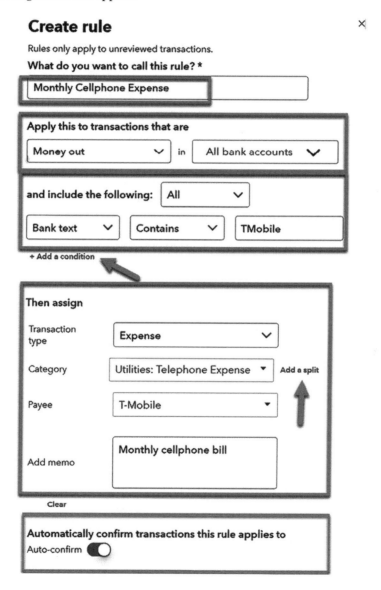

Figure 9.13: Completing the fields required to create a new bank rule

4. The following is a brief explanation of the fields to complete for a new bank rule:

- **What do you want to call this rule?**: The first field allows you to assign a name to the rule. In our example, we are using **Monthly Cellphone Expense**.

- **Apply this to transactions that are**: You can apply rules based on **Money out** or **Money in**, and choose to apply this to **All bank accounts** or a specific bank account. If you have multiple accounts, you can set up rules that are specific to a bank account even when a vendor is paid using multiple bank accounts.

- **Conditions**: You can create several conditions based on **Bank text**, **Description**, or **Amount**. In our example, we have selected **Bank text**.

- **Contains/Doesn't contain/Is exactly**: In the next field, you can select whether the transaction contains, doesn't contain, or is exactly the information that you enter into the next field.

- **Text box**: This field contains text that will appear either in the **Bank text** or **Description** field when the transaction is uploaded into QuickBooks. If you selected the amount as part of your criteria, then you will enter an amount in this field. In our text box, we have entered **T-Mobile**, which is the name of the payee.

- You can click the **Add a condition** link to add multiple conditions. Based on the conditions you have set, QuickBooks will automatically assign a category to the transaction using the information in the next section.

- **Transaction type**: From the drop-down menu, select the type of transaction for which you are creating this rule. In our example, this is **Expense**.

- **Payee**: From the drop-down menu, select the payee for this rule. In our example, the payee is **T-Mobile**.

- **Category**: From the drop-down menu, select the category (account) that best describes the purchase. In our example, we have selected **Utilities: Telephone Expense**.

- **Add a split**: If the transaction should be split between two or more accounts (categories), you can click the **Add a split** link and indicate the accounts that should be used.

- **Add memo**: This field is optional but can be used to provide additional details about the transaction. In our example, we have used **Monthly cellphone bill**.

Now that you have a better idea of how bank rules work and how to create them, in the next section, we will show you how to apply these bank rules to banking transactions.

Pro Tip: If you have multiple bank and credit card accounts that use the same vendor, and you need to record the transactions to different office locations, then you will need to set up rules specific to that bank or credit card account. For example, while the category might be the same, such as **Telephone Expense**, you would still need to set up a rule to categorize one bill to the Texas office and one bill to the California office.

How do you want to apply this rule?

At the bottom of this page is the **Automatically confirm transactions this rule applies to** option. By selecting this auto-confirmation option, QuickBooks will automatically assign the category (account) based on your selections at the top of the page and will automatically record the transaction in QuickBooks without the need to review it first. If you would prefer to review all transactions before they are recorded, turn this feature off.

Pro Tip: I recommend that you review all banking transactions before they are recorded in QuickBooks. After reviewing transactions for the first couple of months, once you are comfortable they are being categorized correctly, you can always change the bank rules to **Auto-categorize and auto-add** later on.

If set up properly, bank rules can automatically categorize and record 80% or more of your bank and credit card transactions. If you have a lot of transactions coming through, this will save you hours of time, which you can spend on other aspects of your business.

Pro Tip: You can sort the transactions by column. It can be beneficial to sort by description or payee to group similar transactions and categorize them in a batch.

Start with one bank rule to see how it works, and then add more as you get comfortable with using them. For example, you could set up a bank rule for your monthly cellphone expenses to start. This type of expense typically is for the same amount and payee and occurs monthly. Using bank rules will also help to expedite the reconciliation of bank and credit card accounts. We will discuss this in more detail in the following section.

Reconciling accounts

Reconciling is the process of making sure your QuickBooks records agree with your bank and credit card statements. At a minimum, reconciling should take place on a monthly basis, if not more often. One of the benefits of using cloud-based accounting software such as QBO is that your banking information is uploaded on a daily basis. This means that you could reconcile as often as weekly, or even daily. There is no need to wait until the bank statement arrives at the end of the month to reconcile your accounts.

Follow these steps to reconcile a bank or credit card account:

1. From the gear icon, select **Reconcile**, as indicated in *Figure 9.14*:

Figure 9.14: Navigating to Reconcile in QBO

2. The **Reconcile** window will appear, as indicated in *Figure 9.15*:

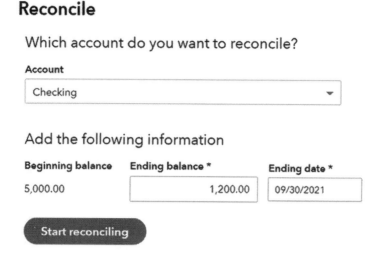

Figure 9.15: Initial reconciliation window

3. If a transaction that was previously reconciled has been changed, QuickBooks will include a message on this screen. Be sure to follow the onscreen instructions to troubleshoot the imbalanced transaction. This issue must be addressed before proceeding with the current reconciliation.

4. The fields that need to be completed in the reconciliation window shown in *Figure 9.15* are as follows:

    *   **Account:** From the drop-down menu, select the bank or credit card account you want to reconcile.

    *   **Beginning balance:** This field will automatically be populated with the ending balance of the previous month. If you have never reconciled the account before, the balance in this field will be the opening balance entered when you created the account in QuickBooks.

    *   **Ending balance:** Enter the ending balance of the bank or credit card statement you are reconciling.

    *   **Ending date:** Enter the ending date on the bank or credit card statement you are reconciling.

5. Click the **Start reconciling** button once all fields have been completed.

6. On the next screen, the following information will appear. The following is a snapshot of the header information when reconciling accounts:

Figure 9.16: Header information in the reconciliation window

7. A brief description of the information found in the header window is as follows:

    -   **STATEMENT ENDING BALANCE:** This field will automatically be populated with the statement ending balance entered on the preceding start reconciliation screen.

    -   **CLEARED BALANCE:** This field will summarize all the transactions that have cleared on your bank or credit card statement.

    -   **BEGINNING BALANCE:** This field will automatically be populated from the prior month's reconciliation. If you have not reconciled this account previously, it will display the beginning balance entered when the account was created in Quick-Books.

    -   **PAYMENTS:** This field will summarize all of the payments/withdrawals that have cleared on your bank or credit card statement.

    -   **DEPOSITS:** This field will summarize all of the deposits that have cleared on your bank or credit card statement.

    -   **DIFFERENCE:** The difference between the statement ending balance and the cleared balance will appear in this field. The goal is to reach a difference of zero. Zero indicates all items that have cleared your bank or credit card statement have been recorded in QuickBooks.

8. The following is a snapshot of the bank and credit card information that appears after the header information:

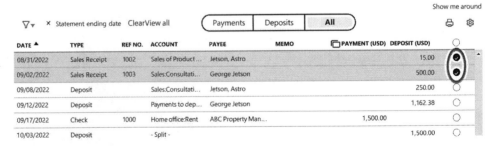

Figure 9.17: Bank and credit card details listed in the reconciliation window

9. The following is a brief explanation of the details in the reconciliation window shown in the preceding screenshot:

- **Transaction type**: At the top of the screen, there are three tabs: **Payments**, **Deposits**, and **All**. You can click on one of the first two tabs to filter by a specific transaction type, or you can select **All**.

- **Transaction details**: The date, transaction type, reference number, category (account), payee, memo, and amount of each transaction that has been recorded in QuickBooks are listed in this section.

10. If a transaction appears on your bank or credit card statement, you need to put a checkmark in the radio button (located in the far-right column) to mark it as cleared in QuickBooks. Each time you mark a transaction as cleared, it will be included in the cleared balance in the header section shown previously. As discussed, after marking all items that have cleared your bank or credit card statement, you should have a difference of zero. If you do not, you are either missing a transaction in QuickBooks or you may have marked a transaction as cleared that does not appear on your statement.

11. Once your difference equals zero, you can click the **Finish now** button to generate the bank reconciliation reports. Click on the drop-down arrow next to the **Save for later** button, as indicated in *Figure 9.18*:

Figure 9.18: The Finish now button

 Pro Tip: If you are having trouble reconciling to a difference of zero, compare the deposit total in the header window to the deposit total on your bank statement. If it matches, then you know there is an issue with withdrawals. If it doesn't match, then you know there is an issue with deposits. Do the same comparison on the withdrawal side. You could be out of balance with both, or with just one transaction type. In addition, if your difference is divisible by nine, it could be a transposition error.

Pro Tip 2: Do not click the **Finish now** button if you don't have a difference of zero. Instead, click the **Save for later** option. You can always come back and resume the reconciliation from where you left off.

12. After successfully reconciling accounts, be sure to save the summary and detail bank reconciliation reports. They will be made available after you complete the bank reconciliation. Bank reconciliation reports are one of several reports that auditors will request during an audit, so it is very important to save these reports to your computer. If you forget to save the reports, you can always access them from within the Banking Center. You can also keep copies of your monthly statements saved in QBO.

13. For a step-by-step recap of how to reconcile an account, watch this Intuit video tutorial: https://quickbooks.intuit.com/learn-support/en-us/banking-topics/reconcile-an-account-in-quickbooks-online/00/186470.

After reconciling an account, you may discover that you need to edit a transaction that was previously reconciled. Be sure that you don't change the amount; otherwise, your account will be out of balance. However, you can edit the category (account) and description fields easily:

1. Navigate to the chart of accounts and click on the **View register** link next to the bank account, as indicated in *Figure 9.19*:

NAME	TYPE ▲	DETAIL TYPE	QUICKBOOKS BALANCE	BANK BALANCE	ACTION
Business Checking	Bank	Checking	15,980.00		View register ▼
Business Savings	Bank	Savings	8,309.00		View register ▼

Figure 9.19: Editing a transaction that was previously reconciled

2. Make the necessary edits and save your changes.

As discussed, reconciling your accounts will help to ensure you haven't accidentally omitted recording any transactions. Plus, it will help you to ensure that your books agree with your financial institution's records. It's important to reconcile all of your bank and credit card accounts on a monthly basis (or more frequently, if possible), in order to catch errors made by the bank or to identify fraudulent transactions.

Troubleshooting tips for reconciling bank and credit card accounts

There will be times when you might encounter an issue with reconciling your bank or credit card statements to QBO. If you are having trouble with getting to a $0.00 difference as shown in step 3 above, here are a few troubleshooting tips you can try:

1. Narrow the search down to the transaction type. To do this, compare the total withdrawals on the bank/credit card statement to the total payments in the reconciliation window, as shown below:

Figure 9.20: Reviewing total payments and total deposits

2. If they do not match, there is an issue with a payment (withdrawal). Do the same comparison for the deposits. Compare the total deposits on the bank statement to the deposits shown in the reconciliation window. If they do not match, you have an issue with deposits.

3. If you discover that you are out of balance for both the payments (withdrawals) and the deposits, tackle them separately. In other words, balance the withdrawals first and then move on to deposits, or vice versa.

4. Look for the exact dollar amount that you are out of balance by. For example, in *Figure 9.21* below, the difference is $3,899.00:

Figure 9.21: Reviewing the difference in reconciling window

In our example, we would look for this amount on the bank statement and within the reconciling window for payments and deposits.

5. Double-check that the statement ending balance, beginning balance, and statement ending date are correct. If you need to make any corrections, click on the **Edit info** button shown in *Figure 9.21* to make the necessary changes.

6. Verify that all of the transactions you have selected in the reconciliation window are actually on the bank/credit card statement. If not, you need to deselect them. It is possible that there is a timing difference, which means they will appear on the statement in the following month.

7. If you find that there is a transaction listed on the bank statement but it is not showing up in QuickBooks, you will need to go to the Banking Center to see if it is listed there. If so, complete the necessary fields (payee, category) to add the transaction. When you return to the reconciliation window, it should be listed there, but you will need to select it to update the totals.

8. If you have been at it for a while, I recommend that you take a break. You can click the **Save for later** option and it will save your work so that you can pick up where you left off. Sometimes, taking a breather and coming back can help you spot what's causing the difference.

Summary

In this chapter, we have discussed how to manage uploaded bank and credit card transactions. You have learned how to match uploaded transactions with transactions previously recorded in QuickBooks. You now know how to make changes to transactions so that the correct payee and category (account) are recorded. You have also learned how to create bank rules in order to reduce the number of transactions you need to review in the Banking Center, which will save you time. Finally, you understand the importance of reconciling bank and credit card accounts on a frequent basis to ensure your records are in sync with your financial institution.

We have met our goal of giving you the knowledge to successfully manage your uploaded bank and credit card transactions. Having this knowledge will help you to save the time you would normally have spent manually entering bank and credit card transactions into QuickBooks.

Reconciling your accounts will also help you become familiar with how much money you are spending, as well as what you are spending it on. Remember, having the ability to control your expenses will help to improve your bottom line.

In the next chapter, we will show you how to generate reports in QuickBooks. There are a number of preset reports in QuickBooks, which means you never have to create a report from scratch. You will learn how to customize existing reports, and then export them as Excel/PDF files or send them as attachments via email.

Join our community on Discord

Join our community's Discord space for discussions with the authors and other readers:

`https://packt.link/quickbooks`

Section 3

Generating Reports in QuickBooks Online

10

Reports Center Overview

Now that you know how to enter income and expenses into QuickBooks, it's time to learn how to generate reports to gain insight into the overall health of your business. Financial reporting allows you to take a step back from the day-to-day bookkeeping tasks and look at your business from a different perspective. By taking the time to generate reports such as a profit and loss (income statement) or the balance sheet report, you can see whether your business has been profitable and, if so, what has made it profitable. On the flip side, you can also dig into why your business has not been profitable and determine what the reasons are for that.

In this chapter, we will show you how to navigate through the Reports Center and give you an overview of the reports available. In addition, we'll show you how to customize reports to meet your business needs. We will also cover how to share reports with your accountant and business stakeholders.

Understanding how to run reports will help you to gain insight into all aspects of your business. Having access to your income, expenses, and other key performance indicators will help you to make good business decisions.

The following topics will be covered in this chapter:

- Navigating the Reports Center
- Reports available in the Reports Center
- Customizing reports
- Exporting reports
- Sending reports via email

By the end of this chapter, you will be able to navigate the Reports Center and know which reports you have access to and how to customize reports to meet your needs. You will also be able to export reports to Excel or PDF format and email reports to stakeholders.

 The US edition of QBO was used to create this book. If you are using a version that is outside of the United States, results may differ.

Navigating the Reports Center

Before we dive into how to navigate the Reports Center, let's cover the five key reports that business owners like yourself should be looking at on a regular basis:

- The **profit and loss report** (also known as the **income statement**)
- The **balance sheet report**, which will provide you with your net equity for the business
- The **accounts receivable aging report**, which will show you the total amount owed by your customers
- The **accounts payable aging report**, which shows what you owe creditors and suppliers
- The **statement of cash flows**, which shows your cash flow activities.

These reports will help you evaluate your business finances and make more informed decisions. In the next few chapters, we will explore generating, customizing, and using each one. As you will see, there are a lot more reports available within the Reports Center, too, which allow you to dig into the details of every aspect of your business.

In this section, we will cover how the Reports Center is organized so that you can easily locate a report. The Reports Center includes several pre-built reports that can give you summarized or detailed information about various aspects of your business. It is organized into three main sections: **Standard, Custom,** and **Management** reports. The majority of the reports are located in the **Standard** reports section.

To access the Reports Center, follow the steps below:

1. Click on **Reports** located on the left menu bar as indicated here:

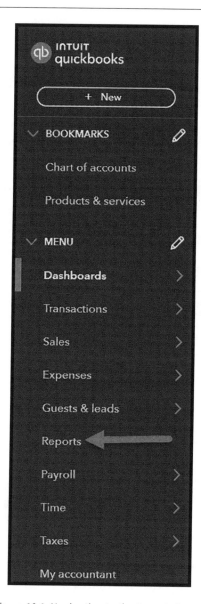

Figure 10.1: Navigating to the Reports Center

2. Click on the **Standard** tab as indicated below:

Figure 10.2: Selecting Standard reports

Standard reports are categorized into the following reporting groups:

- **Favorites**: You can mark your most frequently used reports as favorites and they will be listed in the **Favorites** group. To add a report to your **Favorites** list, simply click the star icon located to the right of each report.

- **Business Overview**: The **Business Overview** group includes reports that provide insight into the overall health of your business. You will find both a detailed report and a summary overview of profit and loss, the balance sheet, and a statement of cash flow reports in this group.

- **Who owes you**: Money owed to you by your customers is also known as **accounts receivable (A/R)**. In this group, you will find reports to help you to stay on top of your A/R balances. The A/R aging detail and summary, open invoices, and collections reports can be found in this group. In *Chapter 12, Customer Sales Reports in QuickBooks Online*, we will show you how to generate these reports.

- **Sales and customers**: The **Sales and customers** group includes detailed and summary reports that provide insight into who your top customers are and what products and services they are buying. Income by customer, products and services lists, and sales by customer are just a few of the reports you will find in this group.

- **What you owe**: Money you owe to others is also known as **accounts payable (A/P)**. In this group, you will find reports to help you to stay on top of your A/P balances. A/P aging, bill payment list, and unpaid bills are just a few of the reports you will find in this group. In *Chapter 13, Vendor and Expenses Reports*, we show you how to run the A/P aging report and several other reports in this group.

- **Expenses and vendors**: The **Expenses and vendors** group includes reports that provide insight into who and what you are spending your money on. Some examples of reports you will find in this group are check detail, expenses by vendor, 1099 detail report, and open purchase orders.

- **Sales tax**: The **Sales tax** group includes reports that provide details on the sales tax your business has collected. Examples of reports found here include the sales tax liability report and the sales tax detail report. In *Chapter 6, Managing Sales Tax,* we covered how to generate these sales tax reports.

- **Employees**: If you have added employees to QuickBooks, this group includes reports that will provide you with employee information. A couple of reports you can find in this group include employee contact lists and time activities. If you manage payroll in QuickBooks, head over to the **Payroll** reports group for more detailed payroll reports.

- **For my accountant**: Reports that assist your accountant in preparing your taxes can be found in the **For my accountant** reports group. In this group, you will find profit and loss, balance sheet reports, and a list of the chart of accounts, along with many other reports. In *Chapter 11, Business Overview Reports,* we will cover how to generate these reports.

- **Payroll**: If you have the **Payroll** feature turned on, you will have access to several detailed and summary payroll reports by employee, location, and class.

3. Click on the **Custom reports** tab located next to **Standard**, as indicated below:

Figure 10.3: Selecting Custom reports

Custom reports will include any report you have customized and saved. We will discuss how to customize reports later in this chapter.

4. Click on the **Management reports** tab located next to **Custom reports**, as indicated below:

NAME	CREATED BY	REPORT PERIOD	ACTION
Company Overview	QuickBooks	This Year ⌄	View ┊ ·
Sales Performance	QuickBooks	This Year ⌄	View ┊ ·
Expenses Performance	QuickBooks	This Year ⌄	View ┊ ·

Figure 10.4: Selecting Management reports

Management reports are the third group of reports, and they include professional report packages that you can download and customize with items such as a cover page and a table of contents. These reports can be used when presenting financial statements to a board of directors or a financial institution when seeking financing. The number of reports you can access depends on your QBO subscription level. In the *Customizing reports* section of this chapter, we will cover how to customize management reports to fit your specific needs.

Now that you understand how to navigate the Reports Center as well as the variety of reports you can run, we will cover what reports are available to you based on your QuickBooks Online subscription in the following section.

Reports available in the Reports Center

In *Chapter 1, Getting Started with QuickBooks Online*, we discussed the four subscription levels you can purchase for QBO: Simple Start, Essentials, Plus, and Advanced. Depending on the subscription level you have purchased, you could have access to anywhere between 20 and 100 or more reports. Simple Start includes more than 20 reports, Essentials includes more than 40 reports, Plus includes more than 65 reports, and Advanced includes more than 100 reports.

The following is a breakdown of some of the reports you will find in each QBO subscription.

QBO Simple Start includes more than 20 reports, some of which are listed here:

Profit & Loss	Sales by Customer
Balance Sheet	Sales by Product/Services
Statement of Cash Flows	Transaction List by Vendor

Customer Balance Summary	Check Detail
A/R Aging Summary	Payroll Reports (if Payroll is on)
Taxable Sales	Customized Reports
Transaction List by Date	Product/Service List
Reconciliation Reports	Deposit Detail

Table 10.1: A list of reports included in the QBO Simple Start plan

In addition to the reports included in Simple Start, QBO Essentials includes over 40 reports, including the following:

A/P Aging	Profit & Loss Detail
Bill Payment List	Sales by Customer Detail
Company Snapshot	Terms Listing
Customer Balance Detail	Trial Balance
Expenses by Vendor	Unbilled Charges
General Ledger	Unpaid Bills
Income by Customer Summary	Vendor Balance

Table 10.2: A list of reports included in the QBO Essentials plan

In addition to the reports included in Simple Start and Essentials, QBO Plus is where the reporting gets even better, with more than 65 reports, including budgeting and reporting by class:

Budget Overview	Purchases by Product/Service
Budget vs. Actuals	Purchases by Location/Class
Class Listing	Sales by Location or Class
Profit & Loss by Class	Time Activities by Customer
Profit & Loss by Location	Time Activities by Employee
Open Purchase Orders	Transaction Detail by Account

Table 10.3: A list of reports included in the QBO Plus plan

In addition to the reports included in Simple Start, Essentials, and Plus, QBO Advanced has more than 100 reports. It also includes a business analytics with Excel reporting tool.

Now that you have a better idea of all the reports you have access to with your QBO subscription, you are ready to learn how to customize the reports. In the next section, we will show you how to customize reports to meet your business requirements.

Customizing reports

As discussed, you don't have to create a report from scratch in QuickBooks Online; you can customize an existing report to get the data that you need. You can save any changes you make to a report so you don't have to recreate it each time.

The following are the steps we need to follow to customize an existing report:

1. Click on **Reports** on the left menu bar to navigate to the Reports Center, as indicated here:

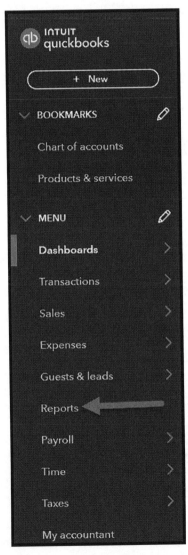

Figure 10.5: Navigating to the Reports Center

2. Select the report you want to customize. In this case, we will customize the **Profit and Loss** report, as indicated:

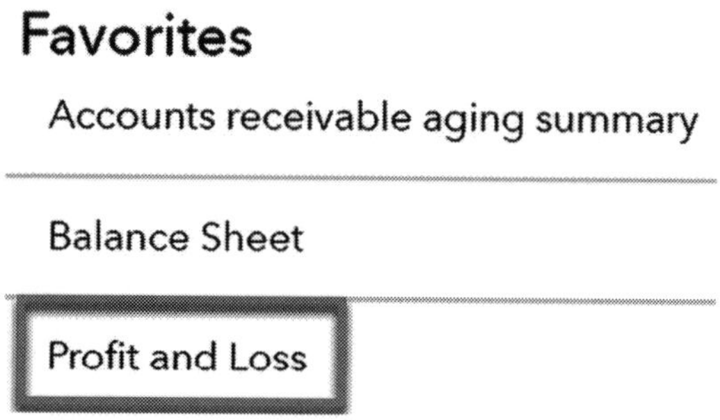

Favorites

Accounts receivable aging summary

Balance Sheet

Profit and Loss

Figure 10.6: Running the Profit and Loss report

3. Click the **Customize** button located in the upper-right corner:

Customize

Figure 10.7: Customizing a report

4. The following customization window will appear:

Customize report
▶ General

▶ Rows/Columns

▶ Filter

▶ Header/Footer

Figure 10.8: Options available to customize the report

In the following sections, we will cover each of the four areas listed in *Figure 10.8* in detail.

General report customizations

In the **General** report customizations, you can select the **Report period**, **Accounting method**, and how you would like numbers formatted on any report:

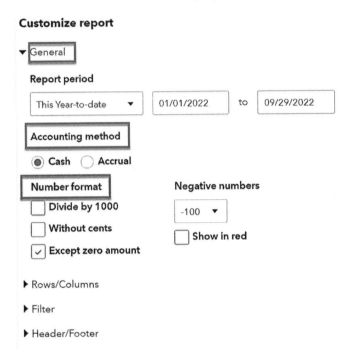

Figure 10.9: General report customizations

The following is a brief explanation of what's included in **General** report customizations:

- **Report period**: Select the period you would like to see in the report. You can do this by selecting the preset time frames from the drop-down menu or entering the dates directly in the fields.

- **Accounting method**: You can select the accounting method you would like to see the report in (**Cash** or **Accrual**). Reports will automatically default to the accounting method chosen when you set up your QuickBooks account. However, you can change this directly on the report. To change the default accounting method, go to **Company settings** and select the **Accounting** tab. In *Chapter 2, Company File Setup*, we showed you how to select the accounting method for your business.

- **Number format**: You can format numbers with three options: dividing them by 1,000, removing the cents, and not showing anything with a zero amount.

- **Negative numbers**: From the drop-down menu, you can choose to show negative numbers in one of three ways. The negative sign can be in front of the number or behind the number, or the negative numbers can be in parentheses, for example, -100, 100-, or (100).

Now that you are familiar with general report customizations, we will discuss how to customize rows and columns next.

Row/Columns report customization

Rows/Columns report customization includes formatting columns, comparing the current data to a previous period, and comparing the number of columns and rows to the grand total on the report:

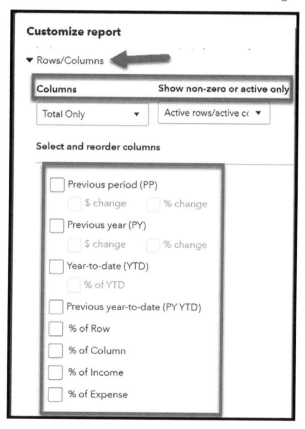

Figure 10.10: Rows/Columns report customizations

The following is a brief explanation of what's included in **Rows/Columns** report customizations:

- **Columns**: Displays column information by showing totals only, by period (days, weeks, or months), or by customer, vendor, or employee.

- **Show non-zero or active only**: Choose to only show non-zero data or all active data (with and without zeros). This option is recommended to keep your reports clean and concise.

- **Period comparison**: This allows you to see how the current period compares to a **Previous period**, **Previous year**, or **Year-to-date**. This change can be shown in either a percentage format, dollar amount, or both.

- **% of Row** or **% of Column**: Select these to see the percentage of each item listed on the report compared to other items on the same row or column of the report.

- **% of Income** or **% of Expense**: Select **% of Income** and the program will calculate the per-centage of each item listed on the report that makes up the total income reported. A similar calculation is done when you select **% of Expense**, but using the total expenses reported.

 For more tips and info on adding columns to reports, watch this Intuit video tutorial: `https://quickbooks.intuit.com/learn-support/en-us/customize-`
`reports/how-to-add-columns-to-reports-comparing-customers-time-`
`periods/00/344896.`

Next, let's discuss the various ways to filter reports.

Using filters to customize reports

To customize reports for specific data, you can filter reports by **Distribution Account**, **Customer**, **Vendor**, **Employee**, and **Product/Service**. To filter a report, put a checkmark in the box to the left of the filter and make your selection from the drop-down menu, as follows:

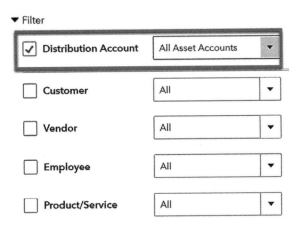

Figure 10.11: Using filters to customize reports

The following is a brief explanation of what's included in filtering reports:

- **Distribution Account**: Click on the drop-down arrow to select the account types you would like to filter on. Some of the options are **All Accounts**, **All Balance Sheet Accounts**, **All Asset Accounts**, and more.

- **Customer**: Click on the drop-down arrow to select specific customers to filter on, or to select all customers.

- **Vendor**: Click the drop-down arrow to select specific vendors to filter on, or to select all vendors.

- **Employee**: Click on the drop-down arrow to select specific employees to filter on, or all employees.

- **Product/Service**: Click on the drop-down arrow to select specific products and services, multiple products and services, or all products and services.

 For additional tips on how to filter reports, watch this Intuit video tutorial: `https://quickbooks.intuit.com/learn-support/en-us/run-reports/how-to-filter-reports-customers-vendors-products/00/344824`.

Next, let's talk a bit about the headers and footers.

Header and footer report customization

You can also customize the header and footer information that appears on reports. This can be useful if you have filtered a report in such a way that the current title is no longer applicable.

To customize the header, you can add a logo, update/change the name of the company that appears on the report, and change the title of the report. You can also choose to have the dates displayed on the report or remove them.

The following is a screenshot of the **Header** information that can be customized on reports:

▼ Header/Footer

Header

☐ Show logo

☑ Company name　　　　Small Business Builders, LLC

☑ Report title　　　　　Profit and Loss

☑ Report period

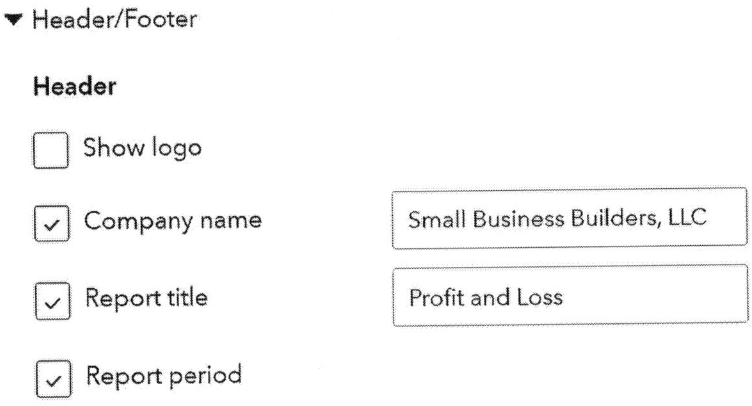

Figure 10.12: Header report customizations

To customize the footer, you can choose whether or not to display the date when the report was prepared, the time the report was prepared, and the report basis.

The following is a screenshot of the **Footer** information that can be customized on reports:

Footer

☑ Date prepared

☑ Time prepared

☑ Report basis (cash vs. accrual)

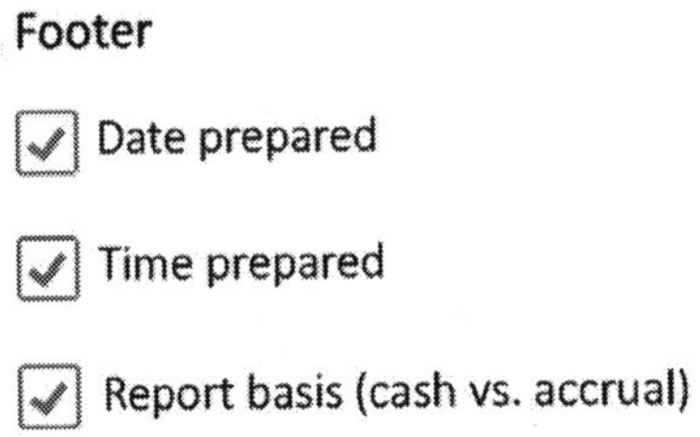

Figure 10.13: Footer customization options

Saving a customized report

After customizing a report, you can save your changes so they will remain each time you run the report. When you run a report, click the **Save customization** button located in the upper-right corner of the screen, as shown below:

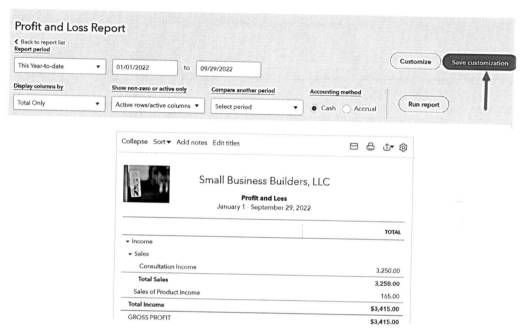

Figure 10.14: Saving your custom report

The window that appears is shown below, along with a brief explanation of each field:

Figure 10.15: Save customization settings

- **Custom report name (1):** The default report name will appear in this field. You can customize the name of the report by adding your business name, for example, **Profit and Loss – Small Business Builders, LLC.**

- **Add this report to a group (2):** Report groups are used to run multiple reports at once. For example, if you typically run the same five reports when closing the books, you can put all five reports in a group and generate them at the same time. Click **Add new group** directly below the field to create a group.

 Pro Tip: Groups are great to use for recurring reports or reports that you share with others. This will help you be more efficient and save you some time.

- **Share with (3):** This field allows you to share the report with other users within your company. Click the drop-down arrow and select specific users or **All**.

Customizing management reports

One of the newest improvements to QBO is the ability to customize an existing management report or build your own. As previously mentioned, management reports can be accessed via the **Management reports** tab located to the right of the **Custom reports** tab, as shown in *Figure 10.16* below:

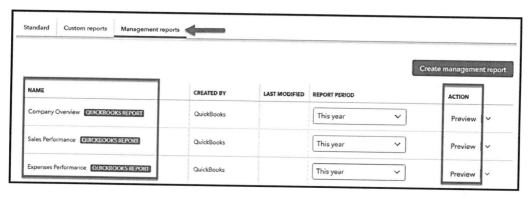

Figure 10.16: Viewing the Management reports tab

As you can see, there are three packages of management reports to choose from. Below is a brief description of what is included in each one:

- **Company Overview**: In addition to a cover page and a table of contents, this package includes a profit and loss report and a balance sheet report. You can choose a report period by selecting it from the drop-down menu, as shown in *Figure 10.16*.
- **Sales Performance**: In addition to a cover page and a table of contents, this package includes a profit and loss report, A/R aging details, and a sales-by-customer summary report.
- **Expenses Performance**: In addition to a cover page and a table of contents, this package includes a profit and loss report, an A/P aging detail report, and an expenses-by-vendor summary report.

To see the reports included in a report package, click on the **Preview** link listed below the **ACTION** column shown in *Figure 10.16*. If you would like to edit the report package, send it via email, or export it as a PDF or Word document, click on the arrow to the right of **Preview** and make your selections.

If you would like to create a custom management report package, follow the instructions below:

1.   Click on the **Create management report** button as shown below:

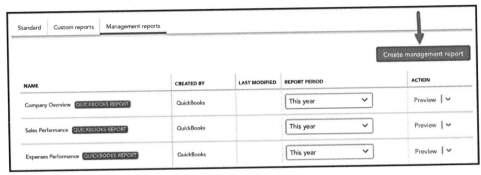

Figure 10.17: Clicking the Create management report button

The following screen displays:

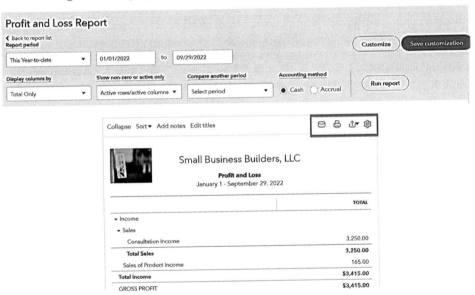

Figure 10.18: Adding a new management report

2.   Complete the fields as follows:

     •   **Template name:** Create a title for the management report (i.e., **Fiscal Year Closing Reports**)

- **Cover page**: Click on the **Cover style** option to choose a cover page. You can also click on **Logo** to include your logo, or you can exclude it.

- **Table of contents**: Choose to include (or exclude) a table of contents.

- **Preliminary pages**: You can add more preliminary pages, for example, a letter to the recipient of the package (i.e., accountant, tax preparer, or board of directors).

- **Reports**: Choose the reports you want to include in the report package. Select from any of the reports that are available in the Reports Center.

- **End notes)**: Any footnotes or additional information you would like to include with the financial statements can be added in this section.

- **Report period**: Choose the time period to run the report package for.

After making your selections, save your new management report package and it will be available on the **Management reports** tab to generate any time you need it.

Now that you know how to customize reports to fit your business needs, you are ready to learn how to share reports. You can export reports to Excel, PDF, or a printer, or email them directly from QuickBooks.

You have several options to choose from when it comes to exporting your QuickBooks data. Like most programs, you can print a hard copy of any report. If you need to manipulate the data or add additional information, exporting the data to Excel might be a good option. If you need to share your data with your accountant, a board member, or anyone who does not have access to QuickBooks, you can save any report as a PDF document and email the report. Finally, you can email a report directly from QuickBooks.

When you select the **Email** option, you can send it to multiple people and copy in anyone that you need to. When sending a report via email, the report will be attached as a PDF document.

Exporting reports

In this section, we will cover how to export reports to Excel and PDF. In the next section, we will show you the step-by-step process of emailing reports directly from QuickBooks.

When you run a report in QuickBooks, the export data menu will automatically appear in the upper-right corner, as indicated here:

Figure 10.19: Multiple ways to export a report from QBO

The following is a brief explanation of each icon:

- **Envelope**: Click on the envelope icon if you want to email a report directly from QuickBooks.
- **Printer**: The printer icon is used if you would like to print a hard copy of a report.
- **Paper**: The icon that resembles a sheet of paper with an arrow going through it is used to export reports to Excel or PDF.

We will discuss exporting reports to Excel first.

Exporting reports to Excel

As discussed in the previous section, if you need the ability to manipulate the data on a report, or add additional columns and rows, you can export reports to Excel.

Follow these steps to export a report to Excel:

1. Navigate to the Reports Center by clicking on **Reports** on the left menu bar, as follows:

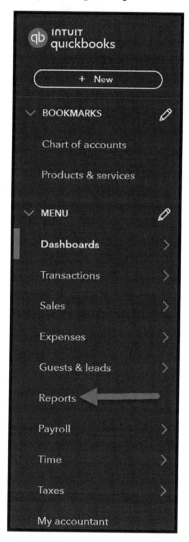

Figure 10.20: Navigating to Reports

2. Select the reporting group that includes the report you wish to export, as follows:

Figure 10.21: Selecting a reporting group

3. Choose the report you wish to export, as follows:

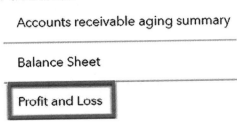

Favorites

Accounts receivable aging summary

Balance Sheet

Profit and Loss

Figure 10.22: Selecting a report to export

4. The report will appear on your screen:

Collapse   Sort▾   Add notes   Edit titles   ✉   🖨   ⬆▾   ⚙

Small Business Builders, LLC

Profit and Loss
January 1 - September 29, 2022

	TOTAL
▾ Income	
▾ Sales	
Consultation Income	3,250.00
Total Sales	**3,250.00**
Sales of Product Income	165.00
Total Income	**$3,415.00**
GROSS PROFIT	**$3,415.00**
Expenses	
Total Expenses	
NET OPERATING INCOME	**$3,415.00**
▾ Other Expenses	
▾ Home office	
Rent	1,500.00
Total Home office	**1,500.00**
Total Other Expenses	**$1,500.00**
NET OTHER INCOME	**$ -1,500.00**
NET INCOME	**$1,915.00**

Figure 10.23: Sample profit and loss report

5. Click on the icon that resembles a sheet of paper with an arrow going through it, as shown below:

Figure 10.24: Clicking on the Export button

6. Choose **Export to Excel**, as follows:

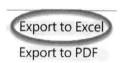

Figure 10.25: Selecting Export to Excel

7. Your report should appear in Excel, as follows:

Small Business Builders, LLC		
Profit and Loss		
January 1 - October 10, 2023		
		Total
Income		
Consulting Services		2,750.00
Sales		225.00
Sales of Product Income		375.00
Total Income	$	3,350.00
Cost of Goods Sold		
Cost of goods sold		100.00
Total Cost of Goods Sold	$	100.00
Gross Profit	$	3,250.00
Expenses		
Rent		
Building & land rent		1,500.00
Total Rent	$	1,500.00
Total Expenses	$	1,500.00
Net Operating Income	$	1,750.00
Net Income	$	1,750.00

Figure 10.26: Profit and Loss report exported to Excel

8.　At this point, you can save the report to your computer and make any necessary changes.

If the report is not immediately displayed on your screen, look at the very bottom (or top) of the screen and there should be an Excel icon. Click on it to display the report in Excel. If the report shows all zeros, click on the **Enable** message that appears at the top of the spreadsheet. That should allow the numbers to populate as expected.

 Pro Tip: After exporting a report, any changes you make in QBO will *not* update the report that was exported. You will need to follow the steps to generate the report and export it to Excel again to see any revisions made.

If you need to send reports to anyone outside of the company, I recommend you export the reports to PDF instead of Excel. This is what we will cover next.

Exporting reports to PDF

If you need to share reports with your accountant, members of your board of directors, or a financial institution, exporting the reports to a PDF file is a great option. The initial steps for exporting reports to PDF are identical to those for exporting reports to Excel (in the previous section):

1.　Click on **Reports** on the left menu bar, make sure you have selected the right reporting group, and choose the report you wish to export. Once the report appears, click on the icon that resembles a sheet of paper with an arrow going through it.

2.　Click on **Export to PDF** as indicated here:

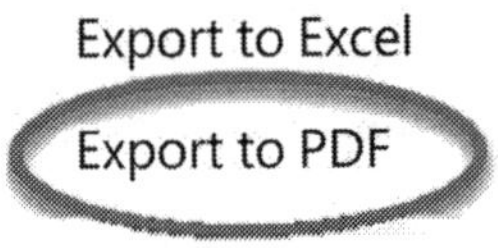

Export to Excel

Export to PDF

Figure 10.27: Exporting a report to PDF

3. The PDF report will appear on your screen, as indicated here:

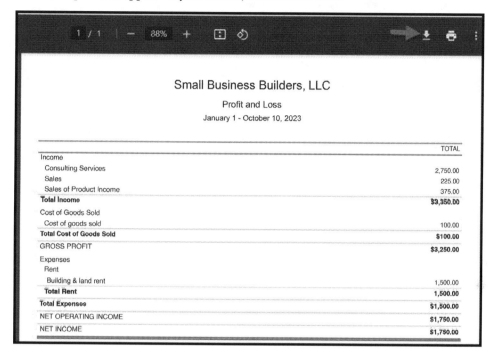

Figure 10.28: Profit and loss report exported to PDF

4. You can save the report to your computer by clicking on the arrow pointing down in the upper-right corner or you can print a hard copy of the report by clicking on the **Print** button, as shown below:

Figure 10.29: Printing a hard copy of the report

That wraps up two of the three primary ways you can export your data out of QuickBooks so that you can share it with your business stakeholders. In the next section, we will cover one final way of sharing reports: by sending them via email directly from QuickBooks.

Sending reports via email

Sending reports via email involves the same steps required to export reports to Excel and PDF format:

1. Click on **Reports** on the left menu bar, make sure you have selected the right reporting group, and choose the report you wish to send.

2. Once the report has appeared, click on the icon that resembles an envelope, as follows:

Figure 10.30: Clicking the email report icon

3. Click on the **Email** option, as follows:

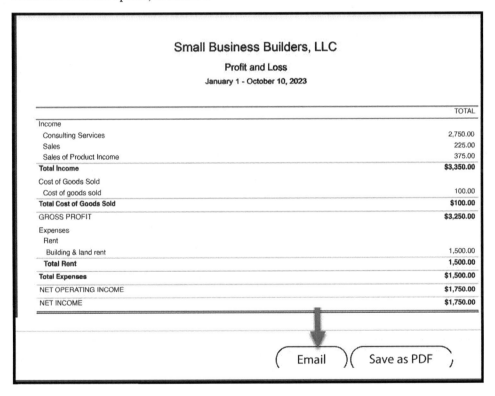

Figure 10.31: Selecting the Email option

The following window will appear:

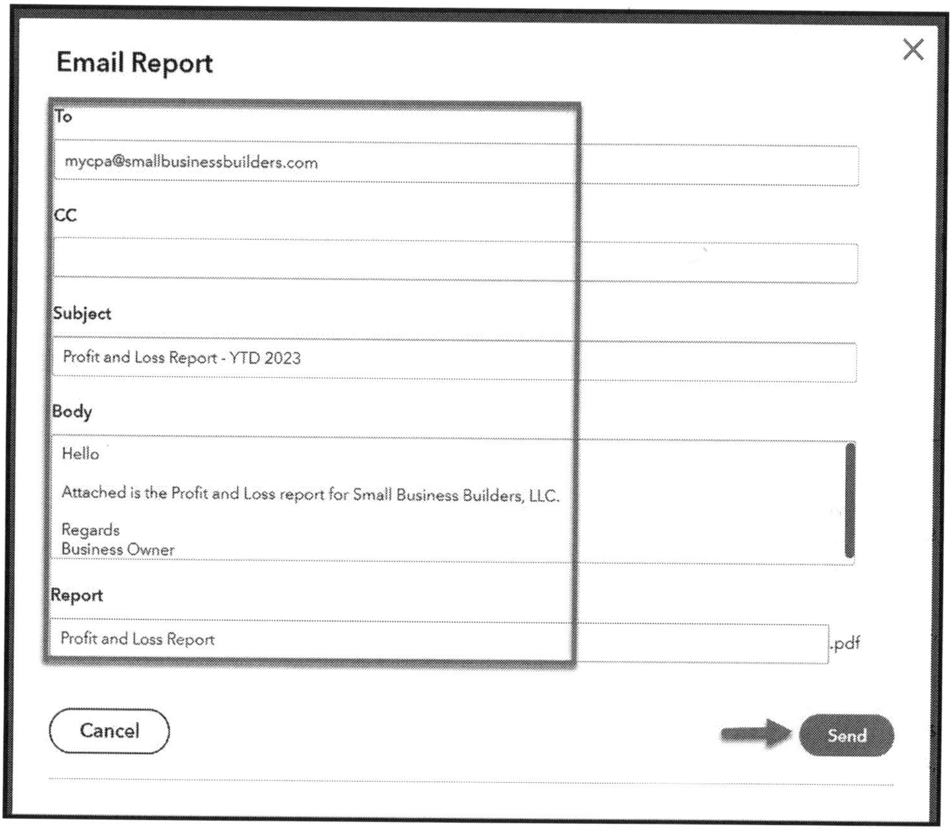

Email Report

To

mycpa@smallbusinessbuilders.com

CC

Subject

Profit and Loss Report - YTD 2023

Body

Hello

Attached is the Profit and Loss report for Small Business Builders, LLC.

Regards
Business Owner

Report

Profit and Loss Report   .pdf

Cancel   Send

Figure 10.32: Completing the required fields to email the report directly from QBO

The following is a brief description of the fields that need to be completed:

- **To**: Enter the email address of each recipient in this field. You can enter multiple email addresses by putting a comma in between each one.

- **CC**: Enter the email address for each recipient that needs to receive a carbon copy of the report. To enter multiple email addresses, put a comma in between each email address.

- **Subject**: This field will automatically be populated with the name of the report. You can make changes to this field.

- **Body**: This field will automatically be populated with a standard message. You can customize the email message to fit your needs.

- **Report**: The report you are emailing will be attached as a PDF document.

4.   After completing all the fields, click the **Send** button to email the report.

Emailing reports can be an easy and secure way to share data with your accountant and stakeholders in your business. The reports are attached in PDF format so they cannot be manipulated.

Summary

We have introduced you to the Reports Center and covered all of the different types of reports available at your fingertips. You have learned how to run reports, edit the data on reports, and save your changes. We have shown you how to share your data by printing a hard copy, exporting the information to Excel, saving to PDF format, and emailing directly from QuickBooks. This will help you to share information safely and securely on a need-to-know basis instead of giving access to your company data.

For an overview of how to best use the Reports Center to generate the reports needed for your business, watch this Intuit video tutorial: `https://quickbooks.intuit.com/learn-support/en-us/run-reports/how-to-use-reports-center-categories-insights-information/00/344862`.

In the next chapter, we will dive deeper into business overview reports. As discussed at the beginning of this chapter, business overview reports provide insight into the overall health of your business. The profit and loss statement, balance sheet report, statement of cash flows, and budgeting/forecasting tools available are included in business overview reports.

Join our community on Discord

Join our community's Discord space for discussions with the authors and other readers:

`https://packt.link/quickbooks`

11

Business Overview and Cash Flow Reports

In *Chapter 10, Report Center Overview*, we explained how to navigate the Report Center, what reports are available based on your **QuickBooks Online (QBO)** subscription level, how to customize reports to meet your business needs, and how to export reports using Excel, PDFs, and email. In this chapter, we will discuss the three primary reports that provide a good overview of your business: **profit and loss statements**, **balance sheet reports**, and **statements of cash flows**. We will explain what information is included in each report, how to customize it, and how to generate the report. In addition, you will learn how to create a budget from scratch so that you can keep track of your income and expenses in relation to the set budget for the year. This information will go a long way in helping you make decisions about your business.

Finally, we will introduce you to the Cash Flow Planner. One of the biggest issues many small businesses face is managing their cash flow. The Cash Flow Planner can help you to predict when you might encounter a cash shortfall so that you can take the necessary remedial steps before it happens. The Cash Flow Planner allows you to create real or hypothetical cash flow scenarios without affecting your actual data in QBO. Additionally, the audit log report provides you with the activity of all QBO users. You can see how long a user was logged in, when they logged out, and the changes (if any) that were made by each user.

By the end of this chapter, you will have a better understanding of what information you will find in the profit and loss statement, balance sheet, and statement of cash flow reports. In addition, you will know how to generate each report as well as create an income and expense budget from scratch.

The following topics will be covered in this chapter:

- Understanding profit and loss statements
- Generating balance sheet reports
- Understanding the statement of cash flows
- Creating a budget
- Using the Cash Flow Center
- Generating the audit log report

 The US edition of QBO was used to create this book. If you are using a version that is outside the United States, the results may differ.

Understanding profit and loss statements

In this section, we will show you how to customize and generate a profit and loss statement. The **profit and loss statement**, also referred to as the **income statement**, or **statement of activities** in the non-profit sector, shows you how profitable a business is over a period of time. This report summarizes all the income accrued and expenses incurred by a business over a specific period of time. The difference between income and expenses is shown on the report as either net profit (when income exceeds expenses) or net loss (when expenses exceed income). Like most reports, you can customize the profit and loss statement to meet your business needs.

 Pro Tip: Before preparing any reports it is important to confirm that your books are reconciled for the reporting period.

Follow these steps to generate and customize a profit and loss statement:

1. Navigate to **Reports** in the left menu bar, as shown in *Figure 11.1*:

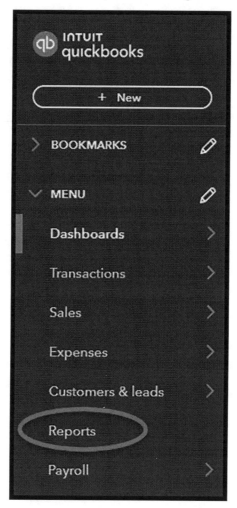

Figure 11.1: Navigating to the Report Center from the left menu bar

2. Scroll down to the **Business Overview** section and select **Profit and Loss**, as shown in *Figure 11.2*:

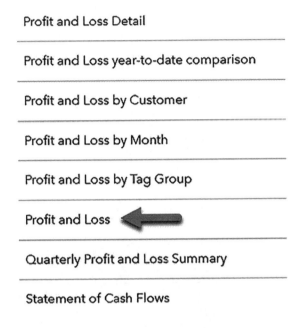

Figure 11.2: Selecting the profit and loss report

As you can see, there are several different types of profit and loss reports that you can run in QuickBooks Online: the **Profit and Loss Detail** report, **Profit and Loss year-to-date comparison**, **Profit and Loss by Customer**, **Profit and Loss by Month**, **Profit and Loss by Tag Group**, and **Quarterly Profit and Loss Summary** are preset custom reports.

3. You can customize the date range, columns to display, and accounting period, as shown in *Figure 11.3*:

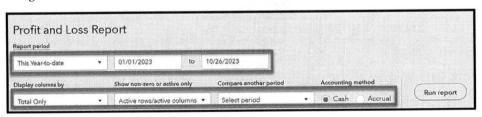

Figure 11.3: Choosing the report's parameters

Brief descriptions of the basic customization options for a profit and loss report are as follows:

- **Report period**: From the drop-down menu, you can choose a preset time period (such as this year) and the from/to date fields will be populated automatically for you. The other option is to type directly into the from/to date fields.

- **Display columns by**: There are a number of options you can choose from when it comes to how to display columns. From the drop-down, you can select days, weeks, months, quarters, years, customers, vendors, employees, and products or services.

- **Show non-zero or active only**: This field allows you to determine whether you want columns and rows to be displayed for all active accounts, regardless of whether they have activity or a zero amount. You can also choose non-zero, which means only accounts that have an amount will show up on the report.

- **Compare another period**: As we discussed in *Chapter 10, Report Center Overview*, you can compare your data to a previous period by making a selection from the drop-down.

- **Accounting method**: As we discussed in *Chapter 10, Report Center Overview*, you can choose the accounting method you would like to run the report for, cash or accrual. You can learn more about the cash and accrual methods in *Chapter 1, Getting Started with QuickBooks Online*.

4. Additional customizations can be made by using number formatting, selecting rows or columns, using filters, and editing header and footer information. Refer to *Chapter 10, Report Center Overview*, for step-by-step instructions on how to customize reports in QuickBooks Online.

The following is a snapshot of a sample profit and loss report that has been generated in QuickBooks Online:

Small Business Builders, LLC

Profit and Loss
January 1 - October 26, 2023

	TOTAL
▾ Income	
Consulting Services	3,250.00
Sales	5,459.84
Sales of Product Income	819.95
Total Income	**$9,529.79**
▾ Cost of Goods Sold	
Cost of goods sold	300.00
Total Cost of Goods Sold	**$300.00**
GROSS PROFIT	$9,229.79
▾ Expenses	
▾ Rent	
Building & land rent	1,500.00
Total Rent	1,500.00
Total Expenses	**$1,500.00**
NET OPERATING INCOME	$7,729.79
NET INCOME	$7,729.79

Figure 11.4: Sample profit and loss report

5. In this profit and loss report, **Small Business Builders, LLC** has a total income of **$9,529.79** and expenses totaling **$1,500**, which yields a net profit of **$7,729.79** for the period January 1 to October 26, 2023. If an income or expense account has a negative balance, it is a good idea to click and check the individual transactions to see whether an item has been categorized to the wrong account. You can drill down to the detailed transactions by clicking on an amount in the report.

 Pro Tip: Watch this step-by-step Intuit video tutorial, which recaps how to run a profit and loss statement: https://www.youtube.com/watch?v=nS GeKUO4HHE&feature=youtube.

Now that you understand the information you will find in a profit and loss statement, as well as how to generate a customized profit and loss statement, we will cover the balance sheet report next. We will show you how to customize a balance sheet report to meet your specific business requirements.

Generating balance sheet reports

A **balance sheet report** summarizes the assets, liabilities, and owner's equity for a business at any point in time. This report allows you to assess the **liquidity** (access to cash or assets that can be quickly turned into cash) of a business, which is important to potential investors and creditors. As with most reports, you can customize the balance sheet report to meet your business needs. We will show you how to generate the report and customize it in this section.

Follow these steps to generate and customize a balance sheet report:

1. Navigate to **Reports** in the left menu bar, as shown in *Figure 11.5*:

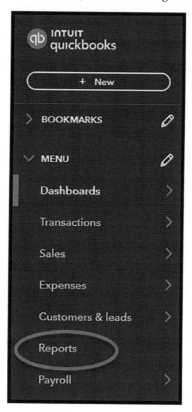

Figure 11.5: Navigating to the Report Center from the left menu bar

2. Scroll down to the business overview section and select **Balance Sheet**, as shown in *Figure 11.6*:

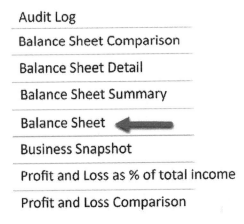

Figure 11.6: Choosing the balance sheet report

As you can see, there are several different types of balance sheet reports you can run in QuickBooks Online. The **Balance Sheet Comparison** report, the **Balance Sheet Detail** report, and the **Balance Sheet Summary** report are preset custom reports.

3. You can customize the date range, columns to display, and accounting period, as shown in *Figure 11.7*:

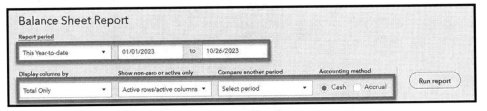

Figure 11.7: Selecting the parameters for the balance sheet report

4. A brief description of the basic customization options for a balance sheet report is as follows:

    - **Report period**: From the drop-down menu, you can choose a preset time period (such as this year) and the from/to date fields will be populated automatically for you. The other option is to type directly into the from/to date fields.

    - **Display columns by**: There are a number of options you can choose from when it comes to how to display columns. From the dropdown, you can select days, weeks, months, quarters, years, customers, vendors, employees, and products or services.

    - **Show non-zero or active only**: This field allows you to determine whether you want columns and rows to be displayed for all active accounts, regardless of whether they have activity or a zero amount. You can also choose non-zero, which means only accounts that have an amount will show up on the report.

    - **Compare another period**: As we discussed in *Chapter 10, Report Center Overview*, you can compare your data to a previous period by making a selection from the dropdown.

    - **Accounting method**: As we discussed in *Chapter 10, Report Center Overview*, you can choose the accounting method you would like to run the report for, cash or accrual. You can learn more about the cash and accrual methods in *Chapter 1, Getting Started with QuickBooks Online*.

5. Additional customizations can be made by using number formatting, selecting rows or columns, using filters, and editing header and footer information. Refer to *Chapter 10, Report Center Overview*, for step-by-step instructions on how to customize reports in QuickBooks Online.

The following is a snapshot of a sample balance sheet report that has been generated in QuickBooks Online:

Small Business Builders, LLC

Balance Sheet
As of October 26, 2023

	TOTAL
▾ ASSETS	
▾ Current Assets	
▾ Bank Accounts	
Business Checking	12,780.94
Business Savings	1,000.00
Total Bank Accounts	**$13,780.94**
▾ Other Current Assets	
Inventory Asset	775.00
Payments to deposit	0.00
Total Other Current Assets	**$775.00**
Total Current Assets	**$14,555.94**
TOTAL ASSETS	**$14,555.94**
▾ LIABILITIES AND EQUITY	
▾ Liabilities	
▾ Current Liabilities	
▾ Other Current Liabilities	
Texas State Comptroller Payable	51.15
Total Other Current Liabilities	**$51.15**
Total Current Liabilities	**$51.15**
Total Liabilities	**$51.15**
▾ Equity	
Opening balance equity	6,775.00
Retained Earnings	
Net Income	7,729.79
Total Equity	**$14,504.79**
TOTAL LIABILITIES AND EQUITY	**$14,555.94**

Figure 11.8: Sample balance sheet report

In this balance sheet report, **Small Business Builders, LLC** has total assets of **$14,555.94**, liabilities totaling **$51.15**, and total equity of **$14,504.79** for the period January 1 to October 26, 2023.

Now that you understand the information you will find in a balance sheet report, as well as how to generate a customized balance sheet, we will cover the statement of cash flows next. We will show you how to customize the statement of cash flows, which gives you insight into the cash flow of a business.

Pro Tip: When examining your balance sheet, you should have backup documentation that supports the numbers. This includes bank statements and reconciliations, A/R aging reports, A/P aging reports, credit card statements, and loan payment coupons, to name a few.

Understanding the statement of cash flows

The **statement of cash flows** is a detail report that shows the cash coming in and going out of your business over a period of time. It groups cash flow into three categories: operating, investing, and financing activities. **Operating** activities include items that are part of the day-to-day business operations, such as cash due from customers (accounts receivable) or money due to vendors (accounts payable). **Investing** activities include the purchase of assets for the business, such as a computer. **Financing** activities include money coming in from a business loan or line of credit.

Similar to the profit and loss and balance sheet reports, you can customize the statement of cash flows to meet your business needs. We will show you how to generate the report and customize it in this section.

Follow these steps to customize and generate a statement of cash flows report:

1. Navigate to **Reports** in the left menu bar, as shown in *Figure 11.9*:

Figure 11.9: Navigate to the Report Center from the left navigation bar

2.   Scroll down to the **Business Overview** section and select **Statement of Cash Flows**, as shown in *Figure 11.10*:

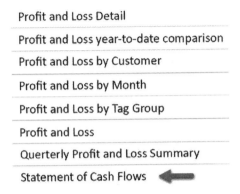

Profit and Loss Detail

Profit and Loss year-to-date comparison

Profit and Loss by Customer

Profit and Loss by Month

Profit and Loss by Tag Group

Profit and Loss

Querterly Profit and Loss Summary

Statement of Cash Flows

Figure 11.10: Selecting the statement of cash flows report

3.   You can customize the date range and columns to display, as shown in *Figure 11.11*:

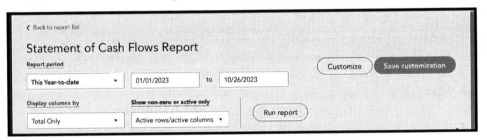

Figure 11.11: Choosing the parameters of the statement of cash flows report

Brief descriptions of the basic customization options for a statement of cash flows report are as follows:

- **Report period**: From the drop-down menu, you can choose a preset time period (such as this year) and the from/to date fields will be populated automatically for you. The other option is to type directly into the from/to date fields.

- **Display columns by**: There are a number of options you can choose from when it comes to how to display columns. From the drop-down, you can select days, weeks, months, quarters, years, customers, vendors, employees, and products or services.

- **Show non-zero or active only**: This field allows you to determine whether you want columns and rows to be displayed for all active accounts, regardless of whether they have activity or a zero amount. You can also choose non-zero, which means only accounts that have an amount will show up on the report.

4. After making your selections, click the **Run report** button.

    A statement of cash flows similar to the following will appear on your screen:

Small Business Builders, LLC

Statement of Cash Flowe
January 1 - October 26, 2023

	TOTAL
▾ OPERATING ACTIVITIES	
Net Income	8,050.00
· Adjustments to reconcile Net Income to Net Cash provided by operations:	
Accounts Receivable (A/R)	-224.75
Inventory Asset	-875.00
Accounts Payable (A/P)	0.00
Texas State Comptroller Payable	55.69
Total Adjustments to reconcile Net Income to Net Cash provided by operations:	-1,044.06
Net cash provided by operating activities	**$7,005.94**
▾ FINANCING ACTIVITIES	
Opening balance equity	6,775.00
Net cash provided by financing activities	$6,775.00
NET CASH INCREASE FOR PERIOD	$13,780.94
CASH AT END OF PERIOD	$13,780.94

Figure 11.12: Sample statement of cash flows

5. In this statement of cash flows report, **Small Business Builders, LLC** has a net cash provided by operating activities amount of **$7,005.94**, there are no investing activities, and a net cash inflow of **$6,775.00** comes from financing activities for the period January 1 to October 26, 2023. The cash at the end of the period is **$13,780.94**.

> **Pro Tip:** Financial statements should be reviewed on a monthly basis at a minimum after all bank and credit card accounts have been reconciled. This will allow you to identify any issues so that you can correct them before filing your tax returns.

Now that you understand the information you will find in a statement of cash flows, as well as how to generate a customized report, we will show you how to create a budget from scratch.

Creating a budget

After you've been in business for a year or two, you may want to take advantage of tools that will help you strategize and plan for the future. You can create a budget in QuickBooks Online from scratch or use existing data from the previous year. When you create a budget, you can keep track of your actual income and expenses to see whether you are coming in over or under budget.

QuickBooks allows you to create budgets for all income and expense accounts. You can also create a budget for specific customers. We will show you how to create a budget from scratch in this section. To access the budgeting feature, you must be subscribed to QBO Plus or QBO Advanced.

Follow these steps to create a budget:

1. Click on the gear icon and select **Budgeting**, as shown in *Figure 11.13*:

Figure 11.13: Navigating to Budgeting from the TOOLS menu

The following screen will appear:

Figure 11.14: The Create a budget button

2. Click on the **Create a budget** button.

3. On the next screen, you will need to select the time period and budget format you want to create:

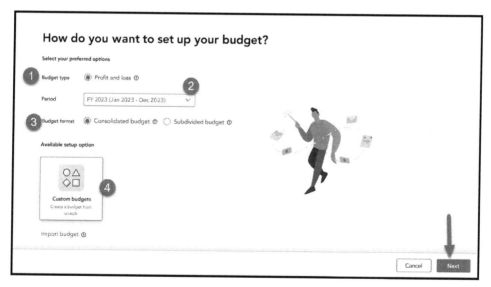

Figure 11.15: Choosing the parameters of the budget

4. Brief explanations of the information included on the preceding screen are as follows:

    - **Budget type (1)**: The budget type available is **Profit and loss**. This will allow you to create your budget based on expected income and expenses so that you can project your expected profit/loss for the time period specified.

    - **Period (2)**: Select the fiscal year the budget is for (for example, **FY 2023 (Jan 2023 – Dec 2023)**). Besides the current year, the other options available from the drop-down are to go back two years or to go forward four years.

    - **Budget format (3)**: There are two formats available: **Consolidated budget** or **Subdivided budget**. A consolidated budget allows you to create a plan at the organizational level. A subdivided budget allows you to create individual budgets based on location, class, department, or customers.

5. Choose the **Import budget** link, if you prefer to create a custom budget from scratch, and the following will appear:

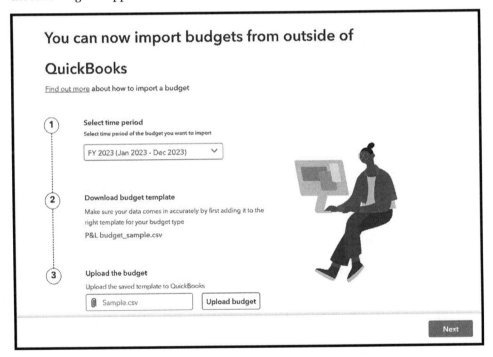

Figure 11.16: Creating a customized budget using the import option

6. After completing the fields, click **Next**.

A screen that resembles the following will appear:

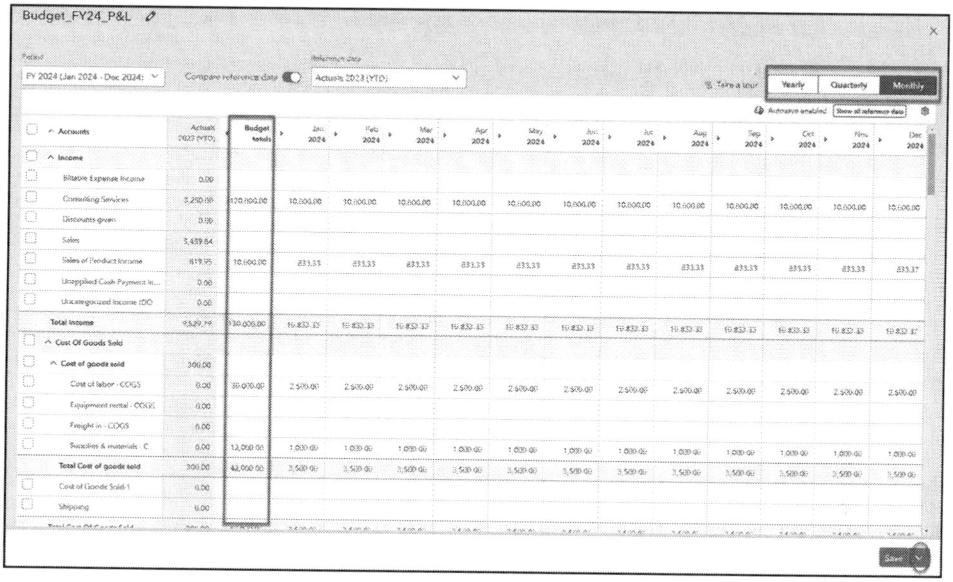

Figure 11.17: Complete budget template

7. Enter an amount in each cell and press *Tab*. If the budgeted amount for each month is the same, enter the total budget amount in the **Budget totals** column and then click the blue arrow that appears to split the total across all 12 months evenly. Be sure to repeat this step until you have completed all the income and expense items.

8. QuickBooks will automatically total each month, along with each income and expense item. Be sure to click the **Save** button located in the bottom-right corner to save your work.

> **Pro Tip:** For certain entities, such as non-profits that need to use up a certain budgeted amount each year, you can put the total budgeted amount in the first month of the fiscal year. Then, your profit and loss budget versus actuals report will show the amount you have remaining in each line item as the year progresses.

9. To close out of the budget, click the drop-down to the right of **Save** and select **Save and close**. The following screen will appear:

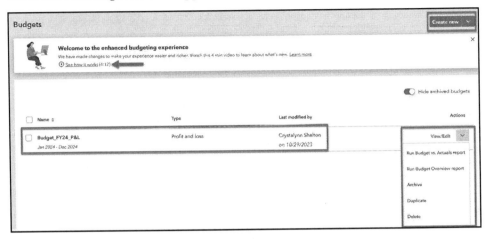

Figure 11.18: Editing an existing budget

10. This screen will show a list of budgets that have been created, including the budget name, type, and the last modification. In addition, you can access your budget reports by clicking on the **View/Edit** button. You can archive, duplicate, or delete budgets from this menu as well as generate reports. There are two reports that you can run to review and manage your budget: a **budget versus actuals** report and a **budget overview** report, as shown above in *Figure 11.18*.

11. A brief description of the information you will find in both reports is as follows:

- **Budget versus actuals report**: The budget versus actuals report includes side-by-side columns, one for the budgeted amount and one for the actuals as of a specific time period. The difference between the budget and the actuals will appear in a variance column. This information can help you determine the areas where you are within your budget or over budget, so that you can make any necessary adjustments.

- Like the budget overview report, you can export the budget versus actuals report to Excel or PDF, Plus, you can email the report directly from QuickBooks.

- **Budget overview report**: After entering your budget, you can run this report to review the budget to ensure that it is accurate. If changes are required, you can go back into the budget template to make the necessary changes. Like most reports in QBO, you can export the budget overview report to Excel or PDF. You can also email the budget overview report directly from QuickBooks.

You now know how to create a budget from scratch for income and expenses, as well as how to generate the budget overview report and the budget versus actuals report.

Using the Cash Flow Center

One of the challenges many small businesses face is staying on top of their cash flow. Within QuickBooks Online, you can access several tools that will help you to stay on top of your cash flow:

1. To access the Cash Flow Center, click on **Dashboards** and select **Cash flow** as shown in *Figure 11.19* below:

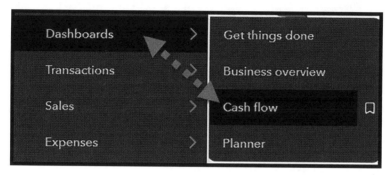

Figure 11.19: Navigating to the Cash Flow Center

The Cash Flow Center will appear as shown below:

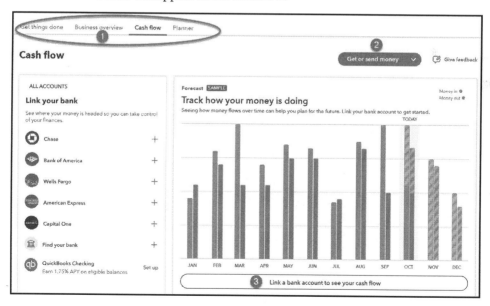

Figure 11.20: Cash Flow Center window

Here is a brief explanation of how this tool works:

- There are three tabs **(1)**: **Get things done**, **Business overview**, **Cash flow**, and **Planner**. The **Get things done** tab has...On the **Business overview** tab, you will have a cash flow graph that shows all 12 months of your fiscal year. You can also link accounts and get or send money, which we will discuss below. The **Cash flow** tab allows you to apply for a checking account with QuickBooks. The **Planner** tab allows you to create real or hypothetical scenarios without affecting your actual QuickBooks data.

- **Get or send money (2)**: Click the drop-down arrow and you will see an option to pay a bill or invoice a customer directly from this screen. Once you have saved the transaction, you can return to this screen to see the impact on your cash flow.

- **Link bank accounts (3)**: As discussed in *Chapter 4, Customizing QuickBooks for Your Business*, you can connect accounts to QuickBooks so transactions will automatically be imported. As you can see, you can also connect accounts within the Cash Flow Center.

2. Below is an overview of the **MONEY IN** section of the Cash Flow Center, as shown in *Figure 11.21*:

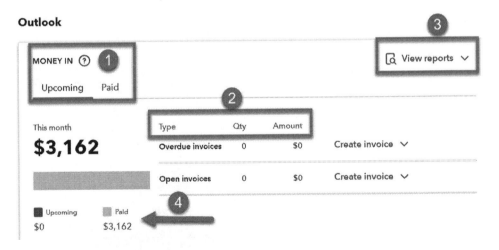

Figure 11.21: Highlighted areas for the MONEY IN section

In the preceding screenshot, the following four sections have been highlighted:

- **MONEY IN (1)**: In this section, there are two tabs – one for upcoming payments from customers and one for payments received from customers.

- **(2)** In this section, customer invoices are categorized as overdue and open. You can also create an invoice by clicking on the blue link.

- **(3)** In the **View reports** section, you can generate three reports: **Open invoices, Invoice list**, and a sales by customer detail report.

- **(4)** In this section, you will see a total of upcoming invoices that are due (**$0** in our example) and the total paid in invoices within the last month (**$3,162** in our example).

3. Below is an overview of the **MONEY OUT** section of the Cash Flow Center:

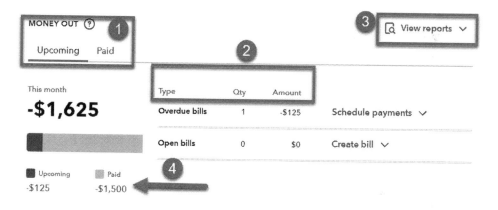

Figure 11.22: Highlighted areas for the MONEY OUT section

4. Like we did in the **MONEY IN** section, we have highlighted four areas in **MONEY OUT**:

- **MONEY OUT (1)**: In this section, you will see two tabs – upcoming payments to be made to suppliers and payments made to vendor suppliers within the last month.

- **(2)** In this section, you will see the quantity and total amount of overdue bills and open bills. You can schedule payments or create bills within this section.

- **(3)** You can generate the unpaid bills, bill payment list, and expenses by vendor summary reports for more details.

- **(4)** This section summarizes the total amount of upcoming bills that will be due and the total amount paid within the last month.

Cash Flow Planner

Within the Cash Flow Center you will find a new and improved Cash Flow Planner. The Cash Flow Planner allows you to create real or hypothetical cash flow scenarios without affecting your QuickBooks data. To get the most out of the Cash Flow Planner, be sure to connect all of your business debit and credit card accounts. In addition, add any real or hypothetical scenarios to get an idea of how your cash flow will be impacted. Best of all, you don't have to worry about it affecting your actual QuickBooks data.

Follow the steps below to access the Cash Flow Planner:

1. Click on the **Planner** tab and the following will display:

Figure 11.23: Accessing the Cash Flow Planner

2. Click on the **Start planning** button as indicated in *Figure 11.23* and the following message will display:

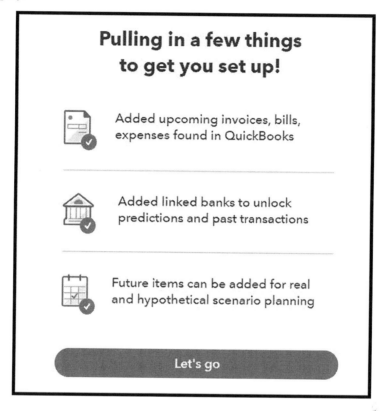

Figure 11.24: Overview of Cash Flow Planner

3. If this is your first time accessing the Cash Flow Planner, you will see the overview shown in *Figure 11.24*. To get the most out of the planner, you should add all upcoming invoices, bills, and expenses to QBO. In addition, linking your bank and credit card accounts will help to predict future income and expenses. Finally, you can add future items that will affect your cash flow.

4. After you click the **Let's go** button shown in *Figure 11.24*, the following will appear:

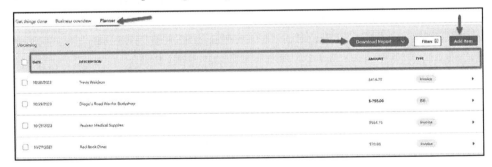

Figure 11.25: Reviewing the Cash Flow Planner

5. Based on the income and expenses you have recorded in QBO, the Cash Flow Planner will display money in (green bar) versus money out (blue bar) transactions for the time period you have selected. In *Figure 11.25*, we have it set for 12 months. However, you can choose this month, 3 months, 6 months, or 24 months. In the upper-right corner, you can switch the planner to **Cash Balance** and you will see the expected cash balance for the time period specified.

6. Scroll down to see the Upcoming activity section as shown in *Figure 11.26*:

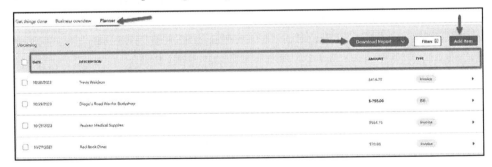

Figure 11.26: Upcoming activity in the Cash Flow Planner tool

This section includes details of how QBO arrived at the money in/money out information shown in *Figure 11.26*. You can click the **Add item** button to add any additional income or expense items that you are aware of (and that are not yet recorded in QBO) to see the impact on your cash flow. Remember, nothing that you do in this area of QBO will affect your books. This is where you get to run hypothetical scenarios to help predict your future cash flow, which will help you to make informed decisions about your business.

Generating the audit log report

The audit log report shows you everything that has happened in your company file so you can keep track of who has been in QuickBooks and what they have been doing. It shows you the date a change was made, the user who made the change, what the change (event) was, and the history if there is more than one change that was made.

Follow the steps below to generate the audit log report:

1. Navigate to **Reports** in the left menu bar, as shown in *Figure 11.27*:

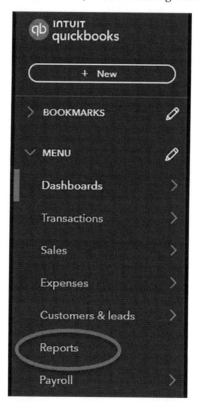

Figure 11.27: Navigating to the Report Center from the left navigation bar

2. Scroll down to the **Business overview** section and select **Audit Log**, as shown in *Figure 11.28*:

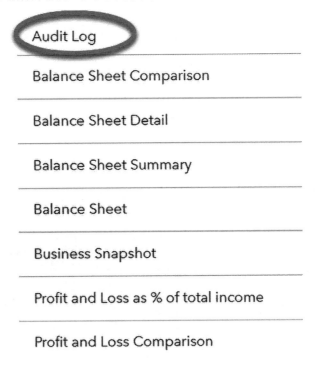

Figure 11.28: Clicking on Audit Log in the Business overview group

3. The audit log report will appear:

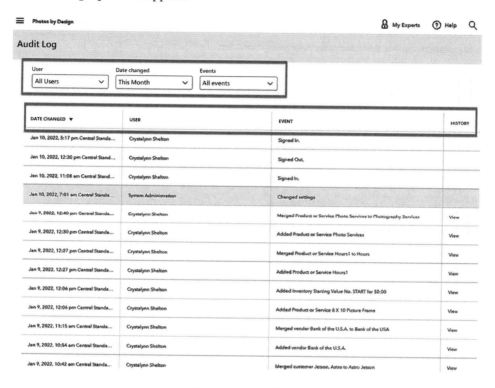

Figure 11.29: Sample audit log report

4. At the top of the report, there are three fields you can use to filter the report by **User**, **Date changed**, and **Events**.

This report will come in handy if there is ever a question as to who changed what in your data file. Unlike most reports in QuickBooks, the only option for exporting this information is by clicking the print button in the upper-right corner to print a hard copy. Emailing and exporting this report to Excel or PDF are not available options.

Summary

As discussed in *Chapter 10, Report Center Overview*, once you have customized the reports you plan to use on a regular basis, it is a good idea to memorize them and/or create a group of reports that will appear in your **Custom reports** tab. In this chapter, we explained the information you can find in the three primary financial reports: profit and loss statements, balance sheet reports, and statements of cash flows.

We also showed you how to customize the reports and generate them. In addition, we showed you how to create a budget from scratch and run budget reports. Finally, we touched on what you can do with the tools available in the QuickBooks Cash Flow Center, and showed you how to generate the audit log report to view the history of changes to your company file.

In the next chapter, we will show you what reports are available in QBO to help you stay on top of customers and sales.

Join our community on Discord

Join our community's Discord space for discussions with the authors and other readers:

`https://packt.link/quickbooks`

12

Customer Sales Reports in QuickBooks Online

In the previous chapter, we covered how to customize and generate key business overview reports, which gave you insight into your entire business. In this chapter, we will focus on reports that provide you with insight into your customers and sales. There are four primary reports we will discuss in this chapter: **accounts receivable (A/R)** aging reports, open invoices reports, sales-by-customer reports, and sales-by-product/service reports. In each section, we will discuss the information you will find on each report, how to customize the reports, and how to generate each report.

Reviewing these reports consistently will let you know who owes you money, who your highest paying customer is, and which products and services are selling the most. Having access to this information will help you to make informed business decisions.

The following topics will be covered in this chapter:

- Generating an accounts receivable aging report
- Generating an open invoices report
- Generating a sales-by-customer report
- Generating a sales-by-product/service report

 The US edition of QBO was used to create this book. If you are using a version that is outside the United States, the results may differ.

In general, you will see the term *customers* used, which refers to the people you provide goods and services for. However, during the setup of Small Business Builders, LLC, we updated the advanced settings to refer to customers as *clients*. Therefore, you will occasionally see the word *client* in place of *customer* throughout this chapter. To learn more about advanced settings, refer to *Chapter 2, Company File Setup*.

Generating an accounts receivable aging report

To stay on top of unpaid customer invoices, you should generate and review the accounts receivable aging report on a *weekly* basis. If the payment terms for most of your customers are Net 30 and you see customers with balances that are 60 days and over, you need to send a payment reminder to customers or pick up the telephone and call them. In *Chapter 2, Company File Setup*, I showed you how to set up automatic payment reminders in QBO.

The **accounts receivable aging report**, also referred to as the **A/R aging report**, categorizes unpaid customer invoices into groups based on the number of days they are past due. In general, there are five main categories: **Current, 1-30 days, 31-60 days, 61-90 days**, and **91 and over**. QuickBooks calculates the number of days they are past due based on the invoice due date.

Follow these steps to generate an A/R aging report:

1. Navigate to **Reports** from the left menu bar, as indicated in *Figure 12.1*:

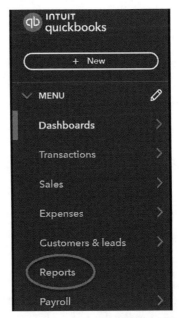

Figure 12.1: Navigating to the Report Center

2. Scroll down to the **Who owes you** section and select **Accounts receivable aging summary**, as indicated in *Figure 12.2*:

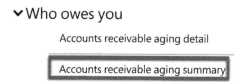

Figure 12.2: Selecting the Accounts receivable aging summary report

3. Notice that there is an **Accounts receivable aging summary** report and an **Accounts receivable aging detail** report. The detail report includes information about each outstanding invoice for all customers. This includes the invoice number, invoice date, due date, and invoice amount.

4. The A/R aging summary report only includes one total for each customer for each of the applicable categories (for example, **Current**, **1-30 days**, and **31-60 days**). However, you can drill down to the details simply by clicking on a dollar amount in the report.

5. You can customize the reporting period, columns, aging method, days per aging period, and number of periods for the A/R aging report, as indicated in *Figure 12.3*:

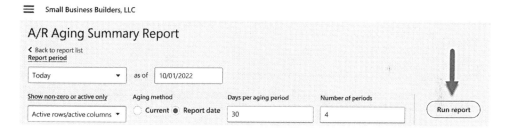

Figure 12.3: Choosing the parameters for the A/R aging summary report

6. The basic customization features available for the A/R aging report are:

- **Report period**: Customize the data range as needed by selecting the reporting period from the drop-down menu. You can choose from 28 options, including the following: **Today**, **This Week**, **This Month**, **This Quarter**, or **This Year**. You can also enter a specific date range by selecting **Custom** from the drop-down menu.

- **Show non-zero or active only**: From the drop-down menu, you can choose to display non-zero only, which means only accounts that have activity will show up on the report. You can also choose to show active accounts with zero activity.

- **Aging method:** You can select **Current**, which will calculate the age of the invoices as of today's date, or **Report date**, which will use the report period to calculate the number of days an invoice is past its due date.

- **Days per aging period:** You can determine the number of days per aging period. In our example, we have 30 days per aging period: **1-30**, **31-60**, **61-90**, and **91 and over**.

- **Number of periods:** You can determine the number of periods for your report. For example, in the A/R aging summary report that we will run next, there are four periods: **1-30**, **31-60**, **61-90**, and **91 and over**.

7. After making your selections, you can click the **Save customization** button and enter a name for this report. Next time you want to run this report, simply click on **Custom reports** and click on the report you wish to run.

8. Click the **Run report** button to generate an accounts receivable aging summary report, similar to the one shown in *Figure 12.4*:

Small Business Builders, LLC

A/R Aging Summary
As of October 1, 2022

	CURRENT	1 - 30	31 - 60	61 - 90	91 AND OVER	TOTAL
George Jetson	950.00					$950.00
Jenny Jetson	400.00					$400.00
Jetson, Astro	1,750.00					$1,750.00
Judy Jetson			2,165.00			$2,165.00
TOTAL	$3,100.00	$0.00	$2,165.00	$0.00	$0.00	$5,265.00

Figure 12.4: Sample A/R aging summary report

 Pro Tip: Credits that appear in the report should be reviewed to determine if the customer has prepaid or overpaid, or if a payment was recorded without an open invoice.

In this sample A/R aging summary report, **Small Business Builders, LLC** has outstanding invoices totaling **$5,265.00**. Of that total, **$3,100.00** is current, there are no invoices 1-30 days past due, **$2,165.00** is 31-60 days past due, and no invoices are more than 60 days past due. The business owner for Small Business Builders should follow up with the customers who have balances in the 31-60 days past due column. In our example, this would be **Judy Jetson** since she has a past due balance of **$2,165.00**.

If it becomes clear that a customer cannot afford to pay their outstanding balance, you will unfortunately need to write off a receivable as bad debt. To learn how to do this, refer to *Chapter 16, Handling Special Transactions in QuickBooks Online*. To avoid incurring a bad debt or sending a customer to a collection agency (collection agencies will go after customers for outstanding amounts due on your behalf; in return, they collect a percentage of the debt as their fee), I recommend you follow up on past due invoices on a weekly basis.

Generating an open invoices report

The **open invoices report** is a list of unpaid customer invoices. It is very similar to the accounts receivable aging detail report, but it does not group invoices by the number of days they are past due. However, the open invoices report does include detailed information, such as customer name, invoice date, invoice number, invoice amount, transaction type, and payment terms. Like the A/R aging report, this report can help you to stay on top of the money owed to you. Next, we will walk through how to customize and generate the open invoices report.

Perform the following steps to customize and generate an open invoices report:

1. Navigate to **Reports** from the left menu bar, as indicated in *Figure 12.5*:

Figure 12.5: Navigating to the Reports Center

2. Scroll down to the **Who owes you** section and select **Open Invoices**.

3. Customize the report period and the aging method of the open invoices report, as indicated in *Figure 12.6*:

Figure 12.6: Selecting the parameters for the open invoices report

4. The basic customizations available for an open invoices report are:

- **Report period**: From the drop-down menu, select the date range you would like to run the report for. You can enter a specific date or choose from 28 options, including the following: **Today, This Week, This Month, This Quarter**, or **This Year**.

- **Aging method**: You can choose to calculate the age of the invoices based on the current date (the date you run the report) or based on the report date you entered into the report period.

5. After making your selections, click the **Run report** button to generate the report.

An open invoices report should look similar to the one in *Figure 12.7*:

Small Business Builders, LLC

Open Invoices
As of October 1, 2022

DATE	TRANSACTION TYPE	NUM	TERMS	DUE DATE	OPEN BALANCE
George Jetson					
09/15/2022	Invoice	1011	Net 30	10/15/2022	950.00
Total for George Jetson					**$950.00**
Jenny Jetson					
10/01/2022	Invoice	1009	Net 30	10/31/2022	400.00
Total for Jenny Jetson					**$400.00**
Jetson, Astro					
09/30/2022	Invoice	1005	Net 30	10/30/2022	1,750.00
Total for Jetson, Astro					**$1,750.00**
Judy Jetson					
08/01/2022	Invoice	1010	Net 30	08/31/2022	2,165.00
Total for Judy Jetson					**$2,165.00**
TOTAL					**$5,265.00**

Figure 12.7: Sample open invoices report

In this sample open invoices report, **Small Business Builders, LLC** has several open invoices outstanding. All customers with open (unpaid) invoices are listed, along with the details of each invoice as of **October 1, 2022**. Open invoices total **$5,265.00**. This amount should equal the total of the A/R summary and detailed reports if they are generated for the same time period.

Review this report on a *weekly* basis and use it to follow up with customers whose invoices are becoming due or past due. If you notice invoices on this report that you have received a payment for, double-check that the payment was recorded in QBO. If it was not, record the payment and then generate this report again to update it. In *Chapter 7, Recording Sales Transactions in QuickBooks Online*, we covered how to apply customer payments to open invoices.

Generating a sales-by-customer/client report

The **sales-by-customer/client report** will give you, as a business owner, insight into who your highest paying customers are. In addition, you will gain insight into customers who seldom make purchases, which can help you when creating a marketing campaign to increase customer sales. The sales-by-client summary report includes a list of your customers and the total amount sold during the time period specified. We will show you how to customize and generate this report next.

Follow these steps to customize and generate a sales-by-client report:

1. Navigate to **Reports** in the left menu bar, as indicated in *Figure 12.8*:

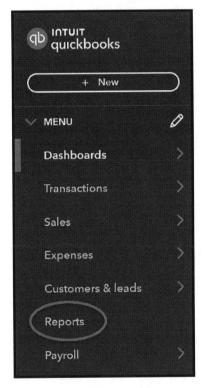

Figure 12.8: Navigating to the Report Center

2. Scroll down to the **Sales and customer** section and select the **Sales by Client Summary** option, as indicated in *Figure 12.9*:

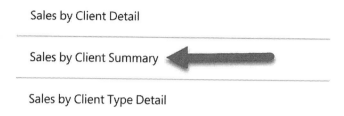

Figure 12.9: Running the Sales by Client Summary report

3. Similar to the A/R aging report, the sales-by-client report also has a sales-by-client detail report. The primary difference between the two reports is that the detail report will display specific invoice information, such as the invoice date, invoice number, and invoice amount, while the summary report does not include this level of detail and is more pertinent for a high-level overview.

4. You can customize the report period, columns displayed, and non-zero rows, compare the current data to a previous period, and select the accounting method to use for the sales-by-client summary report, as shown in *Figure 12.10*:

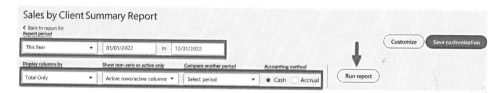

Figure 12.10: Choosing the parameters for the Sales by Client Summary report.

5. The basic customizations available for the sales-by-customer/client summary report are:

    *   **Report period**: Select the time period to run the report for. You can enter a specific date range or choose from 29 options, including the following: **This Week, This Month, This Quarter**, or **This Year**.

- **Display columns by**: Choose how you want the columns to be displayed. From the drop-down, you can choose from the following: **Total, Days, Weeks, Months, Quarters, Years, By customer/client**, or **By product/service**.

- **Show non-zero or active only**: Select this option if you want to display columns and rows for all active accounts or only non-zero accounts.

- **Compare another period**: Compare the current period to a previous period by selecting one from the drop-down. The options available are **Previous Period, Previous Year**, or **Year to Date**.

- **Accounting method**: Choose the accounting method to run the report for, **Cash** or **Accrual**. To learn more about cash versus accrual accounting, refer to *Chapter 1, Getting Started with QuickBooks Online*.

6. You can click the **Save customization** button to save your report selections and follow the on-screen instructions to save the report as a custom report. The next time you want to run the report, click on the **Custom Reports** tab, and all of your custom reports will appear in this tab.

7. After making your selections, click the **Run report** button to generate the report.

   A sales-by-customer summary report, similar to the one shown in the following screenshot, should appear:

Small Business Builders, LLC

Sales by Client Summary
January - December 2022

	TOTAL
George Jetson	1,650.00
Jenny Jetson	500.00
Jetson, Astro	15.00
Judy Jetson	1,000.00
TOTAL	$3,165.00

Figure 12.11: Sample Sales by Client Summary report

In this sample sales-by-client summary report, the total sales for the period **January 1 to December 31, 2022**, is **$3,165.00**. One way of interpreting this report is the following: according to this report, George Jetson is the top customer with sales of **$1,650** for the year, and Astro Jetson has the least amount of sales at **$15.00** for the year.

As a business owner, you could send George Jetson a thank you for being a loyal customer along with a coupon code to use for a future purchase. In addition, you could send Astro Jetson an email that says "We've missed you" or "It's been a while" along with a coupon to use for a future purchase to encourage him to buy something. This is just one of many ways you can use this information to make decisions in your business.

Generating a sales-by-product/service report

The **sales-by-product/service report** gives a business owner insight into which products and services are selling the most, as well as which products and services are not selling. Similar to the sales-by-customer report, you can use this information to create a marketing plan that will help you to sell slow-moving products and services.

This information can also help you determine whether you should add new products and services or eliminate an existing product or service. The sales-by-product/service report includes the quantity sold (if applicable), the total sales amount, the percentage of sales, the average price, the cost of goods sold, and the gross margin of each item sold.

Follow these steps to generate and customize the sales-by-product/service report:

1. Navigate to **Reports** from the left menu bar, as indicated in *Figure 12.12*:

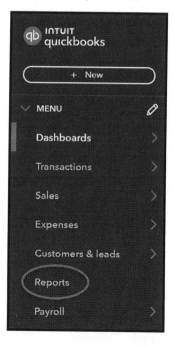

Figure 12.12: Navigating to the Report Center

2. Scroll down to the **Sales and customer** section and select the **Sales by Product/Service Summary** option, as indicated in *Figure 12.13*:

Figure 12.13: Running the Sales by Product/Service Summary report

3. Similar to the A/R aging report and the sales-by-customer report, the sales-by-product/service report includes a detail version. It breaks down each product or service sold, along with the date and amount for each. The summary version is ideal for a high-level overview.

4. Customize the report period, columns displayed, and non-zero rows, and select the accounting method to use for the sales-by-product/service report:

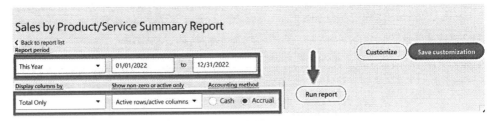

Figure 12.14: Choosing the parameters for the Sales by Product/Service Summary report

Here is a brief explanation of the fields to complete in order to generate a sales-by-product/service report:

*   **Report period:** Select the time period to run the report for. You can enter a specific date range or choose from the following: **Today, This Week, This Month, This Quarter**, or **This Year**.

*   **Display columns by:** Choose how you want the columns to be displayed. From the drop-down, you can choose from the following: **Total, Days, Weeks, Months, Quarters, Years, By the Customer**, or **By the Product/Service**.

*   **Show non-zero or active only:** Change this option depending on whether you want to display columns and rows for all active accounts or only non-zero accounts.

*   **Accounting method:** Choose the accounting method to run the report for, **Cash** or **Accrual**. To learn more about cash versus accrual accounting, refer to *Chapter 1, Getting Started with QuickBooks Online*.

5. As previously, you can click the **Save customization** button to save your report selections and follow the on-screen instructions to save the report as a custom report. The next time you want to run the report, click on the **Custom Reports** tab, and all of your custom reports will appear in this tab.

6. After making your selections, click the **Run report** button to generate the report.

7. A sales-by-product/service report similar to the one shown in the following screenshot should appear:

Small Business Builders, LLC

Sales by Product/Service Summary
January - December 2022

	QUANTITY	AMOUNT	% OF SALES	TOTAL AVG PRICE	COGS	GROSS MARGIN	GROSS MARGIN %
▾ Consulting Services							
Initial Consultation	1.00	1,000.00	12.10 %	1,000.00			
Monthly Bookkeeping Services	3.00	1,400.00	16.94 %	466.6666667			
Tax planning and preparation	2.00	1,950.00	23.59 %	975.00			
Website Development	1.00	3,750.00	45.37 %	3,750.00			
Total Consulting Services		8,100.00	98.00 %				
▾ Workbooks							
Workbook for Business Plan T...	11.00	165.00	2.00 %	15.00	55.00	110.00	66.67 %
Total Workbooks		165.00	2.00 %		55.00		
TOTAL		$8,265.00	100.00 %		$55.00		

Figure 12.15: Sample Sales by Product/Service Summary report

In the preceding **Sales by Product/Service Summary report**, the total sales for the period **January 1 to December 31, 2022**, are **$8,265.00**, and the cost of goods sold totals **$55.00**.

> As a reminder, **cost of goods sold (COGS)** is the total cost a business has paid out of pocket to sell a product or service. It includes any direct costs that a business incurs in the manufacture, purchase, and sale or resale of products.

Website Development had the highest sales of **$3,750.00**, or **45.37%** of total sales. **Initial Consultation** had the lowest sales of **$1,000.00**, which equates to **12.10%** of overall sales. The sales-by-product/service report is the final report that we will cover in this chapter.

> **Pro Tip:** All reports can be memorized and saved in a group for easy access to use on a regular basis. We showed you how to group reports in *Chapter 10, Report Center Overview*.

Summary

Let's recap: we have learned how to customize and generate four key reports that will give you insight into your customers and sales. We have covered the A/R aging report, which provides you with the number of days for which customer invoices remain unpaid. We explained the open invoices report, which shows all unpaid customer invoices. The sales-by-customer report was covered, which includes key sales data for each of your customers. Finally, the sales-by-product/service report was covered, which includes the products and services that are your top sellers. These reports are important in assisting you with staying on top of unpaid customer invoices so that you can get paid faster. It is much easier to maintain a positive cash flow if payments are received on time.

In the next chapter, we will learn how to customize and generate key reports that will give you insights into your vendors and expenses.

Join our community on Discord

Join our community's Discord space for discussions with the authors and other readers:

`https://packt.link/quickbooks`

13

Vendor and Expenses Reports

Having access to reports that give you detailed insight into what your expenses are, who you are paying, and the amount paid to each vendor will help you to control expenses and maintain a profitable business. There are a number of reports in **QuickBooks Online** (**QBO**) that will help you understand what you owe to vendor suppliers and other creditors.

We will dive into the information you can expect to find in each report, how to customize the report, and how to generate reports. We will also discuss ways you can use reports to help you manage your expenses and cash flow. I recommend you run these reports and review them on a weekly basis. Having access to this information will help you to manage your cash flow and stay on top of the money that goes out of your business.

In this chapter, we will focus on the following key reports:

- Understanding the **accounts payable** (**A/P**) aging report
- Utilizing the unpaid bills report
- Understanding the expense-by-vendor summary report
- Utilizing a bill payments report

 The US edition of QBO was used to create this book. If you are using a version that is outside of the United States, results may differ.

Understanding the accounts payable (A/P) aging report

An **accounts payable aging report**, also known as an **A/P aging report**, groups unpaid bills based on the number of days they are outstanding or due. In *Chapter 8, Recording Expenses in QuickBooks Online*, we covered how to record expenses. Similar to the A/R aging report that we saw in the previous chapter, there are five main groups of bills: **Current**, **1-30 days**, **31-60 days**, **61-90 days**, and **91 days and over**. QuickBooks calculates the age of a bill by using the bill's due date. To stay on top of bills, business owners should review this report on a weekly basis and take the necessary steps to pay bills that are nearly due. For bills coming due, you should go ahead and process the payment online with your financial institution or write a check directly from QuickBooks to ensure they arrive by the due date. In *Chapter 8, Recording Expenses in QuickBooks Online*, we showed you how to pay bills.

Follow these steps to generate an A/P aging report:

1. Navigate to **Reports** from the left menu bar, as indicated in *Figure 13.1*:

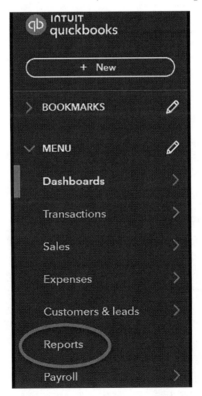

Figure 13.1: Navigating to the Reports Center

2. Scroll down to the **What you owe** section and select **Accounts payable aging summary**, as indicated in *Figure 13.2*:

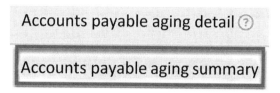

Figure 13.2: Selecting the Accounts payable aging summary report

3. In addition to the **Accounts payable aging summary** report, there is an **Accounts payable aging detail** report. The detail report includes information about each bill for the vendor. This includes the bill date, bill number, due date, and amount due. The summary report, on the other hand, includes the open balance for each vendor, grouped by the age of the bill (**Current, 1-30 days, 31-60 days, 61-90 days**, and **91 days and over**).

4. Click on the **Customize** button and you can customize the report period, format of numbers, columns to display, aging method, days per aging period, and number of periods for the A/P aging summary report. You can also filter by the vendor and configure other general customizations, as indicated in *Figure 13.3*:

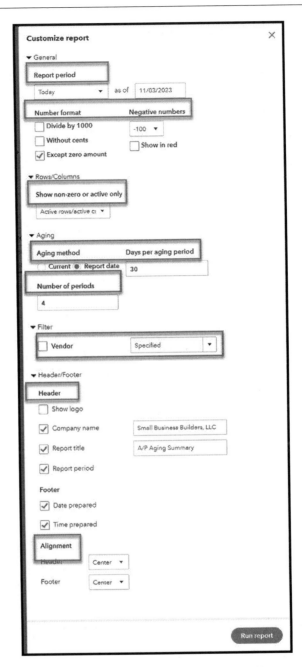

Figure 13.3: Report customization options

The following are brief descriptions of the customizable fields available for an A/P aging summary report:

- **Report period:** You can select preset dates from the drop-down menu, which include **Today, This week, This month, This quarter,** and **This year.** If you prefer a custom date range, select **Custom** from the drop-down and manually enter the dates.

- **Number format:** When it comes to formatting numbers on this report, you can choose to divide the numbers by 1000 or remove the cents so that only whole numbers show up on the report. You can also exclude accounts that have a zero amount (which is selected in *Figure 13.3*; you can also show negative numbers in red by selecting the **Show in red** box).

- **Show non-zero or active only:** You can choose to display non-zero only, which means only accounts with activity for the report period specified will be displayed in the report. You can also choose to show active accounts only, which means any account that was made inactive will not be shown on the report.

  You can learn more about how to make accounts inactive by reviewing *Chapter 4, Customizing QuickBooks for Your Business.*

- **Aging method:** You can choose an aging method of **Current** or **Report date**. **Current** will calculate the age of each bill as of today's date, whereas **Report date** will use the report period to calculate the number of days a bill has remained outstanding (unpaid).

- **Days per aging period:** Customize the number of days per aging period or use the standard 30 days per aging period.

- **Number of periods:** Similar to **Days per aging period**, you can also customize the number of periods in which to group bills. In the preceding example, we have chosen four periods (**1-30, 31-60, 61-90,** and **91 days and over**).

- **Filter:** You can filter the A/P aging report for a specific vendor by selecting the vendor from the drop-down. If you want to review unpaid bills for just a few vendors, you can also choose more than one vendor from the drop-down menu.

- **Header/Footer:** You can customize the header information, such as report title, and the footer information, such as date/time prepared.

Pro Tip: Having the ability to customize the report title comes in handy if this is a report you would like to generate on a regular basis without having to recreate it. Change the title to represent the changes made (i.e., **A/P Aging for Office Supply Vendors**) and click the **Save customization** button to save the report to your **Custom Reports** list.

5. After making your selections, click the **Run report** button to refresh the report.

6. An A/P aging summary report—similar to the following one—will appear:

Small Business Builders, LLC

A/P Aging Summary
All Dates

	CURRENT	1 - 30	31 - 60	61 - 90	91 AND OVER	TOTAL
A+ Printing	1,000.00	-50.00				$950.00
Staples				125.00		$125.00
The Telephone Company	150.00					$150.00
TOTAL	$1,150.00	$ -50.00	$0.00	$125.00	$0.00	$1,225.00

Figure 13.4: Sample A/P aging summary report

7. In this sample A/P aging summary report, **Small Business Builders, LLC** has outstanding bills that total **$1,225.00** with three vendors: **A+ Printing, Staples**, and **The Telephone Company**. Of this amount, a credit for **$50** is 1-30 days past due and **$125.00** is 61-90 days past due. You can click on any dollar amount or the **TOTAL** column to see the details of the bill. To maintain favorable credit terms with vendor suppliers, the business owner needs to make a payment or make arrangements to pay the past due amount.

Before contacting vendor suppliers, you need to run an unpaid bills report to see the details behind the open balances on this A/P aging summary report. We will show you how to generate an unpaid bills report next.

Utilizing the unpaid bills report

An **unpaid bills report** is a list of all bills that have not been paid, as of the date range for the report. It is very similar to an A/P aging detail report, with the exception that it does not group invoices based on the number of days outstanding. The report includes details such as the vendor's name and a list of all unpaid bills, including amount, due date, number of days past due, and open balance. You can use this report to quickly identify bills that are past due. This will allow you to follow up with vendors, to make payment arrangements for any bills that are past due or coming due.

Follow these steps to generate and customize an unpaid bills report:

1. Navigate to **Reports** from the left menu bar, as indicated in *Figure 13.5*:

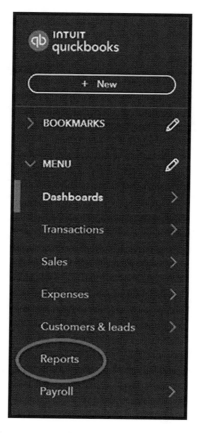

Figure 13.5: Navigating to the Reports Center

2. Scroll down to the **What you owe** section and select **Unpaid Bills**, as indicated in *Figure 13.6*:

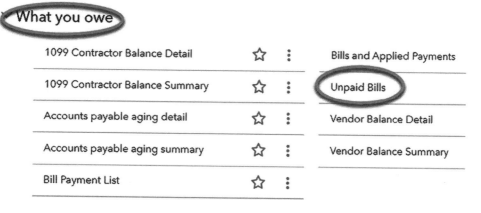

Figure 13.6: Running the unpaid bills report

3. Customize the unpaid bills report by clicking on the **Customize** button and selecting a report period, an aging method, minimum days past due, a filter, and header/footer info, as indicated in *Figure 13.7*:

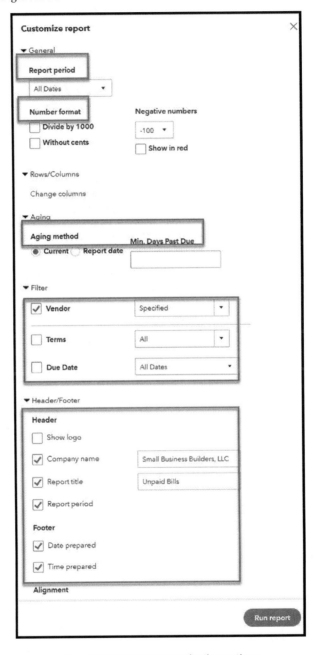

Figure 13.7: Report customization options

The following are brief descriptions of the customizable fields available for an unpaid bills report:

- **Report period**: Select the date range for which to run the report. You can manually enter a date range or choose from the following: **Today, This Week, This Month, This Quarter**, or **This Year**.

- **Number format**: When it comes to formatting numbers on this report, you can choose to divide the numbers by 1000 or remove the cents so that only whole numbers show up on the report. You can also exclude accounts that have a zero amount (which is selected in *Figure 13.3*; you can also show negative numbers in red by selecting the **Show in red** box).

- **Aging method**: The aging method is used to calculate the number of days a bill is past its due date. You can select the **Current** option, which will use today's date, or you can select the **Report date** option. The **Report date** option will use the report period to calculate the number of days the bill remains unpaid.

- **Min. Days Past Due**: If applicable, you can enter a minimum number of days a bill is past due, or you can leave this field blank.

- **Filter**: You can filter the unpaid bills report by selecting a specific vendor, payment terms, and due date of the bill.

- **Header/Footer**: Similar to the A/P aging report, you can show your company logo and company name, as well as customize the report title and the report period, in the **Header** section. You can also choose whether to show the date and time prepared in the **Footer** section of the report.

4. After making your selections, click the **Run report** button to generate the unpaid bills report.

An unpaid bills report, similar to the following one, should appear:

Small Business Builders, LLC

Unpaid Bills
All Dates

DATE	TRANSACTION TYPE	NUM	DUE DATE	PAST DUE	AMOUNT	OPEN BALANCE
▾ A+ Printing						
09/17/2022	Bill	876543	10/17/2022	-12	1,000.00	1,000.00
09/24/2022	Vendor Credit	CM876543		0	-50.00	-50.00
Total for A+ Printing					**$950.00**	**$950.00**
▾ Staples						
08/05/2022	Bill	12345	08/05/2022	61	125.00	125.00
Total for Staples					**$125.00**	**$125.00**
▾ The Telephone Company						
10/01/2022	Bill		10/31/2022	-26	150.00	150.00
Total for The Telephone Company					**$150.00**	**$150.00**
TOTAL					**$1,225.00**	**$1,225.00**

Figure 13.8: Sample unpaid bills report

In this sample unpaid bills report, **Small Business Builders, LLC** has unpaid bills totaling **$1,225.00**. As seen in the A/P aging summary report, the bills pertain to three vendors: **A+ Printing**, **Staples**, and **The Telephone Company**. The oldest bill has been past due for **61** days in the amount of **$125.00**.

This report lists the vendors in alphabetical order and includes the vendor name, contact phone number (not shown), bill date, due date, number of days past due, and outstanding amount. To maintain good credit with your vendor suppliers, you should review this report on a weekly basis and contact vendors to make payment arrangements.

To help you stay on top of what you are spending your money on, you need to review the expenses-by-vendor report. The expenses-by-vendor summary report focuses on what you are spending your money on. Unlike the unpaid bills report, you can gain insight into the types of expenses your business has, such as telephone, office supplies, and rent. We will show you how to run this report next.

Understanding the expenses-by-vendor summary report

In order to maintain a healthy and positive bottom line, you need to be aware of what your business expenses are. An **expenses-by-vendor summary report** provides detailed information about the vendors with whom you are spending your money. This report includes a list of vendors and the total amount you have paid for a specific time period. You can use this report to gauge what your largest expenses are. Plus, you can also use the information in this report to negotiate better pricing with those suppliers from whom you purchase the most.

Follow these steps to generate an expenses-by-vendor summary report:

1. Navigate to **Reports** from the left menu bar, as indicated in *Figure 13.9*:

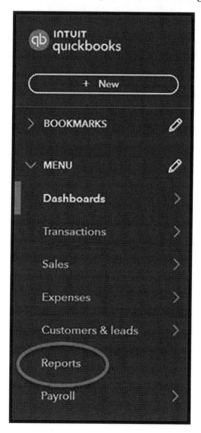

Figure 13.9: Navigating to the Reports Center

2. Scroll down to the **Expenses and vendors** section and select **Expenses by Vendor Summary**, as indicated in *Figure 13.10*:

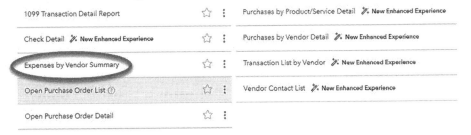

Figure 13.10: Selecting the Expenses by Vendor Summary report

3. You can customize the report by clicking on the **Customize** button and selecting the reporting period, accounting method, number format, columns to display, and period comparison, as indicated in *Figure 13.11*:

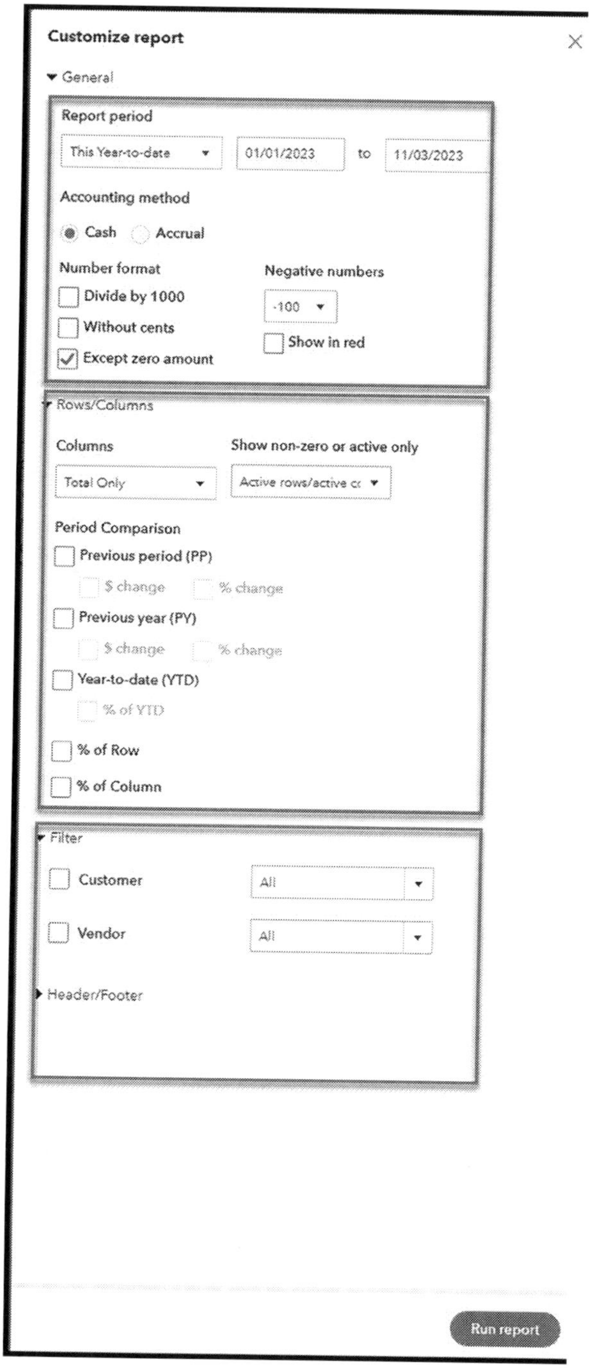

Figure 13.11: Report customization options

The following are brief descriptions of the customizable fields available for an expenses-by-vendor summary report:

- **Report period**: From the drop-down menu, select a reporting period, or manually enter the date range for which to run the report.

- **Accounting method**: Select the accounting method (**Cash** or **Accrual**) for which you would like to run the report. If you are not sure of which method to choose, refer to *Chapter 1, Getting Started with QuickBooks Online*. In this chapter, we explain how to choose the right accounting method for your business.

- **Number format**: Format numbers by dividing by 1,000, displaying them with or without cents, and making negative numbers red. You have three formatting options for negative numbers: **-100**, **(100)**, or **100-**.

- **Columns**: You can format the report to display information by total only, days, weeks, months, quarters, years, customers, or vendors.

- **Show non-zero or active only**: You can choose to display non-zero only, which means only accounts with activity for the period will show up on the report. You can also show active accounts only, which means any account that was made inactive will not be shown on the report.

  You can learn more about how to make accounts inactive in *Chapter 4, Customizing QuickBooks for Your Business*.

- **Period Comparison**: You can compare the current period to a **previous period (PP)**, the current year to the **previous year (PY)**, or view the period as a percentage of the **year-to-date (YTD)**.

Pro Tip: By comparing a current period to a previous period, you are able to gauge whether your expenses are about the same as the previous month, quarter, or year, or whether they are up or down from the previous month, quarter, or year. This can be a good way to identify a potential issue either with expense categorization and/or overspending in some areas.

4. After making your selections, click the **Run report** button to generate the report.

An expenses-by-vendor summary report, similar to the following one, should display:

Small Business Builders, LLC

Expenses by Vendor Summary
All Dates

	TOTAL
ABC Property Management	1,500.00
Staples	125.00
The Telephone Company	150.00
TOTAL	**$1,775.00**

Figure 13.12: Sample expenses-by-vendor summary report

In the sample expenses-by-vendor summary report, the total expenses for **Small Business Builders, LLC** are **$1,775.00**. **ABC Property Management** received the highest payment of **$1,500.00**. The report gives business owners insight into who they are spending their money with. As discussed, this can be helpful when it comes to negotiating a better price for goods and services.

5. If you see an amount listed as **Unspecified vendor** on the report, be sure to click on the amount to verify it is made up of journal entries for items such as payroll. In some cases, it is correct, but it's important to review any amounts listed as unspecified vendors. If the vendor's name was inadvertently not selected, it's important to go ahead and add it. You can click on any amount to drill down to the transaction, which will allow you to make the necessary change.

To drill down to specific payments made to vendors, you can run a bill payments report. We will show you how to generate this report next.

Pro Tip: The vendor summary report is great for reviewing what you have paid vendors for the year to determine who may be subject to 1099s. You can quickly review the report to see who you have paid $600 or more to, which is the threshold for generating a 1099 form. You can learn more about how to process 1099s in *Chapter 14, Managing Employees and 1099 Contractors in QuickBooks Online.*

Utilizing the bill payments report

A **bill payments report** includes detailed payment information about the bills you have paid. The report is broken down by the method of payment (for example, cash, credit card, or check). It includes the payment date, check number (if applicable), vendor, and amount paid. If you want to determine the payments made for a specific time period, this report will give you the information you need.

To generate a bill payments report, follow these steps:

1. Navigate to **Reports** from the left menu bar, as indicated in *Figure 13.13*:

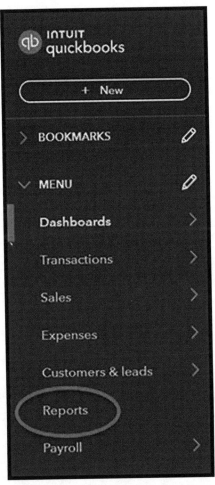

Figure 13.13: Navigating to the Reports Center

2. Scroll down to the **What you owe** section and select **Bill Payment List**, as indicated in *Figure 13.14*:

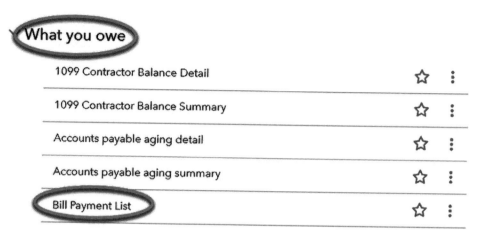

Figure 13.14: Running the bill payment list report

3. On the next screen, you can customize the report period and determine how the report is grouped, as indicated in *Figure 13.15*:

Figure 13.15: Customizing the bill payment list report

The following are brief descriptions of the customizable fields for a bill payments report:

- **Report period**: Select a preset time period, such as **Today**, **This Week**, **This Month**, **This Quarter**, or **This Year**. You can also select **Custom**, and enter a date range.

- **Group by**: When it comes to sorting, you can group the report by **Account**, **Vendor**, **Day**, **Week**, **Month**, **Quarter**, or **Year**.

4. After making your selections, click the **Run report** button to generate the bill payment list report.

A bill payment list report, similar to the following one, should be displayed:

Small Business Builders, LLC

Bill Payment List
All Dates

DATE	NUM	VENDOR	AMOUNT
▾ Checking			
10/05/2023	1	Brosnahan Insurance Agency	-2,000.00
10/06/2023	3	Books by Bessie	-75.00
10/07/2023	6	PG&E	-114.09
09/17/2023	7	Hicks Hardware	-250.00
10/07/2023	45	Tim Philip Masonry	-666.00
07/06/2023	10	Robertson & Associates	-300.00
10/01/2023	11	Hall Properties	-900.00
Total for Checking			**$ -4,305.09**
▾ Mastercard			
10/06/2023	1	Cal Telephone	74.36
10/08/2023	1	Cal Telephone	56.50
10/08/2023	1	Norton Lumber and Building Mate…	103.55
Total for Mastercard			**$234.41**

Figure 13.16: Sample bill payment list report

This report includes the payment date, check number (or payment reference number), vendor, and amount paid. In the sample bill payment list report, **Small Business Builders, LLC** has paid a total of **-$4,305.09** to its vendors from the checking account. When funds are withdrawn from the checking account, a negative amount reduces the balance in the checking account. This is the reason why the total for checks is **-$4,305.09**. On the other hand, a payment made with a credit card increases the balance due on that card, which is represented by a positive number of **$234.41** paid using the Mastercard.

You can run this report for any time period, to gain insight into payments made to all vendors. This information can help you to forecast the amount of cash you need to have available to meet your obligations to vendors.

Pro Tip: Don't forget to click **Save customizations** for reports that you will use on a regular basis. As mentioned previously, this will save your reports to the **Custom** report list so that you don't have to waste time searching for reports and reformatting them each time you need to review them. You can also create custom groups such as closing reports or tax preparation reports so that you can easily generate a group of reports for a particular person or purpose. To understand how to group reports, review *Chapter 10, Reports Center Overview*.

Summary

In this chapter, we have learned about four key reports that will help you to control your business expenses and stay on top of payments to your vendors. We've learned about the A/P aging report, the unpaid bills report, the expenses-by-vendor report, and the bill payments report. We have accomplished this goal by following instructions on how to customize and generate each of these reports. In addition, we have explained how these reports will help you to stay on top of unpaid bills so that you can maintain a good credit history with your vendors.

This chapter wraps up the financial reports series that we kicked off in *Chapter 10, Reports Center Overview*, where we covered the reports available, customizing reports, and how to export reports. In *Chapter 11, Business Overview Reports*, we covered the profit and loss, balance sheet, and statement of cash flows reports. In *Chapter 12, Customer Sales Reports in QuickBooks Online*, we showed you how to stay on top of what your customers owe you by generating an A/R aging report and an open invoices report. Finally, in this chapter, we showed you how to stay on top of the money going out of your business to pay for expenses. Financial reporting is essential in order to stay on top of your cash flow, so it is important to not only know how to generate these reports but also understand how to read them and how often. These past few chapters have aimed to equip you with these skills.

In the next chapter, we will shift gears and discuss another core activity in the financial management of your business: the importance of properly setting up the employees and contractors that work for you.

Join our community on Discord

Join our community's Discord space for discussions with the authors and other readers:

`https://packt.link/quickbooks`

Section 4

Managing Employees and Contractors

14

Managing Employees and 1099 Contractors in QuickBooks Online

Managing payroll is one of the most important aspects of your business. If not done right, it could negatively impact your employees since they may not be paid the right amount. It could also result in interest and penalties if payroll taxes are not filed and paid on time.

There are four main aspects of managing payroll: setting up your employees with the proper deductions and benefit elections, processing payroll by ensuring the hours paid are correct and on time, generating payroll reports to gain an insight into total payroll costs, and filing payroll tax forms and making payments on time. In this chapter, we will cover the information required to properly set up payroll, how to subscribe to an Intuit payroll subscription, payroll reports that will provide you with insight into payroll costs, and the importance of filing payroll tax forms and making payments on time.

If you do not understand how payroll works or you do not wish to do your own payroll, it is highly recommended you subscribe to the QBO Elite payroll plan, which is the full-service payroll option. We will provide additional details about this plan later on in this chapter.

In this chapter, we will show you how the Contractors Center is a one-stop shop to help you set up, manage, and pay independent Contractors. One of the tasks that can be time-consuming is 1099 reporting. We will show you how the Contractor Center automates this process, which will save you the time you normally would have spent tracking down key information so that you can provide 1099 reports to both the contractors and the IRS each year.

In this chapter, we will cover the following topics:

- A checklist of information required to set up payroll
- Signing up for an Intuit (QuickBooks) payroll subscription
- Generating payroll reports
- Filing payroll tax forms and payments
- Setting up 1099 contractors
- Tracking and paying 1099 contractors
- 1099 year-end reporting

 The US edition of QBO was used in this book. If you are using a version that is outside of the US, results may differ.

Setting up payroll

The most important aspect of ensuring an accurate payroll is to set up the payroll properly before you run your first payroll. Setting up a payroll involves gathering information about your employees, such as their names, mailing addresses, and Social Security numbers. As an employer, you will need a federal tax ID number and a business bank account for payroll checks and payroll taxes. You will need to determine what benefits you will offer employees, how often you will pay employees (for example, weekly, bi-weekly, or monthly), and the payment method you will use (for example, paper check or direct deposit).

 Pro Tip: It is best practice to manage payroll out of a separate checking account from all other operating expenses. That way, you ensure the funds for the payroll taxes remain in the account until you remit payment to the state and federal government.

In the following sections, we will provide you with a checklist of information you need to have handy to complete your employer profile and set up employees. However, we will not actually set up payroll in this chapter, because the details will vary depending on your business needs. First, we will show you how to set up payroll in QBO.

Payroll setup checklist and key documents

As discussed, the key to ensuring the accuracy of payroll checks, payroll tax forms, and payments is to ensure your payroll is set up properly. To set up a payroll, you will need to gather information from your employees. Also, you will need to have certain documents and information handy to complete the employer information section. This information may vary state by state, so it is important while following this guide that you refer to your local employment development office for specific requirements.

The following table shows a summarized checklist of the information required to set up your payroll:

Employee info	Employer info
Hire date	**Federal Employer Identification Number (FEIN)**
Form W-4: Employee withholding info	State employer ID number (if applicable)
Salary or hourly rate	Bank account information
Sick leave or vacation accrual rate	Employee benefits
Payroll deductions and contributions	Employee travel reimbursement policy
Payment method	Other compensation: bonuses, commissions
Direct deposit authorization (if applicable)	Other deductions: wage garnishment

Table 14.1: Checklist of employee and employer info needed to set up payroll

The following is a brief explanation of the *employee* information required to set up payroll:

- **Hire date:** This is the official start date for an employee. This information will be used to determine benefits eligibility as well as vacation and sick pay if that is something you offer to your employees.

- **Form W-4:** This is an official form issued by the **Internal Revenue Service (IRS)** to gather employee withholding information, which determines the amount of federal tax withheld from paychecks. You can download this form from http://irs.gov and include it in your employee new hire packet.

- **Salary or hourly rate:** This is the agreed-upon salary or hourly rate for an employee.

- **Sick leave or vacation accrual rate:** The number of hours an employee can earn toward sick or vacation leave.

- **Payroll deductions and contributions**: These are the deductions or contributions for health care, 401(k), or other benefits an employee has agreed to participate in.

- **Payment method**: Most employers will pay their employees in the form of a check or direct deposit. If the employee signs up for a direct deposit, they will need to complete a direct deposit authorization form.

- **Direct deposit authorization**: If an employee would like their paycheck to be electronically deposited into their bank account, this form gives the employer the authority to do so. Employers must keep this form on file along with other payroll information.

> **Pro Tip**: Employee files are important for all businesses and should comply with all federal, state, and local requirements. When in doubt, seek guidance from a **Certified Public Accountant (CPA)** or human resource professional. New hire packets should be part of your normal business practices. These packets will generally include all of the necessary paperwork required under the employment law.

The following is a brief explanation of the *employer* information required to set up payroll:

- **Federal employer identification number (FEIN)**: Employers are required to have a federal tax ID number before they can process payroll for employees. This number is used by the IRS to keep track of employee and employer payroll tax payments and filings. If you don't have an FEIN, you can apply for one at http://irs.gov.

- **State employer ID number**: If you live in one of the eight states that are subject to income tax, you will need to apply for a state employer identification number. Similar to the FEIN, the state employer ID number is used to keep track of payroll taxes.

> **Pro Tip**: Most states have a website where business owners can apply for their state payroll tax IDs. It is important to know which taxes apply to your state and to consult an advisor regarding payroll tax withholding requirements for remote employees.

- **Bank account information**: As discussed, I recommend that you set up a separate bank account to keep track of payments made to employees in the form of payroll checks or direct deposits. Also, all payroll tax payments made to the IRS or your state need to be made out of this account. Since most payments are made electronically, you will need the routing number of your financial institution and the full account number.

  Similar to your business checking account, you will need to add the payroll bank account to your chart of accounts list in QuickBooks. Refer to *Chapter 4, Customizing QuickBooks for Your Business*, where we cover how to add an account to the chart of accounts list.

- **Employee benefits**: Details regarding benefits provided to employees will need to be entered into QuickBooks. This includes the employee and employer portions of health care, 401(k) plans, and sick leave and vacation pay.

- **Employee travel reimbursement policy**: If employees travel on behalf of your business and incur expenses, such as business meals, airfare, and hotel costs, you need to set up your payroll to reimburse employees for these.

  A simpler way to handle employee reimbursements is to process the payments outside of payroll. This would involve setting up an employee as a vendor and writing a check to reimburse them for business expenses paid with personal funds. Refer to *Chapter 5, Managing Customer, Vendor, and Products and Services Lists*, for instructions on how to add an employee as a vendor.

- **Other compensation**: If you pay bonuses or commissions, or make other forms of payment to employees, you will need to include this information in your payroll setup.

- **Other deductions**: On occasion, you may receive wage garnishments for employees who owe back taxes or child support. These are court-ordered requests that you cannot ignore. Instead, you must set up the garnishment amount as a deduction for the employee. These requests will typically have an end date that is based on the total outstanding amount. Be sure to set these payments up exactly as they are outlined in the letter. If you don't, you could be subject to penalties as a result.

Now that you have a better understanding of the key documents and information required to properly set up payroll, you are ready to sign up for an Intuit payroll subscription.

Signing up for an Intuit payroll subscription

Setting up payroll in QBO can be done in six easy steps:

1. Click on **Payroll** on the left menu bar to navigate to the Payroll Center, as shown in *Figure 14.1*:

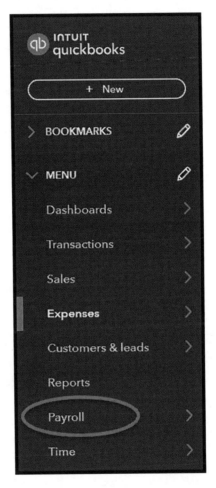

Figure 14.1: Navigating to the Payroll Center

2. Choose the payroll features you need, as shown in *Figure 14.2*:

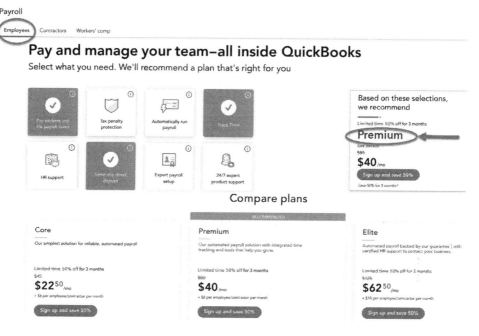

Figure 14.2: Selecting payroll features to begin setting up payroll

Within the screen shown in *Figure 14.2*, you will see a few payroll features automatically selected for you (including **Pay workers and file payroll taxes**, **Track Time**, and **Same-day direct deposit**). You can choose one or more of the additional features shown (**Tax penalty protection**, **Automatically run payroll**, and so on) Based on your selections, the recommended payroll plan will show up to the right of these selections. In our example, **Premium** is the plan recommended for Small Business Builders, LLC.

3. On the next screen, you will have the option of selecting a payroll plan, as indicated in *Figure 14.3*:

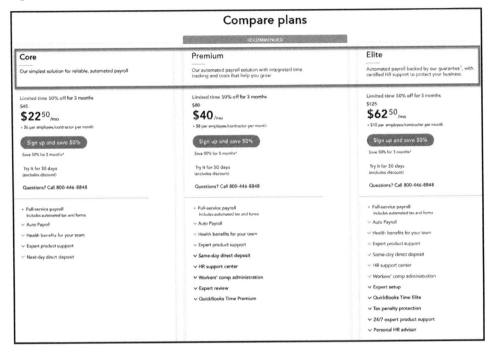

Figure 14.3: Intuit QuickBooks payroll plans

 Note: Pricing is based on the current rates and is subject to change. Please visit https://www.intuit.com/ (click on **Products** and select **QuickBooks**) for the most up-to-date information.

The following is a brief explanation of each QBO payroll plan currently available:

- **Core:** This plan is ideal for employers who prefer to manage their payroll in-house. The subscription fee includes updated payroll tax tables that are used to automatically calculate payroll taxes and payroll checks for you—no manual calculation is required! With this plan, you can process payroll checks, electronically make payroll tax payments for state and federal taxes, and file payroll tax forms for state and federal taxes only. This plan does not offer local tax payments and filings. You will need to print the forms and upload them to the necessary local sites as required. This plan also includes **next-day direct deposit**.

The Core plan is recommended for small payrolls and someone with payroll experience. This is due to the fact that the responsibility for local payroll tax filings and payments will remain with the business owner.

- **Premium**: This plan includes all of the features outlined in the Core plan plus automated local tax filings, **same-day direct deposit, workers' comp administration**, an **HR support center**, a QuickBooks expert who will review your payroll setup, and the ability to allow employees to track time using their mobile device. When setting up payroll, links will be available for applying for certain state ID numbers that are required.

- **Elite**: This plan includes customized setup by a QBO payroll expert, payroll processing, completion of tax forms, and automated payroll tax payments for federal, state, and local governments. In addition, Intuit will process all year-end tax forms and filings such as mailing and filing W-2 forms. Unlike the Core and Premium plans, it includes multi-state payroll filings, the ability to track projects from any mobile device, time tracking, tax penalty protection up to $25,000, access to a personal HR advisor, and 24/7 product support, which can be beneficial if there is an issue with a payroll or an individual paycheck. Voids and corrections must be made by the payroll service.

QuickBooks payroll is available in all 50 states and all payroll plans include the following key features:

- Unlimited payroll runs
- Calculated paychecks and taxes
- Automated taxes and forms
- Workforce portal
- Custom user access by setting permission levels
- Garnishment and deductions management
- Payroll reports

 Pro Tip: It is advised to check local payroll tax filing requirements to confirm that the payroll subscription you have chosen can handle all necessary filings.

Depending on your business needs, setting up payroll and running payroll will vary based on the benefits offered and the applicable taxes. Therefore, we recommend you follow the step-by-step instructions within QuickBooks to learn how to set up and run payroll. To get started, click on the **Payroll** tab located on the left navigation bar. If you run into an issue, contact the payroll support team. You can do this within the software by clicking on the **Help** menu. Be sure to get payroll set up before you start running reports.

 Pro Tip: Unlimited chat and telephone support are available at no additional cost to payroll subscribers of the Core, Premium, and Elite plans.

Generating payroll reports

By now, you know that QBO includes a library of preset reports that provide business owners with insights into every aspect of their business. There are several summary and detailed reports you can generate to gain insight into your payroll costs, payroll deductions and contributions, vacation and sick leave, and payroll taxes. If you have the Core plan, these reports will help you to complete payroll tax forms and make payroll tax payments to the local tax authorities.

 Pro Tip: It's important to note that if you have not signed up for a payroll subscription plan, you will *not* see the payroll reports covered in this chapter. These reports are only available to payroll subscribers.

Follow these steps to generate payroll reports:

1. Click on **Reports** on the left navigation bar, as indicated in *Figure 14.4*:

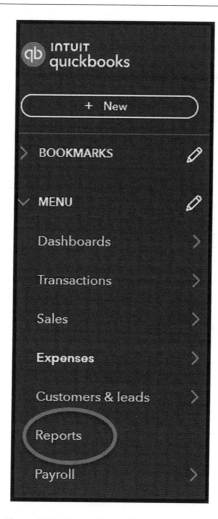

Figure 14.4: Navigating to the Reports Center

2.   Scroll down to the **Payroll** section and you will see several reports, as indicated in *Figure 14.5*:

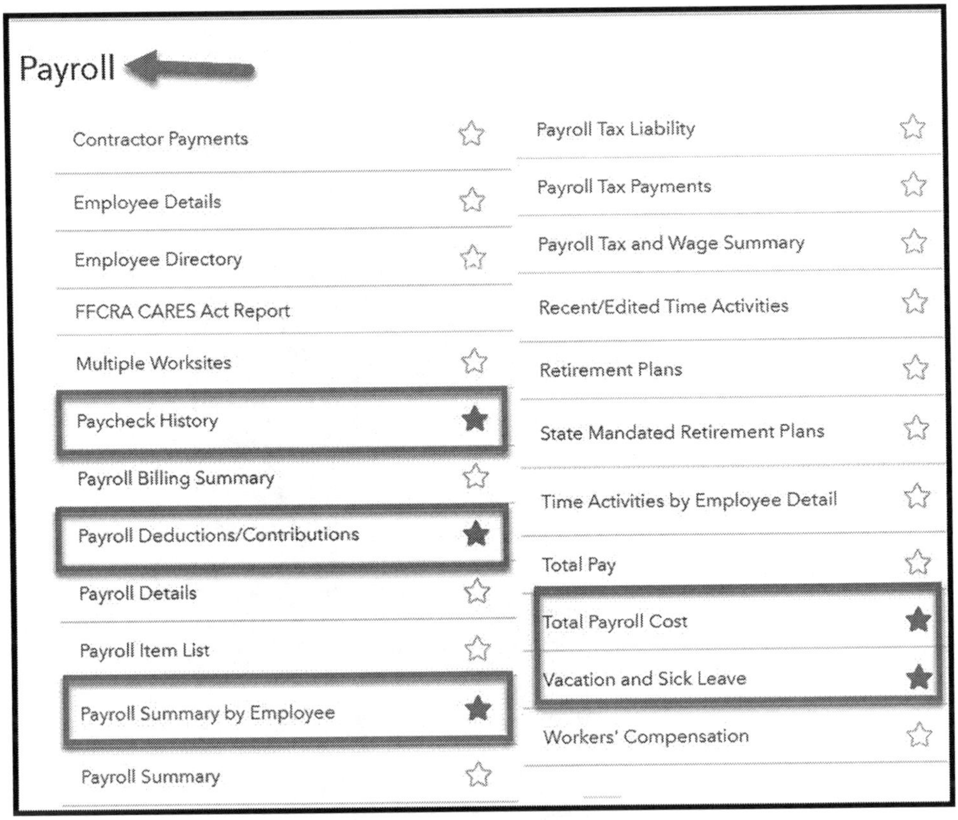

Figure 14.5: Payroll reports available for QBO Payroll subscribers

3.   The following is a brief description of the information you will find on five key payroll reports:

- **Paycheck History**: This report includes a list of paychecks that have been issued. You can use this report to edit check numbers, print pay stubs, and more.

- **Payroll Deductions/Contributions**: This report details payroll deductions by employee as well as employer contributions made for each pay period.

- **Payroll Summary by Employee**: This is a comprehensive report that includes wages, deductions, and taxes totaled by the employee or payroll period.

- **Total Payroll Cost**: This report includes all costs associated with paying employees, such as total pay, net pay, deductions, company contributions, and taxes.

- **Vacation and Sick Leave**: This report details the total vacation and sick pay that has been used as well as the remaining balance left.

4. To generate a report, simply click on the report and select the pay period you would like to see data for. Similar to other QBO reports, you can save payroll reports as PDF files or export them to Excel. Refer to *Chapter 10*, *Report Center Overview*, for step-by-step instructions on how this works.

One of the key benefits of generating reports is that they include the information you need to file payroll tax forms and make payroll tax payments. In the next section, we will discuss your options for filing and making payroll tax payments.

Filing payroll tax forms and payments

Employers are required to file payroll tax forms and make payroll tax payments at both the federal, state, and sometimes local levels. The due dates will vary by employer and are generally based on the dollar amount of the payroll and other factors specific to your business. The good news is that all QBO Payroll plans will take care of calculating, paying, and filing payroll taxes at the state and federal levels. As discussed, the Core plan is the only one that does not automatically take care of the local tax authority.

There are a few key reports that you should generate to help you understand the total cost of payroll to your business. These reports are also shown in *Figure 14.5*:

- **Payroll Tax Liability**: This report provides you with the details of how much payroll tax you are required to pay and how much you have already paid to state and federal tax authorities for a specified period of time.

- **Payroll Tax Payments**: This report provides you with the details of all tax payments you have made for a specific period of time.

- **Payroll Tax and Wage Summary**: This report shows total and taxable wages that are subject to federal and province/region/state withholding for a specific period of time.

While QBO Payroll handles the tax payments and filings on your behalf, it is still your responsibility to make sure that the tax forms and payments are submitted to the proper tax authorities on time. Otherwise, you could be subject to hefty penalties and fines. All payroll plans include unlimited tech support. Therefore, be sure to contact the Intuit payroll support team with any questions or concerns you may have regarding tax.

Managing 1099 contractors in QuickBooks Online

If you hire an individual to perform services for your business and they are not an employee, they are considered an independent contractor, also known as a **1099 contractor**. Payments to 1099 contractors must be tracked so that you can report this information to the IRS at the end of the year.

To ensure payments are tracked properly, you will need to set up contractors in QuickBooks, add an account to post all payments to, pay contractors with a paper check (or an **electronic fund transfer (EFT)**, or debit/credit card), and provide a 1099 form to all the contractors who meet the threshold at the end of the year. If the total payments to a contractor equal $600 or more, you must issue a 1099 form and report this information to the IRS. Failure to track and report payments to 1099 contractors could lead to penalties and fines.

Pro Tip: To determine what constitutes a 1099 vendor vs an employee, be sure to visit http://irs.gov to learn more about whether someone qualifies as a 1099 vendor. The laws around this are updated each year so be sure to visit the IRS website to stay up to date on changes made each year.

Let's get started with setting up 1099 contractors in QuickBooks Online.

Setting up 1099 contractors

It's important to set up 1099 contractors correctly in QuickBooks to ensure payments are tracked for 1099 reporting purposes. Within the last year, there have been *significant* improvements made in QBO to streamline the process of setting up and tracking payments to 1099 contractors. In previous years, you would have to set up a contractor in the Vendor Center and flag the vendor as a 1099 contractor. In the most recent version of QBO, there is now a Contractors Center that allows you to collect the information normally provided on a W-9 form electronically. A W-9 form is similar to a W-4 form for an employee. It includes the vendor's name, mailing address, business entity type (sole proprietor, partnership, S-Corp, or C-Corp), tax ID number, and signature.

To set up a new contractor, you simply send an invitation to them, which requires them to create a user ID and password. Once they do so, they can complete the W-9 form online. Once the form is completed, you will be notified and can go into QBO and view the electronic W-9 form. Within the Contractors Center, you can also process contractor payments and generate reports as needed.

Pro Tip: It is best practice to obtain a completed W-9 form from each contractor before you make your first payment to them. Having this information is important because you will need it to create a 1099 form, if applicable.

Follow these steps to set up a 1099 contractor in QuickBooks:

1. Navigate to **Payroll** and the **Contractors** tab, as shown in *Figure 14.6*:

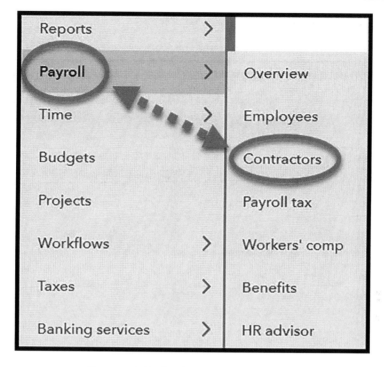

Figure 14.6: Navigating to Contractors Center

2. A screen similar to the one shown in the following screenshot will appear. Ensure that you are on the **Contractors** tab and click **Add your first contractor**:

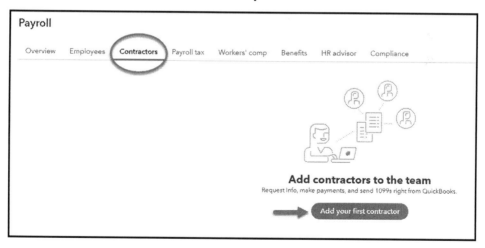

Figure 14.7: Clicking on Add your first contractor

3. The following screen will display. Complete the fields and click on the **Add contractor** button, as shown in *Figure 14.8*:

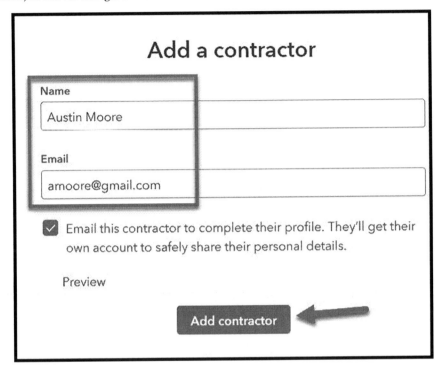

Figure 14.8: Completing the fields to add a new contractor

Pro Tip: Before QBO allows you to add a contractor, you will see a popup that requires you to enter a security code that will be sent to you via text message or email. You will not be allowed to proceed until you enter this code. Once the code is entered, the email invitation will be sent to the contractor, per the note right below the **Email** field shown in *Figure 14.8*.

4. You will see the new contractor listed in the Contractors Center, as shown in *Figure 14.9*:

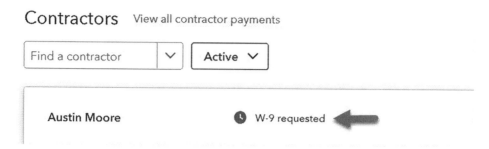

Figure 14.9: Status of the new Contractors listed in Contractor Center

After adding a new contractor, you will see them listed within the Contractors Center along with a note indicating that the W-9 form has been requested.

5. Once the W-9 form has been completed, the status will change to **W-9 ready**, as shown in *Figure 14.10*:

Figure 14.10: Reviewing the W-9 status for contractors

Repeat these steps for each 1099 contractor you pay throughout the year. Once you have added all of your contractors to QuickBooks, you are ready to make payments. We will discuss how to track and pay 1099 contractors next.

Pro Tip: Watch this Intuit video tutorial for a recap of how to add contractors to QBO: https://quickbooks.intuit.com/learn-support/en-us/help-article/account-management/invite-contractor-add-tax-info/L9QgBNvRy_US_en_US

Tracking and paying 1099 contractors

The simplest way to keep track of payments to 1099 vendors is to create an account called **Contractor labor expense**. This account should be added to your chart of accounts list and used to post all 1099 payments. For more information on adding accounts to the chart of accounts, refer to *Chapter 4, Customizing QuickBooks for Your Business*.

You can pay 1099 contractors within the Contractors Center. Follow the steps below to set up a payment to a contractor:

1. Navigate to the Contractors Center (**Payroll | Contractors**).

2. The following screen will display:

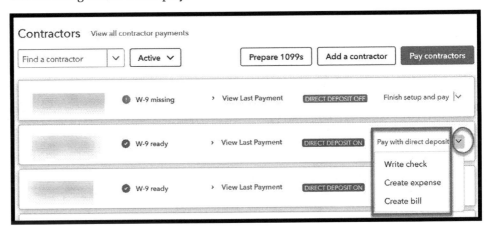

Figure 14.11: Paying contractors within the Contractors Center

3. In the far right column, click on the arrow to select the payment method (**Pay with direct deposit**, **Write check**, **Create expense**, or **Create bill**). Please note that if you would like to pay contractors with direct deposit, you will need to enter their payment details (bank account and bank routing number) before you can do so. This information can be entered by selecting the **Finish setup and pay** link that is shown in *Figure 14.11*.

4. For example, if you select **direct deposit**, you will see the screen shown in *Figure 14.12*:

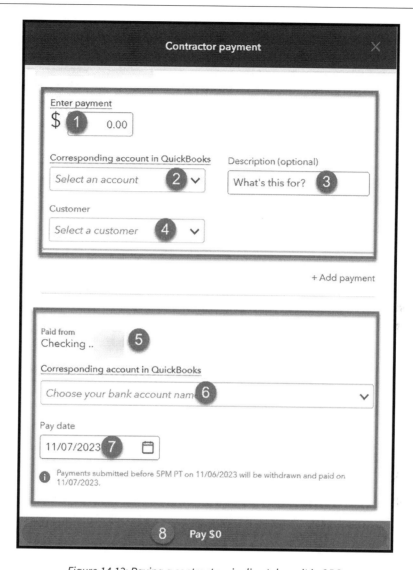

Figure 14.12: Paying a contractor via direct deposit in QBO

5. Complete the fields indicated in *Figure 14.12* as follows:

- **Enter payment (1)**: Enter the total amount of the payment.

- **Corresponding account in QuickBooks (2)**: From the drop-down, select the expense account (i.e., contractors expense, website design, etc.).

- **Description (3)**: Enter a brief description of the type of services provided by the contractor (i.e., monthly social media marketing). This field can also indicate the time period the payment is for (i.e., services for 11/01 to 11/15).

- **Customer (4)**: This field is optional. If you do have customers that you bill back for time worked by contractors, you can select the customer from the drop-down. This payment will also be included in the unbilled expenses account, which you can add to the customer's invoice in order to be reimbursed.

- **Paid from (5)**: You will see the bank account that the payment will be deducted from. This will typically be the business checking account or your payroll account if you have a separate account for employee and contractor payments.

- **Corresponding accounts in QuickBooks (6)**: From the drop-down, select the bank account in QuickBooks that corresponds to the actual bank account the payment will be deducted from in point 5 above.

- **Pay date (7)**: Select the date you would like the payment to be made. Typically, this will be the next business day as long as you submit it before 5 pm PT, as indicated in *Figure 14.12*.

- **Pay (8)**: Click on the **Pay** button to submit the payment.

> **Pro Tip:** After the payment is submitted, you will receive an email indicating that this payment is in process. In addition, the contractor will also receive an email to let them know the payment is in process. The email will include the payment amount and the date the payment has been scheduled for.

Now that you know how to add independent contractors to QuickBooks, set up an account to track payments, and make payments, it's time to discuss what you will do with this information.

1099 year-end reporting

1099 year-end reporting consists of printing and mailing 1099 forms to contractors who meet the $600 threshold and reporting this information to the IRS by January 31st each year.

This date is subject to change, so be sure to visit http://irs.gov each year to confirm the due date. Similar to a **W2 form** or **Wage and Tax Statement** for an employee that includes the amount paid in wages for a calendar year, the 1099 form includes the amount you have paid to a contractor within the calendar year.

This form is used by independent contractors to report their earnings for the year on their tax returns. Failure to provide this information to the IRS and the contractors could result in fines and penalties.

When you are ready to generate 1099 forms, the process is very simple. First, you review the accuracy of your information and the basic contact information for each contractor. Then, you review the payments that have been flagged as 1099 payments. If this information is correct, you can have Intuit process your 1099 forms electronically for a fee. Another option is to manually print and mail the 1099 forms yourself.

There are various types of 1099 forms. The most common are Form 1099-DIV, which is issued for dividends and distributions, Form 1099-INT, which is issued for interest income, and Form 1099-MISC, which is for miscellaneous income.

Pro Tip: Beginning with the 2011 tax year, the IRS requires you to exclude payments made to a 1099 vendor via debit card, credit card, or gift card from Form 1099-MISC. In addition, payments made through third-party payment networks, such as PayPal and QuickBooks Payments, should also be excluded. Instead, these payments are reported by the card issuers and third-party networks on Form 1099-K. The 1099 vendor will receive a copy of Form 1099-K directly from the card issuers.

Follow these steps to learn how to do 1099 reporting:

1. Navigate to the **Contractors Center**, as shown in *Figure 14.13*:

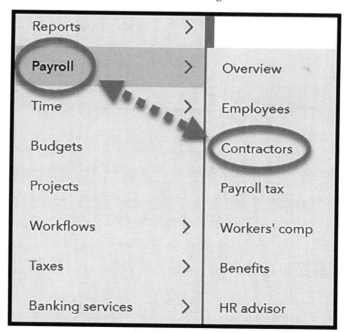

Figure 14.13: Navigating to Contractors Center

2. Click on **Prepare 1099s**, as shown in *Figure 14.14*:

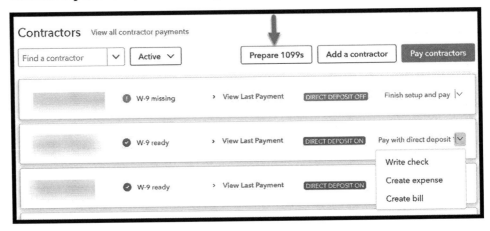

Figure 14.14: Clicking the Prepare 1099s button

3. If this is your first time preparing 1099s, the following screen will appear:

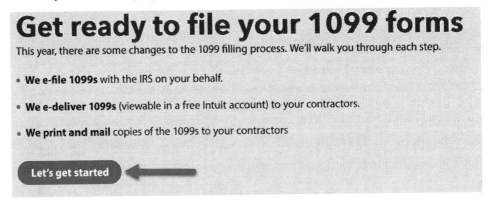

Figure 14.15: Clicking Let's get started to file your 1099 forms

4. Click the **Let's get started** button.

If you have prepared 1099s in QBO before, you will see the deadline for e-filing 1099s and the deadline for printing and mailing 1099s for the upcoming tax season.

5. On the next screen, you can review your company information and make any necessary corrections:

Figure 14.16: Reviewing your company info for accuracy

6. Click the **Save** button when you are done.

7. Click **Next** at the bottom of the screen. Then, select the box and the account you have categorized 1099 payments to, from the list shown in *Figure 14.17*:

Prepare 1099s

Map your QuickBooks contractor payments to 1099 boxes ←

1. First select the checkbox for each type of contractor payment you recorded last year. Each payment type corresponds to two most common types.

2. Then for each payment type selected, select all the QuickBooks expense accounts you used last year. Need more help.

If you're not sure which expense accounts you used, you can run a report of all last year's expenses marked for 1099.

Common payment types

☐ Non-employee compensation (most common) Box 1 1099-MISC

☐ Rents Box 1 1099-MISC

Direct sales

☐ Direct Sales - NEC Box 2 1099-NEC

☐ Direct Sales - MISC Box 7 1099-MISC

Other payment types

☐ Royalties Box 2 1099-MISC

☐ Other Income Box 3 1099-MISC

☐ Medical Payments Box 6 1099-MISC

☐ Substitute Payments in lieu of dividends or interest Box 8 1099-MISC

☐ Crop Insurance Proceeds Box 9 1099-MISC

☐ Gross Proceeds Paid to an Attorney Box 10 1099-MISC

☐ Fishing Boat Proceeds Box 5 1099-MISC

☐ Fish Purchased for Resale Box 11 1099-MISC

Federal tax withheld (very uncommon) When should I withhold taxes?

☐ Federal Tax Withheld - NEC Box 4 1099-NEC

☐ Federal Tax Withheld - MISC Box 4 1099-MISC

Figure 14.17: Mapping QuickBooks contractor payments to 1099 boxes

Pro Tip: In general, you will select the first box, **Non-employee compensation (most common)**, on the 1099 forms you generate for the contractors you have paid. In the drop-down below this box, select the account (category) these payments were posted to (i.e., **Contract labor**). To learn more about which box to select, refer to the IRS instructions for Form 1099. You can find this information at http://irs.gov.

8. On the next screen, review your contractors' information to ensure that it is accurate:

Review your contractors' info

Make sure your contractors' details are correct. To see which contractors meet the 1099 threshold, click **Next**.
Need to add anyone?

Add from Vendor list

CONTRACTOR NAME	ADDRESS	TAX ID	EMAIL	ACTION
Fred Flintstone	456 Bedrock Avenue Beverly Hills CA 90210	95-6789543	flintstone@bedrock.com	Edit
Wilma Flintstone	456 Bedrock Avenue Beverly Hills CA 90210	95-1234567	wflintstone@bedrock.com	Edit

Figure 14.18: Reviewing contractors' info for accuracy

Note that you cannot print 1099 forms if the mailing address and tax ID (or Social Security number) are missing. You must obtain this information prior to printing the 1099 forms.

9. A list of contractors that meet the 1099 threshold will be displayed on the next screen:

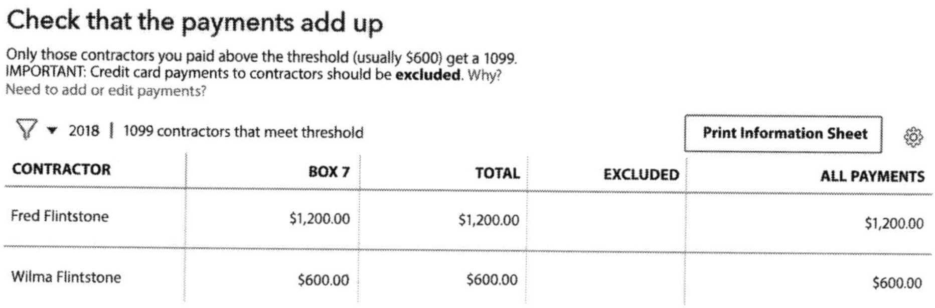

Check that the payments add up

Only those contractors you paid above the threshold (usually $600) get a 1099.
IMPORTANT: Credit card payments to contractors should be **excluded**. Why?
Need to add or edit payments?

▽ ▼ 2018 | 1099 contractors that meet threshold   Print Information Sheet   ⚙

CONTRACTOR	BOX 7	TOTAL	EXCLUDED	ALL PAYMENTS
Fred Flintstone	$1,200.00	$1,200.00		$1,200.00
Wilma Flintstone	$600.00	$600.00		$600.00

Figure 14.19: Reviewing 1099 payments for accuracy

To meet the 1099 threshold, contractors must receive payments totaling $600 or more within the calendar year. If a contractor was paid less than $600, you are not required to issue a 1099 form and the contractor will not show up in the preceding list.

10. On the next screen, select the 1099 plan that works best for you:

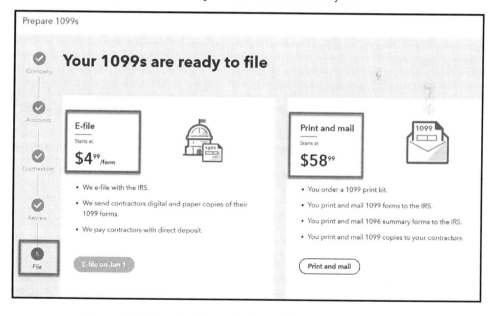

Figure 14.20: Choosing the method you wish to use to file 1099 forms

The two 1099 plans available are:

- **E-file**: This plan starts at $4.99/form and is a full-service plan. Intuit will e-file 1099 forms with the IRS on your behalf, and send contractors digital and paper copies of their 1099 forms. If you choose to, you can also pay contractors with direct deposit at no additional cost.

 Pro Tip: This is the most efficient way to process your 1099 forms. They will be sent to contractors as well as the IRS. You will also have a copy to keep on file for your records. While printing and mailing is an option, it is recommended to file electronically if possible.

- **Print and mail**: This plan starts at $58.99 and is ideal for business owners who prefer to process their 1099 forms in-house. Intuit will mail you a 1099 kit that will include blank 1099 forms you can print on. You are responsible for mailing all 1099 forms to your contractors and sending copies to the IRS before the deadline.

Please note that the pricing of these plans may differ. Visit https://www.intuit.com/ for the most up-to-date pricing plans available. To select a plan, just click the button at the bottom of the plan you want to choose and follow the onscreen prompts to complete filing your 1099 forms.

Summary

To recap, you now know what information is required to set up employees, and what payroll reports are available so that you can gain insight into your total payroll costs, and we discussed the importance of filing payroll tax forms and submitting payroll tax payments on time. Be sure to consult with a CPA, HR professional, or payroll expert to ensure payroll is set up properly. Otherwise, you run the risk of encountering errors, which could result in steep penalties.

In addition to payroll, we have also discussed how to set up 1099 contractors in QuickBooks, how to track payments that have been made to 1099 contractors, the various ways you can pay 1099 contractors, and how to report and file 1099 forms at the end of the year. If you hire individuals such as an attorney or a bookkeeper to provide services to your business, you now know how to set them up in QuickBooks and track payments that are made to them throughout the year. You also know that the threshold for reporting 1099 payments is $600 in payments within a calendar year. Finally, we have shown you how to sign up for the 1099 service provided by Intuit so that you can print and mail 1099 forms.

1099 reporting is just one of many tasks that must be performed at the end of the year. In the next chapter, we will discuss other tasks that must be completed so that we can close the books for the year.

Join our community on Discord

Join our community's Discord space for discussions with the authors and other readers:

`https://packt.link/quickbooks`

Section 5

Closing the Books and Handling Special Transactions

15

Closing the Books in QuickBooks Online

After you have entered all of your business transactions into QuickBooks for the year, you will need to finalize your financial statements so that you can hand them off to your accountant to file your taxes. To ensure you have recorded all business transactions for the financial period, we have included a checklist that you can follow to close your books. Closing your books will ensure that no additional transactions are entered into QuickBooks once you have finalized your financial statements. If you have a bookkeeper or an accountant who manages your books, they should ensure that all of the steps have been completed. In this chapter, we will cover each item on the checklist. This includes reconciling all bank and credit card accounts, making year-end accrual adjustments (if applicable), recording fixed asset purchases made throughout the year, recording depreciation, taking a physical inventory, adjusting retained earnings, and preparing financial statements.

Pro Tip: Many of the tasks in this section are typically performed by an accountant. Adding your tax preparer or **Certified Public Accountant (CPA)** as a user will allow them to access your QuickBooks data – this will allow the accountants to run reports and review the items that are needed, so that they can perform these tasks in preparation for your tax return. Later in this chapter, we will show you how to give your accountant access to your data.

The chapter objectives are summarized as follows:

- Reviewing a checklist to close your books
- Reconciling all bank and credit card accounts
- Making year-end accrual adjustments
- Reviewing new fixed asset purchases and adding them to the chart of account
- Making depreciation journal entries
- Taking a physical inventory and recording inventory adjustments
- Adjusting retained earnings for owner/partner distributions
- Recording journal entries
- Setting a closing date and password
- Preparing key financial reports
- Giving your accountant access to your data

By the end of this chapter, you will know all of the tasks you need to complete in order to close your books for the year. While most small businesses close their books annually, if you close your books on a monthly or quarterly basis, you will still need to follow the steps outlined in this chapter. In the following section, we will cover the details of the checklist.

 The US edition of QBO was used to create this book. If you are using a version that is outside the United States, the results may differ.

Reviewing a checklist for closing your books

As discussed, there are several steps you will need to take in order to close your books for the financial period. How often you close your books (for example, monthly, quarterly, or annually) will determine how often you need to complete these steps. Remember the importance of closing your books, as this will ensure that all transactions for the financial period have been recorded and that your financial statements are accurate, which is important because your accountant will use them to file your business tax return.

The following is a checklist of the steps you need to complete in order to close your books. You should complete them in the order presented:

1. Reconciling all bank and credit card accounts
2. Making year-end accrual adjustments

3. Reviewing new fixed asset purchases and adding them to the chart of accounts

4. Making depreciation journal entries

5. Taking a physical inventory and recording inventory adjustments

6. Adjusting retained earnings for owner/partner distributions

7. Setting a closing date and password

8. Preparing key financial reports

The purpose of closing the books is to ensure that the elements that impact the financial statements are reviewed and deemed accurate before finalizing the financial statements, which will in turn be used to file your business tax return. We will discuss each of these eight steps in detail, starting with reconciling all bank and credit card accounts.

1. Reconciling all bank and credit card accounts

In *Chapter 9, Reconciling Uploaded Bank and Credit Card Transactions*, you learned how to reconcile your bank and credit card accounts. Loans and lines of credit should also be reconciled, and we will cover how to manage a business loan and/or a line of credit from your financial institution in *Chapter 16, Handling Special Transactions in QuickBooks Online*. It's important for you to reconcile these accounts before closing the books so that you can ensure that all income and expenses for the period have been recorded in QuickBooks.

This will ensure that your financial statements are accurate and that you don't miss out on any tax deductions.

2. Making year-end accrual adjustments

If you are on the **accrual** basis of accounting, you need to make sure that all income and expenses that have been incurred for the period are recorded. As discussed in *Chapter 1, Getting Started with QuickBooks Online*, **accrual basis accounting** means that you recognize income when services have been rendered, regardless of when payment is received. The same concept is applied to expenses. For example, if you made a purchase in December but have not yet received the bill for it, you will need to record an adjusting journal entry before you close the books, in order to record the purchase. Some examples of accruals that may be required are inventory purchases that you have received the product for but not the bill and employee wages. Be sure to consult with your accountant for the proper recording of these transactions. We will discuss journal entries in more detail later in this chapter.

Pro Tip: Record all accounts receivable for the end of the period, which means invoicing all customers for work performed. This will ensure that all income is recorded and shows up on your profit and loss (income statement) report. Similarly, be sure to record all accounts payable (vendor bills) for any expenses incurred in the period. This will ensure that all expenses show up on the profit and loss (income statement).

3. Reviewing new fixed asset purchases and adding them to the chart of accounts

If you purchased any fixed assets during the year, you should add these to QuickBooks. As mentioned in *Chapter 1, Getting Started with QuickBooks Online*, fixed assets can be equipment purchased for your business such as computers or printers. Furniture such as a desk or chair are also considered fixed assets. Fixed assets are subject to **depreciation**, which is a **tax-deductible expense**. Depreciation is the reduction of the value of a fixed asset due to wear and tear. Tax-deductible expenses can reduce your tax bill, so you want to make sure that you take all of the deductions to which you are entitled. If you have not recorded new fixed asset purchases, then you will not have depreciation expenses recorded, which means you will miss out on what could be a significant tax deduction. It's also important to conduct a physical check to ensure that all of the assets on the books still exist and have not been disposed of.

Pro Tip: One of the newest features available in QBO is the ability to manage fixed assets. If you are using the QBO Advanced plan, QBO will automatically calculate depreciation and record monthly depreciation expenses for you. Refer to *Chapter 17, QuickBooks Online Advanced*, for step-by-step instructions on how to use this new tool.

For those of you who are not on the QBO Advanced plan, follow the steps below to add your fixed assets to QBO.

Please note that if you have already entered the fixed asset as an expense into QBO, do not record it as a fixed asset. For businesses located in the United States, the IRS recommends that you record purchases as expenses if they are $2,500 or less. Anything that is more than $2,500 you should enter as a fixed asset.

To add fixed assets to QuickBooks, you will need to have the following information on hand:

- Date of purchase
- Purchase price
- Type of asset
- Make and model (if applicable)
- Year

 Pro Tip: Your tax preparer should have a detailed list of fixed assets that have been reported on previous tax returns. It is a good idea to review this list annually to ensure it includes new purchases and/or disposal of assets.

Follow these steps to add a fixed asset to QuickBooks:

1. From the left menu bar, click on **Transactions**, as indicated in *Figure 15.1*:

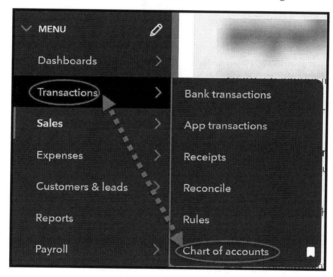

Figure 15.1: Navigating to Chart of accounts

2. Select **Chart of accounts**, and then click the **New** button, as indicated in *Figure 15.2*:

Figure 15.2: Clicking the New button

3.   For a new fixed asset, complete the fields, as shown in *Figure 15.3*:

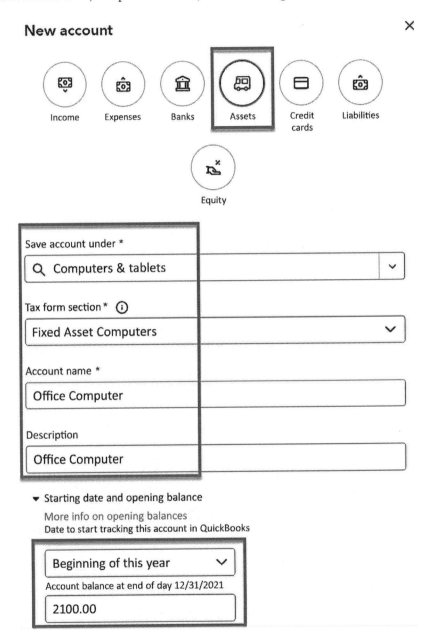

Figure 15.3: Entering details for a fixed asset

The following is a brief explanation of the fields that need to be completed for a new fixed asset:

- **Account type**: Select **Assets**, as shown in *Figure 15.3*.

- **Save account under**: From the drop-down menu, select **Computers & tablets**.

- **Tax form section**: This field should auto-populate based on the information in the **Save account under** field. In our example, **Fixed Asset Computers** is the correct tax form section.

- **Account name**: Type the name of the fixed asset in this field. In our example, this is **Office Computer**.

- **Description**: Type a more detailed description of the fixed asset in this field, or you can enter the account name again. In our example, we have entered **Office Computer**.

- **Starting date and opening balance**: Select the date that the asset was purchased in the starting date field. In our example, this asset was purchased at the **Beginning of this year**. The original cost should be entered into the account balance field, In our example, the original cost is **$2,100**. This amount will be used to calculate depreciation.

4.   Click the **Save and Close** button to add the asset to your chart of accounts list.

Be sure to complete these steps for each fixed asset you have purchased during the accounting period, provided that you have not already entered the items as an expense. Please be sure to consult with your tax professional to ensure fixed asset purchases are recorded properly on your books. After adding fixed assets to QuickBooks, you need to record depreciation expenses for the period.

4. Making depreciation journal entries

Depreciation is the reduction in the value of an asset, due to wear and tear after it has been in service for a period of time. To reflect the reduced value, you must record the depreciation expense in your books. Depreciation is also a tax-deductible expense, which can help to reduce your overall tax liability.

After adding fixed assets to QuickBooks, you need to record depreciation expenses for the period. As mentioned previously, if you subscribe to the QBO Advanced plan, QuickBooks will automatically compute and record depreciation for you. However, if you don't have QBO Advanced, you will need to calculate depreciation manually or have your accountant do this for you. In the *Recording journal entries* section of this chapter, we will show you how to record journal entries in QuickBooks. If you do have QBO Advanced, please refer to *Chapter 17, QuickBooks Online Advanced*, where we will show you how the new fixed asset manager works.

5. Taking a physical inventory and recording inventory adjustments

Reconciling an inventory involves making sure that the products you have on your shelf match what your books reflect as an on-hand inventory. You should take a physical inventory count at least once a year, if not more often. After taking a physical count, any discrepancies between the books and the physical count should be recorded in QuickBooks as inventory adjustments. After recording these inventory adjustments, your books and your warehouse will be in sync.

Follow these steps to record inventory adjustments in QuickBooks:

1. Click on the + **New** button, and select **Inventory qty adjustment** in the **OTHER** column, as indicated in *Figure 15.4*:

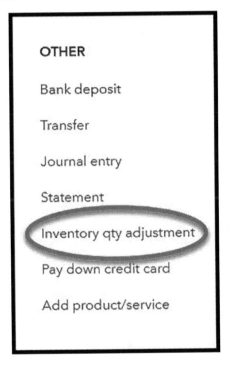

Figure 15.4: Choosing Inventory qty adjustment

2. Complete the fields for the inventory adjustment, as indicated in *Figure 15.5*:

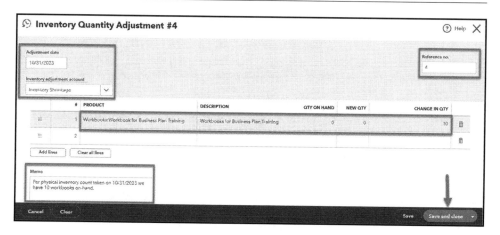

Figure 15.5: Completing the fields to record the inventory adjustment

The following is a brief explanation of the fields that need to be completed in order to record an inventory adjustment:

- **Adjustment date**: Enter the effective date of the adjustment. This date should be on or before the last day of the closing period. In our example, the inventory count was taken on **10/31/2023**.

- **Inventory adjustment account**: **Inventory Shrinkage** is the default account that will appear in this field. However, you can click the drop-down arrow and select a different account, or add a new one.

- **Reference no.**: This field will automatically populate with a number. If you prefer to customize the reference number, you can do so by typing directly into this field.

- **PRODUCT**: From the drop-down menu, select the item for which you are making an adjustment.

- **DESCRIPTION**: This field will automatically be populated based on the description in QuickBooks. You can also enter a description directly in this field.

- **QTY ON HAND**: This field will automatically be populated with what you currently have recorded in QuickBooks. This field cannot be adjusted.

- **NEW QTY**: Enter the quantity, based on the physical count that was taken in this field.

- **CHANGE IN QTY**: QuickBooks automatically computes the adjustment required by taking the difference between the **QTY ON HAND** and **NEW QTY** values entered.
- **Memo**: Enter a brief explanation of why the adjustment was made.

If you have extensive inventory tracking requirements that go beyond what's available in QBO, visit the Intuit app marketplace, where there are over 700 add-on programs that integrate seamlessly with QBO. In *Chapter 16, Handling Special Transactions in QuickBooks Online*, we show you how to navigate the QuickBooks App Center.

6. Adjusting retained earnings for owner/partner distributions

Retained earnings are the cumulative amount of your income and expenses for the prior period(s). This amount will be posted to the retained earnings account at the end of your fiscal/calendar year. QuickBooks will automatically make this entry for you. Depending on the type of organization (corporation, partnership, llc, sole proprietorship, or non-profit), you may need to move this balance to other equity accounts.

To distribute profits to the owners, you will need to create a journal entry to an equity account entitled *owner's draw* or *owner distributions* and offset it with retained earnings. Be sure to consult with your CPA or tax preparer if you are not familiar with this process.

To summarize what we have covered so far: many of the steps in the closing process are designed for you to review the transactions that have been recorded throughout the fiscal year, as well as make adjustments as needed for accruals such as wages, depreciation of fixed assets, and retained earnings of owner/partner distributions. The primary way these closing adjustments are recorded is through journal entries. We will take a brief break from going through the checklist now so that we can discuss this next.

Recording journal entries

A **journal entry** is used to adjust your books for transactions that have not been recorded throughout the year. Depreciation expenses for fixed assets, income and expense accruals, and adjustments to retained earnings are three examples we have discussed in this chapter.

Follow these steps to record a journal entry in QuickBooks:

1. Click the **+ New** button and select **Journal entry**, as indicated in *Figure 15.6*:

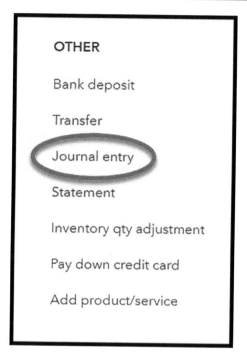

Figure 15.6: Selecting Journal entry in the OTHER column

2. A screen will appear, similar to the one shown in the following screenshot:

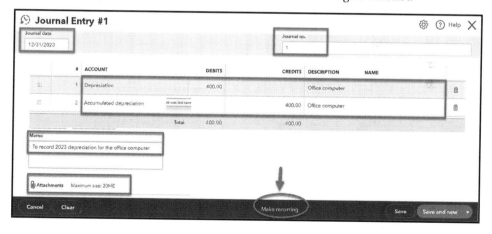

Figure 15.7: Journal Entry template

The following is a brief explanation of the fields that need to be completed in order to record a journal entry:

- **Journal date**: Enter the effective date of the journal in this field.
- **Journal no.**: QuickBooks will automatically populate this field with the next available journal number. If this is the first journal entry you have recorded, you can enter a starting number (such as **1000**), and QuickBooks will increment each journal entry number thereafter. Otherwise, QBO will start with number 1 (as shown in *Figure 15.7*).
- **ACCOUNT**: Select the account from the drop-down menu.
- **DEBITS**: Enter the debit amount in this field.
- **CREDITS**: Enter the credit amount in this field.
- **DESCRIPTION**: Type a detailed description of the purpose of the journal entry in this field. Adding a detailed description is recommended; it is helpful when referring to a journal entry to have an explanation of why it was made.
- **NAME**: If this journal entry is associated with a customer, you can select that customer from the drop-down list in this field.
- **Memo**: Include a brief description of the fixed asset that you are recording this journal entry for.
- **Attachments**: If you have any source documentation you would like to include, you can attach those documents directly to this transaction.
- **Make recurring**: To help you stay on top of these types of adjustments, you can make this journal entry recurring. This means you can set up this journal entry to automatically record on the date you specify. If you don't want QBO to automatically record the journal entry for you, you can also just receive a reminder to record the journal entry. To learn more about how to set up recurring transactions, refer to *Chapter 8, Recording Expenses in QuickBooks Online*.

Be sure to record all journal entries prior to generating financial statements. If you give your CPA or accountant access to your data, they can record all of the necessary journal entries and then generate the financial reports required to file your tax returns. We are now ready to continue with our checklist.

7. Setting a closing date and password

In an effort to maintain the integrity of your data, you should set a closing date and password after you have entered all transactions for the closing period. By setting a closing date, users will receive a warning message if they attempt to enter transactions that affect the closing period. For example, if you set a closing date of **12/31/23**, users will receive a warning message if they attempt to enter any transactions dated **12/31/23** or earlier.

Follow these steps to set a closing date and password in QBO:

1. Click on the gear icon, and then select **Account and settings** in the **YOUR COMPANY** column, as indicated in *Figure 15.8*:

Figure 15.8: Selecting Account and settings in the YOUR COMPANY column

2. Click on the **Advanced** tab, as indicated in *Figure 15.9*:

Figure 15.9: Clicking the Advanced option

3. The **Accounting** preferences are located at the very top of the next screen, as indicated in *Figure 15.10*:

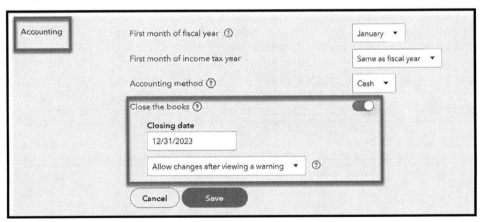

Figure 15.10: Reviewing the Accounting preferences

In the **Close the books** section, you can enter the closing date (that is, **12/31/2023**), which will give users a warning if they attempt to enter transactions dated on the closing date or prior to it. There are two types of warning messages. The first warning message is **Allow changes after viewing a warning**, as shown in *Figure 15.10* above. This message will allow users to proceed with entering the transaction after they close the warning message. The second warning message is **Allow changes after viewing a warning and entering a password**. This message requires users to enter a password to proceed with entering transactions. To choose this option, select it from the drop-down field, as shown in *Figure 15.10*, and enter the password you would like to use.

Pro Tip: Since QuickBooks does not have a formal closing process, choosing the option that requires a password to make changes is highly recommended, keeping users from making changes to prior years where tax returns have already been filed. *Don't give the closing password to anyone who is not authorized to enter transactions after the closing date.*

8. Preparing key financial reports

After you have completed the first seven steps in the closing checklist, you are ready to prepare financial statements. There are three primary financial statements you will need to prepare:

- **The trial balance**
- **The balance sheet**
- **The income statement (profit and loss report)**

In *Chapter 11, Business Overview Reports*, you learned what the balance sheet and income statement reports are, how to interpret the data, and how to generate these reports in QuickBooks. Your accountant, or CPA, will also request a trial balance report. A trial balance report lists all of the debits and credits recorded in QuickBooks for the period. If everything has been recorded properly, debits will always equal credits on this report.

Follow these steps to run a trial balance report in QuickBooks:

1. Navigate to **Reports**, as indicated in *Figure 15.11*:

Figure 15.11: Clicking Reports to navigate to the Reports Center

2. In the **For my accountant** section, click on **Trial Balance**, as indicated in *Figure 15.12*:

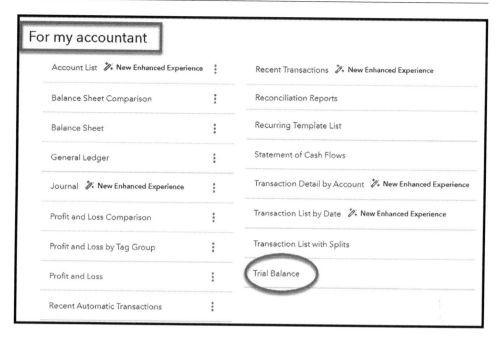

Figure 15.12: Running the trial balance report

3. The trial balance report will appear. Click the **Customize** button:

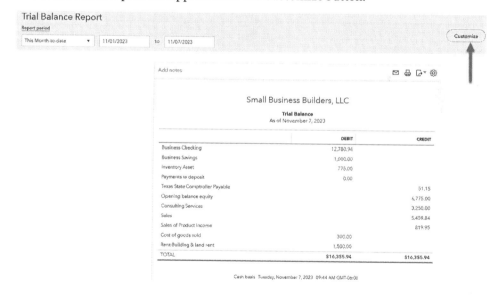

Figure 15.13: Customizing the trial balance report

The following report customization options will appear:

Figure 15.14: Reviewing the report customization options

There are a number of options available to customize the trial balance report. The following is a brief description of some of the information that can be customized:

- **Report period**: You can select a preset report period such as **Last Year** from the drop-down menu, or type a specific date range in the fields to the right of the preset field.

- **Accounting method**: As previously introduced in this book, you can choose the accounting method you want to be applied to the report, **Cash** or **Accrual**.

- **Number format**: There are a variety of options to format the numbers on a report. Omitting the cents and excluding accounts with a zero balance are just a couple of the options shown in the preceding screenshot.

- **Rows/Columns**: Choose which rows/columns are visible on the report.

- **Header**: You can edit the company name and the title of the report in the header section.

- **Footer**: You can choose to show the date/time when the report was prepared.

- **Alignment**: You can decide how to best align the information that appears in the header and footer sections of the report.

4. When you are done with your customizations, click the **Run report** button.

A report similar to the one in *Figure 15.15* will appear:

Small Business Builders, LLC

Trial Balance
As of November 7, 2023

	DEBIT	CREDIT
Business Checking	12,780.94	
Business Savings	1,000.00	
Inventory Asset	775.00	
Payments to deposit	0.00	
Texas State Comptroller Payable		51.15
Opening balance equity		6,775.00
Consulting Services		3,250.00
Sales		5,459.84
Sales of Product Income		819.95
Cost of goods sold	300.00	
Rent:Building & land rent	1,500.00	
TOTAL	$16,355.94	$16,355.94

Figure 15.15: Sample trial balance report

As discussed, the total debits column ($16,355.94) should always equal the total credits column ($16,355.94), as it does in the preceding report. If it does not, you will need to look into any discrepancies. The good news is, 99.99% of the time, this report will balance because QuickBooks does not allow you to post one-sided journals, which means that for every debit, there is always an offsetting credit to keep things in balance.

 Pro Tip: If you do have a trial balance that does not balance, you should calculate the difference between the debits and credits, and then look for that amount on the report. Most likely, there is an amount in one of the columns (debit or credit) that does not appear in the other column.

To summarize, you will need to review three key financial reports before closing your books: the balance sheet, the income statement, and the trial balance report. If you have a CPA or an accountant who reviews your financials and prepares your tax return, you can give that person access to your books so that they can run these reports without having to bother you. We will discuss giving your accountant access to your data next.

 Pro Tip: Always review the information on your reports one last time before sharing them with any third party outside of your organization. You add these reports to a report group and send them out instead of running them individually. Refer to *Chapter 10*, *Reports Center Overview*, for more information on this.

Giving your accountant access to your data

If you have an accountant or tax preparer to whom you need to grant access to your data, you can create a secure user ID and password for them. All you need to do is request their email address so that you can send them an invitation to access your data.

Follow these steps to invite an accountant to access your QuickBooks data:

1. Click on the gear icon, and select **Manage users** in the **YOUR COMPANY** column, as indicated in *Figure 15.16*:

Figure 15.16: Selecting Manage users from the YOUR COMPANY column

2. On the **Manage users** page, click on **Accountants**, as indicated in *Figure 15.17*:

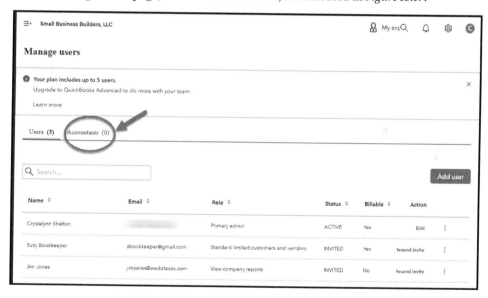

Figure 15.17: Clicking on Accountants

3. Enter your accountant or tax professional's email address, and click on **Invite**, as indicated in *Figure 15.18*, to invite your accountant to access your QuickBooks data:

Figure 15.18: Clicking the Invite button

Your accountant will receive an email, inviting them to access your QBO account. They will need to accept the invitation and create a secure password. Their user ID will be the email address that you entered in the form (shown in *Figure 15.18*).

Once you have given your accountant access to your books, they can simply log in to QuickBooks to get the information they need to prepare your taxes. This is highly recommended if your accountant needs to make any year-end adjustments. You can add/remove permissions access as needed if you prefer them only to have access at tax time. To resend an invite or delete access, go back to the **Accountants** tab, and tick the checkbox to the right of **Resend invite**:

Figure 15.19: Option to resend an invite from the accountant user page

Summary

In this chapter, you have learned about the key tasks that need to be completed to close your books for the accounting period. As discussed, you need to reconcile all bank and credit card accounts, record year-end accrual adjustments (if your accounting is accrual-based), add fixed asset purchases, record depreciation expenses, take a physical inventory and make the necessary adjustments, adjust retained earnings for distributions made to the business owners, set a closing date and password, and prepare key financial statements. You can perform these tasks yourself, or you can give your accountant access to your QuickBooks data to take care of this for you.

This chapter is the last one that covers the QuickBooks features that most small businesses will use. Congratulations on successfully completing all of the chapters thus far! In the next chapter, we will cover some additional topics, such as adding apps to QBO, managing credit card payments, and recording bad debt expenses.

Join our community on Discord

Join our community's Discord space for discussions with the authors and other readers:

`https://packt.link/quickbooks`

16

Handling Special Transactions in QuickBooks Online

So far, we have covered the most common transactions for which small businesses use Quick-Books. However, there are a few more topics that we would like to share with you. While some of these may not apply to your business when you are starting out, it's a good idea to be aware that they exist.

First, we will discuss how to properly set up a business loan or line of credit. If you have a business loan or line of credit, you need to keep track of payments and overall outstanding balances in QuickBooks. Next, we will cover petty cash. Petty cash is often used for small purchases such as stamps or lunch for the office. Due to this, we will show you how to add a petty cash account, record petty cash transactions, replenish petty cash, and reconcile the petty cash account. While you always hope it doesn't happen to you, there may come a time when you are unable to collect payment from a customer. If this happens, you will need to record a bad debt, so we will show you how to properly record bad debt expenses. Finally, we will show you how to record delayed charges. Delayed charges are used to keep track of the services you have provided to customers that you will invoice at a later date.

In this chapter, we will cover the following topics:

- Setting up business loans and lines of credit
- Managing petty cash
- Recording bad debt expense
- Tracking delayed charges and credits

 The US edition of QBO was used to create this book. If you are using a version that is outside the United States, results may differ.

Setting up business loans and lines of credit

If you take out a business loan or line of credit, you need to track the payments that have been made, as well as the outstanding balance owed, in QuickBooks. This will ensure that your financial statements include the money that is owed to all creditors. If this information is not included in QuickBooks, it will not show up on your financial statements. If this information is not reported in your financial statements, you will have inaccurate reports and you could miss out on legitimate tax deductions.

In this section, we will cover how to set up a business loan or line of credit, how to track payments, and how to stay on top of the outstanding balances owed.

Adding a business loan or line of credit to the chart of accounts

The first step to properly tracking loans and lines of credit in QuickBooks is to set them up on the chart of accounts. We will do this next. Follow these steps:

1. Navigate to **Transactions** and select **Chart of accounts**, as shown in *Figure 16.1*:

Figure 16.1: Navigating to Chart of accounts

2. Click on the **New** button located to the right of **Run Report**, as shown in *Figure 16.2*:

Figure 16.2: Clicking the New button

3. Fill in the fields shown in the following screenshot to add a new business loan or line of credit account:

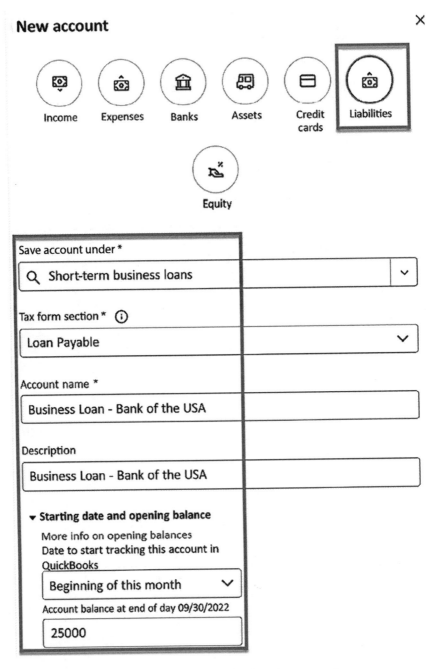

Figure 16.3: Adding a new business loan account

A brief description of the fields in the preceding screenshot is as follows:

- **Account type**: Business loans and lines of credit are money that is owed to a creditor, also known as a liability.

- **Save account under**: There are two types of liabilities; current liabilities and long-term liabilities. Current liabilities have a term of less than one year, while long-term liabilities have a term greater than one year. Depending on the type of loan that you have, you can type in the keyword loan and you will have the option to select **Short-term business loans** (as we have done) or **Long-term business loans** from the drop-down menu.

- **Tax form section**: QuickBooks will automatically populate this field for you, based on the information entered in the previous field.

- **Account name**: In this field, enter the name of the account. This will generally include the type of liability (loan or line of credit) and the name of the financial institution (Business Loan - Bank of the USA, in our case).

- **Description**: In this field, you can simply copy and paste the name or include a more detailed description, such as the account number of the loan or line of credit.

- **Starting date and opening balance**: From the drop-down, select the date you received the loan along with the amount in the field below that. This information will be used to keep track of the balance of the loan as you make payments.

 Pro Tip: Another way to record a beginning balance for a line of credit (or loan) is by categorizing the transaction to the loan account (created above) when you receive the funds in your bank account.

4. Click the **Save and Close** button to add the loan or line of credit account to your chart of accounts list.

If you haven't done so already, you will need to repeat these steps to add an interest paid or interest expense account to the chart of accounts list. You will track the interest portion of your payments in this account. Now, we'll cover how to make payments on a loan or line of credit.

 Pro Tip: It is very important that you track the interest in loans and lines of credit in a separate expense account. The reason for doing this is that interest expense for most liabilities such as this is tax-deductible. If the amount is buried with the principal payments, it will be difficult to go back and calculate later on.

Making payments on a loan or line of credit

In general, you can make payments on a loan or line of credit in the same manner that you pay other creditors. You can write a check or have the funds automatically deducted from your bank account. Here, we will walk through how to record a payment.

Follow these steps to make payments on a loan or line of credit with a check:

1. Click on the **+ New** button and then select **Check** in the **Vendors** column, as shown in *Figure 16.4*:

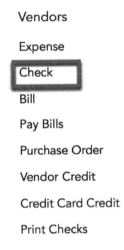

Figure 16.4: Navigating to Check

2. Fill in the fields for the loan payment:

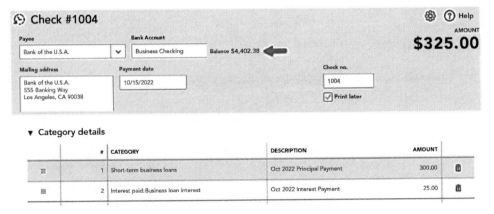

Figure 16.5: Completing the Check form to record payment for the loan

A brief description of the fields you need to complete to record a payment for a loan or line of credit is as follows:

- **Payee**: From the drop-down menu, select the payee. If you haven't added the payee to QuickBooks, you can do so here by selecting **Add new** from the drop-down menu.

- **Bank Account**: If you have more than one bank account, you need to select the bank account that you want to write the check from in the drop-down menu. When you select the bank account, the current balance will appear to the right of the field, as indicated in the preceding screenshot.

- **Mailing address**: This field will automatically be populated with the address on file for the payee you've selected. If you don't have an address on file, you can type the information directly into this field. However, it's best to go to the vendor profile and add the address information there. If you type it in this field, the address will not be saved to the payee's profile.

- **Payment date**: Enter the check date or the date the payment was deducted from your bank account.

- **CATEGORY**: In this field, you need to select accounts that are affected by this payment. In general, that will be the loan payable account (principal) and an interest expense account. The portion of the payment that applies to the principal amount should be allocated to the loan payable account. The portion of the payment that applies to the interest should be allocated to the interest paid account.

- **DESCRIPTION**: Type a brief description of what the payment is for in this field.

- **AMOUNT**: Enter the amount you wish to pay in this field.

If your loan payments are automatically withdrawn from your bank account, you will enter these payments as an expense. You will repeat step 1 but instead of selecting **Check**, you will select **Expense**. The fields you will complete are similar to the fields required on the **Check** form.

 Pro Tip: In order to accurately record the proper amounts for the principal and interest accounts, you may need to refer to your loan statement to see how your payment was applied. Be sure to do this so that your books match up with those of the financial institutions.

One final step you should do to ensure that the business loans and lines of credit on your books match your statements is to reconcile these accounts on a monthly basis. The steps to reconcile business loans and lines of credit are identical to reconciling your bank accounts. Refer to *Chapter 9, Reconciling Uploaded Bank and Credit Card Transactions*, for step-by-step instructions on reconciling.

Remember, it's important for your financial statements to be as accurate as possible. This means including all of the money that is owed to creditors, such as loans and lines of credit. In addition, to deduct the interest expense, you need to keep track of it in QuickBooks.

If you tend to pay cash for small incidentals for the office, such as a Starbucks run for the office or stamps, you need to set up a petty cash fund to keep track of these types of expenses. We will show you how to manage petty cash in QuickBooks next.

Managing petty cash

Petty cash is a small amount of money that's used to cover incidentals such as postage, lunch for the office, or other items. Petty cash is generally no more than $500 and is kept under lock and key and managed by the business owner or someone designated by the owner. Like all business expenses, you need to keep track of all your receipts so that you can record the expenses in QuickBooks.

In this section, we will discuss how to track petty cash, record petty cash expenses, and reconcile the petty cash account. Let's get started by creating a petty cash account.

Adding a petty cash account in QuickBooks

In order to track petty cash in QuickBooks, we need to add a petty cash account to the chart of accounts.

Follow these steps to add a petty cash account:

1. Navigate to **Transactions**, as shown in *Figure 16.6*:

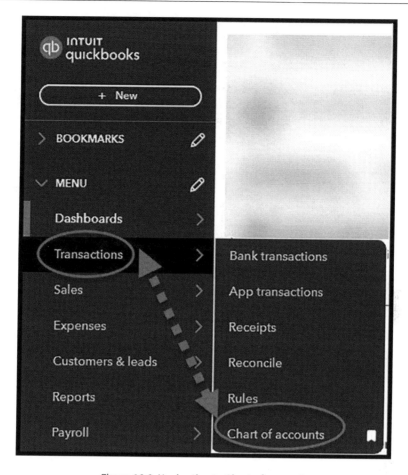

Figure 16.6: Navigating to Chart of accounts

2. Select **Chart of accounts** and then click the **New** button, as shown in *Figure 16.7*:

Figure 16.7: Clicking the New button

3. Fill in the **New account** setup window, as shown in *Figure 16.8*:

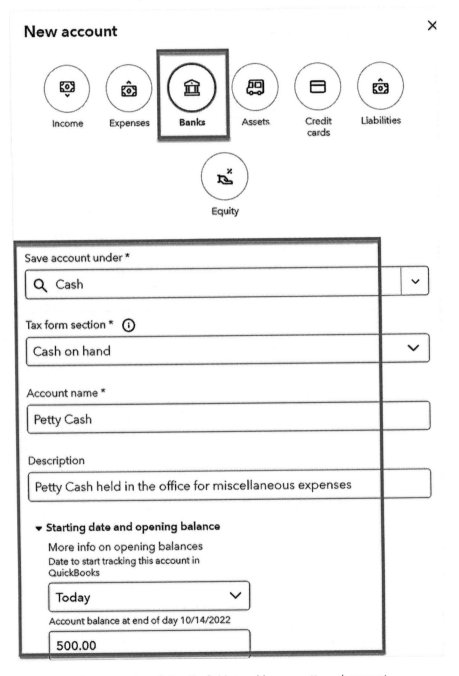

Figure 16.8: Completing the fields to add a new petty cash account

The following is a brief explanation of the information you will need to fill in:

- **Account type**: From the drop-down menu, select **Banks** as the account type. All petty cash accounts should be categorized as bank accounts and treated as such.

- **Save account under**: Type the keyword `Cash` and select it from the drop-down menu.

- **Tax form section**: QuickBooks will automatically populate this field based on the information entered in the previous field.

- **Account name**: In this field, you can put `Petty Cash` as the name of the account and any additional details required.

- **Description**: If there is additional information that will help you to identify this account, you can include it in this field or use the account name.

- **Starting date and opening balance**: Enter the date that you established the petty cash fund along with the amount.

Pro Tip: Instead of entering a starting balance in this account, you can record a transfer from a business checking account to the petty cash account in QuickBooks. In general, this is the most likely place that the cash will originate from.

4. Save your changes to add the petty cash account to the chart of accounts list.

Pro Tip: If you are using apps such as PayPal, Zelle, or Cash App, you will set these accounts up in the same manner as we have done the petty cash account. It's important to treat these accounts like your bank account by recording all transactions and reconciling these accounts monthly or more often.

Note that if you do not pay for expenses from your Zelle or Cash App accounts, you do not have to set these up as separate bank accounts, assuming the money received from these apps is deposited directly into your business checking account.

Now that you have created a petty cash account, you are ready to record the purchases that are made using petty cash.

Recording petty cash transactions

Receipts for petty cash expenditures should be kept in the same place as the petty cash is kept: under lock and key. If possible, you should enter the petty cash receipts into QuickBooks on a weekly basis. To minimize manual data entry, you should use the receipt capture feature in QBO. This feature allows you to upload the paper receipt to QBO. QBO will read the data on the receipt to assist you with categorizing it. Refer to *Chapter 8, Recording Expenses in QuickBooks Online*. If petty cash is not used that often, monthly should be sufficient.

Follow these steps to record petty cash transactions:

1. Navigate to the chart of accounts, as we did in the previous section.

2. Click on the **View register** link to the right of **Petty Cash**, as shown in *Figure 16.9*:

Figure 16.9: Clicking on the View register link

3. Click on the arrow next to **Add check** and select **Expense**, as shown in *Figure 16.10*:

Figure 16.10: Clicking the drop-down arrow next to Add check and selecting Expense

4. Fill in the remaining fields, as shown in *Figure 16.11*:

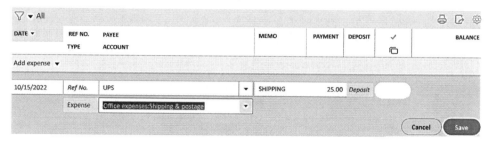

Figure 16.11: Completing the fields to record the expense

Explanations of the fields to fill in are as follows:

- **DATE**: Enter the date of purchase in this field.
- **REF NO.**: If you have a reference number such as an invoice number or account number, enter it in this field.
- **PAYEE**: Select the payee from the drop-down menu. If the payee has not been set up in QuickBooks, begin typing the name of the payee. You will see an option to add the payee to QuickBooks.
- **ACCOUNT**: Select the account the expense should be charged to from the **Chart of accounts** drop-down menu.
- **MEMO**: Type a brief description of what was purchased in this field.
- **PAYMENT**: Enter the amount of the purchase in this field.

5. Be sure to click the **Save** button to record the transaction.

Repeat the preceding steps to record each petty cash receipt in QuickBooks.

Replenishing petty cash

Eventually, you will get to a point where you've run out of petty cash or you don't have enough to pay for an item. Before replenishing petty cash, make sure you have entered all of the receipts for petty cash purchases that have been made thus far. Similar to a bank account, you can record a transfer in QuickBooks so that you can transfer money from a checking account to a petty cash account. Of course, to get the actual cash, you will need to make a withdrawal from your business checking account to replenish the actual funds.

To record a transfer from the business checking account to petty cash, follow these steps:

1. Navigate to the petty cash register by going to the chart of accounts and clicking **View register** to the right of **Petty Cash**, as you did in the previous section.

2. Click on the drop-down arrow and select **Transfer**, as shown in *Figure 16.12*:

Figure 16.12: Clicking on Add transfer and selecting Transfer

3. Fill in the fields shown in the following screenshot to record the transfer:

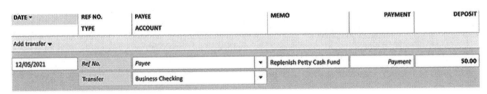

Figure 16.13: Completing the fields to record the transfer

Brief explanations of the fields you need to fill in to complete the transfer are as follows:

- **DATE:** The date the funds will be deposited into the petty cash account.
- **PAYEE:** Since you are the payee, you can leave this field blank.
- **ACCOUNT:** Select the bank account where the funds will be drawn from. In our example, it is the business checking account.
- **MEMO:** Include a brief description, such as **Replenish Petty Cash Fund**.

  If you have recorded all the money that you have paid out of petty cash, this transaction will increase the balance back to the cash on hand in your petty cash box.

- **DEPOSIT:** Enter the amount that is being transferred to the petty cash account.

4. Once you have completed all of these fields, click the **Save** button to complete the transfer. You will need to match this transfer to the bank transaction, which we showed you how to do in *Chapter 9, Reconciling Uploaded Bank and Credit Card Transactions*.

Now that you know how to add the petty cash account to the chart of accounts, record petty cash expenses, and replenish the petty cash fund, you need to know how to ensure that it stays in balance. Like most bank accounts, this will require you to reconcile the petty cash account.

Reconciling petty cash

As we mentioned previously, petty cash is similar to bank and credit card accounts that you track in QuickBooks. You need to ensure these accounts remain in balance. To do that, you must reconcile them. In *Chapter 9, Reconciling Uploaded Bank and Credit Card Transactions*, we showed you how to reconcile these accounts in QuickBooks. Refer to that chapter for step-by-step instructions on how to reconcile your petty cash account. I recommend that you reconcile your petty cash account *before* you replenish it. This will ensure that you have accounted for all the expenses that have been paid for using petty cash and that you have all the receipts to support these purchases.

While you will hope to avoid such a situation, there may come a time when a customer cannot afford to pay their outstanding balance. If this happens, you will need to write off the receivable as bad debt. We will discuss how to record bad debt expenses next.

Recording bad debt expenses

If you're in business long enough, there will come a time when a customer is unable or unwilling to pay you. If you use cash-based accounting, you don't need to record bad debt expenses because you don't have accounts receivable. However, if you do extend credit to your customers and, after attempting to collect the payment, you become aware that you will not be able to collect payment, you should write off the bad debt. This will ensure that your financial statements remain accurate and that revenue is not overstated.

There are three steps you need to follow in order to write off bad debt: first, you need to add a bad debt item to the products and services list; next, you need to create a credit memo; and finally, you need to apply the credit memo to the unpaid customer invoice. We will walk you through these steps in this section.

Creating a bad debt item

The first step of recording bad debt expenses is to add an item to the products and services list for tracking.

Follow these steps to create a bad debt item:

1. Click on the gear icon and select **Products and Services**, as shown in *Figure 16.14*:

Figure 16.14: Navigating to the Products and Services list

2. Select the item type, as shown in *Figure 16.15*:

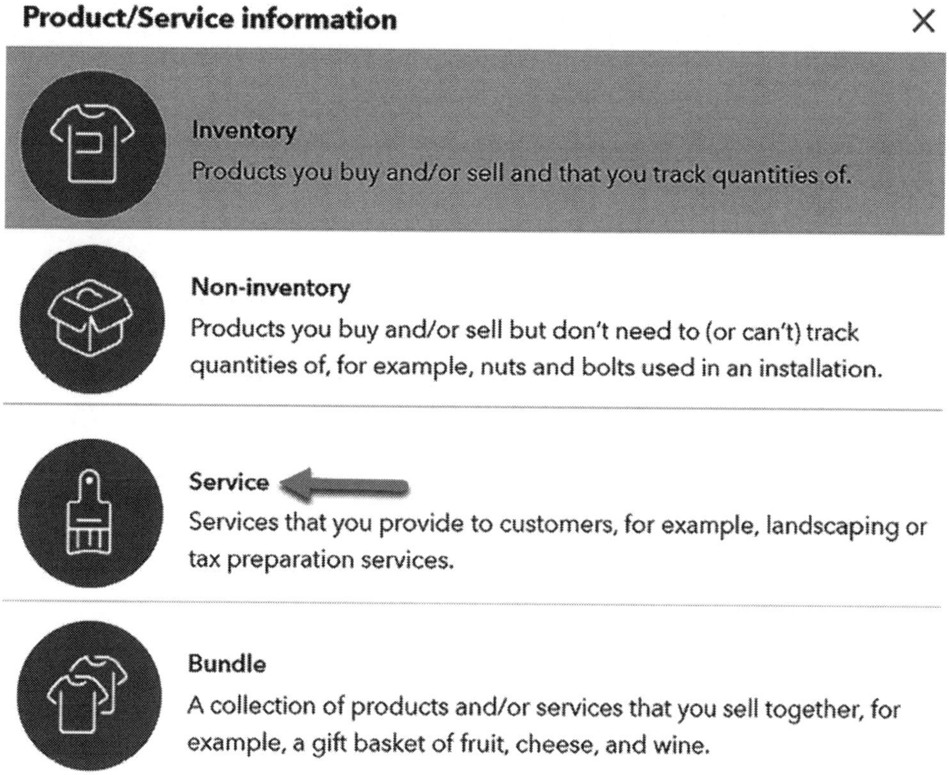

Product/Service information

Inventory
Products you buy and/or sell and that you track quantities of.

Non-inventory
Products you buy and/or sell but don't need to (or can't) track quantities of, for example, nuts and bolts used in an installation.

Service ⟵
Services that you provide to customers, for example, landscaping or tax preparation services.

Bundle
A collection of products and/or services that you sell together, for example, a gift basket of fruit, cheese, and wine.

Figure 16.15: Selecting Service as the item type

As you can see, there are four item types to choose from. **Service** is the item type we will use for bad debt expenses.

3. Fill in the following fields to add **Bad Debt** to the items list:

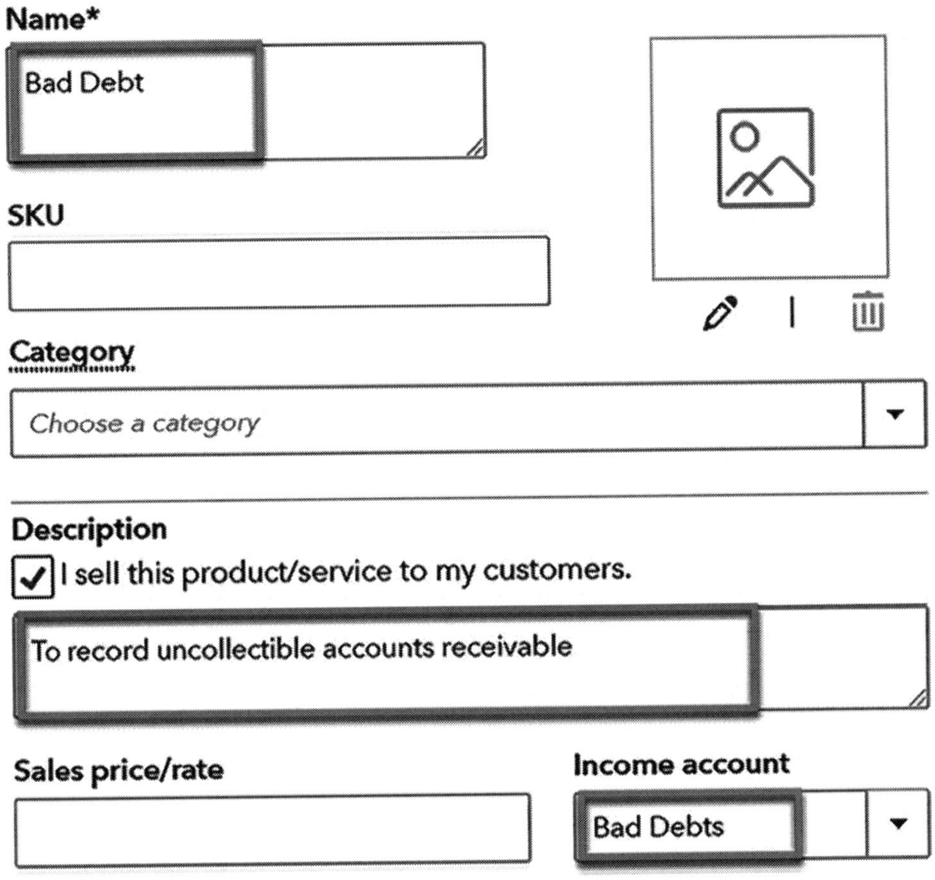

Name*

Bad Debt

SKU

Category

Choose a category ▼

Description

☑ I sell this product/service to my customers.

To record uncollectible accounts receivable

Sales price/rate

Income account

Bad Debts ▼

Figure 16.16: Completing the fields to add Bad Debt to the Products and Services list

4. Brief descriptions of the fields to fill in are as follows:

    - **Name:** Enter Bad Debt or Bad Debt Expense in the item's **Name** field.

    - **Description:** Enter a brief description of the types of transactions that will be recorded using this item.

- **Income account**: From the drop-down, select **Bad Debts**. This should be an expense account on the chart of accounts list. If you did not create this account, click on the drop-down arrow, scroll up, and select **Add new** to create the bad debt expense account.

Now that you've set up the new **Bad Debt** expense item, you can use this item to record the bad debt on a credit memo form.

Creating a credit memo

In addition to recording bad debt, a credit memo is generally used to refund a customer for items purchased that were returned or services that were not rendered in full. After creating the credit memo, we can apply it to the unpaid customer invoice.

Follow these steps to create a credit memo:

1. Click on the **+ New** button and select **Credit Memo**, as shown in *Figure 16.17*:

Create

Customers

Invoice

Receive Payment

Estimate

Credit Memo

Sales Receipt

Figure 16.17: Navigating to Credit Memo

2. Fill in the fields shown in *Figure 16.18*:

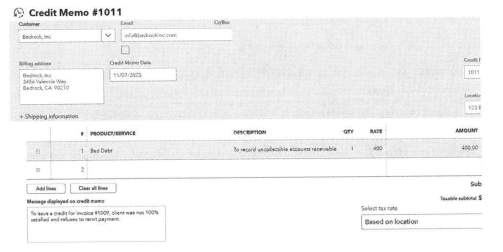

Figure 16.18: Completing the fields in the Credit Memo form

Brief explanations of the fields to fill in to complete the credit memo are as follows:

- **Customer**: Select the customer from the drop-down menu.

- **Email**: The email address that you have on file will automatically populate this field. If you don't have an email address on file, you can type one in directly.

- **Billing address**: The billing address you have on file will automatically populate this field. If you don't have a billing address on file, you can enter one in this field.

- **Credit Memo Date**: Select the date you would like to record this credit memo.

- **PRODUCT/SERVICE**: Select the **Bad Debt** item you created in the previous section from the drop-down menu.

- **DESCRIPTION**: The description field should automatically be populated with the description of the **Bad Debt** item.

- **QTY**: Select **1**.

- **RATE**: Enter the amount of the invoice that you want to write off in this field.

- **AMOUNT**: This field will automatically be populated with the amount you entered into the **RATE** field.

- **Message displayed on credit memo**: Provide a brief explanation for the bad debt to be written off in this field.

3.   Once you've filled in all the fields in the credit memo, save it.

We will show you how QuickBooks applies the credit memo to the customer's open invoice next.

Applying a credit memo to an outstanding customer invoice

The final step in writing off bad debt is to remove the open invoice from accounts receivable. In most cases, QBO will automatically apply credits to open invoices if you have turned this feature on. In *Chapter 2, Company File Setup*, we showed you how to turn on the **Automatically apply credits** feature. If you choose not to use this feature, you can manually apply the credit memo to the open customer invoice. Follow these steps to see how to apply the credit memo to the open customer invoice:

1.   From the left menu, select **Sales**, as shown in *Figure 16.19*:

Figure 16.19: Navigating to Sales

2. On the next screen, click on the **All sales** tab, as shown below:

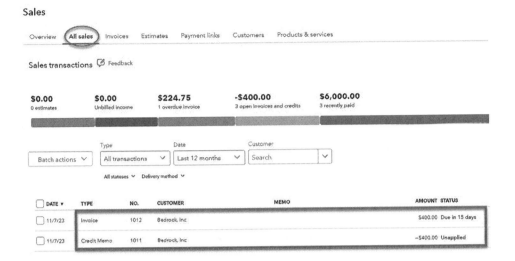

Figure 16.20: Selecting the invoices and/or credit memos to process

In *Figure 16.20*, you can see the invoice and the credit memo listed for **Bedrock, Inc.** However, the invoice remains open with a status of **Due in 15 days** and the credit memo has a status of **Unapplied**.

Follow the steps below to apply the credit memo to the open invoice:

1. Click on **Receive payment**, as indicated in *Figure 16.21* below:

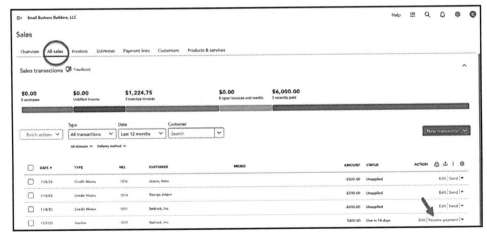

Figure 16.21: Selecting Receive payment

2. The **Receive Payment** window will be displayed, as shown in *Figure 16.22*:

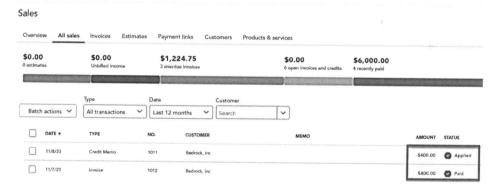

Figure 16.22: Completing the fields in the Receive Payment window

3. Select the invoice (**Invoice # 1012**) and the open credit (**Credit Memo # 1011**), as shown in *Figure 16.22*. The amount received should be **0.00** since they will offset each other.

4. After clicking on **Save and Close**, the following screen will be displayed:

Sales

Overview	All sales	Invoices	Estimates	Payment links	Customers	Products & services

$0.00	$0.00	$1,224.75		$0.00	$6,000.00
0 estimates	Unbilled income	3 overdue invoices		6 open invoices and credits	4 recently paid

	Type	Date	Customer		
Batch actions ∨	All transactions ∨	Last 12 months ∨	Search ∨		

	DATE ▾	TYPE	NO.	CUSTOMER	MEMO	AMOUNT	STATUS
☐	11/8/23	Credit Memo	1011	Bedrock, Inc		-$400.00	✓ Applied
☐	11/7/23	Invoice	1012	Bedrock, Inc		$400.00	✓ Paid

Figure 16.23: Reviewing the updated status for the invoice and credit memo

The status of the invoice is now **Paid** and the status of the credit memo is now **Applied**.

To summarize, it's important that you write off accounts as soon as they become uncollectible. This will ensure that the accounts receivable balance is not overstated. If you are an accrual basis taxpayer, you will not want to pay tax on income that you will never receive.

Pro Tip: If the customer has already paid the invoice and you need to refund their money, do not create a credit memo. Instead, create a refund receipt. To do this, click on the **+New** menu, select **Refund Receipt**, and complete the form as shown below.

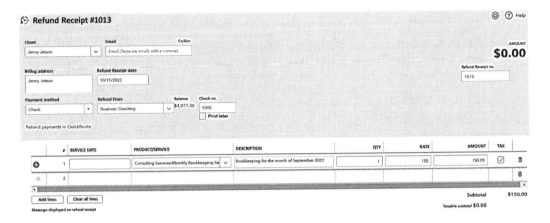

Figure 16.24: Creating a refund receipt

If you provide ongoing services to customers on a weekly or bi-weekly basis but don't want to invoice customers that often, you should consider using delayed charges. Delayed charges allow you to accumulate charges in QuickBooks (without affecting the financial statements). Once you are ready to bill a customer, you can easily transfer the delayed charges to an invoice. We will discuss delayed charges and credits in detail next.

Tracking delayed charges and credits

Delayed charges and credits are used to keep track of services that are provided to customers so you can bill them sometime in the future. For example, if someone provides weekly pool maintenance to customers but does not want to bill them until the end of the month, delayed charges are ideal for keeping track of the services that are provided each week. These weekly services can easily be added to an invoice when it's time to bill the customer.

Follow these steps to record delayed charges:

1. Click on the **+ New** button and select **Delayed charge**, as shown in *Figure 16.25*:

Figure 16.25: Navigating to Delayed charge

2. Fill in the necessary fields to record the delayed charge, as shown in *Figure 16.26*:

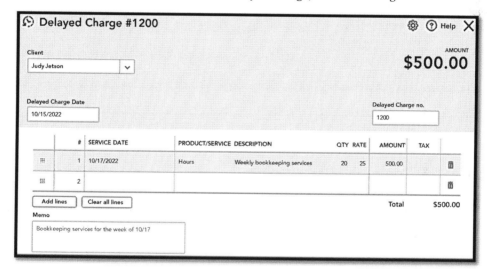

Figure 16.26: Completing the Delayed Charge form

Brief descriptions of the fields to fill in are as follows:

- **Customer/Client**: Select the customer from the drop-down menu.
- **Delayed Charge Date**: Select the date the services were provided.
- **PRODUCT/SERVICE**: Select the type of service that will be provided from the drop-down menu.

- **DESCRIPTION**: This field should automatically be populated with the description that was used to set up the product/service. However, you can also enter a description directly in this field.
- **QTY**: Type a quantity into this field, if applicable.
- **RATE**: Enter the total amount or the hourly rate for the service.
- **AMOUNT**: This field is automatically calculated by taking the quantity and multiplying it by the rate.
- **Memo**: Enter a brief description in this field.

When you save a delayed charge, it is a non-posting transaction, which means it doesn't affect the financial statements. Next, we will show you how to add delayed charges to an invoice:

1. From the **+New** menu, select **Invoice**. Select a customer from the drop-down menu and you will see a drawer open to the far right, listing the delayed charges that haven't been billed:

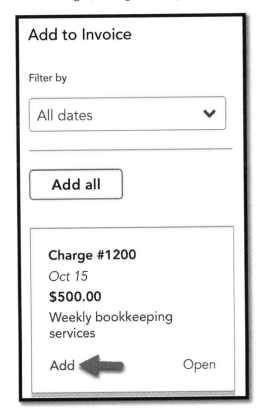

Figure 16.27: Selecting the delayed charges to bill the customer for

2. On this screen, click the **Add** button to add the charges to an invoice.
3. Save the invoice to record an increase in accounts receivable and income.

   If you would like to review a list of unbilled charges before creating an invoice, you can do so by running an **Unbilled charges** report. We will show you how to generate this report next.

4. Click on **Reports**, scroll to the **Who owes you** section, and select **Unbilled charges**, as shown in *Figure 16.28*:

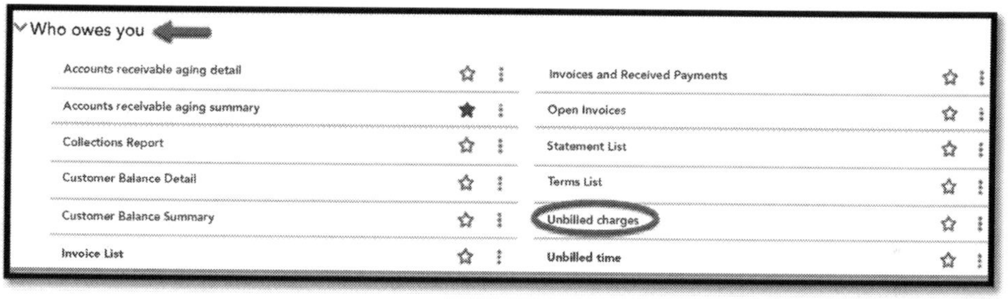

Figure 16.28: Navigating to the Unbilled charges report

5. The **Unbilled Charges** report will appear:

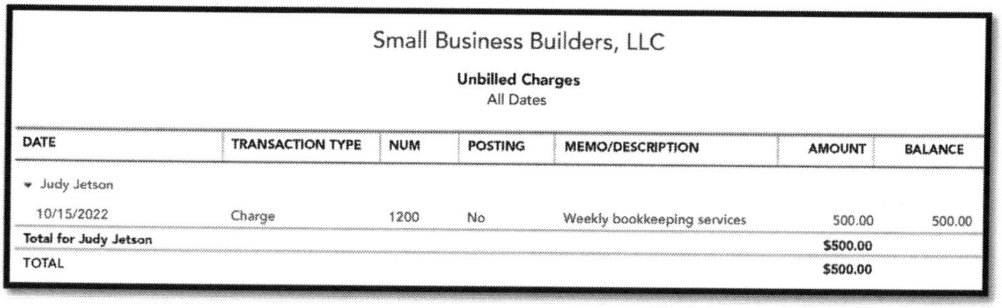

Small Business Builders, LLC

Unbilled Charges

All Dates

DATE	TRANSACTION TYPE	NUM	POSTING	MEMO/DESCRIPTION	AMOUNT	BALANCE
▾ Judy Jetson						
10/15/2022	Charge	1200	No	Weekly bookkeeping services	500.00	500.00
Total for Judy Jetson					**$500.00**	
TOTAL					**$500.00**	

Figure 16.29: Sample Unbilled Charges report

That's how delayed charges work. One last thing you need to know is that if you need to reverse a delayed charge, you can do so by recording a delayed credit. Similar to delayed charges, navigate to the **+New** menu and select **Delayed credit**. Follow the onscreen instructions to record the delayed credit. Delayed charges are used a lot in landscaping and maintenance industries for routine services that are billed monthly.

Summary

In this chapter, you have learned how to handle many special transactions in QuickBooks Online. You may be able to take advantage of a few of these now or keep them in your back pocket for later on when you need them. To recap, you now know how to set up and track payments for a business loan or line of credit. For those incidental purchases, you can create a petty cash account, track purchases, and reconcile the account, just like bank accounts. We also discussed the importance of recording bad debt expenses, which you now know how to record in QuickBooks to ensure that your financials are accurate. Finally, you learned how to record delayed charges and credits to track services that are provided to customers that will be billed sometime in the future.

In the next chapter, we will provide you with an overview of some of the key features included in QuickBooks Online Advanced. While this subscription plan is more expensive, it offers some powerful capabilities to streamline your business accountancy. Setting up customized fields, managing customized user permissions, using workflow automation, and reclassifying transactions are just a few of the features that we will cover in detail.

Join our community on Discord

Join our community's Discord space for discussions with the authors and other readers:

`https://packt.link/quickbooks`

17

QuickBooks Online Advanced

QuickBooks Online (QBO) Advanced is the top-tier QuickBooks Online subscription plan. As mentioned in the first chapter, it includes all of the features found in QBO Simple Start, QBO Essentials, and QBO Plus, in addition to many more features. Some of the features are as follows: you can add up to 25 users, it includes 48 additional custom fields, you can create customized performance charts, it has granular user permissions similar to QuickBooks Desktop Enterprise, it has workflow automation to reduce manual tasks, it offers the ability to import invoices and budgets, and it allows you to do batch data entry. These are just a few of the many features included in QBO Advanced.

QBO Advanced is ideal for businesses that are currently using QBO Plus and have outgrown it, as well as current QuickBooks Desktop Enterprise customers looking to move to the cloud. The ideal business has more than 10 employees, sales receipts that exceed $500,000, and annualized revenue that continues to increase substantially.

QBO Advanced includes several features that are ideal for small businesses that are growing at a rapid rate. The features we will cover are used for different purposes and are only available in the QBO Advanced subscription:

- Accessing the QBO Advanced test drive account
- Managing fixed assets
- Setting up customized fields
- Managing customized user permissions
- Using workflow automation
- Importing invoices and budgets into QBO

- Batch-creating invoices in QBO
- Reclassify transactions
- DocuSign integration
- Using online backup and restore
- Utilizing the Performance Center and custom charts
- Business analytics with Excel (Spreadsheet Sync)
- Email scheduling for standard and custom reports
- Priority Circle membership

 The US edition of QBO was used to create this book. If you are using a version that is outside the United States, results may differ.

Accessing the QBO Advanced test drive account

To demonstrate the key concepts outlined in the introduction to this chapter, we will use the QBO Advanced test drive account. This account includes data for Craig's Design and Landscaping Services, a fictitious business. There are a couple of ways in which you can access the test drive account. You can log in to your existing QBO account, click the **Help** icon, and type test drive in the search field. The second way to access the test drive account is to paste the URL into a new web browser page. Copy the URL in *step 4* and bookmark it for next time.

Follow these steps to access the QBO Advanced test drive account:

1. Log in to your existing QBO account.
2. Click on the **Help** icon located in the upper-right corner of the home page, as indicated here:

Figure 17.1: The Help icon

3. In the search box, type test drive and you will see **Test drive QuickBooks Online**, as indicated in *Figure 17.2*:

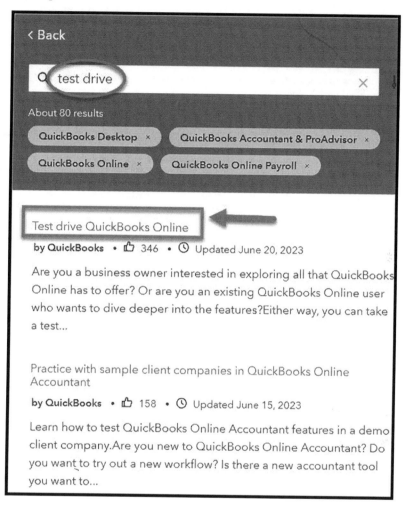

Figure 17.2: Accessing the test drive from QB Assistant

The following page will appear:

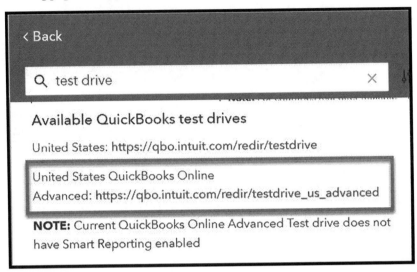

Figure 17.3: The QuickBooks Online test drive page

4. Click on the link as indicated in the preceding screenshot to access the United States QuickBooks Online Advanced test drive. If you are currently logged in to QBO, you will be logged out of your company file.

> Pro Tip: You can only access one QBO file at a time in the same browser. If you would like to open more than one QBO file at a time, use a different browser or open an incognito window.

The following welcome page will appear for **Craig's Design and Landscaping Services**, a fictitious company:

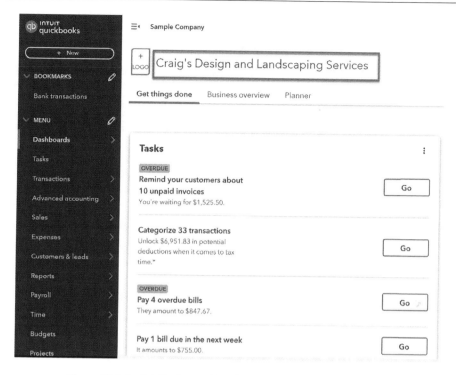

Figure 17.4: Craig's Design and Landscaping Services welcome page

While you will be able to complete most of the exercises in this chapter using the QBO Advanced test drive account, there are a few features that are not fully functioning. In these sections, we have provided you with step-by-step instructions and screenshots where possible. Please also note that your work in the test drive account is saved as long as you remain logged in. Once you log out of the test drive account, your work will no longer be accessible.

Now that we have shown you how to access the QBO Advanced test drive account, we will take you through several exercises to demonstrate the key concepts of this chapter.

Managing fixed assets

In *Chapter 15, Closing the Books in QuickBooks Online*, we explained what a fixed asset is and showed you how to add new and existing fixed assets to the chart of accounts. To recap, a fixed asset can be a vehicle that you use for your business, office furniture such as desks and chairs, or a computer. In general, the purchase amount for these items may be larger than your day-to-day business expenses. Fixed assets are subject to **depreciation**, which is the reduction of the value of a fixed asset due to wear and tear. Depreciation is a tax-deductible expense so this is one of the reasons why you want to be sure to account for it on your books.

One of the newest features available to QBO Advanced subscribers is the ability to generate a depreciation schedule in QBO for all of your fixed assets. QBO will automatically record depreciation for your assets on a monthly basis. If you would like to add multiple fixed assets at the same time, you can use the fixed asset template to manually enter the information or you can copy and paste from an Excel spreadsheet. In this section, we will cover how to navigate to the fixed asset manager, set up a new fixed asset, schedule depreciation for a fixed asset, and add multiple fixed assets at the same time.

Follow the steps below to add a *new* fixed asset, which means that there is no depreciation to calculate:

1. From the left navigation bar, click on **Advanced accounting** and select **Fixed assets**, as shown in *Figure 17.5*:

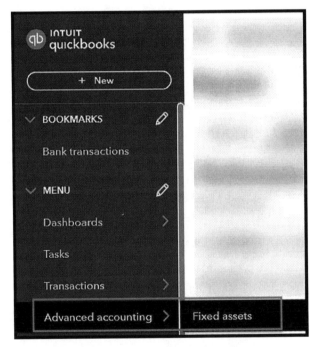

Figure 17.5: Navigating to Fixed assets

2. The following screen will display:

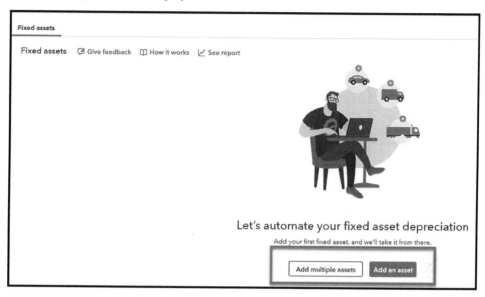

Figure 17.6: Fixed asset manager displays

3. Click the **Add an asset** button and complete the fields on the **Setup** tab, as indicated in *Figure 17.7*:

Figure 17.7: Setting up a fixed asset

4. Save the information that you entered, and the depreciation schedule will display as shown in *Figure 17.8*:

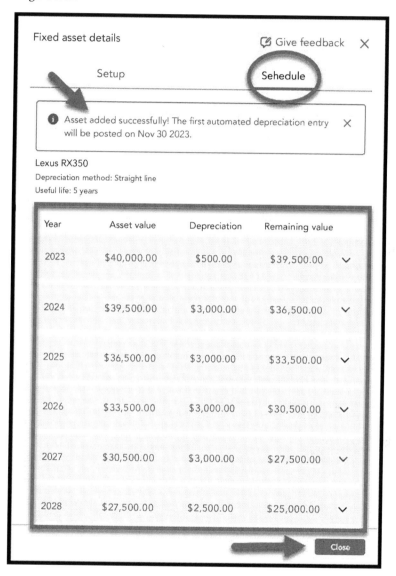

Figure 17.8: Depreciation schedule displays

At the very top of the schedule, you will see a confirmation that the asset was successfully added. In addition, the date that QBO will post the first automated depreciation journal entry will also be displayed.

5. If you click on the arrow to the far right of the remaining value, you will see the dates and amounts for which QBO will record depreciation for each year. For example, for the remainder of 2023, QBO will post depreciation in the amount of $250 on November 30 and December 31.

Figure 17.9: Details of automated future depreciation journal entries

6. Click the **Close** button and the fixed assets list will be displayed, as shown in *Figure 17.10*:

Figure 17.10: Review fixed asset listing

At this point, you should review the information shown here to ensure it is correct. If you need to make any changes, click on the **View** link right below the **Action** column and click on the **Setup** tab to make any necessary changes.

As mentioned previously, if you need to add multiple assets to QBO, you can use the fixed asset template. Follow the steps below to use the fixed asset template:

1. Click on **Add multiple assets** from within the fixed asset manager, as shown in *Figure 17.11*:

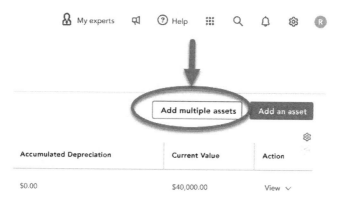

Figure 17.11: Selecting Add multiple assets

2. The fixed asset template displays:

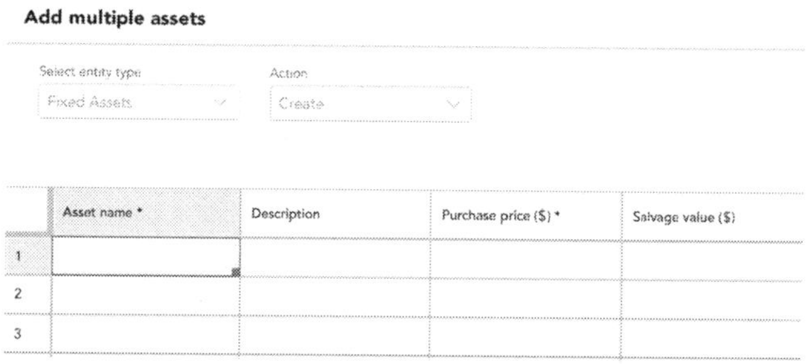

Add multiple assets

Select entity type: Fixed Assets

Action: Create

	Asset name *	Description	Purchase price ($) *	Salvage value ($)
1				
2				
3				

Figure 17.12: Displaying the fixed asset template

The fixed asset template works just like an Excel spreadsheet. You can either copy and paste the information from another spreadsheet into this template or you can manually enter the data. You can customize the columns shown as well as reorder them to fit your preference. Please note that all available columns are not shown in *Figure 17.12*.

Pro Tip: To recap the steps we have covered in this section, watch this Intuit video tutorial: `https://quickbooks.intuit.com/learn-support/en-us/help-article/fixed-assets/add-manage-fixed-assets-quickbooks-online-advanced/L19788yU0_US_en_US`.

Now that you are familiar with adding fixed assets to QBO so that it can automatically calculate and record depreciation, we will discuss how to add customized fields to QBO.

Setting up customized fields

Custom fields can be used to filter customers, sales, purchasing, expense, and vendor reports. QBO Advanced is the only QBO subscription that includes customized fields. A total of 48 custom fields can be created in QBO Advanced. Custom fields are split between customers, sales, purchase/expense, and vendor fields. A total of 12 custom fields are available for each of these 4 groups.

Follow the steps given here to add a custom field:

1. In the upper-right corner of the QBO screen, click on the gear icon, as indicated here:

Figure 17.13: The gear icon

2. Select **Custom fields**, as indicated in the following screenshot:

Figure 17.14: Custom fields in the LISTS menu

3. If this is your first time adding a custom field, the following window will appear. To learn more about how custom fields work, click the **See how it works** link to watch a two-minute video:

Figure 17.15: Custom fields window

4. Click the **Add custom field** button, as indicated in the preceding screenshot.

The following window will appear:

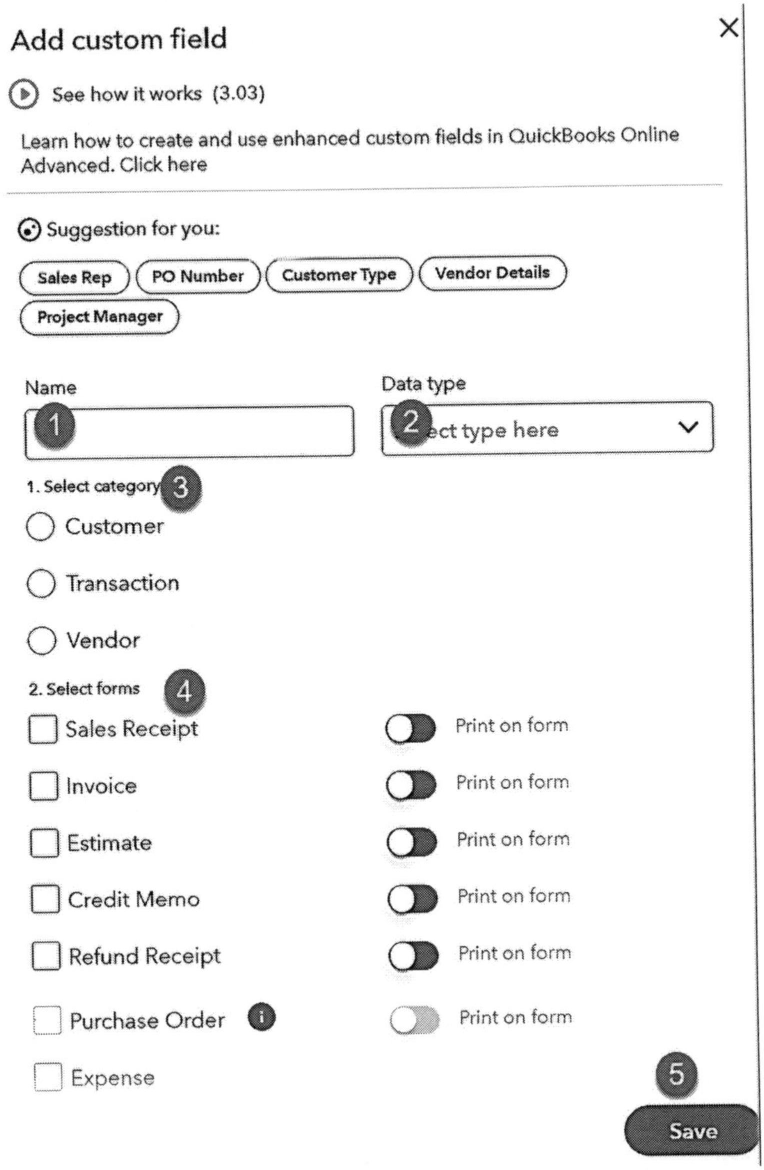

Add custom field   ✕

⊳ See how it works (3.03)

Learn how to create and use enhanced custom fields in QuickBooks Online
Advanced. Click here

⊙ Suggestion for you:

(Sales Rep)   (PO Number)   (Customer Type)   (Vendor Details)
(Project Manager)

Name   Data type

[**1** _____]   [**2** ect type here   ⌄]

1. Select category **3**

○ Customer

○ Transaction

○ Vendor

2. Select forms **4**

☐ Sales Receipt   ⬤ ◯ Print on form

☐ Invoice   ⬤ ◯ Print on form

☐ Estimate   ⬤ ◯ Print on form

☐ Credit Memo   ⬤ ◯ Print on form

☐ Refund Receipt   ⬤ ◯ Print on form

☐ Purchase Order ⓘ   ◯ ⬤ Print on form

☐ Expense   **5**

                                                       (Save)

Figure 17.16: The Add custom field window

Pro Tip: At the top of the screen, there is a **See how it works** link. This is a
step-by-step video tutorial that will show you how to add a custom field.

Below is a brief description of the fields that need to be completed:

- **Name (1)**: Type the name of the custom field here (for instance, Sales Rep).
- **Data type (2)**: When it comes to the type of data entered, you have four options to choose from: text and number, number only, date, or dropdown list. Since we are creating a list of sales reps, we will select a drop-down list. When you choose **Dropdown list**, a couple of blank fields will appear. Type C. Shelton into the first field and J. Jones into the second field, as shown here:

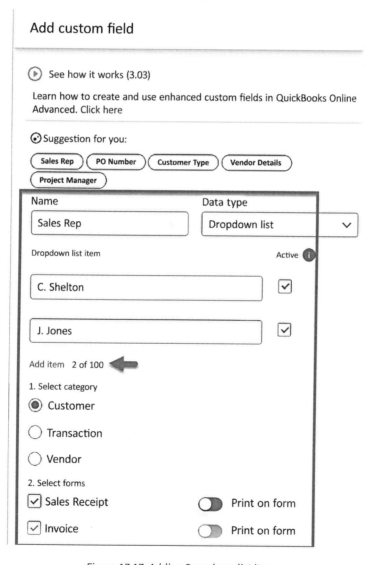

Figure 17.17: Adding Dropdown list items

Notice that directly below the drop-down list, there is an option to add an item. Currently, we are only using two fields, but you can add up to 100 items in a drop-down list.

- **Select category (3)**: You can choose to create the custom field to be used for a customer, a transaction, or a vendor; choose **Customer**.
- **Select forms (4)**: You can choose to use the custom fields on a variety of forms. In addition, you can choose to have the field printed on the forms or just have it displayed in the software only.

5. Choose **Sales Receipt** and **Invoice**. We don't want to print these fields on forms, so leave the toggles as they are.

6. Click the **Save** button **(5)** to save the custom fields, and the following screen will be displayed:

Figure 17.18: Reviewing custom fields created

In our example, we have created a custom field called **Sales Rep** that will appear when creating sales receipts and invoices. By including the **Sales Rep** field on these key documents, it will also show up on reports.

Reports can be filtered by the **Sales Rep** field so that you can review sales for each sales rep individually or as a collective group.

Here is a table that includes examples of the types of custom fields you can create:

Field	Examples
Customer	Sales Rep, Contract Renewal, Birthday, Policy, or Contract Numbers

Sales	Sales Rep, Job Site Foreman, Contract Number, Project Supervisor, or **Purchase Order (PO)** number
Purchase/Expense	A/P Contact, Contract Number, PO number
Vendor	A/P Contact, Sales Rep, Contract Number, Expiration Date

Table 17.1: Custom field examples

In this section, we have shown you how to create customized fields for various stakeholders. In the next section, we will talk about how to customize user permissions.

Managing customized user permissions

QBO Advanced gives you more control over what areas of QuickBooks you can give users access to. In *Chapter 4*, *Customizing QuickBooks for Your Business*, we discussed ten user types available in all subscriptions: company administrator, standard all access, standard limited customers and vendors, standard limited customers only, standard limited vendors only, standard no access, track time only, view company reports, primary admin, and accountant.

In addition to these user types, QBO Advanced also includes four additional user roles: Accounts Receivable (A/R) Manager, Sales and Inventory, Workers and Sales reports, and Custom roles.

A brief explanation of these roles follows:

- **A/R Manager**: This role allows the user to access the entire sales cycle, with the exception of sales and bank deposits. Sales and bank deposits give the user the ability to receive payments in undeposited funds and create bank deposits.

- **Sales and Inventory**: This role combines sales and inventory access into a single role so that stock levels can be updated as needed.

- **Workers and Sales reports**: This role can be used for sales managers with sales reports access. It allows them to make vendor payments, calculate commissions, and add commissions to paychecks.

- **Custom roles**: This role enables the admin to assign permissions for a broad range of roles.

Now, we will show you how to create and assign a custom user role to a user. Follow these steps to create a custom user role:

1. In the upper-right corner of the dashboard, click on the gear icon, as indicated below:

Figure 17.19: The gear icon

2.   Select **Manage users**, as indicated here:

Figure 17.20: Manage users in the YOUR COMPANY menu

3.   The Customize user permissions window will appear:

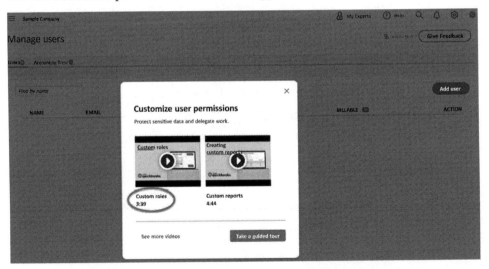

Figure 17.21: The Customize user permissions window

4.   You can click on the **Custom roles** video for instructions on how to add a role.

Click the **X** in the upper-right corner to close the pop-up window and then click the **Add user** button located on the right side of the **Manage users** screen, as indicated below:

Figure 17.22: The Add user button

5. The following screen will appear:

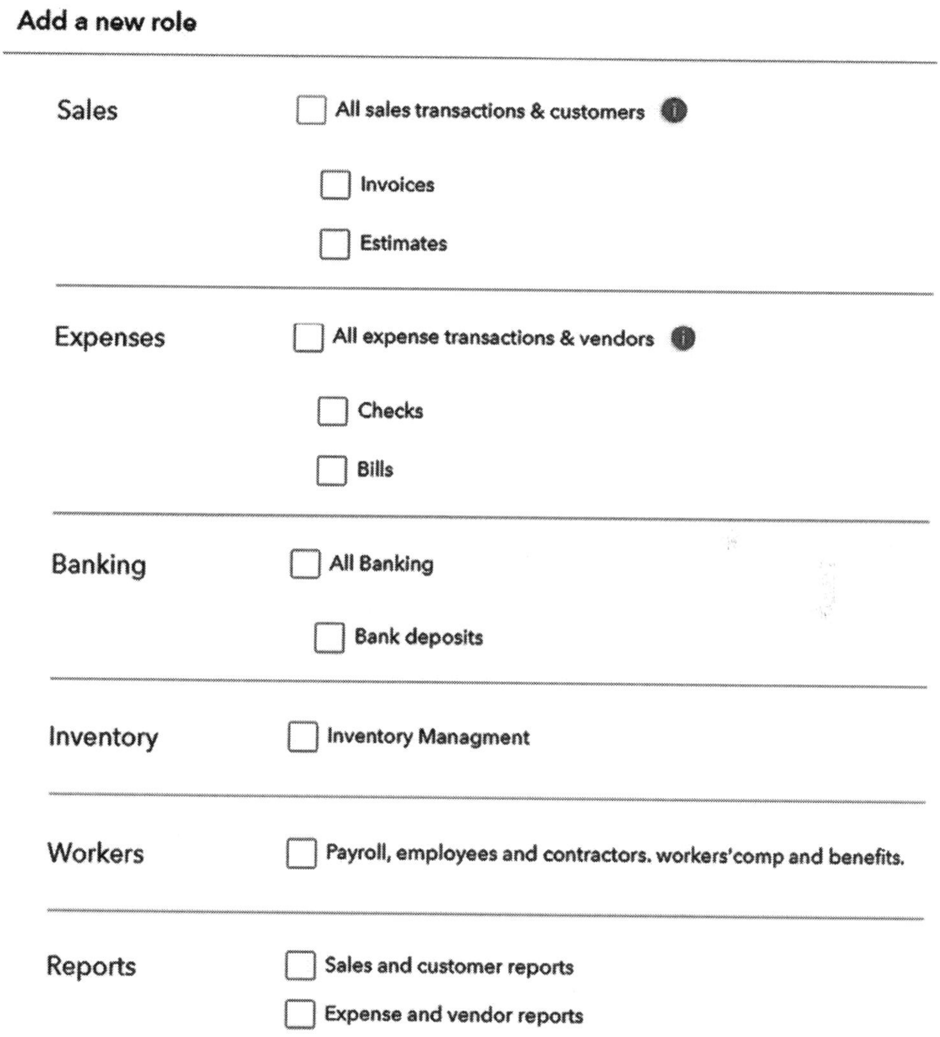

Add a new role

Sales	☐ All sales transactions & customers 🛈
	☐ Invoices
	☐ Estimates

Expenses	☐ All expense transactions & vendors 🛈
	☐ Checks
	☐ Bills

| Banking | ☐ All Banking |
| | ☐ Bank deposits |

| Inventory | ☐ Inventory Managment |

| Workers | ☐ Payroll, employees and contractors. workers'comp and benefits. |

| Reports | ☐ Sales and customer reports |
| | ☐ Expense and vendor reports |

Figure 17.23: The Add a new role screen

Put a checkmark next to the areas of QuickBooks you would like to permit this role to access.

6.   Follow the onscreen prompts to save the new role.

Now that you have created a new role, you can assign it to a user. Follow these steps to assign the new role to a user:

1.   From the **Manage users** screen, click on the **Users** tab and then click the **Add user** button, as indicated here:

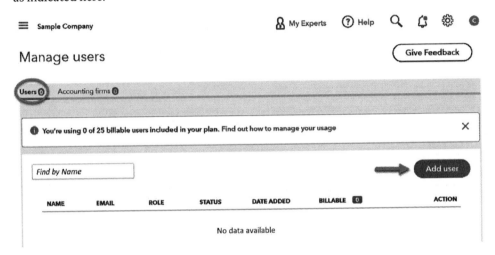

Figure 17.24: The Add user button

2.   The **Add a new user** window will appear. Click the drop-down in the **Custom role** field, as indicated here:

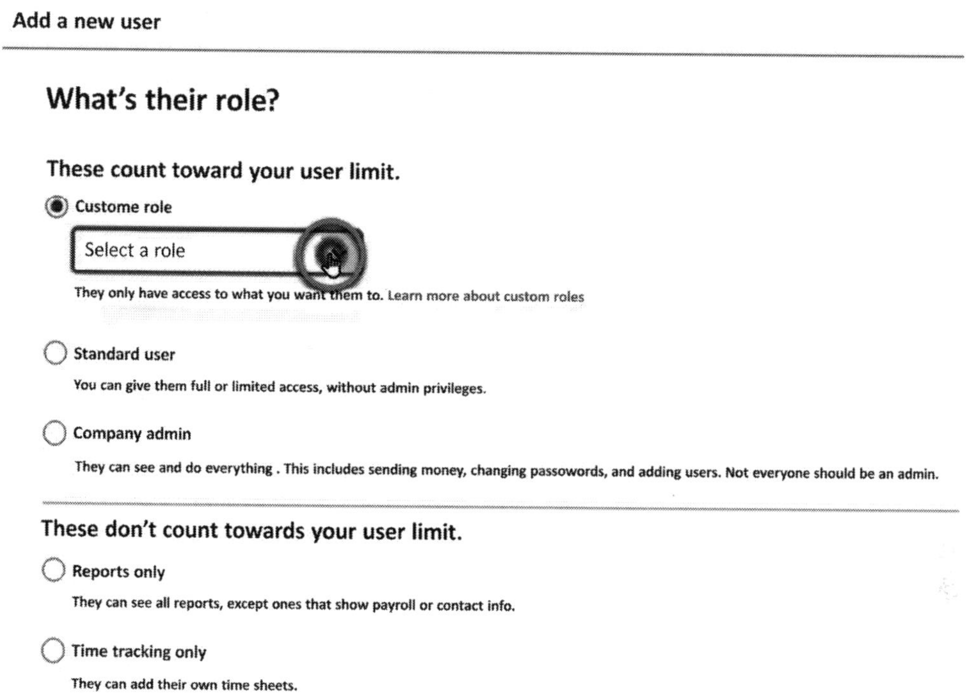

Add a new user

What's their role?

These count toward your user limit.

◉ Custome role

> Select a role

They only have access to what you want them to. Learn more about custom roles

○ **Standard user**

You can give them full or limited access, without admin privileges.

○ **Company admin**

They can see and do everything . This includes sending money, changing passowords, and adding users. Not everyone should be an admin.

These don't count towards your user limit.

○ **Reports only**

They can see all reports, except ones that show payroll or contact info.

○ **Time tracking only**

They can add their own time sheets.

Figure 17.25: The Custom role field

3. Select the custom role that you created in the previous step and choose **Next**.

   The following screen will appear:

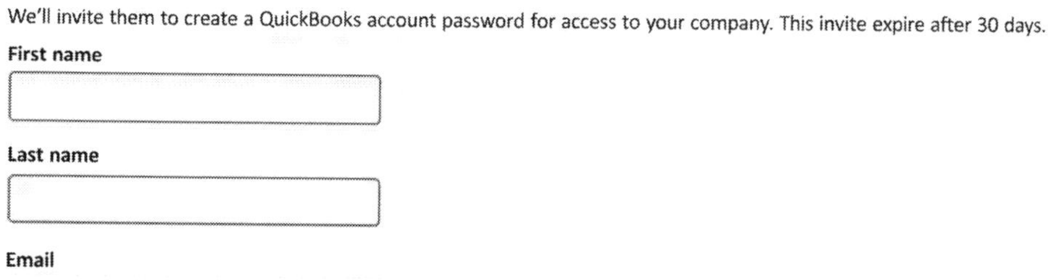

   We'll invite them to create a QuickBooks account password for access to your company. This invite expire after 30 days.

   First name

   [   ]

   Last name

   [   ]

   Email

Figure 17.26: Adding contact info

4. Complete the fields with the user's name and email address. When you click the **Save** button, an email invitation will be sent to the user.

If the new user does not accept the invitation within 30 days, it will expire. If this happens, you can resend the invite directly from the **Manage users** page. Just navigate to the gear icon and click **Manage users**. The status of all email invitations will be listed.

An improvement made to the custom sales role is the ability to delegate sales form duties to sales reps by location, allowing them to create estimates, invoices, sales receipts, credit memos, refunds, and more for their own sales territories.

This new feature gives you the following capabilities:

- Sales users now have the ability to receive invoice approval tasks, if they are set up to approve invoices.
- Sales users can be notified of past-due invoices by admin users via tasks.
- Sales managers can be added with only the locations they are authorized to manage.

Below is a snapshot of this new functionality:

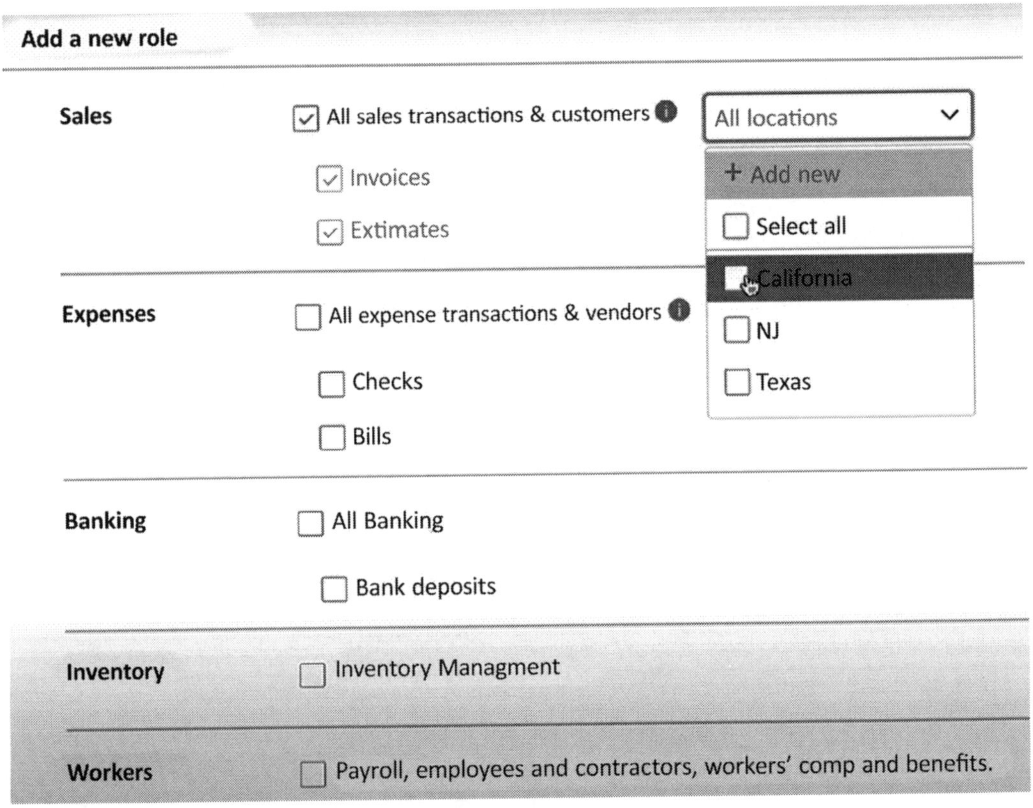

Figure 17.27: Adding a location to a sales role

You can see how you can add the specific locations to a sales role so that each salesperson can see the territory they are responsible for and no more. You can access this new feature within the **Manage users** page.

Using workflow automation

Workflow automation is used to remind those responsible for tasks that those tasks need to be completed. Reminders to pay a vendor, make a bank deposit, or approve invoices can automatically go out via email, mobile devices, or push notifications to one or more persons who are responsible for completing a given task.

Follow these steps to access workflows:

1. Click on the gear icon.

2. Select **Manage workflows** in the **TOOLS** column, as indicated here:

Figure 17.28: The Manage workflows option in the TOOLS column

3. If this is your first time creating a workflow, the following window will appear; if not, you will see the **Create workflow** button:

Figure 17.29: The Workflows window

Click the **Create workflow** button.

4. The following **Workflows** screen will appear:

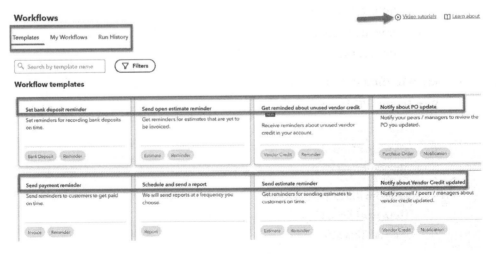

Figure 17.30: The Workflows screen

There are three primary sections in a workflow: **Templates, My Workflows,** and **Run History**. A brief explanation of each of these sections follows:

- **Templates:** This tab lists the predesigned workflows that can be adopted or used. A list of some of the templates available, along with a brief description, is as follows:

    - **Pay vendor reminder:** Automatically reminds the party responsible to pay bills when they become due.

    - **Payment received:** Automatically notifies customers that a payment has been received on their account.

    - **Payment due reminder:** Automatically notifies customers when their invoice is overdue.

    - **Overdue invoice memo:** Automatically stamps a memo on an invoice when it becomes overdue. The overdue memo is visible on the invoice when it is printed or emailed.

    - **Bank deposit reminder:** Automatically reminds the responsible party to create bank deposits after the undeposited funds account exceeds a predetermined value. This notification is sent via email or a push notification. A link to the undeposited funds screen is included in the notification.

    - **Auto send unsent invoices:** Automatically sends invoices that have been marked to send later to customers.

    - **Unsent invoices reminder:** Automatically sends the responsible party a notification regarding invoices that are due and need to be sent to customers. This notification is sent via email or a push notification.

    - **Invoice approval:** Automatically sends a reminder to the responsible party that invoices are awaiting approval.

- **My Workflows:** This tab lists all the workflows that have been created.
- **Run History:** This tab will track the history of each workflow that has been used.

Pro Tip #1: Invoices created by an administrative person are automatically approved. In addition, recurring invoices do not go through the approval process.

Pro Tip #2: If there is a workflow that does not currently exist, you can create a custom workflow. Click the custom workflow button shown in *Figure 17.31* and follow the on-screen instructions.

Follow these steps to initiate a workflow:

1. Click on the **Templates** tab, then click on the workflow template you wish to select, as indicated in the following screenshot:

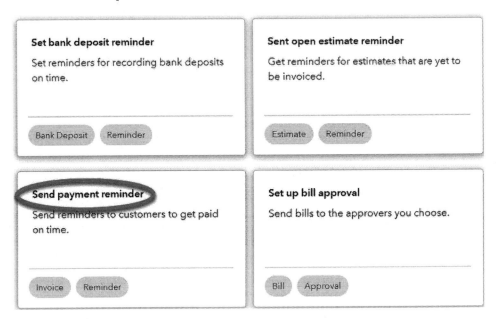

Figure 17.31: The Templates tab

2. The template will display as shown in *Figure 17.32*:

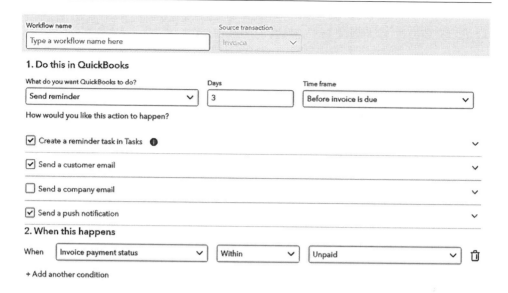

Figure 17.32: The Send payment reminder template

Here is a brief explanation of the information shown in *Figure 17.32*:

- **Workflow name**: Enter the name you would like to use for this new workflow. For example, `Customer payment reminder`.

- **1. Do this in QuickBooks**: In this section, you will select the parameters around what action you would like the workflow to perform and how you would like the action to happen. For example, *Send reminder 3 days Before invoice is due*. This will be done by creating a reminder task in **Tasks**, sending the customer an email, and using a push notification such as a text message.

- **2. When this happens**: This section determines under what conditions the action identified in *step 1* will take place. In our example, *when an invoice payment status is unpaid*. You can add additional conditions as needed by clicking on the + **Add another condition** link directly below this step.

3. Click the **Save and Enable** button located at the bottom of the screen and the customer payment reminder workflow will appear in the **My Workflows** tab.

Importing invoices and budgets into QBO

In *Chapter 5, Managing Customer, Vendor, and Products and Services Lists*, we covered importing customers, vendors, and products and services into QuickBooks. In this section, we will show you how to import invoices into QuickBooks. Importing your data into QuickBooks can save you a lot of time that would have been spent manually entering this information into QuickBooks. In addition to saving time, importing data will ensure more accuracy and consistency than manual data entry. If you use budgets in your business, you may want to consider importing your budget data into QuickBooks. Importing budgets is only available in QBO Advanced.

Follow these steps to import invoices into QuickBooks:

1. From the gear icon, select **Import data**, as indicated in the following screenshot:

Figure 17.33: The Import data option under TOOLS

2. The **Import Data** screen will appear:

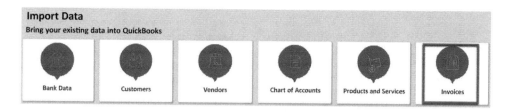

Figure 17.34: The Import Data screen

3. Select **Invoices**.

The following window will appear:

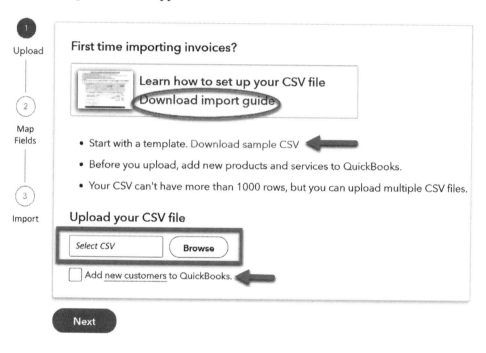

Figure 17.35: Importing invoices – the Upload step

Three steps must be completed to import invoices into QuickBooks. First, download the import guide to learn tips and tricks for importing. Second, download the sample CSV template so that you can see how your data should be formatted before uploading. Last, upload your invoice information in CSV file format.

For your convenience, you can also find both the import guide and the sample CSV in the GitHub repository for this book: `https://github.com/PacktPublishing/Mastering-QuickBooks-2024-Fifth-Edition/tree/main/Chapter17`.

4. Click the **Browse** button and select the CSV file saved on your computer. The filename should appear in the box to the left of **Browse**, as indicated in the following screenshot:

Upload your CSV file

| Sample Invoice Impor | **Browse** |

☐ Add new customers to QuickBooks.

Figure 17.36: Uploading a CSV file

 Pro Tip: By checking the **Add new customers to QuickBooks** checkbox, QuickBooks will add any new customers you have included in the file that are not currently set up in QuickBooks to your customer list.

Next, you will map the fields in your CSV file with the fields in QuickBooks. The final step is to review the data to ensure accuracy before submitting it for import. Let's go through all these steps:

1. The **Map your column headings** screen will appear:

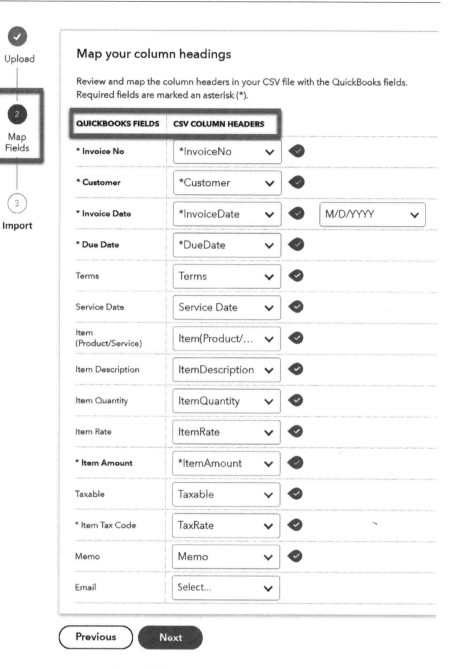

Figure 17.37: Map your column headings

In this step, you will map the columns in your CSV file with the fields in QuickBooks. Do this by clicking on the drop-down field below the CSV file column to make your selections. For example, the column that includes your invoice number should be mapped to the **Invoice No** field in QuickBooks.

2. While you could ideally map all of the fields listed here, the only required fields are the ones that have an asterisk (*) next to them: **Invoice No, Customer, Invoice Date, Due Date, Item Amount,** and **Item Tax Code.**

3. Click **Next** and the following screen will appear:

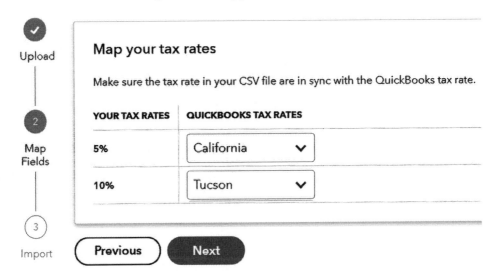

Figure 17.38: Map your tax rates

4. If you have sales tax rates, this screen will pop up. Select the appropriate state from the drop-down menu, as shown in the preceding screenshot.

5. Click **Next** and the following screen will appear:

Figure 17.39: Importing invoices – the Import step

Be sure to verify that the total number of invoices that will be imported is correct before starting the import.

6. Once you click the **Start import** button, there is *no way to undo this action*. Therefore, make sure that the number of invoices you are importing is correct.

7. Click the **Start import** button to import the invoices into QuickBooks. Once the import is complete, the following message appears:

Figure 17.40: Invoice import complete

8. Click **OK** and you will return to the **Import data** screen.

One thing to keep in mind is that if an invoice has more than one line item, you must include one row for each item on the invoice. There is a maximum of 1,000 rows allowed per CSV file. Therefore, if your file exceeds 1,000 rows, you will need to create a new CSV file and upload them separately. Refer to the import guide for more details on troubleshooting errors when importing data into QBO. The invoice import guide can be found here: `https://github.com/PacktPublishing/Mastering-QuickBooks-2024-Fifth-Edition/tree/main/Chapter17`.

Importing budgets into QBO

You can save time by importing company-wide and generic budgets rather than using actual reporting. This feature is ideal for non-profit organizations that need to manage profit and loss budgets.

In *Chapter 11, Business Overview Reports*, we covered how to create a budget from scratch. However, if you build your budget in a different program and would like to import it into QBO, you can do that with a QBO Advanced subscription. The file format must be a CSV file or it will not work.

Please note that the **Import budget** feature is disabled for the test drive account, so you will not be able to follow along if you are using it. Screenshots in this section have been taken using a non-test drive account.

Follow the steps below to import a budget:

1. To access the **Import budget** feature, click on **Budgets** on the left navigation bar and choose **Import budget**, as shown below:

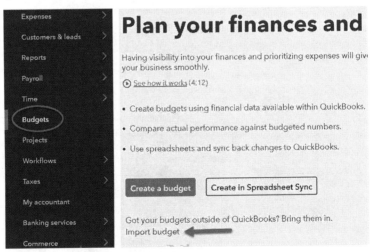

Figure 17.41: Importing a budget

2. Your data should resemble the image of the budget template below:

Figure 17.42: Budget template

As outlined in *Figure 17.42*, there are three steps you need to complete to import a budget from outside of QuickBooks:

1. **Select time period**: From the drop-down menu, select the time period of the budget that you want to import. Currently, you can go back 2 years and you can go forward 4 years.

2. **Download budget template**: Click on the P&L budget_sample.csv link to download the budget template. You will need to enter your budget information into this template to ensure it is in the right format to import into QBO.

3. **Upload the budget**: Click in this field to attach the completed budget template. Click the **Upload budget** button to import your budget into QBO. Follow the on-screen prompts to complete the process.

After importing your budget into QuickBooks, you will be able to run a budget versus actuals report to see how well your actuals are tracking against your budget. Refer to *Chapter 11, Business Overview Reports*, to learn more about how to generate budget reports.

You can save a ton of time creating recurring invoices in QuickBooks by using the batch-create invoice feature. We will cover this topic next.

Batch-creating invoices in QBO

Batch-creating invoices is an alternative to importing invoices into QBO. It's ideal for businesses that need to create several invoices that will include the same (or similar) services. For example, a property owner may need to bill their tenants for monthly rent. If you have 10 tenants that pay $1,000 a month, you can quickly generate 10 invoices using batch-create.

Follow these steps to generate a batch of invoices:

1. Click the **+ New** button located on the left navigation bar, as indicated below:

Figure 17.43: The New button

2. Select **Batch transactions** under the **OTHER** column, as indicated in the following screen-shot:

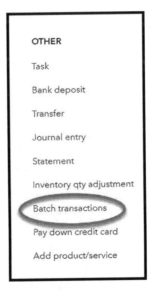

Figure 17.44: Selecting Batch transactions

3. The **Batch Transactions** screen appears, as follows:

Figure 17.45: The Batch Transactions screen

This screen resembles and works like an Excel spreadsheet. First, you will select the *transaction type* you are creating or importing. There are six to choose from: **Invoices**, **Bank Deposits**, **Sales Receipts**, **Checks**, **Expenses**, and **Bills**. Next, you will select the *action* you wish to take: **Create**, **Modify**, or **Delete**. If you have the invoices in an Excel or CSV file, you can use the **Import CSV** option to upload the information, which will prevent you from manually entering it. The options allow you to add/remove columns as needed.

To complete the spreadsheet, put your cursor in each field and enter the information required, pressing *Tab* to move between fields.

For example, in the following screenshot, we have created an invoice to bill a customer for weekly gardening services at $200:

Figure 17.46: Example of a completed invoice

1. To create a duplicate invoice for other customers, click on the number to the left of the customer name and the following dialog box will appear:

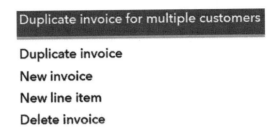

Figure 17.47: Invoice options

You can duplicate this invoice for multiple customers, duplicate this invoice, create a new invoice, add a new line item to the existing invoice, or delete the invoice.

2. Click the **Duplicate invoice for multiple** customers option.

The following window will appear:

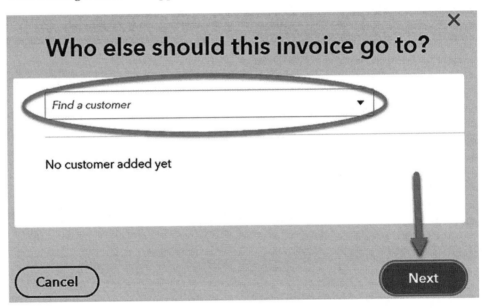

Figure 17.48: Duplicating an invoice for multiple customers

3. From the drop-down menu, select each customer for whom you would like to create the invoice, as shown in *Figure 17.49*:

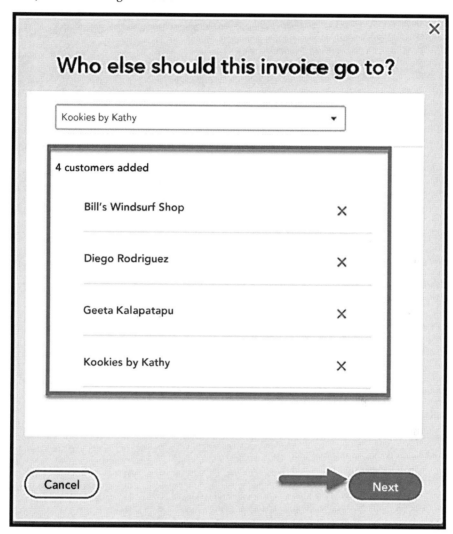

Figure 17.49: Select customers to create batch invoices for

4. After you click the **Next** button, the following screen will appear:

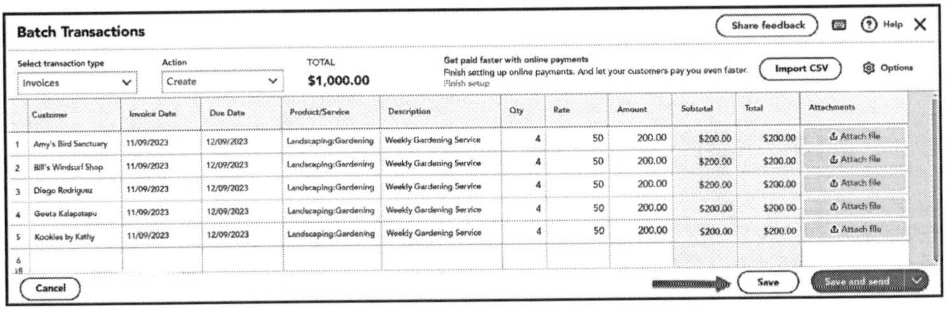

Figure 17.50: Successfully duplicated invoices

There will be an invoice listed for each customer selected in the previous step. You can add additional customers, save your work, and come back later on to make additional changes, or you can save and send the invoices via email to your customers.

If you prefer to import invoices instead of entering them manually, the batch invoicing sample template can be found here: `https://github.com/PacktPublishing/Mastering-QuickBooks-2024-Fifth-Edition/tree/main/Chapter17`.

Next, we will cover an existing feature in QBO that is now available to QBO Advanced subscribers – reclassifying transactions.

Reclassify transactions

The **Reclassify transactions** feature is not new. However, in the past, it was only available for accountant users; now it is available to admin users who have a QBO Advanced subscription. The **Reclassify transactions** feature allows you to modify a batch of transactions all at once. For example, if you find that the expense account for checks written to a vendor has been categorized incorrectly, you can use **Reclassify transactions** to make the correction for a batch of checks at once.

Follow the steps below to access the **Reclassify transactions** feature:

1. Click on the gear icon and select **Reclassify transactions**, as shown below:

Figure 17.51: Selecting Reclassify transactions

2. The following screen will appear:

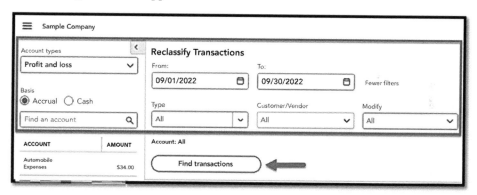

Figure 17.52: The Reclassify Transactions screen

A brief explanation of the information required in this screen is as follows:

- **Account types**: From the drop-down, you can select profit and loss accounts or balance sheet accounts. If you need to reclassify accounts that are both profit and loss and balance sheet accounts, you will need to do them separately.
- **Basis**: Select the accounting method that you use – **Accrual** or **Cash**. This will determine which accounts appear during the search.
- **From/To**: Select a date range to search for transactions.
- **Type**: Narrow your search by selecting the type of transactions. From the drop-down, your options are bill, check, credit card credit, credit memo, deposit, expense, invoice, journal entry, refund, sales receipt, and vendor credit.
- **Customer/Vendor**: You can filter by a specific customer/vendor or select **All** from the drop-down.
- **Modify**: From the drop-down, you can choose to modify all data or just the accounts.

3. Click the **Find transactions** button to search for any transactions that meet the criteria.

The Reclassify tool will save you time that you would have spent manually making corrections to your data. It is a great tool to use when you need to do a quick cleanup as you discover errors, or at the end of the year to ensure the accuracy of your financial statements before filing your tax return. If you don't have QBO Advanced, you can still edit the original transactions or use a journal entry to reclassify them.

DocuSign integration

One of the newest features in QBO Advanced is the integration of DocuSign. You can now easily sign, send, and manage digital documents directly from your QBO Advanced account. E-signatures allow signees to receive and sign documents from any computer or mobile device with an internet connection.

Please note that the DocuSign feature is disabled for the test drive account, so you will not be able to follow along if you are using it. Screenshots in this section have been taken using a non-test drive account.

Below is a screenshot of what this feature looks like when the DocuSign app is downloaded and implemented:

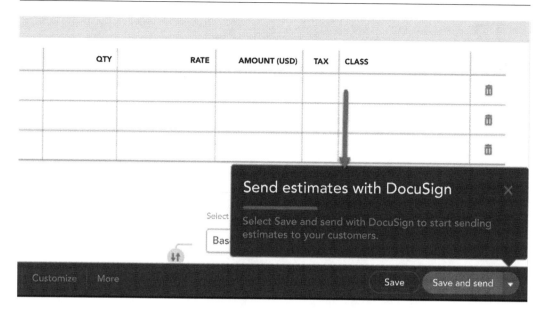

Figure 17.53: DocuSign notification

In the bottom-right corner of the preceding screenshot, there is a notification that alerts the user that they can send estimates to their customers with DocuSign.

 Pro Tip: Watch this Intuit video tutorial to learn how to connect DocuSign to QBO Advanced: https://www.youtube.com/watch?v=9hbGrRVuYqo.

Using online backup and restore

Similar to QuickBooks Desktop products, you can save a backup copy of your QBO data with your QBO Advanced subscription. This feature gives your accountant or administrative personnel the ability to continuously back up data and then restore it to a point in time as needed. Online backup and restore captures transaction data, list data, and other elements such as attachments, company information, exchange rates, and preferences. However, it does not record things such as custom reports, recurring transactions, and bank feeds.

You can access the backup tool from the gear icon. After clicking on the gear icon, select **Back up company**, listed in the **TOOLS** column.

Here is a brief description of the three types of backups available:

- **Backup**: This type of backup saves everything in the chart of accounts. You can also undo unwanted changes made to vendors, customers, settings, and other data if you need to.

- **Restore**: This backup allows you to roll back a backed-up company to any time (down to the minute) since its first backup.

- **Copy**: This feature allows you to copy an existing QBO Advanced company and use it to start a new one.

 Pro Tip: Watch this Intuit video tutorial to learn how to back up, restore, and copy your QBO Advanced file: `https://www.youtube.com/watch?v=4FBq8ey0S0s`.

After reviewing your options for backing up and restoring your QBO data, you should be able to use this information to determine which type of backup will work best for you. While one of the benefits of using QBO is that your data is automatically stored in the cloud through Intuit, you can also keep a backup on hand if you prefer to do so.

Utilizing the Performance Center and custom charts

QBO Advanced offers the ability to create custom **Key Performance Indicator (KPI)** dashboards and other user-defined charts. This will give you insights into those areas that might require additional oversight or management. The Performance Center is only available in QBO Advanced. One of the features within the Performance Center is custom charting. Custom charting allows you to visualize your financial data in chart format, which can be easier to understand than just plain numbers. You can create a chart that allows you to include up to 10 groups of values on a single chart.

For example, revenue can be tracked by products and services, classes, locations, projects, and employees. You can also micro-filter specific customers, classes, locations, and more.

The following datasets can be used to create custom charts:

- Expenses
- Revenue
- Gross profit
- Net profit
- Accounts receivable
- Accounts payable
- **Cost of goods sold (COGS)**
- Current ratio
- Quick ratio

When you set up your QuickBooks account, you select the industry your business falls into. This allows you to compare benchmark info when running reports in the Performance Center. QBO uses real-time data for custom charts, which means report visualization is 100% accurate. Currently, existing reports are updated every 4 hours.

Follow these steps to access the Performance Center:

1. From the left menu, click on **Reports** and select the **Performance center**, as indicated in the following screenshot:

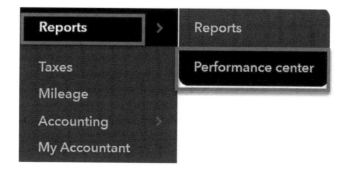

Figure 17.54: Navigating to the Performance Center

2.   Select the **Add New Chart** button.

3.   Select from one of the datasets shown in the following screenshot:

Figure 17.55: Choice of datasets for the dashboard

4.   Click Continue.

5.   After selecting **Revenue**, the following window is displayed:

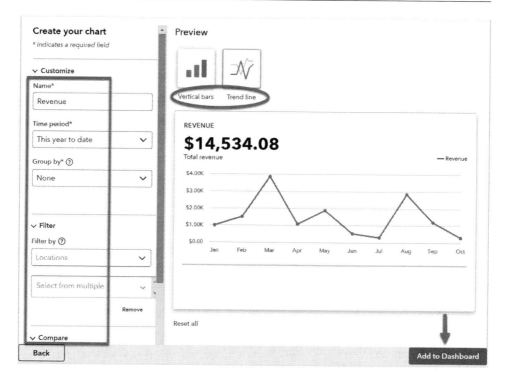

Figure 17.56: Customizing a revenue chart

This window contains the following customization options:

- **Name**: Type a name for the chart, for example, Revenue.

- **Time period**: From the drop-down, select the time period for which you wish to see data – for example, **This year to date**.

- **Group by**: Select how you would like the report to be grouped.

- **Filter**: You can filter data in a number of ways. For revenue, the options are items, clients, or income.

- **Compare**: You can compare the data to previous periods in this section. For example, you can compare revenue for this year with last year.

6. Click the **Add to Dashboard** button to add this chart to the **Performance center** dashboard, as shown in *Figure 17.57*:

Figure 17.57: Adding a revenue chart to the dashboard

Now that we've covered the basics of how to utilize the Performance Center and custom charts so that you can visualize your financials, we will discuss how to create business analytics using Excel.

Business analytics with Excel

Business analytics with Excel, also known as **Spreadsheet Sync**, can be used to track business performance by using Excel to create custom charts and graphs with your QuickBooks data. You can use pre-made templates to build consolidated reports for multiple companies or for a single entity. With *Business analytics with Excel*, you will be able to access KPIs that will enable you to make informed business decisions using real-time information.

Follow the steps below to access *Business analytics with Excel*, also known as **Spreadsheet Sync**:

1. Click on the gear icon and select **Spreadsheet Sync**, as shown in *Figure 17.58*:

TOOLS

Manage workflows

Reclassify transactions

Order checks

Import data

Import desktop data

Export data

Reconcile

Budgeting

Spreadsheet Sync

Audit log

Back up company

SmartLook

Resolution center

Figure 17.58: Selecting Spreadsheet Sync from TOOLS

2. The following window is displayed:

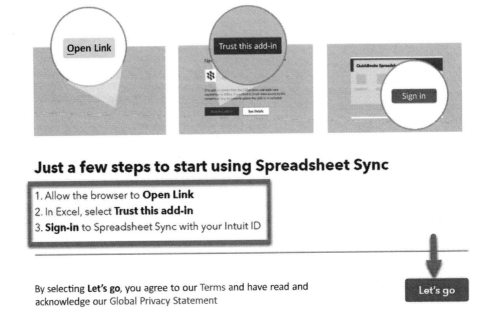

Just a few steps to start using Spreadsheet Sync

1. Allow the browser to **Open Link**
2. In Excel, select **Trust this add-in**
3. **Sign-in** to Spreadsheet Sync with your Intuit ID

By selecting **Let's go**, you agree to our Terms and have read and acknowledge our Global Privacy Statement

Let's go

Figure 17.59: Startup tips for Spreadsheet Sync

In *Figure 17.59*, there are three steps that you need to take to start using Spreadsheet Sync. You select **Open Link**, **Trust this add-in**, and **Sign in** to Spreadsheet Sync using your Intuit ID.

3. Click the **Let's go** button to begin the process.

After you click the **Let's go** button, Microsoft Excel will open. From this point, you can pull in data from QuickBooks to build reports or edit existing data. Edit multiple items and select the **Sync** button to send the updates back to QuickBooks. If you have multiple companies, you can send data for both companies to Excel to create consolidated financial reports.

Watch both of the Intuit video tutorials for step-by-step instructions on how to get the most out of Spreadsheet Sync.

Pro Tip #1: Watch this Intuit video tutorial, which will walk you through the steps to get started with Spreadsheet Sync: `https://youtu.be/IZsXw9UmLRE`.

Pro Tip #2: Watch this Intuit video tutorial, which will show you the features of Spreadsheet Sync: `https://youtu.be/_MCX9aAuQSo`.

Email scheduling for standard and custom reports

One of the newest features included with QBO Advanced is the ability to schedule custom and standard reports to automatically go out to an individual or a group. To set up an email schedule for a report, you need to choose who should receive the report and how often they should receive it. After this one-time process is complete, the report will be sent automatically to the individual or group you have specified.

Follow the steps below to create a schedule for a custom report:

1. Select **Reports** from the left menu bar and click on the **Custom reports** tab, as shown below:

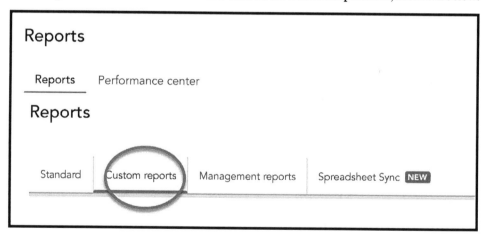

Figure 17.60: Navigating to the Custom reports tab

2. A list of all custom reports will be displayed, as shown below:

Figure 17.61: List of custom reports

3. Click the **Edit** button next to the report you want to schedule and the following will display:

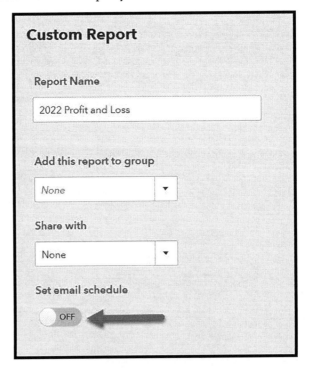

Figure 17.62: Navigating to the Set email schedule otpion

You can edit the report name, add the report to a group of reports, or share it with another user. In *Chapter 10, Report Center Overview*, we explain these options in detail.

4. Click on the toggle below the **Set email schedule** section at the bottom to turn on this feature and complete the fields as follows:

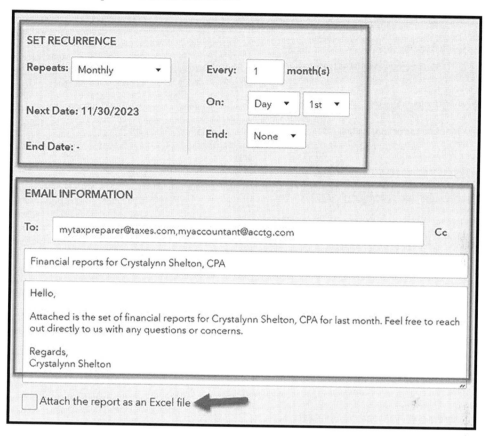

Figure 17.63: Configuration options for email schedules

There are three main areas that need to be completed:

- **Set Recurrence**: In this section, you will select how often you would like the report to be sent to the recipients. The options are daily, weekly, monthly, or twice a month. The **Every** field allows you to choose the frequency (once a month, twice a month, every 3 months, etc) You can select the specific date and include an end date or leave it as **None**.

- **Email Information**: In this section, you will type the email address of each person who should receive the report. Click on **CC** to carbon copy additional people (like yourself). The **Subject** field will automatically populate but you can edit it as needed. You can also customize the email message or keep the default message.

- **Attach the report as an Excel file**: By default, all reports are attached as a PDF. However, if you prefer an Excel format, just click this box and the recipients will receive the report in an Excel format.

5. Be sure to save your changes, and the report will go out on the date specified in the **Next Date** field, as shown in *Figure 17.63* above.

Priority Circle membership

Another feature that sets QBO Advanced apart from other QBO subscriptions is it includes membership in Priority Circle. Priority Circle membership gives you access to three types of services: a dedicated account team, 24/7 premium support, and QBO on-demand training.

These services are ideal if you have a medium or large team that needs to get up and running on QuickBooks quickly. Unlimited access to these services is included in the QBO Advanced subscription, so there is no additional charge.

Here is a brief description of the services included in Priority Circle membership:

- **Dedicated account team**: This includes access to a team of QBO experts who can provide answers to the most common product-related questions. These experts will be familiar with your business when you call in, which will ensure that the answers you receive are applicable to your business needs.
- **24/7 premium support**: This service includes front-of-the-queue access from the support team. This team is trained to answer all of your technical questions related to QuickBooks.
- **On-demand training**: This service includes access to a suite of self-paced training videos that will teach you the basics of QuickBooks, QuickBooks Payroll, and the QBO Advanced features. It has an annual value of $3,000 and includes the following courses:

    - Mastering Accounting Basics for QBO
    - Mastering QBO Level 1
    - Mastering QBO Level 2
    - Mastering QBO Payroll
    - QBO Advanced Features

You can access your **Priority Circle** benefits directly from the gear icon, as shown below:

Figure 17.64: Naviagating to Prioty Citcle from the gear icon

Keep in mind that the Priority Circle team is not able to answer questions related to your business strategy, tax, accounting, or which apps to choose. You will need to consult with a QuickBooks Pro Advisor or your accountant on these matters.

Summary

In this chapter, we have provided you with a detailed look at the features that are only available in the top-tier QBO plan, QBO Advanced. The topics we covered included accessing the QBO test drive, managing fixed assets, using customized fields on forms, setting custom user permissions to control what areas of QuickBooks you give other users access to, how to use workflow automation to streamline deadline-driven tasks, importing invoices and budgets to save time, utilizing batch-entry transactions to create invoices, reclassifying transactions, DocuSign integration, the options you have for backing up your QBO data, how the Performance Center and custom charts work, an overview of *Business analytics with Excel*, and what's included in Priority Circle membership. Now that you have a better understanding of what's included in QBO Advanced, it will help you determine whether it is the right subscription for your business.

This is the final chapter of this book. Be sure to review the appendices that follow. The *Shortcuts and Test Drive* appendix provides a list of keyboard shortcuts, a link to the QBO test drive, and a link to purchase QBO at a discount. In the final appendix, we have provided you with an outline of the objectives covered on the **QuickBooks Certified User (QBCU)** exam. If you are an aspiring bookkeeper or accountant, you may want to consider becoming a QuickBooks Certified user. We have covered more than 95% of the QBCU objectives in this book, and the quick reference guide in the appendix can assist you with locating the information throughout this book.

We've completed our journey of learning how to set up, manage, and use QBO in our business. I want to congratulate you on investing the time and effort to make your business finances a priority. I wish you much success and hope you will join our Discord space so that we can continue to provide you with great tips and tricks for using QBO.

Join our community on Discord

Join our community's Discord space for discussions with the authors and other readers:

`https://packt.link/quickbooks`

Appendix

Shortcuts and Test Drive

QuickBooks Online keyboard shortcuts

Keyboard shortcuts help speed up navigation, which will save you time when you're using **Quick-Books Online (QBO)**. For example, instead of using the mouse to click multiple times before you get to the chart of accounts or a new invoice template, you can use the keyboard shortcut to display these areas of QBO a lot faster.

The following screenshot shows a list of the QBO keyboard shortcuts. To access them directly in your QBO file, press the *Ctrl + Alt + ?* keys simultaneously (keys may differ on a Mac).

Keyboard Shortcuts

To use a shortcut, press and hold **ctrl/control** and **alt/option** at the same time. Then press one of the keys below.

On main pages, like the dashboard or customers

SHORTCUT KEY	ACTION
i	Invoice
w	Check
e	Estimate
x	Expense
r	Receive payment
c	Customers
v	Vendors
a	Chart of accounts
l	Lists
h	Help
f	Global search
d	Focus the left menu
? or /	This dialog

On transactions, like an invoice or expense

SHORTCUT KEY	ACTION
x	Exit transaction view
c	Cancel out
s	Save and new
d	Save and close
m	Save and send
p	Print
? or /	This dialog

Figure A.1: Keyboard shortcuts

You can also access keyboard shortcuts from the gear icon. Within the gear menu, select **Additional info**, which is located below the **Your Company** column.

QBO test drive

Before signing up for a QBO subscription, you can check out the QBO test drive, which we introduced in *Chapter 17, QuickBooks Online Advanced*. The test drive account contains sample data for a fictitious company.

Here, you can enter test transactions before you put them in your actual QBO file. For example, you can enter a credit memo or a journal entry to see how it affects the books before entering the transaction in your QBO file. Just click on the following link (depending on your region) and follow the onscreen instructions:

- United States: `https://qbo.intuit.com/redir/testdrive`
- United States QuickBooks Online Advanced: `https://qbo.intuit.com/redir/testdrive_us_advanced`

The US edition of QBO was used to create this book. If you are using a version that is outside the United States, results may differ.

Discount on a QBO asccount

You can use my referral link to save money when you sign up for a new QBO account: `https://quickbooks.grsm.io/crystalynnshelton4264`.

Join our community on Discord

Join our community's Discord space for discussions with the authors and other readers:

`https://packt.link/quickbooks`

Intuit QuickBooks Online Certified User Exam Objectives

The Intuit QuickBooks Certified User certification is a credential that is recognized in the industry as a way for bookkeepers and accountants to demonstrate their proficiency in the Intuit Quick-Books accounting software. Once you have achieved this certification, you will receive access to a digital badge that you can put on your resume, social media profiles, and your website. This certification will automatically set you apart from other candidates looking to obtain employment as a bookkeeper or accountant.

In this chapter, we have included a list of the objectives that are covered on the exam. In addition, we have provided the corresponding chapter where you can find the information on each topic in our book, *Mastering QuickBooks® 2024*.

For more information on how to take the exam, visit the Certiport website: `https://certiport.pearsonvue.com/Certifications/Intuit/Certifications/Certify/QuickBooks-Certified-User`

Objective		Chapter
1	**Intuit QuickBooks Online Administration**	
1.1	**Set up Intuit QuickBooks Online**	
1.1.1	Recognize features and benefits of Intuit QuickBooks Online Plus	1, 16
1.1.2	Describe licensing requirements for setting up an entity in Intuit QuickBooks Online	1
1.1.3	Describe the process of migrating a company to Intuit QuickBooks Online	3
1.1.4	Describe the access of each default user role	4
1.2	**Manage Intuit QuickBooks Online**	
1.2.1	Identify the company information that you can and can't edit	2
1.2.2	Recognize the benefits of the Close the Books feature	15
1.2.3	Compare and contrast the cash and accrual accounting methods	1
1.2.4	Identify the purpose of project tracking, class tracking, and locations	2
1.2.5	Describe how to activate project tracking, class tracking, and locations	2

1.2.6	Identify the tasks performed by automation	17
1.3	**Manage lists**	
1.3.1	Identify the lists that you can import	4, 5
1.3.2	Identify the content of various lists	4, 5
1.3.3	Identify the appropriate lists for different purposes	4, 5
1.3.4	Identify when and how to add, edit, delete, and merge list items	4, 5
1.3.5	Manage the Chart of Accounts	4
1.4	**Manage recurring transactions**	
1.4.1	Describe reasons for making transactions recurring	8
1.4.2	Define types of recurrence	8
1.4.3	Describe how to implement recurring transactions	8
1.5	**Manage journal entries**	
1.5.1	Identify the information required for journal entries	15
1.5.2	Describe how to implement journal entries	15
1.6	**Connect Intuit QuickBooks Online to apps**	
1.6.1	Identify the purpose of apps	4
1.6.2	Identify where to get apps	4
1.6.3	Identify the risks and benefits of extending functionality through apps	4

2	**Sales and Money In**	
2.1	**Set up customers**	
2.1.1	Identify the importance of the Display Name field	5
2.1.2	Differentiate between billing and shipping addresses	5
2.1.3	Define and describe the use of customer payment terms	5
2.1.4	Identify taxable and non-taxable customers	5
2.1.5	Define and describe the correct use of sub-customers	5
2.2	**Set up products and services**	
2.2.1	Describe and differentiate between products and services	5
2.2.2	Identify the information required to set up products or services	5
2.2.3	Describe reasons for setting up products or services	5
2.2.4	Contrast inventory products and non-inventory products	5
2.3	**Manage sales settings**	
2.3.1	Customize sales forms	7

2.3.2	Customize email message forms	2
2.3.3	Describe the purpose of activating customer discounts	2
2.3.4	Describe the Intuit QuickBooks Payments feature and how it differs from traditional payments	2, 7
2.4	**Record basic money-in transactions**	
2.4.1	Describe the money-in transaction workflow	7
2.4.2	Record and manage invoices and sales receipts	7
2.4.3	Receive, record, and manage payments, undeposited funds, and deposits	7
2.4.4	Record credit memos and refund receipts	7

3	**Vendors and Money Out**	
3.1	**Manage vendor records**	
3.1.1	Describe how to identify existing customers as vendors	5
3.1.2	Describe when and how to merge vendor accounts	5
3.1.3	Describe how to add or change vendor payment terms	5
3.1.4	Describe how and why to identify vendors as 1099 contractors	5, 14
3.2	**Manage expense settings**	
3.2.1	Describe how and why to activate expense tracking by customer	2
3.2.2	Describe when and how to make expenses and items billable	2
3.2.3	Describe how to identify unbilled billable expenses	2
3.3	**Record and manage basic money-out transactions**	
3.3.1	Describe the money-out transaction workflow	8
3.3.2	Identify types of money-out transactions	8
3.3.3	Compare and describe the appropriate use of checks and bill payments	8
3.3.4	Describe the effects of recording bills, checks, and credit card transactions	8
3.3.5	Differentiate between expense transactions and bank feed transactions	8
3.3.6	Describe how to record check, credit card, and debit card expense transactions	8
3.3.7	Describe the use and effects of vendor credits and refunds	8
3.3.8	Describe why and how to void, delete, and edit money-out transactions and the impact thereof	8

4	Bank Accounts, Transaction Rules, and Receipts	
4.1	**Implement financial account connections**	
4.1.1	Identify the types of financial accounts Intuit QuickBooks Online can connect to	4
4.1.2	Describe the benefits of connecting Intuit QuickBooks Online to accounts	4
4.2	**Manage bank feeds**	
4.2.1	Process bank feed transactions	9
4.2.2	Define and describe the use of bank rules	9
4.3	**Manage receipts**	
4.3.1	Identify methods of uploading receipts	8
4.3.2	Describe how to record transactions from uploaded receipts	8

5	Basic Reports and Views	
5.1	**Describe the content and purpose of reports**	
5.1.1	Describe the content and purpose of financial reports	6, 10, 11
5.1.2	Describe the content and purpose of money-in reports	12
5.1.3	Describe the content and purpose of money-out reports	13
5.2	**Customize and deliver standard reports**	
5.2.1	Customize standard reports	10
5.2.2	Identify report delivery formats	10
5.3	**Access other reports and views**	
5.3.1	Describe the content of the Audit Log	11
5.3.2	Describe the content and functionality of the dashboards	1

Join our community on Discord

Join our community's Discord space for discussions with the authors and other readers:

`https://packt.link/quickbooks`

packt.com

Subscribe to our online digital library for full access to over 7,000 books and videos, as well as industry leading tools to help you plan your personal development and advance your career. For more information, please visit our website.

Why subscribe?

- Spend less time learning and more time coding with practical eBooks and Videos from over 4,000 industry professionals
- Improve your learning with Skill Plans built especially for you
- Get a free eBook or video every month
- Fully searchable for easy access to vital information
- Copy and paste, print, and bookmark content

At www.packt.com, you can also read a collection of free technical articles, sign up for a range of free newsletters, and receive exclusive discounts and offers on Packt books and eBooks.

Other Books You May Enjoy

If you enjoyed this book, you may be interested in these other books by Packt:

NetSuite for Consultants – Second Edition

Peter Ries

ISBN: 9781837639076

- Understand the NetSuite ecosystem, including the platform and its primary modules, and associated features
- Learn how to gather and document requirements, including understanding an organization's industry, transactions, and people
- Learn about the methodologies that go into creating a project plan for a NetSuite implementation
- Fulfill client requirements with expanded coverage on managing employees, customer projects, and budgeting

- Discover how to create custom automations and perform data migration with SuiteQL scripts
- Perform integrations with expanded coverage on how we use the REST API for business purposes
- Recognize the procedures for testing and development
- Refine your skills with NetSuite tips and tricks and make each implementation process a success

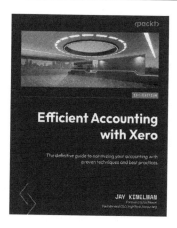

Efficient Accounting with Xero

Jay Kimelman

ISBN: 9781801812207

- Understand why Xero is the best choice in accounting software for your SMB
- Easily set up or convert to Xero for a service- or product-based business
- Reconcile cash and related transactions effortlessly
- Track and depreciate capital assets purchased by and used in the business
- Produce customized reports tailored to your specific need
- Use Xero to make informed and timely decisions and become a better business owner or advisor

Learn Microsoft Power Apps - Second Edition

Matthew Weston

Elisa Bárcena Martín

ISBN: 9781801070645

- Understand the Power Apps ecosystem and licensing
- Take your first steps building canvas apps
- Develop apps using intermediate techniques such as the barcode scanner and GPS controls
- Explore new connectors to integrate tools across the Power Platform
- Store data in Dataverse using model-driven apps
- Discover the best practices for building apps cleanly and effectively
- Use AI for app development with AI Builder and Copilot

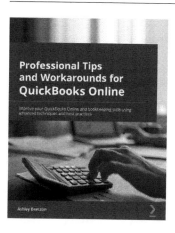

Professional Tips and Workarounds for QuickBooks Online

Ashley Beetson

ISBN: 9781801810371

- Discover how to correctly set up QuickBooks Online with opening balances
- Adapt QuickBooks Online to meet specific industry needs, from manufacturing and retail using inventory to helping lawyers and property agents handle client funds
- Get the most out of features such as Projects and Multicurrency
- Review reports within QuickBooks Online, understand why errors occur, and learn how to resolve them
- Get to grips with key accounting principles and concepts tailored for bookkeeping and accounting beginners
- Find out how the audit trail works and explore all of the information it holds

Packt is searching for authors like you

If you're interested in becoming an author for Packt, please visit authors.packtpub.com and apply today. We have worked with thousands of developers and tech professionals, just like you, to help them share their insight with the global tech community. You can make a general application, apply for a specific hot topic that we are recruiting an author for, or submit your own idea.

Share your thoughts

Now you've finished *Mastering QuickBooks 2024*, we'd love to hear your thoughts! Scan the QR code below to go straight to the Amazon review page for this book and share your feedback or leave a review on the site that you purchased it from.

https://packt.link/r/1835469957

Your review is important to us and the tech community and will help us make sure we're delivering excellent quality content.

Index